G.21

£8=
coo book

NAPOLEON
AND THE
ARCHDUKE
CHARLES

NAPOLEONIC LIBRARY

NAPOLEON AND THE ARCHDUKE CHARLES

A History of
the Franco-Austrian Campaign
in the Valley of the Danube in 1809

F. Loraine Petre

Greenhill Books, London
Presidio Press, California

This edition of *Napoleon and the Archduke Charles*
first published 1991 by Greenhill Books, Lionel Leventhal Limited,
Park House, 1 Russell Gardens, London NW11 9NN
and
Presidio Press,
31 Pamaron Way, Novato, Ca.94949, U.S.A.
This edition © Lionel Leventhal Limited, 1991

British Library Cataloguing in Publication Data
Petre, F. Loraine (Francis Loraine)
Napoleon and the Archduke Charles. – New ed. – (Napoleonic Library).
1. Napoleonic Wars. Franco-Austrian campaign
I. Title   II. Series
940.2

ISBN 1-85367-092-8

Publishing History
Napoleon and the Archduke Charles was first published in 1909
(John Lane: The Bodley Head) and is reproduced now complete
and unabridged.

Greenhill Books
welcome readers' suggestions for books that might be added to this Series.
Please write to us if there are titles which you would like to recommend.

Printed by Biddles Limited, Guildford, Surrey

STEPHEN TRINDER

AUTHOR'S PREFACE

THE campaign which forms the subject of this volume is one which has received scant notice in England, and has been a good deal misunderstood. The misunderstanding has been mainly due to Napoleon's successful misrepresentation of the earlier part as one of his greatest and most successful efforts. The publication of the full correspondence of the time in Colonel Saski's *Campagne de* 1809, and General Bonnal's criticism in his *Manœuvre de Landshut*, effectually show that the Emperor was guilty of lapses which did not occur in 1805 or 1806. Besides these works, there are many excellent accounts of older date in French, which have been consulted by the author. The most notable are Pelet's history of the campaign, and Koch's *Memoirs of Masséna*.

The campaign is of special interest as being the only one, except the Austrian retreat from Italy in 1797, in which Napoleon was personally opposed to his ablest continental opponent.

The publication, under the patronage of the Archduke Charles' family, of Colonel von Angeli's *Erzherzog Karl als Feldherr*, and of the collected writings of the Archduke, has thrown much light on the Austrian side. The history commenced by Binder von Krieglstein ("*B. K.*" in the notes), a Prussian officer, and completed by a brother officer, deals with French, Austrian, Bavarian, and Wurtemberg sources of information. There are several recent Austrian works, especially that of Mayer-

v

hofer von Vedropolje, which are of great value in the study of the campaign.

Of the maps attached to this volume, No. IV. is a reproduction of part of the Bavarian Staff map. So is the inset to No. III., whilst the rest of that map is based upon the same foundation. I have gratefully to acknowledge the courtesy of the Topographical Department of the General Staff at Munich in allowing me thus to use their map. Most of the other maps are based, either on the great atlas of the *Memorial du dépôt de la Guerre*, or, in the case of No. V., on the Atlas of Koch's *Memoirs of Masséna*. Most of the drawing and reduction has been done for me by my son, Mr R. L. Petre, an officer of the South Wales Borderers. All but two of the illustrations are, as in the case of my two former works, reproductions from pictures in the collection of Mr A. M. Broadley, of The Knapp, Bridport, who has courteously allowed them to be used. The view of the Danube at Saal, showing the defile through which Davout's baggage column passed on the 19th April 1809, and that of the headquarters at Rohr, are two out of a number taken by myself during a tour in September 1907.

F. L. P.

CONTENTS

CONTENTS

ILLUSTRATIONS

Appearing between pages xvi and 1

*From photographs by the author.
The remaining illustrations are reproduced
by the kind permission of A. M. Broadley Esq.,
from prints, engravings etc., in his collection.

MAPS AND PLANS

Appearing at end of Volume

Map I

General Map of Central Europe

Maps II

The Valley of the Danube from Ratisbon to Komorn.
Plans for Battles of Ebelsberg, Raab, and Snaim.

Map III

Map for the Campaign of Eckmühl.
Enlarged (Bavarian Staff) Map of Neighbourhood of Abensburg.

Map IV

Country Round Thann and Eckmühl (Bavarian Staff Map).

Map V

Plan for Battles of Essling and Wagram.

NAPOLEON AND THE ARCHDUKE CHARLES

THE ARCHDUKE CHARLES
(From Mr. Broadley's Collection)

THE DANUBE AT SAAL (LOOKING DOWN STREAM)

THE POST HOUSE, ROHR (THE FARTHER HOUSE)
Headquarters, in 1809, of Archduke Charles, 18th April;
The Emperor Napoleon, 20th April

GENERAL MOUTON
(From Mr. Broadley's Collection)

FRANCIS THE FIRST
EMPEROR OF AUSTRIA

(From Mr. Broadley's Collection).

THE BATTLE OF ESSLING-ASPERN
(From Mr. Broadley's Collection)

MARSHAL OUDINOT
(From Mr. Broadley's Collection)

GENERAL LASALLE
(From Mr. Broadley's Collection)

NAPOLEON
& THE ARCHDUKE CHARLES

CHAPTER I

THE ORIGIN OF THE WAR

WITH the signature of the Treaty of Tilsit and the secret clauses attached to it, Napoleon seemed to be, at last, the arbiter of the destinies of all Europe, from the Pyrenees to the Niemen, and from the Baltic to Sicily. He had crushed and dismembered Prussia, who, for the present, was no longer worthy of his consideration. In Germany every state which was not under his direct rule was either under that of his puppets, or else was his ally, willing or unwilling, with the sole exception of Austria, who had deemed it wise, in 1806 and 1807, not again to measure swords with the imperial armies which had so recently inflicted on her a disastrous defeat.

Italy was completely controlled by Napoleon through his stepson Eugène Beauharnais, Viceroy of the Kingdom of Italy, and his brother Joseph, soon to be succeeded by Murat, as King of Naples.

Holland was nominally the kingdom of another brother; Westphalia, comprising Prussia's former possessions west of the Elbe, and the territories of the Elector of Hesse-Cassel, was in the hands of Jerome, a puppet even more amenable than Louis. Saxony, now increased by the Grand Duchy of Warsaw, was the latest addition to the Rhenish Confederation, into which Napoleon had now swept all the minor German States, of which Bavaria was the most important.

Denmark was the bone of contention between Napoleon and England, and her fleet was shortly to pass into the hands of the latter. Neither she nor Sweden was held of much account by the chief contracting parties at Tilsit ; for both were to be compelled to close their ports against England if the latter did not fall in with the views of Napoleon, and if Sweden made difficulties, Denmark was to be made to declare war on her.

In Eastern Europe, Russia had been worsted in the late contest, but she was in a very different position from unfortunate Prussia. At Eylau the Russian army had inflicted a check on the Emperor's victorious career, though it is true that without the arrival, in the nick of time, of Lestocq's Prussians, Bennigsen would probably have been disastrously defeated. Heilsberg had been another partial check for the French, though the memory of it was wiped out by Napoleon's great victory, a few days later, at Friedland. Still, even Friedland bore no resemblance to Jena in the complete rout of the beaten side. Therefore, at the Tilsit negotiations, whilst the Prussian monarch and the queen, who was worth many such as her husband, were treated by the conqueror with contempt and insult, the Tsar was received very differently. He was flattered and cajoled by one whose personal fascination, when he chose to use it, rarely failed to gain over even those most prejudiced against him. Alexander made no secret of his own prompt surrender, or of his regret for his former prejudices.

Before the greedy eyes of the Russian was dangled the bait of a possible partition of Turkey, whilst he was assured on the subject of a contemplated restoration of the old Polish kingdom. He, the defeated party, lost no territory and paid no money indemnity ; on the contrary, he was presented with a new slice of Poland—at the expense of Prussia.   What poor concessions were made to Prussia, notably the return to her of Silesia, were attributed by Napoleon to the Tsar's intercession, whereby the Emperor killed two birds with one stone, by flattering Alexander and passing one more insult upon the unhappy Frederick William.   By one of the secret clauses Alexander and Napoleon bound themselves to an offensive and defensive alliance against any other European power on whom either of them might make war.

Yet, withal, the Tsar was not so completely hoodwinked and satisfied as Napoleon would wish him to have been.   He never liked being dragged into Napoleon's Continental System, which, however much it might be supposed to favour the French Emperor's struggle against England, could certainly never be anything but harmful to Russia.   Nor did Alexander trust his new ally in the matter of Turkey, and it seems pretty certain that Napoleon had no intention of letting the Russians into Constantinople, or of partitioning Turkey at all, until he saw much more clearly how it might affect his own dreams of Eastern empire.   This threatened partition of Turkey, too, was a useful weapon against Austria, to whom it could not fail to be a matter of vital interest, and an impenetrable barrier against any awkward rapprochement between her and Russia.   With regard to Denmark, or at least her fleet, the designs of the new allies were frustrated by England's seizure of the ships.

Napoleon had now drawn into his great scheme for the exclusion of British commerce from the ports of Europe every power east of the Pyrenees except Sweden and Turkey.   There still remained the Iberian Peninsula, or rather Portugal ; for Spain was already under the Napoleonic influence.   A scheme for Portugal's partition, instigated by the Prince of the Peace, had only been postponed on account of the campaigns in Prussia and Poland. Now the Emperor returned to it.

It is unnecessary for our purposes to describe the expedition of Junot, which led to the flight of the Portuguese reigning family to South America, or the subsequent events ending in the Convention of Cintra.

Nor would there be any advantage in detailing the course of the intrigues and violence by means of which Napoleon succeeded in cajoling the wretched Charles IV. of Spain and his son Ferdinand, himself but a poor creature, into renouncing their rights to the throne. Joseph Bonaparte was now transferred from Naples to Madrid, whilst Murat presently became king, and by no means a bad king, of Naples. But the Emperor, in the arrogance which now more and more characterised him, and of which we shall have much more to say in connection with his military character, reckoned without the Spanish people. The idea of their seriously contesting his ability to dispose of their throne as he thought fit never seems to have occurred to him as worthy of his consideration.

He was soon to be disillusioned as to the possibility of a serious rising, for all Spain rose against him. He was still at Bayonne, the scene of the shameful abdication of Charles and Ferdinand, when Bessières' victory at Medina del Rio Seco confirmed him in his opinion that the revolt against his authority could soon be suppressed without his personal intervention. But, on July 19, Dupont, with 20,000 French troops, surrendered to the Andalusian insurgents at Baylen. Napoleon was naturally furious at so serious a reverse, inflicted on one of his best divisional generals, the man who, even in the last campaign, had distinguished himself so greatly, notably when, at Friedland, his promptitude had saved Ney's left from a serious danger. This was followed by Joseph's evacuation of the capital which he had so recently

reached, and by the French repulse from Saragossa.
Still the Emperor affected to despise the Spaniards, and
to be satisfied that the French misfortunes were solely
due to the incompetence of his brother, and his generals
and advisers. Whatever he might say, it was clear that
he must do something to retrieve disasters which, if they
had not been incurred whilst he was personally in command, had yet broken the spell of the supposed invincibility of the French. Germany was seething with
discontent under the tyranny of the French occupation,
Austria was arming, and Napoleon had already, even in
May 1808, heard of her proposal to raise a fresh levy of
180,000 landwehr.

This arming of Austria was amongst the reasons which
led Napoleon to take measures for reassuring his position
towards Alexander, who had more than once shown
symptoms of restiveness. Napoleon, fully aware of his
own personal power of fascination, arranged for a meeting
with the Tsar, at Erfurt, in the latter part of September
1808. There the two Emperors, the principal figures,
were surrounded by a temporary court in which kings
and German princes, marshals and ministers of state,
played only minor parts.

There was plenty of display and pomp, but there was
also a great deal of business transacted between the principal actors. There was no lack of intrigue, and both
Napoleon and Alexander were suspicious. The part of
the business which concerns us chiefly is the clause in
the convention finally drawn up which bound the Tsar to
take a hand against Austria should she attack Napoleon.
The agreement, which was signed on the 12th October
1808, provided that, "in the event of Austria making
war on France, the Emperor of Russia undertakes to
declare against Austria, and to make common cause with
France, that event being equally one of those to which
the alliance uniting the two empires applies."

The support thus acquired by Napoleon was of vital importance to him, for on it he relied to stave off an Austrian war, at least until his hands were freed from the chains of the Spanish imbroglio. Not only that, but the alliance with Russia would help to check the spirit of revolt against his authority, which was growing fast in the recently-conquered German states, under the influence of men of the stamp of Stein and Scharnhorst, of Blücher and Gneisenau, of Jahn and Schill, most of them Germans of non-Prussian origin. The example of the Spaniards, and the reverses of the French arms in the Peninsula, had afforded much encouragement and hope to this band of German patriots. From Frederick William himself they had little to expect, and, if the liberation of Germany from the French yoke had depended on him, it would perhaps never have been effected ; for even in 1813 it was not he, but his subjects and his ministers, who led the revolt.

For the present, Germany's best hope lay in the resistance which Austria might be able and willing to oppose to the conqueror and oppressor. The House of Habsburg had witnessed the gradual dismemberment of its possessions by the treaties of Campo Formio, of Lunéville, and of Pressburg. By the first, Austria had lost to France Flanders and her Italian possessions, in return receiving Venice. At Lunéville she again yielded up the left bank of the Rhine, and Italy was lost to the west of the Adige. After Austerlitz, the Peace of Pressburg deprived her of the Tyrol, the Vorarlberg, and other adjoining territories, which went to the new kingdom of Bavaria. To Wurtemberg were ceded territories in Swabia, and to Baden other lands in the direction of Constance. Austria's Venetian provinces were also wrested from her, and she gained practically nothing but Salzburg. Altogether, she lost by this treaty nearly 30,000 square miles of territory and a population approaching 3,000,000. Her total population in the beginning of 1809 has been estimated at 22,576,500.

The constitution of the Rhenish Confederation had resulted in the abdication by Francis II. of his shadowy title of Holy Roman Emperor, and his assumption of the Imperial Crown of Austria only, as Francis I.

After Pressburg, Austria had seriously set to work to reorganise her resources and her administration, but her finances were crippled and her army shattered for the time being. She required time before she could venture on a renewal of the struggle with France. Had she been in the least ready, Napoleon's campaigns of 1806-7, in Prussia and Poland, offered her a splendid opportunity for falling on his right flank and rear in Germany. How anxious he was to keep her quiet, even in her weakened condition, has been described in the author's previous volumes on those campaigns. There also will be found an account of the measures which he took in Italy to hold a large portion of the Austrian army on the southern frontier. The risk of a fresh war with France, in 1806 or 1807, was too great; for defeat then could hardly have meant to the Imperial House anything but extinction at the hands of Napoleon. With the victory of Friedland and the Peace of Tilsit, the temptation to risk interference against the victorious Emperor was removed. Austria must now quietly prepare for a 'revanche' at some more favourable opportunity.

For a definite and immediate cause of Austria's attack on the French in April 1809 it is useless to search. Her object was simply a rectification of what she had been compelled to agree to in the end of 1805. Colonel Saski puts the case clearly. "Since 1805 Austria had worked at her military organisation, and her sole thought, encouraged by England, the soul of all the coalitions at that time, was to tear up the Treaty of Pressburg." As

regards Austria he is correct, though, seeing that England
only concluded formal peace with Austria after her fresh
defeat by Napoleon, he seems hardly accurate as regards
British encouragement, at least in a substantial sense.
As Napoleon began to involve himself in the Spanish
affair, Austria perceived that the time was approaching
when her great enemy was likely to be hampered by
difficulties in his rear which had not existed in any of
his previous wars in Italy or Germany.

He first shows in his correspondence that he was
anxious on the subject of Austrian armaments in May
1808. Towards the end of that month, he writes to his
Minister for Foreign Affairs that he hears, from sources
other than his ambassador at Vienna, that Austria is
contemplating a fresh levy of 180,000 militia. If the
ambassador, Andréossy, found that there was truth in
this story, he was to demand that the levy be not made ;
for, Austria already having 300,000 men enrolled, it was
clear that further military preparations must be directed
against France. The Emperor threatened, if the levy of
180,000 were persisted in, to raise fresh troops in
France, and to mobilise the contingents of the Rhenish
Confederation. That would be an expensive operation,
of which the cost must fall on Austria herself.

A month later, he was again alarmed by reports of
the constitution of magazines in Bohemia, and the collection of horses and supplies of all sorts. He seems to
have been particularly badly served by Andréossy at
Vienna, for on both occasions the reports came from
elsewhere, on the second from the French Minister at
Munich.

The Emperor next sent a warning to Bavaria to be
in readiness in case Austria should move ; for, as in
1805, Bavaria must necessarily bear the first brunt of
the attack. He also finds fault with the Austrian
observance of the continental blockade at Trieste. On

the 11th July he again reverts to the question of the militia levies, and a week later he directs the re-armament of the Silesian fortress of Neisse, which he still held. On the 10th August he jubilantly informs Champagny, his Minister of Foreign Affairs, that he has received from the Tsar an assurance of active alliance in the event of war with Austria. All the information he received from his numerous agents, and especially from Davout, commanding in Germany, confirmed him in his belief that Austria was preparing for war. The Emperor was now back in Paris, and, on the 16th August, at a reception of the ' corps diplomatique,' he conversed at length with Metternich, the Austrian Ambassador, or rather he delivered a long lecture to that diplomat. The substance of the conversation is stated in a despatch from Champagny to Andréossy. If that statement is anything like accurate, it is an extraordinary instance of the arrogance which prompted the use of language to the ambassador of a power with which the Emperor was still at peace, such as, at any other period, must infallibly have led to war. In this report the Emperor is represented, of course with his own sanction, as upbraiding Metternich with Austria's preparations, and rudely waving aside as ridiculous the ambassador's protestations of his master's peaceful intentions. Napoleon scoffs at the idea of the military measures being merely defensive, for Austria had nothing to fear from himself or anyone else. He is full of threats as to how he will reply, by armament, to the action of Austria ; he vaunts his friendship with Russia ; he even goes so far as to insinuate that that power may justly take umbrage at the Austrian preparations as a danger to herself. His conclusions as to the meaning of Austria's movements were correct enough in fact, but his language is devoid of all diplomatic restraint.

Early in September he writes long letters to Jerome

and to the kings of Bavaria, Saxony, and Wurtemberg, in which he estimates that, including the troops of the Confederation, he will have 300,000 men available during January in Germany. Again, he boasts of the friendly feeling of the Tsar towards him. This vaunt is so frequently repeated about this period as, by the mere fact of its reiteration, to raise a suspicion that Napoleon is not quite so sure about it as he professes. At the end of his letter to Jerome, he indicates that Austria seems more pacifically inclined, and he hopes by October to be able to send better news of the prospects of peace.

On the 22nd September the Emperor left Paris for Erfurt. To that meeting-place Francis I. had not been invited personally or by deputy. Nevertheless, he sent there Baron Vincent as the bearer of a letter to Napoleon. The letter was humble enough, protesting the writer's devotion to Napoleon, and the peaceful nature of his own measures. On the latter subject Vincent would be able to give further assurances. Doubtless the assurances were left to Vincent's discretion when he should have observed how the wind blew, for he, having been employed in a similar capacity during the campaign in Poland, was well acquainted with the ways of the French court or camp. As the political weather at Erfurt did not favour Austria, the assurances seem to have been conveyed in terms which lulled, to some extent, Napoleon's suspicions. He writes to the Princes of the Confederation that the Austrian militia has been disbanded, and will not be again assembled. The Confederation troops might, therefore, be withdrawn from the camps in which they had been concentrated, and allowed to return to their ordinary cantonments. At the same time, the Princes were to make it clear, through their ministers at Vienna, that any unusual armament on the part of Austria would entail a fresh concentration of their troops.

On the 12th October, the last day of the Erfurt assembly, the "Grand Army" of the Prussian and Polish campaigns was abolished in name, and in its place was constituted the "Army of the Rhine." The Emperor, as a sop to Russia, proposed to withdraw generally behind the Elbe, though he would still keep 10,000 men on the Oder as garrisons of the fortresses of Glogau, Küstrin, and Stettin. A division would remain in Pomerania, 12,500 men at Magdeburg, two small corps in the Hanseatic cities and Hanover, and 23,000 cavalry, of which 10,000 would be cuirassiers. The garrison of Danzig would also remain. That would make altogether an army of 70,000 or 80,000 men. The command of this army was given to Davout.

For the moment the war cloud seemed to have blown aside in Germany, and the Emperor, arriving in Paris on the 25th October, felt secure enough to leave again for Spain three days later.

It is clear, however, from his letter to Davout of the 25th October, that he was not altogether satisfied. In his previous campaigns in Germany he had had nothing to trouble him seriously in his rear beyond the Pyrenees. Now it was very different, for he had the Spanish rising to cope with, and the task of restoring the prestige of his arms, which had suffered so seriously by the capitulation of Baylen, the retirement of Joseph from Madrid to the upper Ebro, the repulse at Saragossa, and Junot's capitulation at Lisbon. He certainly did not want war with Austria for the present, at least not till he had had time to crush all opposition in Spain and Portugal, and to drive the English into the sea. He hoped to stave it off until he had attained these objects, but he was disappointed and compelled to return to France to look after affairs there, and to prepare to meet the Austrians on the Danube, leaving the pursuit of Sir John Moore to Soult, and the attempt to subjugate the

Spanish people to Joseph and a team of unruly marshals who could be kept in order by no hand but Napoleon's own.

What was the real position in Austria, the country which was causing Napoleon such anxiety? As in Prussia in 1806, so in Austria in 1808 there were two distinct parties, of peace and of war. The resemblance is intensified by the fact that, as Queen Luise was the centre of the Prussian war party, so the Empress Maria Ludovica, the consort of Francis I., was the chief supporter of that of Austria. Handsome, charming, proud, and energetic, she exercised considerable influence over the Emperor, and was a most useful ally to Count Philip Stadion, the leading statesman of the party. The other principal personages of the party were Metternich, the Austrian ambassador in Paris, Freiherr von Balducci, a member of a Corsican family settled in Hungary, General von Kutschera, and Count Ferdinand Palfy. The peace party, on the other hand, consisted chiefly of soldiers, at the head of whom was the Archduke Charles, the commander-in-chief. He was followed by his brothers, the Archdukes John, Joseph Palatine of Hungary, and Rainer.

The differences between these parties were based rather on their views of expediency than on any repugnance to war, or any special desire for peace. Stadion believed less in steadfast internal reform and reorganisation than in a bold foreign policy as a means of restoring the fallen fortunes of his country and his sovereign. He was always an advocate of a strong Germany under the joint leadership of Austria and Prussia, and he had strong hopes, destined for years to come to disappointment, of a general rising of Germany against Napoleon. Charles, on the other hand, was no less a patriot than Stadion, but believed his country was not yet ready for a fresh war against the

mighty warrior who, less than three years before, had
beaten her to the ground. The Archduke felt that he
would himself, as the only general who was fit to lead
the armies of Austria against a commander such as
Napoleon, have to bear the whole burden of military
operations. He recognised that there was still much to
be done in administrative and financial reform, as well
as in army reorganisation. Stadion, however, thought
more of the opportunity offered by Napoleon's entangle-
ment in the Peninsula, and of the possibilities of a
German uprising similar to that of Spain. He estimated
that Napoleon could not, in the beginning of a war in
Germany, bring more than 197,000 men on to the field,
inclusive of the Rhenish Confederation contingents.
Metternich put the French and allied forces at 206,000
men at first, and wrote that, "the forces of Austria, so
inferior to those of France before the Spanish rising,
will be at least equal to them in the first movements."

Stadion's influence, backed by that of the Empress,
was great. Charles' had to some extent waned, and his
relations with the Emperor had lost in cordiality. Still
he must be gained over, in so far that he might be relied
on to carry out his part if war should come.

The differences of these two parties were public pro-
perty in Germany, and Napoleon had little difficulty in
keeping himself informed as to the progress of the dispute.

Could Austria hope to enter on a fresh campaign
with any ally at her back? From England perhaps
some financial aid might be got, though even her treasury
was at a low ebb just then. She might perhaps make a
diversion in Hanover or Holland, but that was not to be
relied on, and the unfortunate expedition to Walcheren
was actually only undertaken when it was all over with
Austria.

Prussia was broken and dismembered by the late war.
Her army was ruined, she had no money, and she had

lost half her former possessions. The patriots would have thrown in their lot with Austria at all hazards, but Frederick William was not going to risk his own throne, and, when Major v. der Goltz concluded an arrangement under which Prussia was to assist Austria with 80,000 men,[1] the Prussian King would have none of it. As for Russia, the Tsar was formally bound to Napoleon by the treaty signed at Erfurt. He was sounded by Stadion through Prince Schwartzenberg, who was sent to induce Alexander to ally himself with Austria, or at least to promise neutrality in the event of a fresh Franco-Austrian war. Alexander could not well, if he had desired it, get out of his Erfurt promise, and, moreover, he saw that Austria could not make a better bid regarding Turkey than Napoleon. Accordingly, Schwartzenberg returned with nothing better than Alexander's advice to Austria to keep the peace. This was on the 12th February 1809, when war was already decided on. When, finally, finding himself unable to resist the influence of Stadion, the Archduke Charles wrote that, " he washed his hands like Pilate,"[2] Austria stood absolutely alone against Napoleon and his allies, threatened by them on all her frontiers. It was on the 8th February 1809 that Austria finally decided on war, though it was not commenced till the 9th April. Metternich, who had returned to Vienna, seems to have given the final push which drove the Emperor to this decision. The grounds of the decision were :—

1. The estimates, already given, of Napoleon's strength at the commencement of war ;

2. the disinclination of the French nation for a new war, which had been impressed on Metternich by expressions of discontent in Paris, notably by Talleyrand ;

---

[1] Half regulars and half landwehr, the latter's muskets to be supplied by Austria.

[2] *B. K.*, i. 20.

3. Metternich's belief that under no circumstances would Russia take a decided part against Austria.[1]

Napoleon certainly did not want war at this juncture, for, though he wrote to the King of Bavaria, on the 15th January 1809, that he had "destroyed the Spanish armies and defeated the English army," it is highly improbable that he would have left Spain, as he did on the 16th January, but for the disquieting news from France, and regarding Austria.

[1] *Ibid.*, p. 29.

CHAPTER II

THE ARMIES AND THEIR LEADERS

(1) THE FRENCH ARMY

ON the 18th February 1808, Napoleon issued a decree for the reorganisation of the French infantry on the basis of a regiment of five battalions, of which four were to be " bataillons de guerre " with six companies each, and the fifth a four-company depôt battalion. A further decree was issued, on the 26th January 1809, for the immediate formation of fifth battalions of such regiments as still had only four. All these new battalions required new men and must take long to complete. The organisation was not complete till July 1809, when the war was over. In order to get the necessary men, fresh conscriptions had to be raised.

In September 1808, the Emperor obtained a senatus consultum placing at his disposal 20,000 men from each of the conscriptions of the years 1806-1809, 80,000 in all. These were, of course, men who had not yet been called up with the conscripts of the years referred to. At the end of December 1808, he called out 80,000 conscripts from those due in the year 1810, nearly two years before their time. They would, therefore, be immature youths.

It will be remembered that, immediately after the Erfurt meeting with Alexander, Napoleon had formally done away with the Grand Army which had fought the campaigns of 1806 and 1807. The troops remaining in Germany, other than those in the Hanseatic cities, were

to be known as the Army of the Rhine.   Its organisation
was fixed by decree of the 12th October 1808.

Its composition was as follows :—

(1) The 3d corps of three divisions :
 Morand's, with headquarters Magdeburg.
 Friant's, headquarters Baireuth.
 Gudin's, headquarters Hanover.

(2) St Hilaire's division, drawn from the now dissolved
 4th corps, headquarters at Stettin, with garrisons
 in Stralsund, Küstrin, and Glogau.

(3) Oudinot's division, which had been formed in November 1806, from the "compagnies d'élite" of the
 3rd battalions of the regiments of the Grand Army,
 headquarters at Hanau.

(4) Two divisions of heavy cavalry in Hanover and one
 in Baireuth—14 regiments in all.

(5) Three brigades (10 regiments) of light cavalry,
 widely distributed over North Germany and the
 Archduchy of Warsaw.

(6) An independent garrison for Danzig, under Rapp.

All these were under the chief command of Davout.
There were, in addition, some 10,000 French and Dutch
troops, under the separate command of Bernadotte, in
the Hanseatic cities, chiefly in Hamburg and Lübeck.
The two remaining divisions of the 4th corps (Legrand's
and Carra St Cyr's) were presently withdrawn to Metz.
Two other divisions (Molitor's and Boudet's), drawn from
the army of Italy and stationed about Lyons, made up
a reserve force of four divisions, which was available
wherever required.

Besides part of the 4th corps, there had been withdrawn from Germany the whole of the 1st, 5th, and
6th corps, and the Guard.   These were on their way to
Spain, where the capitulation of Baylen and the evacuation of Madrid had necessitated the assembly of a large
army.

B

Few readers, probably, would care to follow all the details of organisation which are given in Colonel Saski's work on the war of 1809, and we do not propose to give them.

On the 1st January 1809, Napoleon estimates the strength of the armies he expects to have in Germany and Italy by the end of March thus :—

I. GERMANY.

Army of the Rhine, exclusive of Oudinot	89,000
Oudinot's corps, now a separate command . . .	30,000
Divisions of Legrand and Carra St Cyr, to be brought from France	10,000
Bernadotte's corps	10,000
Confederate contingents	100,000
Total . .	239,000

Or, including Artillery, Engineers, etc., say 260,000.

II. ITALY.

Armies of Italy and Dalmatia	60,000
Divisions of Molitor and Boudet from Lyons . . .	23,000
Italians	20,000
Confederated States	20,000
	123,000

Or, as Napoleon loosely puts it, 150,000.

Altogether, there would be over 400,000 men to meet Austria in Germany and Italy.

The estimate was an extremely exaggerated one, as will appear presently, but it is interesting to note, as an example of the optimism which now formed a marked characteristic of the Emperor. It was stated in a letter to the Minister of War, not in a published document. Therefore it must be taken to represent correctly Napoleon's actual views, and not as a mere piece of "bluff" intended to frighten Austria and keep her quiet. The next corps to be formed was to be commanded by Masséna and styled "Corps of Observation of the

Rhine," assembling at Strasburg by the 15th March.
Its component parts were (1) the divisions of Legrand
and Carra St Cyr; (2) those of Boudet and Molitor,
now no longer destined for the Army of Italy; (3) a
brigade of four regiments of light cavalry stationed at
this time (February 23rd) about Lyons; (4) troops of
the Baden, Hesse Darmstadt, Saxon Ducal Houses, and
Nassau contingents.   As a reserve were organised
17 demi-brigades, stationed partly in France, partly
in Italy.   These were made up of companies drawn
from 5th battalions.   The whole of these 17 demi-
brigades consisted of conscripts of 1810.   These
"provisional" demi-brigades had 3 to 4 battalions of
4 to 6 companies, each of 140 men.   The result of
drawing on the depôt battalions was that regiments were
left without adequate means of replacing losses.

On the 21st March, the "Army of the Rhine," added
to Masséna's corps and the German contingents (Saxony
excepted), became the "Army of Germany," and was
presently transformed into a new "Grand Army."

On the 15th April, six days after the commencement
of war, but before there had been any real fighting, the
strength of the Army of Germany "present under arms"
was as follows :—

	Infantry.[2]	Cavalry.[3]	Total.	Guns.
2nd corps [1] (Oudinot). . .	16,005	5,293	21,298	42
3rd corps (Davout) . . .	51,968	8,629	60,597	75
4th corps (Masséna) . . .	34,805	2,765	37,570	66
7th corps (Bavarians, Lefebvre).	24,334	3,269	27,603	76
Wurtemberg corps (Vandamme)	10,028	2,214	12,242	16
Rouyer's division (German) .	3,820	—	3,820	(?) 6
Dupas' division (French) . .	4,713	1,378	6,091	(?) 12
Nansouty's Cuirassiers . .	—	5,085	5,085	18
	145,673	28,633	174,306	311

[1] Called " 2nd " here for convenience. At present it was only provisional.
[2] Includes field artillery, parks, and engineers.
[3] Includes horse artillery.

The divisions of Dupas and Rouyer were not yet in the Danube valley, to which they were marching from the north. Their absence reduced the available forces to about 164,000. In Saxony, available for operations against Austria, were about 20,000 men of the contingent. In Poland, for operations towards Galicia, were about 19,000 Poles under Poniatowski.

The army of Italy under Eugène Beauharnais numbered about 68,000, including fortress garrisons, though Eugène never commanded so many in the open field. In Dalmatia Marmont commanded about 10,500 men.

Altogether, therefore, Napoleon had in active operation against the Austrian frontiers some 275,000 men who were constantly being reinforced by drafts from France, and by the Guard marching back from Spain. In Spain Napoleon had nearly 300,000 men.

It is now necessary to consider the composition of this great army, of which the main portion, that on the Danube, was slightly smaller than the army which advanced from the Upper Main against Prussia in October 1806. Of the 174,000 men of the army of Germany, 54,287[1] were troops of the Rhenish Confederation, not far short of one third. There can be no doubt that the best of these, in 1809, were distinctly inferior to the best French troops. The pick of the French troops were probably the immortals of Auerstädt, the three divisions (Morand, Friant, and Gudin) of Davout's " 10th legion " of the Modern Cæsar. The other divisions composed exclusively of French troops were those of St Hilaire and Demont in Davout's corps, of Claparède and Tharreau in Oudinot's, of Molitor and Boudet in Masséna's, and of Dupas. Of the German auxiliaries General Bonnal considers Vandamme's Wurtemberg division to have been the best. They frequently

---

[1] The 7th corps (Bavarians), Wurtemberg division, Rouyer's division altogether 43,315. Besides these were 10,972 Baden and Hesse Darmstadt troops in Masséna's corps.

elicited warm praise from their chief, a hard man who demanded much. Their light infantry brigade distinguished itself by marching 50 miles in 38 hours, on the 21st and 22nd April, including a fair proportion of fighting and cross country work. Morand's and Gudin's divisions, about the same time, covered 94 miles in five days, on nearly all of which they had heavy fighting. On one of these days they covered 30 miles, much of the distance across fields.

Next to the Wurtembergers, General Bonnal places Wrede's Bavarian division, and last the two other Bavarian divisions. The Saxons only came on to the field on the Danube in the later part of the campaign. If Napoleon believed in the loyalty of his German auxiliaries, his marshals did not always do so. Austria made vigorous appeals to them to throw off the French yoke and join in a war of liberation. We shall find that, on one occasion at least, when the retreat of Wrede's Bavarians was reported, Davout openly expresses his suspicion of " quelque noire trahison." [1]

The fighting value of the French infantry was much weakened, as compared with what it had been at Austerlitz and Jena, by the large admixture of immature conscripts. Of the 80,000 conscripts of 1810 to be called up, 47,119 were to belong to the army of the Rhine, 15,793 to the army of Italy, 3913 to the army of Spain, and 7000 to the Guard.[2] The majority of these would go to the depôt battalions in France in the first instance, but, in a note by the Minister of War on the army of the Rhine,[3] it is said to be absolutely necessary to send 11,340 conscripts of 1810 direct to Germany, as well as 2625 of those of the preceding

[1] *Saski*, ii. 214.
[2] *Saski*, i. 25, n. 1.—The total here given is just under 74,000, which is probably all that could be expected out of a call for 80,000.
[3] *Saski*, i. 31.

four years who, if not immature in years, would be only partially trained. Another report[1] shows that more conscripts of 1810 would have to be sent to Masséna. These figures are by no means complete, and it is probably impossible to ascertain precisely how many young or half trained conscripts there were in the army at any given date. It is only certain that there were large numbers of such weakening elements which did not exist in the army of Jena, still less in that of Austerlitz, though they had begun to appear in 1807. They would still have been few if the Emperor's criminal policy towards Spain had not imposed upon him the necessity of maintaining a large army there as well as in Germany. Many things in this campaign point clearly to the Emperor's consciousness of the deterioration of his infantry. Amongst them is his adoption, before Wagram, of the Prussian system of regimental guns. Had he adopted it merely because he thought it essentially good, he would have done so before this war. He did not, but waited till after his repulse at Essling. Amongst his orders on the subject there is a passage which seems to show that the guns were given, not for their destructive power, but for the confidence they might be expected to give to the infantry to which they were attached. The Emperor writes on the 26th May[2]: "It is a matter of indifference to a battalion whether it has four-pounders, or three-pounders, or six-pounders." Again his formations in heavy columns show, as has often been noted, that the men could not always be trusted in difficult situations in the smaller columns of former days. The most notable instance is Macdonald's attack on the Austrian centre on the second day of Wagram. In that column 8 battalions in line, one in rear of the other, formed the front of a hollow square, the sides of which consisted respectively of 6 and 7 battalions in column.

---

[1] *Saski*, i. 104.   [2] *Corr.* 15,257.

The losses in such a formation, under a tremendous artillery and infantry fire, were necessarily immense, and the 8000 men who originally composed it were reduced to 1500. With the armies of Jena or Austerlitz it would have been simple waste of men to send them to the attack in such a formation ; with the army of Wagram the close association of large numbers was the only way to keep together the deteriorated infantry. Napoleon could ill afford such losses, but he felt that he must adapt his formations to the quality of his men. It was at this period that the French soldiers of the Empire first showed that they were capable of fleeing in the wildest disorder. They had done so the evening before Macdonald's attack, when the attack on the Russbach position was beaten off, and there was a regular " sauve qui peut " even amongst Oudinot's grenadier battalions. Such a panic is almost inconceivable amongst the men who fought for Napoleon at Austerlitz and Jena.

The French cavalry, on the battlefield at any rate, seems to have deteriorated less than the infantry. It consisted, in the first part of this campaign, only of light and heavy. There was only one dragoon regiment belonging to Baden. After Essling, dragoons arrived with the army of Italy. The light cavalry was mounted chiefly on French horses, but there was a considerable proportion of North German horses, procured in the campaigns of 1806-7. The heavy cavalry rode Norman and Flemish horses,—great weight carriers, but heavy and slow. After a long day's work before the charge in the evening of Eckmühl they were unable to get beyond a trot.[1]

As a means of getting information, Napoleon's cavalry

---

[1] Most of the French heavy cavalry were protected by cuirasses with back pieces. It was only, however, after 1809 that, at Nansouty's suggestion, the Carabiniers received cuirasses.—(Thoumas, *Les Grands Cavaliers de l'Empire*, Nansouty, p. 19.)

were never very good, and they had certainly not improved since the campaign of Ulm.

The artillery of 1809, with the exception of the horse batteries, was extremely deficient in mobility. There were no means of carrying the men, other than drivers, on the gun carriages, limbers, or ammunition waggons ; consequently even a trot was out of the question for any distance.[1] During the earlier part of the campaign the French guns were inferior in number to the Austrian. In April, Napoleon could oppose only 311 guns in all to 366 of the Austrians on the right, and 136 on the left bank of the Danube. It was not till Wagram that he had 554 against 414. At Essling he was largely outnumbered in guns, and much of his time between Essling and Wagram was occupied with increasing his artillery.

His system of massing great batteries to tear a gap in the enemy's line, reached its greatest development in the 100-gun battery on the second day of Wagram. He wrote to Eugène :[2] "Artillery, like the other arms, must be collected in mass if one wishes to attain a decisive result." But the deterioration of his infantry was also responsible to some extent for his action, as is evidenced by a letter to Clarke, dated 18th August : " The less good troops are, the more artillery they require There are corps d'armée with which I should require only one-third of the artillery which would be necessary with others." [3]

Whatever the discipline in the French army may have been at the commencement of operations, it soon relaxed under the stress of heavy marching and fighting. It had been the same after Jena, as has been described in the author's histories of that campaign and its sequel in Poland. In the present campaign, by the time Napoleon

[1] Bonnal, p. 357.   [2] *Corr.* 15,358, dated 16th June 1809.
[3] *Corr.* 15,678.

had reached Vienna the straggling and marauding had
become so bad that, in an order dated 14th May 1809,
the following passage occurs :—" The Emperor sees with
regret the disorders occurring in rear of the army ; they
are becoming such as to demand his attention.   Bad
characters seek to dishonour the army, and, instead of
being with their colours before the enemy, they remain
in the rear, where they commit every kind of excess, and
even of crime."   The order goes on to form five travelling
courts martial, with an escort of 150 men each.   The
orders for their procedure are simple : " Every straggler
who, under pretext of fatigue, leaves his corps for the
purpose of marauding, will be arrested, tried by court
martial, and executed on the spot." [1]

The following account of how Napoleon's army marched
from Ulm to Vienna in 1805, is probably equally applicable to the march from Ratisbon to Vienna in 1809.
" Ulm taken and negligently occupied, the army of
Bonaparte, the victorious army, was disbanded, and
appeared to me no longer anything but an army in rout,
but in rout in advance instead of in retreat.   This torrent
took the direction of Vienna, and henceforth there was
nothing but an ' arrive qui peut ' by roads full and en-
cumbered.   Our German army alone marched like regular
troops." [2]   Yet the writer, a French ' emigré ' in the
employ of Bavaria, describes later his utter astonishment
when, at the first sound of alarm, all this apparent disorder disappeared at once, and in its place stood regiments,
divisions, and corps, all in perfect order.

(2) THE AUSTRIAN ARMY

Austria's misfortunes in 1805 under the latest army
organiser, Mack, had the result of inducing the Emperor

[1] *Saski*, iii. 366.
[2] Comeau, *Memoires des Guerres d'Allemagne*, p. 219.

Francis at last to give a free hand to his brother Charles in the matter of rebuilding the military system of his country. He was henceforth to be solely responsible to the sovereign for all military matters. He was appointed "Generalismus," and was formally placed above the "Hofkriegsrath," which had so seriously interfered hitherto with generals in the field, and had mismanaged affairs generally.

Charles and Stadion were in accord in their belief that an effectual resistance to Napoleon could only be carried out by a national, as opposed to a purely professional army, and their hopes rested on the possible[1] creation of a nation in arms. Naturally, in a country like Austria, any such scheme was sure to incur vehement opposition from a bureaucracy reared in the principles of absolutism. The words "freedom," "people," and "Fatherland," now for the first time resounding through Austria, were repugnant to the opponents of the reformers. Moreover, there were many difficulties due to the heterogeneous composition of the Austro-Hungarian monarchy. There was in the German provinces a general willingness to incur the sacrifices required by a national service. In Hungary there was much less enthusiasm. The Hungarians thought only of themselves, and were for postponing all sacrifices until the actual approach of an enemy should endanger their native land. They seemed to consider their "Insurrection" would suffice.

If little was possible in the way of raising a landwehr in Hungary, nothing at all could be done in Galicia, where there was a general hope amongst the Poles that victory for Napoleon would mean the restoration of the Polish Kingdom. In a war against Napoleon the Imperial House could only rely thoroughly on its German subjects, and to a moderate extent on those of its Hungarian

---

[1] This account of the Austrian army of 1809 is a summary of the more important part of *B. K.*, i., pp. 48-73.

Kingdom.   Its Polish provinces were a positive source of weakness and danger.

Practically, therefore, only the German provinces could be employed for the creation of landwehr, and the Hungarian and Croatian " Insurrections " must be utilised as they stood, and for what they were worth, which was not very much.   In numbers they were supposed to amount to 100,000.   As a matter of fact they only produced 40,000.

The landwehr in the German provinces was constituted by an order of 9th June 1808, which was the cause of Napoleon's remonstrances at that period.

Altogether there were about 200,000 men raised thus, and, adding the " insurrections," the total of these popular forces was 240,000.   Of the landwehr some 15,000 were employed with the active army at the beginning of the war.   Taken as a body, however, this militia force was then of small military value, and, at most, was capable of local defence and of supplying losses in the regular army.   The Minister of War described it as " a body without a soul," not worth all its heavy cost, and a useless burden on the regular army.   The officers were of all sorts, many of them old and useless for war.

There was little of the spirit of war in the landwehr, and discipline was very bad.   One battalion attacked and wounded its chief with the bayonet.   Two others refused to march.   Eleven Bohemian battalions could only be got to march when regular troops were added to them.   Even then they only averaged about 500 men each, and those badly equipped and armed.

The general conclusion arrived at by Binder von Krieglstein is that the landwehr of 1809 was only fit for filling gaps in the regular army, and for that only on condition that the admixture of landwehr was made in small bodies.

In the later stages of the war the gaps in the regular

army had to be largely filled by landwehr battalions ; out of 175 battalions at or near Wagram there were 31 of landwehr, Vienna volunteers, or free corps.

The regular army presents quite a different picture. At its improvement the Archduke Charles had been working, off and on, ever since 1801. In the earlier years he had been hampered in various ways, and in 1805 the unfortunate Mack had tried his hand at the work. Now, however, since the beginning of 1806, Charles had a free hand, in so far as Austria's financial position would allow.

Of infantry regiments there were 46 German, 15 Hungarian, 17 " Border," and 2 garrison. These existed in 1805, but to them had been added since that year 9 " Jäger " battalions, the origin of which is to be traced to the sharpshooters of the Tyrol.

The cavalry consisted of 8 cuirassier, 6 dragoon, 6 chasseur, 12 hussar, and 3 uhlan regiments.

The artillery was divided into 4 regiments and 1 " bombardier " corps.

In 1805 Austria's army on a war footing was nominally 433,387 men, but she was scarcely able actually to put in the field 200,000. In 1809 she had

> 279,472 infantry,
> 36,204 cavalry,
> 12,800 artillerymen.

Altogether, including engineers, etc., she had 339,073. Behind these there stood in the interior of the country very considerable, though perhaps not very efficient, reserves.

The revised infantry drill book made provision for something on the model of the French skirmishing tactics, but the provisions for drawing in skirmishers, and for limiting their proportion to the main body, were not calculated to encourage the dash and enterprise

which had earned for the French 'tirailleurs' their
soubriquet of 'enfants perdus.' The French did not
limit the proportion of skirmishers, and in the wood
fighting near Laichling, on the 21st April, practically the
whole of some of Friant's battalions were dissolved into
skirmishers or small groups. The same thing had
occurred at the battle of Thann.

In the cavalry there was, notwithstanding the Archduke's horse-conscription, a shortage of horses, and the
Austrian horsemen were deficient in numbers as compared to the French.

The artillery had undergone a thorough overhauling,
and its field guns reached the large number of 760.
The organization was good, but, being new, the higher
officers were not sufficiently accustomed to it for a
proper arrangement and leading of the artillery in
battle.

The staff seemed to consider that their best qualifications consisted in mathematical knowledge, good writing,
topography, etc., and they believed that therein lay the
secret of the French success. Their practical qualifications were slight, and when Charles, in the spring of
1809, attempted to vitalise his staff by broad measures,
it was too late. The arrangements for issuing and
forwarding orders were very inferior.

The army commanded by the Archduke was as an
instrument of war very superior to the army of 1805,
but was still inferior to Napoleon's. The Austrian
soldier was as well trained as the French ; physically, he
was at least as good as his enemy ; the Austrian army
organization equalled the French ; there was nothing to
choose between the armament of the two armies ; in
artillery the Austrians at first had a preponderance of
guns.

It was on the moral, rather than on the physical side
that the soldiers of Francis I. lagged behind those of

Napoleon. With the Austrian, the idea of patriotism, as opposed to mere loyalty to a sovereign, was of recent birth ; with the Frenchman the spirit of the days when France stood alone against Europe still survived. It had not yet been realised in the army that it was for the Emperor's, not for France's, benefit that the doors of the Temple of Janus stood constantly open. The French soldiery were reared in the tradition of victory, based on a long series of stupendous successes. The faith of the common soldier, and of his officers, in the invincibility of their great leader was still unshaken. With the older men, the heroes of Italy, of Austerlitz, of Jena, and of Friedland, this faith remained constant to the end. They could never believe that the disasters of 1812-1815 were ever due to any shortcomings on Napoleon's part. That was only to be believed by conscripts, or foreign contingents. Breathing the atmosphere of such traditions, the French army believed itself invincible, under the leadership of the Emperor, and the effects of that belief in themselves and in him were made manifest in the activity and energy of every man, from the marshal to the private soldier, in the determination to conquer, in the assurance of victory which pervaded all ranks.

The Austrian army, on the other hand, had few traditions of victory, no leader in whom it placed implicit trust. It was long since it had tasted the sweets of victory, and the successes of Charles against Moreau, or Jourdan, or Masséna had never been such overwhelming victories as Napoleon's over Beaulieu, or Mélas, or Mack. The Austrian soldier was animated by the hope of avoiding defeat, rather than by the determination and assurance of victory which inspired his enemy. That was a spirit which gave but slight hope of success. The Austrian was by nature slow, and wanting in the animation, the vivacity, and the endurance of the Frenchman.

His slowness was as much part of his nature as rigidity was of the Prussian's, or doggedness of the Russian's. Consequently, the army, as a whole, was terribly slow. Its rapid movements were only in retreat.   It took seven days to march forward from the Inn to the Isar ; its left wing covered the same distance in the reverse direction in two.   Then it was a rout.   The army fought well at Essling, and again at Wagram, but on the former occasion it had the advantage of immense numerical superiority, and on the latter it had the encouragement of recent victory.   In both battles it was fighting in an open plain, better suited to its slow movements in great lines and masses than the close country in which the " battue " of Abensberg afforded such a terrible example of dissolution.   In close, wooded country the superior intelligence and individuality of the French carried everything before them.

The Austrian forces at the beginning of the war were the following :—

I. ARMY OF GERMANY (ARCHDUKE CHARLES).

(a) In Bohemia.

	Infantry.	Cavalry.	Total.	Guns.
I. corps (Bellegarde) .	23,600	2,100	25,700	68
II. corps (Kolowrat) .	20,600	2,700	23,300	68
	44,200	4,800	49,000	136

(b) South of the Danube.

	Infantry.	Cavalry.	Total.	Guns.
III. corps (Hohenzollern) .	23,903	1,010	24,913	96
IV. corps (Rosenberg) .	19,020	1,869	20,889	68
Vecsey's brigade (detached from II. corps) . .	5,894	1,025	6,919	—
V. corps (Archduke Louis) .	24,383	2,042	26,425	68
VI. corps (Hiller) . .	23,374	2,189	25,563	80
I. Reserve corps (Liechtenstein) . . .	12,998	2,566	15,564	34
II. Reserve corps (Kienmayer)	6,950	2,460	9,410	20
	116,522	13,161	129,683	366

(c) Towards Munich.

Jelacic (from VI. corps) .	9,962	1,039	11,001	16
Grand total army of Germany	170,684	19,000	189,684	518

II. ARMY OF ITALY (ARCHDUKE JOHN).

VIII. corps (Chasteter) .	18,250	1,942	20,192	62
IX. corps (Gyulai Ban of Croatia . . .	24,348	2,758	27,106	86
In Tyrol (part of VIII. corps)	9,800	370	10,170	17
In Dalmatia . .	7,000	300	7,300	14
	59,398	5,370	64,768	179

III. ARMY OF GALICIA.

VII. corps (Archduke Ferdinand) . . .	30,200	5,200	35,400	94

IV. RESERVES.

Landwehr, etc. . . .	188,525	3,318	191,843	—
Hungarian Insurrection .	20,810	15,207	36,017	—
Croatian do. . .	9,760	1,627	11,387	—
Slavonic do. .	5,000	—	5,000	—
	224,095	20,152	244,247	—

(3) THE COMMANDERS

The sun of Napoleon's military glory reached its zenith in 1806 and 1807. From then onwards it began to decline. His genius, " like a flaring firebrand, certainly made, when in full blaze, an overwhelming impression upon the spectator, but also consumed rapidly away, and, though fitfully throwing a few bright showers of sparks as high as ever, finally sank down into extinction." [1]

In the Emperor's correspondence, and in his strategy of 1806, we find the idea of the " bataillon carrée " most

[1] Yorck, *Napoleon as a General*, ii. 270.

fully developed, the assembly of his army in a state of semi-concentration such that it seemed to be almost a matter of indifference to the commander from which direction he was attacked. Whether the storm broke on his front or on either flank, his arrangement of his corps was such that he could always depend on its being met by a force of at least 50,000 men, and 50,000 French soldiers of 1806 could always be depended on to hold any force the enemy was likely to bring against them longer than was necessary to enable their reinforcement by the other sides of the " battalion square."

Again, the Emperor in 1806 kept his eye steadily fixed on the one essential of successful war, the attainment and the destruction of the enemy's army. He never, in those days, allowed his attention to be diverted by secondary objectives, which must infallibly be attained as a consequence of decisive victory over the enemy's main army. It is true that he wrote of marching on Berlin or Dresden, as if those geographical points were his objective ; but the whole spirit of his orders, and of his actions, indicates that the Prussian and Saxon capitals were not, in his eyes, the real objective. They were merely indicated as directions, the following of which was sure to bring about the battle he so eagerly desired. The moment he found that the enemy's army was retreating westward, he abandoned the road to Berlin for that to Erfurt. In 1809, and till the end, his military faith was the same as in 1806 ; but, after that year, we see him lapsing at times from the practice of his own principles. He became false to himself. The idea of the " battalion square " still pervaded his orders to Berthier for the strategical deployment of his army in April 1809. The centre of assembly was to be Ratisbon or Donauwörth, according as the Austrians commenced operations after or before a certain date. Berthier, managing to misunderstand him, distributed the army in two

c

"battalion squares" separated by a distance, and by a close country, rendering their mutual support impossible. Once Napoleon realised Berthier's extraordinary dispositions, he strove to correct them, and to form the "battalion square" between the two alternative points originally indicated. Yet, when his object was practically realised, we find him failing, sending Masséna on a circuitous march, which again separated the army. For Berthier's failure the marshal alone has generally been held responsible; but that is not quite fair. It was partly due to a rapidly-growing defect in the Emperor's orders. The fact is that Napoleon now began to think so much more rapidly than it was possible for his secretaries to take down his orders that these became elliptical to a degree that rendered them sometimes incomprehensible to others. To Napoleon himself, carrying in his mind the whole train of thought which led up to them, they were as clear as daylight. But he could not, or would not, lower himself to the level of the recipients of the orders, or explain their object in language beyond the possibility of misapprehension. Few of his marshals were capable of fully following the workings of his mind. Masséna and Davout, perhaps Soult and Lannes, generally could do so, but sometimes even Davout failed to fill in the blanks. Examples of this will be found in the campaign of 1809. The Emperor did not seem to realise this, except in the case of men like the Viceroy of Italy, in his orders to whom he condescended to explain matters in the fullest and simplest of words. In those cases, he realised that he must use language suited to the beginner.

We shall find the Emperor, in 1809, guilty of serious lapses from the practice of his own guiding principles. In 1806, he gave the direction of the Prussian capital as that to be followed with a purpose which we have already indicated, namely the certainty that somewhere on, or near, that line he would find, and beat, the Prussian army, and that its destruction must bring about the capture of Berlin, and all other secondary objects.

In 1809, he again indicated the enemy's capital as the direction to be followed, as soon as he should be able to pass from the defensive to the offensive. His orders of the 1st March, for the fortification of Passau, show clearly, according to General Bonnal,[1] that he had, even then, made up his mind to march direct on Vienna by the right bank of the Danube, without regard to the enemy's movements. The idea dominated him throughout, and caused him to throw away, in the end of April, chances of a decisive battle which would then probably have made an end of the war, without the defeat of Essling, or the far from decisive victory of Wagram, a defeat and a victory causing losses which the Emperor could ill afford. That leads us to another failing of Napoleon which became more and more marked as time went on. His wonderful successes in every previous campaign, and the height to which his power had risen, by the practical subjection of all Europe to his dominion, tended to fan the flame of his pride, to make him deem himself invincible and infallible, to cause him to assume that what he desired was certain to happen. The wish now began to be father to the thought. Of this we shall find numerous instances in this campaign, the most notable, perhaps, being when, notwithstanding Davout's positive assertions that the greater part of the Austrian army was in front of himself, the Emperor persisted in believing that Charles was in full retreat on Vienna by the right bank of the Danube. His constant over-estimates of his own forces, not in bulletins but in letters to his generals and ministers, are other examples of this failing.

Another evil effect of Napoleon's growing pride was

[1] *Bonnal*, p. 28.

the contempt which he exhibited for his enemy. On more than one occasion, he wrote of Austrian regular troops as " cette canaille," and spoke of their commanders with equal contempt. He seemed to think that Austria had stood still, and was now just what she had been 10 years before. He failed to realise that she had profited by the lessons he had taught her, and that her armies, and her commander-in-chief, were very different from the troops and leaders of 1796 and 1805.

Napoleon had only once before, in 1797, been personally opposed to the Archduke Charles in the field. Then the Austrian prince had taken over command of an army already demoralised by frequent disaster, and with no part left but to retreat on the capital, delaying and harassing the enemy as much as possible. Under these circumstances Charles had had no fair chance of showing his worth.

Young as Napoleon was when he first commanded in chief, his opponent of 1809 was two years his junior in age, and had held command of an Austrian army at twenty-five. Napoleon was nearly twenty-seven when he first led the army of Italy to victory. That Charles was ever quite in the same grade with Napoleon, as a general, probably no one will venture to maintain. He succeeded against the minor French generals. He beat Moreau in 1796, Jourdan in 1796 and 1799 ; he checked Masséna in 1799 and 1805, but in this, his last, campaign of 1809 he was to show how very far he was behind the Emperor, even when the latter was beginning to decline. The schools of war in which the two men began their military life were very different. Napoleon, the child of the Revolution, began his practical soldiering with armies which had already revolutionised war. Charles, on the other hand, was brought up in the strictest principles of war, as they were understood in the first nine decades of the eighteenth century, and as they continued to be understood for some time afterwards outside France.   It is all to Charles' credit that he surpassed nearly all his contemporaries in Austria and Prussia in throwing off the shackles of the old school, and assimilating the principles practically demonstrated by the French Revolutionary armies, and perfected by Napoleon.   But he never completely rid himself of the bonds of his early training.   He started the present campaign with the very correct intention "to seek out and engage the enemy,"[1] but, when it came to practice, he frequently deferred the day of battle, seeming to look upon it as an evil to be put off as long as possible, rather than the supreme object, the attainment of which, at the earliest favourable moment, was above all things to be desired.   That was Napoleon's desire in 1806 ; in 1809 he sometimes let the opportunity slip.

The Archduke thus states his views as to the object of war in his *Principles of Strategy*[2]—"The principal object of a plan of operations is often the attainment of a geographical point, but that is not an absolute condition of every enterprise.   In a war of invasion the capital is the decisive point to be aimed at, and the conclusion cannot be avoided that, whatever be the internal condition of an empire, the occupation of the capital inflicts a fatal blow on its real and reputed power. But such an objective is a remote and ideal rather than a direct one for operations which should before all things be directed against the organised forces of the enemy. Thus in a well-conceived plan of campaign the position of those forces will alone decide the objective of the earlier operations, and it is only possible to select the most advantageous geographical points after having disorganised and destroyed the adversary's means of defence."

Charles had to contend against many difficulties which

[1] *B. K.*, i. 320.   [2] Vol. i. p. 30, note, of the French translation.

Napoleon, as Emperor, knew not. The Austrian was a soldier first and last, and very little of a statesman. Yet he was a man of many, and sometimes curious tastes, as is evidenced by his collected writings, ranging from treatises on strategy and tactics to essays on the Gospels. He was surrounded by an atmosphere of intrigue, military as well as political, which, to his open character, was repugnant. He had succeeded at last in getting rid of the influence of the " Hofkriegsrath," the " Aulic Council," which in former wars had so fatally tied the hands of himself and others ; but he was still hampered by the presence in the field of his Imperial brother, rarely capable of resisting the temptation to interfere in what he did not understand. If a subordinate French general was untrustworthy, or suspected of disloyalty, Napoleon summarily got rid of him.[1] Charles had no such power, and he constantly suffered from the enforced retention of men, like Hiller, his avowed opponents.

Charles's subordinates, taken all round, were very inferior to those of Napoleon. The latter may not have been fitted for independent command, though that can hardly be said of Davout and Massena, but they were, as a rule, admirable instruments of execution, under the guidance of their great chief, and they were capable of making the best of a bad situation when landed in it. That was certainly not the case with the Austrian corps commanders. There can be no possible comparison between the conduct of Hiller between Abensberg and Landshut, and that of Davout on the 19th-22nd April, when exposed to the attack of the greater part of the Austrian army. Binder v. Krieglstein holds that only two Austrian generals, Stutterheim and Radetzky, showed

---

[1] As an example see Koch's *Masséna* regarding the way in which Napoleon got rid of Becker, Masséna's Chief of Staff, probably unjustly. The real reason probably was that Napoleon noticed Masséna's indolent tendency to leave the command of his corps in Becker's hands.

any capacity in the campaign.   Nepotism was rampant in the Austrian army of 1809, and Charles found himself hampered by incompetent commanders like his brothers Louis and John, and the Empress's brother Ferdinand.

Another disadvantage from which Charles suffered was his own bad health.   He had been compelled by it to resign his command in 1800, and he was subject to epileptic fits.   There seems strong reason to believe that, during the greater part of an important day in April, he was suffering from such a fit, and had locked himself into his own quarters, the result being that nothing was done, in his absence, by his subordinates.   There was no one to take his place, as Gneisenau took Blücher's after Ligny, when the old marshal was suffering from the effects of his fall.   Unlike Napoleon, Charles was often undecided; sometimes he yielded to his natural indolence, as when he told Rosenberg at Eckmühl to get out of his difficulties as best he could.   Napoleon was always to be found in the forefront of a battle, Charles, as at Eckmühl, was sometimes miles in rear of the field on which his personal presence was desirable.   That was certainly not due to any lack of personal courage, for excess of bravery was in him, at times, a fault.   At Essling, and again at Wagram, he threw himself at critical moments into the thick of the fray, seizing a standard and leading his wavering troops back into the hottest fire.   By his personal example he saved an apparently desperate situation, when his subordinates had lost control of their troops.   Nevertheless, even in 1809, the day had long gone by when personal combat was a fitting part for the commander of a great army.   That part Napoleon had played as a young general at Arcola ; as Emperor he never did so.

Something must now be said of the subordinate commanders individually.   From among the French corps commanders several names are missing of those

who played a prominent part in the campaigns of
1805-7. Ney, Soult, Mortier, Victor, Augereau, and
Suchet were in Spain; Murat was governing his new
Kingdom of Naples. On the other hand, Berthier,
Davout, Masséna, Oudinot, Bernadotte, and Lefebvre were
still with the army, to join which Lannes, Bessières, and
Lasalle hastened back from the Peninsula. Later on,
appear generals who took no part in the recent wars,
Eugène Beauharnais, Macdonald, and Marmont. Berthier
was still Chief of the General Staff, and, before Napoleon's
arrival at the front, commanded the army for his master.
That soon brought out his incapacity for separate command,
and showed him to be nothing more than an excellent secre-
tary for the drafting and conveyance of the Emperor's
orders. Even in this department, however, with all his
industry, and all his long acquaintance with Napoleon's
methods, he was far from infallible. We shall see
presently how completely he failed to realise the spirit
of the Emperor's orders. Yet, some allowance must be
made for him on account of the elliptic form in which
those orders reached him. Davout hinted that he misunderstood the Imperial orders, but Berthier did not take
the hint. Once he found himself actually commanding
in the field, after the commencement of hostilities, he
completely lost his head and maddened generals, officers,
and men alike with a succession of orders and counter-
orders which wore them out and brought them back in the
end to where they started from. It is difficult to imagine
a more pitiful picture than that afterwards drawn of
him by his then aide-de-camp, Lejeune —" I was much
distressed to see this man, so courageous, so calm in the
midst of fire, whom no danger could intimidate, trembling
and bending under the weight of his responsibility."

Masséna,[1] the 'doyen' of the corps commanders,

---

[1] It seems more convenient to write of the marshals by their surnames than
by the titles conferred on them.

Napoleon still estimated at the value of the hero of
Rivoli, of Zurich, and of Genoa, but others seem to have
recognised the deterioration since those days. The
Emperor wrote to Eugène, " I know that in Italy you
affect to despise Masséna. If I had sent him, what has
happened [Eugène's defeat at Sacile] would not have
occurred. Masséna has military talents before which we
must bow down ; his failings must be forgotten, for all
men have some." Yet Napoleon had seen little of
Masséna lately. The marshal was neither at Austerlitz
nor at Jena and played but a minor part in Poland.
Consequently, the Emperor had had few opportunities of
observing the deterioration of the last few years, due to
self-indulgence and avarice as much as to the wear and
tear of war. Masséna was now 51 years of age, still
young as we reckon generals now. Under the impulse
of a great stimulus he would still rise to the occasion, as
at Essling and at Wagram, but in ordinary circumstances
his native Italian indolence had grown on him. He
never during this campaign signed a general order to his
corps. He left that work, and probably also a great deal
of the framing of orders, to Becker, his Chief of Staff.
He was dilatory in his movements, failed to ride with his
advance guard, even when he had special orders to do so.
On the 21st April, his late rising and late arrival at the
front left his advance guard to hesitate, in the absence
of orders, and lost a good chance of destroying Hiller's
corps. Yet, with all the shortcomings which he cannot
have failed to notice, Napoleon's continued confidence in
Masséna is evidenced by his appointment, in 1810, to
the Spanish command. Wellington's estimate placed
him above all the marshals who commanded there, but
it must be remembered that Masséna was then in his
decadence, and that Napoleon would probably have better
consulted his own interests by sending Davout. Perhaps
obstinacy had something to do with the choice.

As for Davout, the "little, smooth-pated, unpretending man, who was never tired of waltzing," there had been some scoffing amongst the other marshals when he was raised to that dignity. His conduct at Auerstädt silenced the scoffers and marked out Davout as the first of the corps commanders. He never had an opportunity of proving his worth in separate command, except at Hamburg. His strategical insight equalled Masséna's, and it was he who warned Berthier, in vain, that he was off the track. His character was higher and more stable than Masséna's, and he would probably have managed the unruly team of marshals and generals in Spain better than the latter, who constantly rubbed them up the wrong way. Of his conduct on the critical days of the 19th-22nd April 1809 it is impossible to speak too highly. He was not afraid to stick to his own opinion, even against the Emperor's, as to the Austrian movements before and after Eckmühl, and Napoleon admitted his value by sometimes asking his opinion.

Lannes arrived at the front, from Spain, just as the fighting began. The "pigmy" that Napoleon said he found was now the "giant" whom he lost by a stray round shot at Essling. That the Emperor felt his loss deeply can hardly be doubted when one notes the constant references to Lannes' death in the correspondence. A few words in a bulletin sufficed to notify the death of a man like St Hilaire, who, to great military capacity, added an uprightness and sweetness of disposition which endeared him to all. Lannes, too, was beloved by his men, and, if he was not a general of the first order, he was at least remarkable for his constancy in command, as witness Saalfeld, Jena, and Pultusk. He never feared to speak his mind to Napoleon, and that fact seems to add improbability to the story of his reproaches on his deathbed ; for, had he thought as he is said to have spoken, he would have said his say without waiting till he knew that death was about to carry him beyond the reach of Napoleon's anger.[1]

Marmont, Oudinot, and Macdonald all gained their marshal's batons after Wagram. Marmont wrote much on war, but was not remarkably successful as a general, and suffered one very notorious defeat at Wellington's hands. Napoleon had always had a liking for him, though his letters in this campaign contain many a stern censure of Marmont's delays. Nor can Oudinot or Macdonald lay any claim to great reputation as generals. The last named was, above all the marshals, notable as upright and honest beyond suspicion. Bernadotte was again in trouble with the Emperor at Wagram, as he had been at Austerlitz and Jena, and was sent home in disgrace. His abilities were undoubtedly great, but for his character as a man it is impossible to feel any respect.

Lefebvre did well on the whole in the first days of the campaign, indeed showed himself clearer headed than Berthier, but he incurred many sharp censures for dilatoriness in the Tyrol. They were sometimes due to Napoleon's persistent over-estimate of the forces under Lefebvre's command. One of Lefebvre's letters throws a curious side light on the scramble for rewards, and the intrigues amongst the generals of the French army. He writes to Napoleon—" I shall be unfortunate if your Majesty does not honour me with rewards ; my staff had nothing in Spain, and this war here is still more disheartening. My two aides-de-camp, Maingarnaud and Montmarie, are wounded ; Fontanges, adjutant, also has a contusion ; the Bavarians also loudly demand crosses from me, and, as a chief (Wrede) of that army is jealous of me, the failure of my demands, rather than his very

[1] On this subject see Rose's *Napoleon*, ii. 192-193. That writer, on the whole, seems to disbelieve the story. It is unnecessary to discuss it further here.

ordinary military talents, gives him a weapon against me."[1] Napoleon had a better opinion of Wrede, though, when the Bavarian tried to stop him at Hanau, in 1813, the Emperor made short work of him. To Eugène de Beauharnais, Josephine's son, then aged twenty-seven, was given the command of the Army of Italy. It was his first command in chief, and, though the Emperor commended his conduct of the campaign, it was rather to the incapacity of the Archduke John, and to the misfortunes of Charles, compelling John's retreat, that Eugène owed his satisfactory issue from operations in which both sides vied with one another in the commission of blunders.

Limits of space confine us to a mere mention of the cavalry generals. Bessières was perhaps a better general than Murat, though he had not the latter's reputation as a 'sabreur.' Lasalle (killed at Wagram), the man who took Stettin with a handful of hussars in 1806, Napoleon described as "an officer of the highest merit, and one of our best light cavalry generals." Nansouty, Espagne (killed at Essling), Montbrun, Marulaz, and St Sulpice were the best known of the others. Montbrun did very well before Eckmühl. Of the commanders of infantry divisions, the most notable were Morand, Friant, Gudin, St Hilaire (killed at Essling), and Vandamme. The violent and brutal temper of the last had brought him into collision with every marshal he had served under, a fact which perhaps induced Napoleon to keep him in command of the Wurtemberg division, attached to no corps. The generals of division and brigade had not fallen away from the high standard of 1806-7, and the same can be said of the other superior officers. The officers of lower grades, in the French divisions, were still to a great extent excellent, but some of those sent to the front from depôts, at the head of newly formed corps, were distinctly below the standard of the old stagers of

[1] *Saski*, ii. 276.

Austerlitz and Jena. The officers of the allied troops had gained in value by their association with the French in the field, a gain which, later on, was turned against Napoleon.[1]

The loss of French officers, in proportion to men, was remarkably high, especially at Wagram, a fact which once more points to the deterioration of the rank and file, calling for self-sacrifice by their leaders.

Of the Austrian commanders subordinate to the Archduke Charles there is little to be said, for few, if any, of them rose above mediocrity. The name of Radetzky, the victor of Novara in 1849, is perhaps the only one which will be remembered. He did well as Chief of the Staff to Schwarzenberg in 1813-14. Stutterheim, who did well, and has written a good history of the war, did not long survive it. Wimpffen and Grünne, Charles' chief staff officers, had not even Berthier's qualifications. They exercised some influence, not for good, on Charles, but they did so, not so much by openly arguing out their views with him, as by putting him in a position, as at Wagram, in which he had no option but to act as they ..ished. Their action in some degree resembled that of Massenbach in the Prussian army of 1806. Of the Archduke John nothing favourable can be said. He at first beat Eugène in Italy, but the action of Sacile shows him in the light of a blunderer, who only won because his adversary made even greater mistakes. He was conceited as well as incompetent, fancying himself something of a soldier, a title to which, according to Binder v. Krieglstein, he had not the slightest claim. In his campaign in Hungary he kept wasting time by putting forward wild schemes. When these were negatived by Charles, he had the disloyalty to appeal to Cæsar, in the shape of the Emperor Francis. The latter, fortunately,

[1] *Bonnal*, p. 352.

had the good sense to snub his younger brother and to tell him to obey orders. John's presence at Wagram some hours earlier than he began to put in an appearance would probably not have influenced the result; for his force was very inferior to what Napoleon believed it to be. Nevertheless he was to blame for not arriving.

Another brother, the Archduke Louis, commanded the V. corps during the Ratisbon campaign. He, too, was remarkable chiefly for the slowness of his movements.

Hiller, to whom Louis was subordinated, was openly opposed to Charles, and, after the separation of his wing at Landshut, seized the excuse for corresponding with the Emperor, instead of with Charles. His conduct of the retreat on Vienna was not marked by any ability, and he lost the opportunity of rejoining Charles by Linz. Instead of that, he fought at Ebelsdorf, where his ineffi- cient command resulted in a sound beating in an immensely strong position. He resigned his command, just before Wagram, on the ground of ill-health, conduct very different from that of Masséna, who insisted on commanding the French 4th corps from a carriage when, owing to a fall, he was unable to mount his horse. Klenau, who succeeded Hiller, is spoken of by Binder v. Krieglstein as one of the best of the Austrian generals, but does not appear to have done anything very remarkable.

Rosenberg, commander of the IV. corps, bore the brunt of the fighting at Eckmühl and at Wagram. On the former occasion he was left by Charles to get out of a very awkward position as best he could. On the whole, he did as well as could be expected under the circumstances. The unfortunate Thierry was sacrificed in front of Abensberg and not properly supported. Then he was, rather unfairly, blamed for the disaster which followed.

Schustekh, whose name frequently occurs, was a tough

old fighter of the Blücher type, but quite unsuited to separate command.   The regimental officers seem to call for no special remark.   Even allowing for their inferiority in numbers to the French, their losses at Wagram were much less.   The way in which the Austrian retreat on Landshut became a mere panic flight does not speak much in their favour.

CHAPTER III

PREPARATIONS ON BOTH SIDES TO THE END OF MARCH 1809

NAPOLEON was still at Valladolid when, on the 15th January, 1809, he began his active preparations for war with Austria. At this moment he was fully convinced that Austria meant war. He was right in that, though he was not so well justified in his profession of belief that he had completed his task in Spain.

On this day he writes to the King of Bavaria that he had "destroyed the Spanish army and beaten that of England." He goes on to warn the King that he will have to mobilise the Bavarian army, and expresses a hope that he may rely on its numbering 40,000 men. At the same time, orders were sent to Davout for the despatch southwards, as if *en route* for Italy, of Oudinot's infantry, three regiments of cavalry, and 18 guns. Oudinot, however, was to stop when he reached Augsburg and await further orders. Needless to say, orders to proceed to Italy never reached him, and were never intended to be issued. The real object of his movement was to support Bavaria, which, as in 1805, would probably be the first object of Austria's attack.

The Emperor left Valladolid secretly on the 16th January, reaching Paris on the 23rd. Almost every day brought further confirmation of Austria's hostile intentions. As we know, the final decision in favour of war was arrived

at in Vienna on the 8th February, though of course that
was not made public.

But just at the time of the Emperor's arrival in Paris
there happened to be a temporary lull, as he saw some
reason to think Austria was less active in her preparations,
and, if not needlessly alarmed, might still be kept from
war till May or June. Above all things the Emperor
desired time, for he had much to do before he would be
really ready. By the 13th February, these hopes were
dissipated, and orders for preparations followed in rapid
succession. One aimed at raising the battalions of the
Army of the Rhine to their full complement of 840 men
by drafts from the regimental depôts in France. Oudinot's
battalions, on the other hand, could only be raised to 560,
as the depôts of regiments now in Spain could only supply
him with two, instead of four, companies each. He could only
have two divisions, instead of three as originally designed.
The Guard was ordered to return from Spain as far as
Mont de Marsan, north-east of Bayonne. Other orders
provided for the formation of the 4th battalions of Davout's
21 regiments. Letters to Eugène at Milan, and to Louis
at the Hague, directed them to take measures towards
the financial discredit of Austria, and the prevention of
her raising a loan. Lastly, on the 23rd February, came
the formation of Masséna's " Corps of Observation of the
Rhine," and, on the 3rd March, the project for the reserve
corps, at the expense of the final exhaustion of the depôts.
The constitution of these corps has already been noted.[1]

The Emperor now commenced the assembly of his
army, not its concentration for immediate operations, but
its location in cantonments spread widely enough for convenience of subsistence, over an area from which it could
be united in a few marches on a point to be decided on.
This general assembly was to be completed by the 20th

[1] The orders of the 1st March for the fortification of Passau will be more
conveniently dealt with later.

D

March, and Napoleon no doubt had Donauwörth on the Danube in his mind's eye as the central point. He shows this in his letter of the 6th March to Davout, which was not intended for publication, in which he directs the Marshal to send to Donauwörth the greater part of the magazines existing at Magdeburg, Forcheim, Kronach, Bamberg, and Wurzburg. His orders for the collection of biscuit at Ulm, Ingolstadt, Passau, Munich, and Augsburg were sent, through his minister Otto, to the King of Bavaria, and were much more likely to leak out than those sent to Davout. The biscuit alone which Davout had to send to Donauwörth more than equalled the whole amount ordered at the other five places, and the Emperor says plainly to the marshal : " My intention is that the first magazine of the Army of the Rhine shall be formed at Donauwörth.   There will be at that point a magazine of clothing, a magazine of food, and a magazine of cartridges."

General Bonnal [1] opines that the fact of collection of supplies at Ulm, Ingolstadt, Augsburg, and Munich was intended to come to the ears of the Austrians, to induce them to believe in a French concentration between the Danube and the Isar, and thus, perhaps, to induce them to bring the greater part of their forces to the right bank of the Danube.

The four divisions of Legrand, Carra St Cyr, Molitor, and Boudet were to move up from France to Ulm by the 20th March.

Davout was to assemble his corps on Bamberg as a centre, the Saxons near Dresden, and the three Polish divisions near Warsaw.

Oudinot's corps, with Espagne's cuirassiers, was to be at Augsburg, behind the Lech, the bridge heads on which were to be repaired.   The Wurtemberg division to be at Aalen, Ellwangen, and Neresheim.   The three Bavarian divisions at Straubing, Landshut, and Munich.

[1] P. 31.

For the present, the mission of the Polish corps, under Poniatowski, far away from the rest of the army, was to threaten Cracow. The two Saxon divisions had to defend Dresden against a sudden attack. That capital being of doubtful safety, the King of Saxony and his family were advised, at the first rumour of invasion, to seek a safe retreat on the Rhine.

As for the rest of the army, the idea was to cover the assembly by Davout's corps north of the Danube, and by the Bavarians south of it.[1]

Davout carried out his task by using Jacquinot's light cavalry for a line of outposts along the Austrian frontier, touching the Saxon outposts on the left, and the Bavarian on the right. Some 30 miles behind these stood Friant's division, about Bayreuth, and Pajol's light cavalry, about Amberg. In second line, 30 miles farther back again, were Morand at Bamberg, and Gudin at Nürnberg.

On the 17th March, Napoleon sent orders for St Hilaire's division, and the heavy cavalry of Nansouty and St Sulpice, to be moved south, from near Magdeburg, to fill the space between Nürnberg and the Danube.

On the 18th March, the Emperor formed, at Wurzburg, a new division of 9000 men under Rouyer. This

---

[1] Napoleon, as is pointed out by Colonel Foch in his *Conduite de la Guerre*, guarded his "assembly of the army" ("strategical deployment") by a shield held well in advance. That is, he was not content to select an area of assembly so far removed from the frontier that he would have time to complete it before the enemy could traverse the intervening space, if not seriously opposed. That was one factor in his dispositions, but he also gained time by provisions for checking the enemy's advance. This he did by the employment of a general advance guard of the army, consisting of one or more corps, which could offer a serious resistance and delay the enemy's advance. In this case, he had two such advance guards, Davout north of the Danube and the Bavarians towards the Inn frontier. Colonel Foch severely criticises Moltke's strategical deployment, in July 1870, on the ground that it was protected by the factors of time and space only, and not by any powerful advance guard of the army, such as Napoleon would have employed to gain time for his assembly of the army.

comprised the contingents of some of the smaller German states, and was attached to Davout's corps.

Yet another small reserve division was formed on the 21st March under Demont. It consisted of the 4th battalions of Davout's infantry. The Emperor gave as his reason for forming it that the divisions of Morand, Friant, and Gudin would otherwise become too unwieldy. General Bonnal[1] says this is false, and that the real motive was to impose on the enemy by an apparent increase in the strength of his army, by the creation of a fresh division, which in reality added nothing.

Just at this moment the Emperor came to the conclusion that Austria could not be ready before the end of April, and he ordered cantonments to be spread wider, so that the troops could subsist on the country. Almost immediately afterwards, however, reports from the Bavarian General Wrede asserted that Austria was ready to begin at any moment, and would probably advance from Bohemia. Two days later, Napoleon heard that one of his couriers had been stopped at Braunau. Preparations therefore recommenced with vigour.

The guard was ordered to be sent from Bayonne to Paris in carts, doing triple stages. Oudinot was ordered to move over to the right back of the Lech, so as to economise supplies on the left bank, in case the line of the river had to be defended. Masséna was to call up the Baden and Hesse-Darmstadt troops for incorporation in his corps, and to keep always ready four days' supply of bread and the same of biscuit. The engineer and bridging corps were assigned to the several corps d'armée.

Let us now see what were the Austrian movements up to the same period, the end of March 1809.

Of the nine corps d'armée, and the two so-called

---

[1] P. 37.

Reserve corps, constituting the Austrian regular army, two were assigned to the command of the Archduke John on the Italian frontier and in the Tyrol, whilst one was given to the Archduke Ferdinand in Galicia. The remainder (corps I.-VI. and the two Reserve corps) made up the army of Germany.

As in the case of the French, we shall confine ourselves, for the moment, to a brief statement of actual movements, leaving discussion of the plan of campaign till later.

Even in January, the assembly of the corps, the calling in of men on furlough, and other preparations for war had begun. It soon became apparent that the third battalions of the Galician regiments, the landwehr battalions to be attached to the regular army, and some of the "Border" regiments would be late. There was a threatened deficiency of 30,000 men. As the success of the original idea, of falling on and destroying the army of the Rhenish Confederation before Napoleon could bring reinforcements, depended on promptitude, it was first of all resolved not to await these troops. Later on this decision was reversed.

The army was to be openly placed on a war footing on the 1st March, but many troops were already marching so early as the 25th, and even the 20th February.

The Archduke Charles' first orders were for the corps to assemble as follows :—

I. corps on 10th March at Saaz.

II.   „   1st   „   Pilsen.

III.   „   17th   „   Prag.

IV.   „   27th   „   Pisek.

V.   „   22nd   „   Budweis.

VI.   „   18th   „   Wels.

I. Reserve corps on 17th March at Iglau.

II.   „   „   18th   „   Enns.

Under that arrangement, all but the VI. corps at Wels, and the I. Reserve corps at Enns, would be north of the Danube.

In the middle of March all this was changed, and it was decided to leave only the I. and II. corps north of the Danube, and to march the III., IV., V., and I. Reserve corps, viâ Linz, across the river, to join the VI. and II. Reserve and advance on the Inn.

On the 31st March, the Austrian positions were as follows :—

    I. corps at Saaz.
    II.   „   Pilsen.
    III.   „   Linz.
    IV. corps south of Budweis, marching on Linz.
    V. corps following the IV.
    VI. corps between Wels and Gmünden.
    I. Reserve corps near IV. and V.
    II. Reserve corps near Enns.

The rate of marching was not rapid, and some of the corps were still waiting for part of their regiments. The average daily march, up to the Inn, varied from only 5 miles, in the case of the V. corps, to 9½ in that of the II. Reserve corps.

At the same time the French positions were—

3rd corps (Davout)—(1) Jacquinot's light cavalry, along the Austrian frontier north of the Danube.

(2) Pajol's light cavalry round Amberg.

(3) Friant south of Baireuth.

(4) Morand south of Neumarkt.

(5) Gudin between Morand and Friant.

(6) St Hilaire (a march north of Bamberg) and the heavy cavalry of St Sulpice and Nansouty approaching the space between Nürenberg, Pleinfeld and Ingolstadt.

(7) Rouyer's new division marching on Wurzburg.

(8) Demont's reserve division towards Ansbach.

Hesse Darmstadt troops at Mergentheim, marching

to join Masséna. Badeners also marching from Pforz-
heim.

Wurtemberg Division (Vandamme) round Heiden-
heim.

On the right bank of the Danube were—

Masséna at Ulm, along the Danube nearly down to
the mouth of the Lech, and up the Iller. Oudinot was
at Augsburg and on the right bank of the Lech, with
Espagne's cuirassiers about Pfaffenhofen.

7th corps—Bavarians (Lefebvre)—one division each
at Munich (Prince Royal), Landshut (Deroy) and
Straubing (Wrede), with cavalry outposts towards the
frontier, communicating on their left with Jacquinot's
on the left bank of the Danube. Dupas' French
division, marching from Hamburg, was still far away
north of the Main.

The Saxons (Bernadotte) were at Dresden.

CHAPTER IV

THE THEATRE OF WAR AND THE PLANS
OF CAMPAIGN

THE theatre of the campaign which we are about to describe is mainly situated in the valley of the Danube, from Ulm in the west to Komorn in the east, some 90 miles as the crow flies below Vienna. Nearly everything of importance occurred in a strip of country never more than 50 or 60 miles broad on the right bank of the great river, or on the very edge of the left bank.

Beyond these limits were the operations of Lefebvre in the Tyrol, the retreat of the Austrians through Bohemia from Ratisbon to Vienna, and, at the close of the war, back to Znaim. There were also the advance of Eugène Beauharnais from Italy and the operations in Poland and Saxony; but, after all, these were mostly secondary operations, and what we are primarily concerned with is the country on the two banks of the Danube, and for 50 or 60 miles south of its right bank. Above all, what is important is the space on the perimeter of which are situated Donauwörth, Augsburg, Munich, Landshut, Ratisbon and Ingolstadt.

For the invader of Austria coming from the west, the Danube is, or at least was in 1809, of almost incalculable importance; for, as long as he could keep himself on the river, he had it as the best possible means of supplying himself with food, ammunition, and stores of all sorts. Even troops could be brought down by it more

56

quickly than they could march; for it is a rapid river in its upper course, falling 950 feet between Ulm and Vienna, which leaves only 450 feet for the fall between the Austrian capital and the sea, a distance nearly thrice as great. To the defender it could never, before the days of steam, be of the same value, as the current is too strong to enable him to use it as a means of bringing up supplies.

At Ulm the influx of the Iller causes the Danube to become navigable for flat bottomed barges of 100 tons. The river there looks at least as large as the Thames at Richmond. By the time Ingolstadt is reached, the river has already increased to a breadth of 140 yards, and 10 miles short of Ratisbon, it is shown in the photograph facing p. 56. At Ratisbon itself it separates into two branches on either side of an island.

The Danube is said to have some 400 tributaries, many of which are themselves first-class rivers, descending from areas in Switzerland or the Tyrol, which, in the spring, are still covered deeply with the winter's snows. The melting of these, with the first heats of May and June, necessarily causes the sudden inpouring of vast quantities of water, with consequent sudden and great rises in the Danube. How nearly one of these floods of the melting snows proved the destruction of Napoleon's army will be seen later. The Emperor had only campaigned previously on the Danube in the autumn and winter, and he refused to take heed of the warnings which he received of the suddenness of floods in the early summer. Napoleon himself writes of the river at Vienna on the 1st July as being four feet above extreme low water and thirteen below high flood level.[1] It rose three feet in the night of the 21st-22nd May.

When it is stated that the river from Ulm to

[1] 24th bulletin, corr. 15,487.

Passau flows through the plain of Bavaria the word
'plain' must not be taken as indicating a dead level
on either side for many miles, such as is seen in
the case of the rivers of Upper India. This so-called
plain of Bavaria is extremely uneven, and often of very
markedly hilly character. It is true that in places, about
Ingolstadt for instance, there is a plain, on one or both
banks, of five or six miles in breadth which is absolutely
flat ; but in the distance, even there, are low hills which
presently close in upon the river. These plains are a
sheet of peat soil with bogs in places which, in 1809,
were larger than they are now since drainage operations,
for instance in the Donaumoos between Donauwörth and
Ingolstadt, have turned them into rich cultivated land.
This peat is characteristic not only of the valley of the
Danube itself but also of the tributary valleys. In that
of the Isar, for instance, there was the great Dachaumoos
near Munich.

The principal tributaries of the Danube on its right
bank, within the limits of the theatre of war, are the
Iller, reaching it just above Ulm ; the Lech flowing past
Augsburg to a short way below Donauwörth ; the Isar
passing Munich and Landshut in a north-easterly course
to the Danube near Plättling ; the Inn flowing parallel
to the Isar and debouching at Passau, the eastern frontier
town of Bavaria ; the Traun and the Enns with mouths
some distance below Linz ; and the Raab, joining the
main river near the fortress of the same name. All
these are considerable streams ; the Isar and Inn are
first-class rivers. Between these are many smaller
tributaries, such as the Paar, the Ilm, the Abens, the two
Labers, and the Vils, of less magnitude, but still, with
their open marshy valleys, constituting serious military
obstacles, especially in wet weather, such as prevailed in
April 1809.

The chief tributaries on the left bank are the Altmühl,

the Naab, the Regen, and the March, all considerable streams, though of less importance to us, because there were fewer operations on that side of the Danube, and because, not being snow-fed, they had less influence on the rise and fall of the Danube.

The hills between the southern tributaries, which about Augsburg are quite insignificant, gradually increase in height as we go eastwards, and the same may be said of the left bank. In the country south of Ratisbon they rise to 300 or 400 feet above the valley, and they are still higher south of Passau and Linz. A great part of the river between Ratisbon and Vienna is, as the Saale was described in 1806, " profondement encaissé." Below Passau the river increases immensely in width and volume owing to the inflow of the Inn. It is nearly 400 yards broad as it leaves Passau, though it narrows to 200 or 250 in the lower gorges. Between Ratisbon and Passau the left bank is covered by the hilly wooded country of the Bavarian forest, with that of Bohemia farther north. Immediately east of Vienna, on the left bank, is the great plain of the Marchfeld, bounded on the west by the Bisamberg, on the north by hills, on the east by a spur of the Carpathians running south to Pressburg, and on the south by the Danube. On the right bank, east of Vienna, begins the lesser plain of Hungary, crossing to the north bank also beyond Pressburg. Here, too, on the south side of the Danube, is the Neusiedl lake, the only sheet of water of any importance in this campaign.

All the hill country is well wooded, and in many parts, especially on the left bank, there are extensive forests. At and below Vienna the river splits up generally into several channels separated by islands. The total width is many hundreds of yards.

Roads, in 1809, were few and far between, that is to say ' chaussées ' suitable for the passage of all arms in all conditions of weather. In the area between Ratisbon, Ingolstadt, Munich, and Straubing, in which occurred the all-important operations in the second half of April, there were only the following ' chaussées ' :—

(1) Ratisbon to Straubing.

(2) Abensberg to Straubing.

(3) Abensberg to Landshut.

(4) Munich to Landshut.

(5) Munich to Ingolstadt, with a branch to Abensberg.

Anything short of a ' chaussée ' meant, in 1809, a very poor road, or a mere village track. Even at the present day the metalled roads are not very numerous, and such a thing as a metalled cross lane does not exist. The author, even in September 1907, found it too risky to attempt riding his bicycle, in fine weather, over many of the roads which the troops had to follow in 1809. In wet weather, such as prevailed in April 1809, the labour of dragging artillery and waggons, or even of marching infantry, would be immense.

North of the Danube the roads seem to have been even worse than those of the left bank. Davout writes, on the 14th April, to Berthier [1] :—" The roads leading to Ratisbon (*i.e.* north of the Danube) are detestable. There is only one reaching the town, and that is nothing but a defile for the last five miles."

The permanent bridges over the Danube in 1809 were at Ulm, Donauwörth, Ingolstadt, Kelheim, Ratisbon, Straubing, Passau, Linz, Mauthausen, Krems, Vienna, Pressburg, and Komorn. There were several other temporary bridges. Napoleon was more than once seriously hampered by the destruction of bridges over the Danube or its tributaries. He was delayed on the Salzach,[2] again on the Enns, and his defeat at Essling

---

[1] *Saski*, ii. 147.

[2] A large tributary of the Inn joining it from the south-east after passing Salzburg.

was largely due to the fact that he failed to seize, as he had done in 1805, the crossing at Vienna, with its consequent power of passing his army to either bank at will.

When Napoleon invaded Saxony in October 1806, he was campaigning in a country of which he had no personal knowledge. It was different in 1809; for he had, in 1805, first conducted the campaign of Ulm, and then marched the whole way down the Danube to Vienna. Of the value to him, in an invasion of Austria of the Danube he was thoroughly satisfied. On the 1st March 1809, he writes: "Passau is an important post, especially for the offensive. In marching into Austria nothing can be more advantageous than to follow the Danube. From this moment, the army cannot want for ammunition or food, and can manœuvre as desired. In this plan of campaign Passau is called upon to play a great part. As centre of the army, it ought to contain all the magazines and be its storehouse. Everything should arrive by the Danube."[1]

From this passage General Bonnal[2] infers that Napoleon had already determined to march on Vienna by the right bank of the Danube, as he had done in 1805.

From the first, the Emperor recognised that, in the coming war, Austria would probably be ready to move before he himself was, and that he must commence the campaign on the defensive—a new experience for him. But his mind dwelt ever on the passage, at the earliest possible date, from the defensive to the offensive. In 1806, he knew he could be ready as soon as, or sooner than Prussia, and he was able to assemble his army close against the enemy's southern frontier. In 1809 it was different; for he saw clearly that it was impossible to concentrate on Austria's western frontier. He must

[1] *Saski*, i. 78.   [2] P. 28.

abandon part of Bavaria to begin upon ; how much of it he must abandon would depend on circumstances, that is on the date on which Austria commenced hostilities and crossed the frontier. But he looked forward to the day when, having passed from the defensive to the offensive, he would himself with his army be east of Passau, the Bavarian frontier fortress. He could not afford to let it pass into Austrian hands at any price, commanding as it did passages of the Danube and its great affluent the Inn. Therefore he ordered the place to be very carefully fortified. The works were designed (1) for the defence of the peninsula between the Danube and the Inn, on which the main town stands, (2) for a bridge head on the right bank of the Inn, (3) for defence of the peninsula between the left bank of the Danube and the Ilz, thus forming a tête de pont to the Danube bridge. These works, with a garrison of 3000 men, would be safe from a ' coup de main,' and would compel a regular siege, if Passau was to be taken. Before that could happen, the Emperor clearly expected to relieve it.

At the end of March his position was this. In the first place, he was convinced that, at first, his strategy must be defensive. In the second place, he could not be certain whether the Austrians would break out with the main body of their forces south of the Danube or from Bohemia. If they chose Bohemia they might advance along the Danube, or they might fall upon Saxony, in the hopes that North Germany would rise. They might advance on the south of the Danube, or they might use both banks. What he had to do, therefore, was to unite his army in positions from which he could concentrate in three or four days, according to circumstances, when the enemy's plan was disclosed.[1] Up to the

[1] General Bonnal explains in several places that a "réunion de l'armée" meant, with Napoleon, something quite different from a close concentra-

present, his information pointed to an Austrian advance from Bohemia. On the 23rd February Andréossy gave the distribution of the Austrian armies thus :—

In Galicia	50,000	men.
In Bohemia . . .	165,000	,,
In Upper and Lower Austria	50,000	,,
Inner Austria and Villach .	95,000	,,
Total .	360,000	,,

Of the massing of troops near the Bohemian frontier Napoleon had confirmation on the 14th March, and on the 21st Wrede, at Straubing, reported again the probability of attack from Bohemia towards the Danube. On the 30th March, Napoleon still believed in hostilities commencing north of the Danube ; for he had no certain knowledge of the countermarch, now in progress viâ Linz, of four Austrian corps. He had already made endeavours to draw the Archduke to the south. He had, as has been mentioned, made no particular secret of the collection of supplies at Ulm, Ingolstadt, Augsburg, and Munich. He had also written to the King of Wurtemburg that he would be able to be *on the Inn* with 150,000 men, besides the Rhenish contingents, by *the end of February*. Both these statements were false ; for the Emperor when he wrote, on the 15th January, had already determined in his own mind to unite his army between Donauwörth and Ratisbon, and he knew he would not have 150,000 French by the end of February.

tion. The " bataillon carrée " was not a concentration for battle, but a preliminary assembly of the corps in such positions that, in whichever direction they were attacked, there was always available a force strong enough to hold any strength the enemy was likely to bring to bear, until complete concentration could be effected in the threatened direction. Colonel Foch (*Conduite de la Guerre*, p. 25) identifies Napoleon's " réunion de l'armée " with the German " strategical deployment " and the inappropriate French expression " concentration."

He apparently expected the King to let out these statements, one of which might draw the Archduke to the
Inn frontier, and the other might frighten Austria.[1]
Had he found an offensive campaign possible, he would,
no doubt, have wished to concentrate as near the frontier
as possible, but, seeing that he must commence on the
defensive, the question was how far forward he dared
unite his army.   The farther the better, for the surrender
of Bavarian territory, even temporarily, to Austria was
bad, and would not add to his popularity in Bavaria.
The line of defence must depend on the date on which
Austria declared war ; the earlier she moved the farther
back, looking to his own preparations, Napoleon must
organise his defensive.

His first care was for his magazines of food and
ammunition, which form the subject of his letter of the
28th March to Daru,[2] the Intendant-General.   Donauwörth is indicated again as the centre of the army, and
Napoleon writes : " If the Austrians attack before the
10th April, the army must concentrate behind the Lech,
its right occupying Augsburg, the left on the right bank
of the Danube on Ingolstadt-Donauwörth."

With ample magazines at Ulm, Donauwörth, and
Augsburg he would be able to manœuvre on either bank
of the Danube, and, if the Austrians advanced at so early
a date, the magazines at Munich and Ingolstadt could be
withdrawn behind the Lech.   Between Augsburg, Donauwörth, and Ulm he required, for an army of 200,000,
five days' supply of biscuit and twenty of flour.

On the 17th March, Berthier, Prince of Neufchatel,
was formally appointed Chief of the General Staff of the
Army of Germany.   On the 30th he received his instructions, and next day he betook himself to Strasburg, the
Emperor still staying in Paris ; for he did not wish to
risk precipitating an Austrian attack by his own move-

[1] *Bonnal*, p. 21.   [2] *Saski*, i. 463.

ment eastwards, and even Berthier's arrival in Bavaria might be taken as an indication of his master's early approach. Therefore Berthier was to stop at Strasburg for the present.[1]

Berthier's instructions of the 30th March require most careful consideration.

First of all, reviewing the general situation, the Emperor concludes that Austria will not make war without withdrawing her ambassador (Metternich), or without a formal declaration. The sequel showed him to be wrong on both points. At the same time he admits that war is imminent. He also infers that Austria will be ready to move on the 15th April. (He was again wrong, as the Inn was crossed on the 10th.)

---

[1] Another reason for his stopping at Strasburg was that he would there, and not beyond, be in communication by ærial telegraph with the Emperor. The telegraph was working in clear weather, as far as Strasburg and on to Huningen, but the latter place was not on the line of communication of the army.

The ærial telegraph, as used by the French in 1809, was the invention of Claude Chappe, a French civil engineer. The signalling instruments were a main movable arm with two subsidiary arms attached to its ends. The combinations of these in different positions enabled the communication of signals from station to station, provided the weather was clear. At night lanterns were attached to the semaphores. The whole erection resembled the railway signals at a junction. The first line was set up in 1793, from Paris to Lille, was extended to Dunkirk in 1798, and to Brussels in 1803. Other lines ran from Paris to Brest, Lyons, Strasburg, the last being extended to Huningen in 1805. In that year also the Paris-Lyons line was carried on to Milan. The first telegraphic message of importance sent through reported, to the Committee of Public Safety, the surrender of Quesnoy in 1794. The wording of this telegram is characteristic of the times. "Austrian garrison of 3000 *slaves* has laid down its arms and surrendered at discretion." The battle of Moskirch was reported, in 1800, in a telegram of 56 words, transmitted in less than three hours. The stations appear to have been always less than 7½ miles apart, for that was the extreme distance at which lanterns could be seen at night.

The signalling arrangements were adaptable, in miniature, as field telegraphs, but Napoleon does not seem to have used them. The Austrians, during the period when Charles was on the Marchfeld, had an observatory on the Bisamberg, from which the French movements, on and near the Danube t Ebersdorf, were signalled with great rapidity by telegraph.

E

He must be ready himself to move on the 15th. He, therefore, orders the Guard and his own horses to be at Strasburg on that date.

Next, he recapitulates the positions of his forces as they should be on the 1st April. These have already been given.[1]

The following measures are required :—

1. Augsburg. Fortifications to be hurried on so as to render it safe from a 'coup de main.' They were already in active progress.

2. All the bridge heads on the Lech to be completed and armed. This work also was near completion.

3. Passau citadel to be armed and provisioned for a two or three months' siege. This was in view of the prospective offensive, the date of which could not, at present, be foreseen. The fortifications had already been far advanced.

4. Ingolstadt to be provided with good bridge heads, so as to allow of an issue on either bank of the Danube.

The orders to Daru of the 28th March, regarding supplies, are then recapitulated.

Then Napoleon goes on to state his views and intentions. "My design is to carry my headquarters to Ratisbon and there to centralise all my army." That was his aim *if the enemy did not anticipate him by attacking before the 15th.*

" Headquarters at Donauwörth and the line of the Lech is the position to occupy if the enemy should anticipate me ; but, if the Austrians do not stir, I desire that General Oudinot and General St Hilaire should unite at Ratisbon." The Emperor calculated that, with these two, he could have at Ratisbon, about the 10th April, 30,000 infantry and seven regiments of cavalry, and Bessières could arrive the same day with the whole of the cavalry

[1] *Supra*, p. 54.

reserve. Davout, with headquarters at Nürenberg and his extreme left at Baireuth, watching the exits from Bohemia by Eger, would only be three marches from Ratisbon. The three Bavarian divisions would be one, two, and three marches off respectively. Masséna at Augsburg would be five ordinary marches, or four " marches de guerre," away. " Thus headquarters at Ratisbon would be in the midst of 200,000 men,[1] astride of a great river, guarding the right bank of the Danube from Ratisbon to Passau, and we should be in a position safe from any anxiety about the movements of the enemy, with the advantage of the Danube carrying promptly to the army everything necessary."

Then the writer flies off at a tangent to express his views as to what would happen if the enemy " who is ready " were to move " to-day."

He soon returns to the Ratisbon idea. " Once the army is cantoned around Ratisbon what will the enemy do? Will he move on Cham? If so, we shall be in a position to unite all our forces against him, in order to stop him in positions which we shall have reconnoitred on the Regen."

This movement is explained by General Bonnal [2] thus : Oudinot, the reserve cavalry, and the nearest Bavarian division, would hold the enemy on the Regen, whilst Davout, marching by Amberg, and Masséna by Hemau, would hurry up to fall on his right flank.

The instructions go on : " Will he move upon Nürnberg? He will find himself cut from Bohemia." That is, whilst Davout at Nürnberg held him in front on the Rednitz, Oudinot, the cavalry, the Bavarians from Ratisbon, and Masséna from Augsburg, would fall on his left flank and rear.

" Will he march on Bamberg? He will equally be cut off," by an analogous movement.

[1] The " battalion square " of the Jena campaign.   [2] P. 52.

" Will he choose to march on Dresden? Then we shall enter Bohemia and pursue him into Germany." This requires no comment.

" Will he act in the Tyrol at the same time as he debouches from Bohemia?" In that case the Emperor admits he will easily reach Innsbruck with 10 or 12 regiments, but that could be disregarded whilst the main advance in Bohemia was being dealt with. Once the Bohemian army had been beaten, a French force could be spared to deal with the Tyrol detachment, by moving on Salzburg to cut it off.

" Lastly, if the enemy appears to wish to take for his action the extremities of the right and left, we must accept the centre, having the Lech to retreat upon, and holding Augsburg by a garrison, so as to be sure of always having that town at our disposition."

The phrase "accepter le centre" is a curious one, but the meaning is clear. General Bonnal [1] discusses this alternative, pointing out that Napoleon's meaning was that if the enemy attacked by Nürnberg on the (French) left, and by Munich or Landshut on the right, the two wings would have to retreat fighting on the position of the Lech between Augsburg and Donauwörth. There the army would be protected on the north by the Danube, the bridges of which would have been destroyed during the retreat. In front it would be protected by the marshy valley of the Lech. With fortified bridge-heads at Donauwörth, Rain, and Augsburg on the Lech, the French would be able to manœuvre on either bank of that river against the Austrian left, separated from its right by the Danube, and spread over a wide area. In the meanwhile, Davout was to command all troops north of the Danube, Masséna all to the south. Neither could be well subordinated to the other, looking to the great distinction of both, and the Emperor would be at

[1] P. 53.

Strasburg by the 15th April, on the point of taking over command, before the two would have to act together.

The rest of the instructions deal with supplies and the organisation of what is now called the "Grand Army."

Stripped of their reasoning and digressions, the instructions may be very shortly summarised, in so far as they deal with the general arrangements which Berthier would have to make.

First, if the Austrians moved before the 15th April, the army was to be assembled within a few marches of Donauwörth.

Secondly, if they did not move by the 15th, the assembly was to be centred on Ratisbon.

Subsequent events were in accordance with the first supposition, and we shall see how Berthier attempted to obey orders, as he understood them. There was a third supposition, which evidently the Emperor thought improbable, namely that the enemy "who are ready" might move at once. We know now, what the Emperor did not know on the 30th March, that this was impossible, as the Archduke was in the midst of his counter-march from Bohemia to the Inn. General Bonnal,[1] however, demonstrates that Napoleon's assumptions as to the course of events in the supposed case were vitiated by an unjustifiable optimism, especially his assumption that Davout would know of the advance from Pilsen as soon as it commenced, at a distance of five marches from Cham. He was not in the least likely to hear of it till the frontier was passed.

If the army was to be assembled within concentrating distance of Ratisbon (*i.e.* at Nürnberg, Ratisbon, and Augsburg) by the 10th, the movement would have to commence on the 5th.

General Bonnal[2] remarks that, whilst Napoleon only

[1] P. 55. [2] P. 57.

deals with two cases, viz., the Austrian advance between the 30th March and the 5th April, and on or after the 15th April, Berthier, if he had been more clear-sighted, should have set before himself the alternatives (1) the enemy commences operations between the 5th and 10th April, (2) he does so between the 10th and 15th. In fact, in order to effect the assembly of the army, he really required ten days' notice of the Austrian advance, and not only five. That is General Bonnal's argument; but it must be remembered, on the other hand, that Napoleon, with his past experience of Austrian slowness of movement, probably never thought of their being able to move at the rate habitual with his own armies, though, for safety, he assumed they would when he wrote instructions.

The instructions, as they stand, would have been read aright by Davout or Masséna, but Berthier was not a man of the military intelligence of these two marshals. Speaking of these instructions, and thinking also of others of the same period, General Bonnal[1] says: "Napoleon, when fired by inspiration, besides dictating with a bewildering rapidity, employed, in order to express his thoughts, a form too concise and full of implications (sous-entendus). To such a degree does he do so that many passages of his most important instructions require, in order to make them comprehensible, amplification by the imagination. Was Marshal Berthier of sufficient intelligence to understand the spirit of instructions dictated under the circumstances we have mentioned? It is permissible to doubt it, looking to what is known of the mistakes, sometimes gross, which he committed in the issue of orders prepared by him, in a way, under the Emperor's dictation." That hits the nail on the head. Napoleon was writing over the head of his Chief of the Staff,

[1] P. 48.

forgetting that the latter was not a strategist, but a mere glorified clerk. Poor Berthier has had to bear all the blame of the mistakes made at the commencement of this war. He was the author of them certainly, but he must receive some sympathy, seeing that he was completely out of his depth; and for putting him there his master must bear a large share of the blame.

The first idea of the Archduke Charles was to make an early attack on the Army of the Rhine, and to destroy it before Napoleon could bring up reinforcements. Therefore, he ordered the assembly of the corps numbered I.-V. at Saaz, Pilsen, Prag, Pisek, Budweis, and of the I. Reserve corps at Iglau, on dates between the 1st and the 27th March. Only the VI. and the II. Reserve corps were to assemble, at Wels and Enns, on the south bank of the Danube.

On the 3rd February, Charles ordered Mayer, his Chief of Staff, to work out a plan, on the supposition that Prussia would take a hand in the war on Austria's side. The end of numerous discussions between Charles and Mayer, on the latter's plans, was that Mayer was, by the orders of the Emperor of Austria, summarily sent off to take command of a remote fortress. Nevertheless, after Wagram, he was recalled to the army. In his place, on the 20th March, was appointed Prohaska, a pedant and a man of no personality.

Soon after this, two possible plans of campaign came under discussion. The reasons for and against each of them were stated by Stutterheim, who, though not on the staff, had much influence.

First plan. To attack south of the Danube.

Points in favour of this—

    (1) Better and safer base.

    (2) If the enemy had designs on Switzerland or the Tyrol, he could be reached.

(3) The army would be in communication with Archduke John. Roads better than on the north bank.

(4) This is the shortest line from Vienna to Strasburg.

Against—

(1) A delay of 12 to 14 days in transferring the corps.

(2) More rivers to be crossed on the south, and, therefore, more actions to be fought.

(3) The enemy has many strong positions on this side.

Second plan. To debouch from Bohemia.

Reasons in favour—

(1) The operation is bolder and leads more quickly to a decision.

(2) The enemy has few good positions.

(3) The Austrians would be nearer Franconia, Hesse, and Saxony, where a popular rising was anticipated.

(2) They would cut off the French forces in North Germany.

(5) The operation is to be recommended on moral grounds, because of earlier arrival on the theatre.

Against—

(1) The base is short and difficult to debouch from.

(2) The separation of the main army from the Archduke John, which would necessitate a corps on the Danube as a link.

Binder von Krieglstein[1] remarks that the essential difference between the two is clear—one is bold but risky; the other is safe and means endless delay. The

[1] *B. K.*, i. 95.

less bold plan was chosen, and the countermarch by Linz decided on. The positions of the various corps at the end of March have already been stated.[1]

It has been said that this change of plans caused the Austrians a delay of 21 days, but Binder von Krieglstein notes that, according to the " Operations Journal " of the main army at the end of March, the greater part of the army was not ready for battle. For such an army it is infinitely better to be based with the capital directly in rear. On the whole he seems to think that, unless it could march faster in Bohemia than it did to the Inn, it did not lose much in the time in which it could reach the frontier ; at the most, he thinks not more than a week. On strategical grounds he prefers the advance from the Inn.

[1] *Supra*, p. 54.

CHAPTER V

EVENTS UP TO THE 19th APRIL

SO early as the 1st April, the Emperor found himself under the necessity of modifying his instructions of the 30th March. He now writes to Berthier, who only reached Strasburg on the 4th, that he is to place Davout's headquarters at Nürnberg forthwith, to send St Hilaire's division, Nansouty's six heavy, and Montbrun's seven light cavalry regiments to Ratisbon. Davout was to take post with one division at Baireuth, one at Nürnberg, and one between that place and Ratisbon. Dupas, who was marching from the Hanseatic cities with a French division, was directed to hurry up to Wurzburg. According to the instructions of the 30th March, Oudinot was to have been with St Hilaire at Ratisbon. *Now* he was not, the reason being that he was below his expected strength, and had only 18,000 men, including 2000 or 3000 still on their way to join him. Special arrangements were ordered for reinforcing him up to a strength of 28,000 by the end of April. Meanwhile, he must not be pushed forward with little over half his full strength. Davout's right wing must take his place, as covering force, at Ratisbon. A second letter, dated 2nd April,[1] enforces the necessity of having St Hilaire, Nansouty, and Montbrun at Ratisbon between the 6th and 10th April. About this time the Emperor must have received Davout's letter of 27th March indicating

[1] See Napoleon's letters to Berthier of 1st and 2nd April. *Saski*, ii. 3-6.

the appearance of an Austrian movement leftwards, *i.e.*
towards the Danube. This was the first indication that
the enemy might be meaning to advance south of the
river. Accordingly, Bertrand[1] is sent to reconnoitre a
defensive position with its right on Kufstein (a Bavarian
fortress), centre on the Chiem lake, and left near Marktl,
at the confluence of the Alz with the Inn. Napoleon
sent two more officers on the 4th to study the Inn
frontier and the enemy's movements near it.

On the 6th April, Berthier is ordered to bring one
or two of Davout's divisions, and St Sulpice's cuirassiers,
to within one day's march of Ratisbon. These were
intended to take the place of Oudinot, whose presence
at Ratisbon was contemplated in the orders of 30th
March.

As soon as Berthier heard of the arrival at Ratisbon of
St Hilaire, Nansouty, and Montbrun, he was to move army
headquarters forward to Ingolstadt. General Bonnal[2]
takes this to indicate (1) that Napoleon still believed
the greater part of the Austrians were in Bohemia ; (2)
that he still hoped they would not commence hostilities
before the 15th April.

Meanwhile, on the 3rd April, Davout had sent to the
Emperor a most important despatch. In it he says that
all reports concur in saying the Austrians had sent a
large portion of their troops to the right bank of the
Danube, and, apparently, had changed their plan of
operations. This despatch, according to General Bonnal,[3]
was received by Berthier on the 16th, and he adds " it is
permissible to believe " that Berthier did not pass it on
to Napoleon, either from incapacity, or on account of
jealousy of Davout. The grounds for this assumption
are not stated. Saski[4] heads the despatch as directed
to the Emperor personally, and it begins " Sire." It

---

[1] Chief engineer officer.   [2] P. 65.
[3] P. 67.   [4] ii. 11.

seems rather a bold assumption that Berthier would dare to suppress a letter addressed to the Emperor personally. Certainly Napoleon makes no allusion to it, and, if he had seen it, his indifference to so important a matter would be indicative of a great falling off of his activity. General Bonnal apparently thinks it impossible that the Emperor could have been guilty of such an omission, if he had ever seen the letter. Besides the news about the Austrian movements, the despatch forwards reports of the secret police at Berlin, and gives other possibly important news which it seems almost impossible to believe Berthier would dare to keep back.[1] General Bonnal says the Emperor had gone to sleep till he was rudely awakened by the outbreak of hostilities. He lays the blame on Berthier, whom he suspects of suppressing Davout's report. The report may never have reached Napoleon, but it seems hardly possible to believe that Berthier deliberately kept it back.

It would be useless, and of no interest, to trace the course of the leisurely marches which brought the Austrian armies into the position from which they were ready to advance across the frontier, both north and south of the Danube. On the 9th April, an aide-de-camp of the Archduke Charles carried to Otto, the French Minister at Munich, and to Lefebvre, commanding the Bavarians, a formal notice that the Austrian commander had orders to advance into Bavaria, and to treat as enemies all who should oppose him. On the same day a similar notice was sent by Bellegarde, the Austrian

---

[1] The letter is also interesting as showing how thoroughly Davout understood the discontent in Germany. He writes : " As for the project of some Prussian officers of seizing our fortresses, which is mentioned in a letter from Berlin of the 24th March, I have ordered all the commandants to be on their guard against the people of these places, to take hostages on the slightest appearance of popular movements, and to shoot all attempting to debauch the troops, or incite the people to revolt ; finally to blow up the garrison and the inhabitants sooner than allow the success of a treasonable project."

commander north of the Danube, to Pajol, commanding the French outposts. These notices were all the declaration of war that was made, and the frontier was actually crossed on the following morning without opposition.

At this moment the Austrian army was thus distributed :

On the Bohemian frontier, near Tachau and Pfraumberg, the I. and II. corps under Bellegarde, having in round numbers 44,000 infantry, 5000 cavalry, and 136 guns.

On the Inn, from Schärding to Braunau, in order from right to left, Vecsey's brigade (detached from II. corps), I. Reserve corps, IV., III., V., VI., and II. Reserve corps. Altogether about 116,000 infantry and 13,000 cavalry with 366 guns.

Detached towards Salzburg was Jelacic's division of the VI. corps with about 10,000 infantry and 1000 cavalry.[1]

Allowing for artillerymen, engineers, train, etc., the Archduke Charles must have had about 150,000 men south of the Danube and over 50,000 north of it. His designs are to be found in his orders of 27th March.[2]

Bellegarde was to attack the nearest corps of the enemy, and to order his subsequent movements so as not to remain long at a distance from the Danube, on which the main army would act. He was to act boldly and energetically, so as to relieve the main army, which, in

---

[1] These are the strengths, in infantry and cavalry, given by Binder von Krieglstein (i. 103). Angeli (iv. 39) gives them lower, but he appears to have taken the present states of the 12th April ; for his figures agree with those which B. v. K. says are clearly laid down there. The last-named authority is unable to account for the disappearance of more than 15,000 men between the 10th and 15th, except on the supposition that they were frittered away in small detachments. Some can be accounted for.

[2] B. K., i. 100.

the meanwhile, would cross the Inn, in order "to seek and fight the enemy."

As for Jelacic, he was not, at first, to advance by Rosenheim and Wasserburg, but was to send a reconnaissance towards Munich, and, later on, to advance with the whole division on the Bavarian capital. He would form a flank guard on the left of the main army.

On its right flank it would be guarded, and linked to the corps beyond the Danube, by Vecsey's brigade moving between it and the river.

Passau was to be blockaded by a detachment of three battalions, one squadron, and some pioneers, in conjunction with a Bohemian landwehr brigade across the river.

The main army itself was timed to arrive on the left bank of the Isar about Moosburg, Landshut and below, on the 17th. In these eight days the army would march on the average 63 miles, just about 8 miles a day. The rate of progression hoped for was very slow, as compared with what the French were accustomed to, but the Archduke was probably not justified in expecting more from such slow-moving troops as the Austrians.

On the 10th April, Napoleon telegraphed to Berthier as follows :—" I think the Emperor of Austria will attack shortly. Proceed to Augsburg, in order to act in conformity with my instructions, and, if the enemy has attacked before the 15th, you must concentrate the troops on Augsburg and Donauwörth, and let everything be ready to march. Send my Guard and horses to Stuttgart." That telegram, which should have been beyond all possibility of mistake, came to grief, for the telegraph was not working, owing, probably, to thick weather.[1] The message reached Strasburg only at noon on the 13th, and Berthier was then on his way to Augsburg,

---

[1] The fact that the telegraph was not working was reported to Napoleon on the 11th. *Saski*, ii. 122, n. 1.

where he received it at 6 A.M. on the 16th.   He had left
Strasburg on the 11th.

When Napoleon sent his telegram, he simultaneously
wrote an order to Berthier, which reached the latter at
11 P.M. on the 13th, two and a half days sooner than
the telegram !   The order professed to enclose a copy
of the telegram, but, apparently, the copy was forgotten
in despatching the letter.   Now this letter was what
Berthier misunderstood, and what led him into the terrible
blunders he presently committed.   Had he had the
telegram before him at the same time as the letter, and
observed that they both bore the same date and hour,
he must have known that the Emperor would not con-
tradict himself flatly in the way Berthier assumed he had
done when he received the telegram, fifty-five hours later.

Just before he left Strasburg (11th April), Berthier
wrote to the Emperor that he had given Masséna the
command on the right bank (including Vandamme's,
Oudinot's and Lefebvre's forces), and Davout that on the
left.   Masséna was to move up to the Lech ; Davout,
St Hilaire, and the cavalry to fall back on Ingolstadt, if
pressed.   Wrede's division to fall back from Straubing
on Ingolstadt ; the other two Bavarian divisions were
already on the march for the Lech.

This, as General Bonnal contends,[1] may not have been
an exact compliance with the orders of the 30th March,
which Berthier professed to follow ; but, at least, the
orders were reasonable, and not widely different from
what Napoleon intended in the event of an Austrian
attack before the 15th.

Now we come to the letter of the 10th, which Napoleon
intended as an amplification of the missing telegram.
After saying the Austrians appeared to be attacking at once,
and might already have done so (as they really had), the
Emperor says Masséna and the Wurtemberg corps should

[1] P. 69.

move to Augsburg, and Berthier should go there himself. All this had been done or ordered.

As for Davout and St Hilaire, Berthier was to warn them that, if the Austrians attacked before the 15th, everything should fall back on the Lech. Berthier's orders only required the addition of directions to retire beyond Ingolstadt in order to be as required.

Dupas was to be warned to avoid exposing himself on his march to Wurzburg. But the Emperor had a preconceived idea that the Austrians would not advance before the 15th, and he goes back to what was to happen then. "As the Austrians are very slow," he writes, "it is possible they might not attack before the 15th; then it would be different, for I am about to start myself. If the enemy does not make any movement,[1] you will still make that of the Duke of Rivoli on Augsburg, of the Wurtembergers on Augsburg, or Rain, as you may judge most suitable, and that of the light cavalry and the divisions of Nansouty and St Hilaire on Landshut, or Freising, according to circumstances. The Duke of Auerstädt will have his headquarters at Ratisbon, his army will be gathered at one day's march round that city, *and that under all circumstances*. The Bavarians will make no movement if the enemy makes none. As for Rouyer's division, it will approach Donauwörth, if unable to await[2] Dupas' division."

The instructions for action in the event of the Austrians not attacking before the 15th differ considerably from those of the 30th March. General Bonnal assumes the Emperor had got some general idea that the Austrian forces on the Inn would be larger than originally sur-

---

[1] *I.e.* before the 15th.

[2] "Attendre" is the word given in *Saski*, ii. p. 124. General Bonnal (p. 70) reproduces it as "atteindre," which seems less good sense. There are other unimportant alterations in General Bonnal's transcription, *e.g.* "Maréchal Masséna" for "Duc de Rivoli" and "Maréchal Davout" for "Duc d'Auerstadt."

mised. Why not admit at once that he had received
Davout's report of the 3rd April? To assume he had
not seems unwarranted, whilst to admit he had at once
clears up his new orders, by showing exactly how he got
to his new view. Davout could not say positively the
Austrians had mainly gone to the south of the Danube,
but he thinks it probable, and that is just the sort of
information General Bonnal assumes the Emperor to
have received by unspecified reports " whether from his
ambassadors, or from his marshals, or by violating
despatches destined for M. de Metternich." [1]

Napoleon, therefore, now inclined to the belief that
the attack from the Inn would be more serious than he
had thought so far, perhaps that it would be the main
attack, re-arranges his troops, as General Bonnal shows,
so as to give more support to his covering corps on the
Inn. The Bavarians would now have St Hilaire and the
two cavalry divisions to support them as they fell back.
Davout, within a day's march of Ratisbon, would still be
opposed to the advance from Bohemia, and would be in
a position also to send further support to the southern
covering corps, if it should turn out that an excessively
large proportion of the Austrians was on that side. The
passage in the Emperor's letter which played havoc with
Berthier was that which said that Davout was to be
placed within a day's march of Ratisbon, " *and that
under all circumstances.*" These last words Berthier
seems to have supposed included the circumstances of
an Austrian attack before the 15th. Clearly that was
not so ; what was evidently meant was "under all circumstances, subject to the premiss that the Austrians
did not begin operations before the 15th."

If they *did* begin before the 15th then the first part of the
orders held good, and " everything should fall back on the
Lech." Berthier completely failed to see this meaning,

[1] P. 72 ; *cf.* supra, p. 75.

F

thereby, and by his subsequent dispositions, demonstrating his utter failure to grasp the main principle of the strategy of the commander with whom he had been in the closest personal relations for the last thirteen years. Yet the Emperor must bear his share of the responsibility, in that he failed to remember that Berthier's intellect was incapable of following the rapid reasoning of his own, and that, if he wanted his Chief of the Staff to act intelligently, he should have explained much more fully and clearly the reasons which lay at the back of his change of arrangements.

Curiously enough, if the letter sent Berthier off on the wrong tack about Davout, it set him right as to Oudinot. At 9 P.M. on the 13th, Berthier wrote to Napoleon that he had ordered Oudinot to join St Hilaire at Ratisbon in four days. At 11 P.M., the same night, he received the Emperor's letter of the 10th. Thereupon, he at once issued orders to Davout to place his troops within a day's march of Ratisbon, and wrote to Oudinot cancelling the order to march on Ratisbon.

Poor Berthier was rapidly losing his head, and kept fiddling with the reins of his team, on a road which he did not understand, until they had very little chance of knowing what he wanted, any more than he himself knew. He did feel clearly that the position was beyond him, and, at midnight on the 14th, he writes to the Emperor : " In the position of affairs, I greatly desire the arrival of your Majesty, in order to avoid the orders and counter-orders which circumstances, as well as the instructions and orders of your Majesty, necessarily entail." The little attempt to shift the blame on to the Emperor's shoulders is amusingly like a child. It was not Napoleon's orders that were to blame, except in the matter of their being expressed in a form which was beyond Berthier's power of comprehension. General Lejeune, at this time one of Berthier's aides-de-camp,

wrote in his memoirs regarding him : " The anxieties
of Prince Berthier were then redoubled, and I was much
distressed to see a man so courageous, so calm under fire,
whom no danger could intimidate, trembling and bending
under the weight of his responsibility. . . . In this re-
grettable perplexity we made constantly, during four
days and four nights, the journey backwards and forwards
between Ingolstadt, Donauwörth, and Augsburg, in order
to be present everywhere where danger might occur."
The picture of Berthier, between the 13th and the 17th
April, hurrying hither and thither himself, marching and
counter-marching his troops till they were weary and
utterly confused, is enough to damn for ever his claims
to be a general.

In his letter of midnight on the 14th, he explains,
to the Emperor, his orders to Oudinot to march on
Ratisbon, orders which he cancelled almost as soon as
issued :—" Your first instructions being formal, I had set
Oudinot's division in motion to march on Ratisbon, but
your letter of the 10th, arriving two hours later, caused
me to suspend execution of my order."   Yet what were
the " formal instructions " referred to ?   They were those
of the 30th March, and they said : " Headquarters at
Donauwörth, and the line of the Lech is the position to
be occupied in the event of the enemy anticipating me
(*i.e.* attacking before the 15th) ; but if the Austrians do
not stir (again before the 15th), I desire that General
Oudinot and General St Hilaire should unite at Ratisbon."   Surely Berthier could not hold that the Austrians
had " not stirred " when they had crossed the frontier on
the 10th, and Berthier himself wrote that they appeared
to be trying to turn him by Suabia and Switzerland.
Those were the very conditions to which the Emperor
had referred, on the 30th March, when he wrote : " Lastly,
if the enemy appears to wish to take the extremities of
the right and left for action, it is necessary to accept the

centre, having for retreat the Lech, and holding Augsburg by a garrison, etc."

Davout understood the Emperor's system better than Berthier did. He received Berthier's orders of the 13th at Ingolstadt, and replied that, though he feared he would find Ratisbon already evacuated, he would do his best to unite his army there by to-morrow (15th). At the same time he said : " It appears to me that the best manœuvre would be to debouch by Ingolstadt"; and again, " In this state of things I think the best thing to do would be to debouch by Ingolstadt, and it would be easy to unite the whole army there." After describing the badness of the roads to Ratisbon by the left bank, he does not think it possible to get his forces there under forty-eight hours. He also says : " I await with impatience your Highness' reply." That is, he hoped Berthier would see the force of his view, and agree to an assembly on Ingolstadt. It must be explained that, under previous orders of Berthier, Davout's forces were thus placed at the time of writing——Friant at Neumarkt, St Hilaire at Hemau, with Nansouty behind him, Gudin, Demont, and Morand between the Altmühl and Ingolstadt, and St Sulpice at the last-named place. The light cavalry covered the front, in a semi-circle from Amberg to the Danube below Ratisbon, at which place was Pajol. From those positions it was clear that Davout was right when he said that it would be easy to unite at Ingolstadt, and that even Friant was much nearer in time to Ingolstadt than himself to Ratisbon.

Davout washes his hands of the result of Berthier's order. " If your Highness persists in the execution of your orders, I shall execute them without any fear for the consequences." Then he propounds a conundrum which must have sorely puzzled Berthier. " Lastly, supposing the enemy debouches at several points, and in great force, on the Isar, as he is said to be doing, I beg your High-

ness to let me know what I should do." In a later
letter, of the same date, he says that Ratisbon is held all
right, and he will have Morand and Gudin there by the
15th, and Friant en route at Daswang, with rearguard at
Neumarkt "to-day." Davout had over-estimated the
rapidity of march, as will be seen.

To describe at length the marches and counter-
marches of the French between the 9th and the 16th, or
the slow advance of the Austrians from the Inn to the
Isar, would not be of much profit, and perhaps somewhat
tedious. There was no collision worthy of mention
south of the Danube. On the north there was a rearguard action, fought by Friant at Kastel on the Amberg-
Neumarkt road.

We will pass over all this, to state the positions reached
by the two armies, in so far as they were on the immediate
theatre of operations, on the night of the 15th April.

French—

Friant still at Neumarkt, with Piré's cavalry brigade
towards Nürnberg.

Pajol (light cavalry), and Nansouty (heavy cavalry), on
the Regen, north of Ratisbon.

St Hilaire in Ratisbon, on the south bank.

Morand near Hemau.

Gudin about Vohburg on the Danube.

St Sulpice at Ingolstadt.

Demont at Eichstadt on the Altmühl.

All these were north of the Danube, except St Hilaire
and part of Gudin's division.

Lefebvre's three divisions of Bavarians stood thus—

Prince Royal, Munich.

Deroy, opposite Landshut, on the left bank of the
Isar. (He had retreated from the town, but been sent
back there by order of Berthier.)

Wrede had fallen back from Straubing to Abensberg,
leaving only a few cavalry out on the Little Laber.

Far in rear of these were Oudinot and Masséna, on the Lech, and to the west of it, between Augsburg and Landsberg, with Marulaz's light cavalry still farther south.

Vandamme was west of the mouth of the Lech.

Austrians—

I. corps (Bellegarde) just reaching Amberg, with outposts on the Nürnberg and Neumarkt roads.

II. corps (Kolowrat) arriving at Schwandorf.

South of Danube—

Vecsey's brigade approaching the Isar at Plättling.

IV. corps (Rosenberg) between the Vils and the Isar near Dingolfing.

V., III., I. and II. Reserve corps approaching Landshut.

VI. corps (Hiller) just across the Vils, marching on Moosburg, with advanced posts across the Isar there.

Jelacic's division only about a march short of Munich, on the Wasserburg road.

On the 16th occurred the first important action at Landshut. The town had been occupied on the evening of the 15th by Radetzky's advance guard of the V. corps.[1]

The bridges having been partly destroyed by Deroy when he evacuated Landshut, the Austrian passage could not be effected that night in face of Deroy. At Landshut the valley of the Isar is some $2\frac{1}{2}$ to 3 miles broad, as flat as a billiard table. The hills on the right bank rise some 200 feet above the river, which flows close to their foot, leaving only a space of a few hundred yards, on which the town is built, a typical Bavarian one, with houses rising in high gables with several tiers of windows in the steep and lofty roofs. The " schloss " stands 200 feet directly above the town, on a hill precipitous towards the river. The hills beyond the valley rise much more gradually.

---

[1] With 2 companies, 1 squadron.

The Isar, "rolling rapidly," as Campbell rightly describes it, separates, as it reaches the town, into two branches, surrounding an island, on which stands the suburb known as "Zwischen den Brücken." Several bridges lead from the town to the island, and from the island to more suburbs beyond. There are others over small canals. Deroy, not meaning to retreat without some show of resistance, put a battalion in the island, and the rest of his first infantry brigade in the suburbs on the left bank, about where the railway station now stands. The 2nd brigade and Sendewitz's cavalry brigade were at Altdorf, at the foot of the slope on the left bank of the valley.

On the other side, Radetzky, about 11 A.M., opened fire with his artillery from the hills above Landshut to cover the repair of the Lendbrücke, the single bridge just above the bifurcation of the river. By 1.30 he had succeeded in repairing it in face of a rather feeble opposition.

At 2 P.M., Deroy heard that an Austrian force which had crossed at Moosburg was threatening his retreat. He, therefore, fell back, before Radetzky's advance, towards Pfeffenhausen. There were a few unimportant cavalry skirmishes in the evening. During the night, Deroy found himself at Pfeffenhausen, whence he continued his march to Siegenburg. Wrede was on his left at Rottenburg, the Crown Prince far away on his right at Pfaffenhofen, whither he had retreated from Munich.

In the fight at Landshut neither side brought into action more than 3000 or 4000 men, and the loss did not exceed 150-200 killed and wounded in either force.[1]

---

[1] Lefebvre was with the Crown Prince's division. A letter from him to the Emperor, dated 17th April, gives an account of the wanderings of the Bavarian divisions since the 10th. They had remained at Munich (Crown Prince), Landshut (Deroy), and Straubing (Wrede) till the 14th when, finding the Austrians pressing on him, Lefebvre started to retire on the Lech, the two right divisions on Augsburg, and Wrede by Ingolstadt, Neuburg and Rain. Then

On the evening of the 16th, more progress had been made towards the separation of the two French wings which Berthier had innocently planned.

Jelacic on the Austrian extreme left had occupied Munich unopposed on the night of the 15th-16th. Hiller's main body had not yet reached Moosburg, though he had cavalry over the river as far as Au. He reached Moosburg about 11 P.M.

The V. corps was between Altdorf and Ergolding, well across the Isar; the III. was in Landshut, and the two reserve corps between Landshut and Geisenhausen. Rosenberg with the IV. corps had crossed unopposed at Dingolfing, and, marching very slowly, reached Essenbach and Wörth late in the evening. Vecsey's brigade, far away to the right, had passed Straubing and was near the Danube, beyond the mouth of the Great Laber. On the other side of the Danube, Bellegarde, from Schwarzenfeld, announced that he would reach Ratisbon by Donaustauf on the 17th or 18th. Kolowrat was between Schwandorf and Burglengenfeld.

Of the Archduke Charles' intentions the only intimation is in a letter to his brother the Emperor saying " I am uniting the army corps to-morrow in a position beyond Landshut."

The positions on the evening of the 17th were as follows :—

French. Davout's corps—Morand, Gudin, St Hilaire and St Sulpice, in or close to Ratisbon. Friant at Hemau, with Jacquinot's cavalry behind him at Tenning. Pajol's

came orders from Berthier to re-occupy Landshut, and cover Ratisbon. On the morning of the 16th, Deroy who had evacuated the previous evening, was again marching on Landshut, the Crown Prince on Freising. Wrede had already marched on Abensberg. Then, on the 16th, as Deroy once more retreated, the Crown Prince also fell back, and it was intended to concentrate the other two divisions, by evening on the 17th, at Vohburg. Lefebvre found Demont holding Ingolstadt. He had been ordered there by Davout, who, not understanding Wrede's retreat from Straubing, suspected "quelque noire trahison," with which Demont was to deal firmly. *Saski,* ii. 214 and note.

light cavalry on the Regen, and Montbrun's on the Straubing road.   The three Bavarian divisions were, Prince
Royal at Geisenfeld, Deroy at Vohburg, Wrede at Neustadt marching for Vohburg.   Demont and Vandamme
were at Ingolstadt and Donauwörth respectively, with
Nansouty between them on both banks of the Danube.
Masséna and Oudinot as on the previous day.

Austrians. Bellegarde at Amberg with cavalry at
Pfaffenhofen and Velburg. Kolowrat at Nittenau, with
a detachment advancing from Falkenstein towards the
lower Regen.   The III., IV., V., and I. and II. Reserve
corps were closely concentrated beyond the Isar valley
opposite Landshut, across the roads from Landshut to
Siegenburg, Rohr, and Ratisbon.   Their outposts were
actually on or over the Abens from Mainburg to
Abensberg, and on the Great Laber towards Eckmühl.
Hiller was at Moosburg and Jelacic at Munich.   Vecsey
between Straubing and Ratisbon.

The position of Napoleon's army was now, thanks to
Berthier's misunderstandings, hazardous in the extreme,
though orders had by this time been issued to endeavour
to remedy the situation.   Mark out on a sketch-map the
French and Austrian positions as given above, and the
danger will be clear to the least advanced student of
strategy.   It must be remembered that Davout could
not concentrate at Ratisbon in less than a day, owing to
the distance from it of Friant and Jacquinot.   He might
of course leave these two without risk of their being cut
off by the Austrians, provided he diverted their march on
Ratisbon and sent them to Ingolstadt, or, at any rate,
behind the Altmühl.   But then his own force would be
so much the less.   At the other end of the line, the
position was similar; for Masséna and Oudinot were
still in widely distributed cantonments.   Of Masséna's
corps the outlying divisions were at the following
distances from Augsburg—

Legrand, headquarters 14, farthest regiment 20 miles.
Carra St Cyr,   „   14,   „   „   24 „
Molitor,   „   24,   „   „   28 „
Boudet,   „   18,   „   „   23 „
Marulaz (light cavalry), headquarters 34 miles.

Even if Davout and Masséna had been closely concentrated, the position would have been bad enough. As it was, they would each require a whole day's marching in order to concentrate at their respective centres—Ratisbon and Augsburg.

There would then be approximately 50,000 men at Ratisbon; 55,000 about Augsburg; 13,000 infantry and 5341 cuirassiers between Donauwörth and Neuburg; 3200 (Demont) at Ingolstadt; and 27,000 Bavarians between Geisenfeld and Neustadt. On the other hand, leaving out of consideration the I. and II. corps north of the Danube, Vecsey's brigade, and Jelacic's division, the Archduke Charles had a closely concentrated body of nearly 90,000 beyond the right bank of the Isar valley in front of Landshut, and Hiller with over 20,000 a march to his left rear. Two *very* easy marches would take his main body to the Danube at Kelheim; two marches would take it to Ratisbon, whilst between Augsburg (Masséna) and Ratisbon (Davout) were four "marches de guerre," even for French troops. In this space there was nothing to oppose this great Austrian force except the three Bavarian divisions, 27,000 men, supported, perhaps, by Demont's 3200[1] from Ingolstadt. Vandamme, at Donauwörth, was as far off as Masséna. But the period of Berthier's feeble command was at an end, and the master was already gathering the reins into his own powerful hands. Yet, even he could hardly have saved disaster but for Austrian slowness.

The Emperor left Paris at 4 A.M. on the 13th April,

[1] They could really do nothing as they were required to hold Ingolstadt.

reached Strasburg on the morning of the 15th, was at Ludwigsburg[1] very early on the 16th, and at Donauwörth at 5 A.M. on the 17th.   Considering that an express train leaving Paris at 8 P.M. only reaches Ulm at 3 P.M. next day, the rapidity with which Napoleon travelled in his carriage can be imagined.   He never rested, and, during the few hours he was at Ludwigsburg, he found time to send a despatch to Berthier in answer to that of 9 P.M. on the 13th in which the Prince of Neufchatel announced that he was sending Oudinot to Ratisbon.

Napoleon already partially realised the false position which Berthier was getting the army into.   He condemns the proposed march of Oudinot, and the order to Lefebvre to re-occupy Landshut.   Why Wrede was to return to Straubing he did not know, for he was ignorant of the reasons for evacuating it.   He lays down what he would have considered a perfect arrangement of the army. "Everything would have been perfect if the Duke of Auerstädt had been near Ingolstadt, the Duke of Rivoli, with the Würtembergers and Oudinot's corps, near Augsburg . . . so that the exact contrary of what you have done (*i.e.* marching Oudinot to Ratisbon) should have been done."   Berthier certainly had cancelled his order to Oudinot, but a glance at the map will show how very far the actual positions of the army were from what Napoleon would have deemed perfection.   When the Emperor reached Donauwörth on the morning of the 17th, he found Berthier gone to Augsburg.   He could get no reliable information as to positions, though he was inundated with incorrect accounts.   Vandamme told him the enemy was in Ratisbon !   He took the only means available, in Berthier's absence, by sitting down to study that marshal's correspondence in the office, which he had fortunately not taken to Augsburg. He now learnt that Davout had first, under Berthier's

---

[1] Near Stuttgart.

orders, retired behind the Altmühl, covered by Friant's division at Neumarkt. He had then been sent to Ratisbon by the left bank of the Danube over very bad cross roads. Friant also had been called in towards Ratisbon, but was not yet at Hemau. His exact position could not be known to Napoleon, but he was presumably on the road from Neumarkt to Ratisbon.

The Emperor's first move was to send Savary off to Davout to warn him of the absolute necessity of getting into touch with the centre, even if he had to abandon Ratisbon. In that case, he was to destroy the stone bridge there, so as to prevent the Austrians from Bohemia falling on his rear. Savary never reached Davout till the afternoon of the 19th, when his mission had ceased to be of possible use.

At 8 A.M., news had come from Lefebvre that an Austrian force of unknown strength had issued from Landshut, driving Deroy before it. This "column of Landshut," as the Emperor calls it, he seems to have estimated to be only a single corps, the advance guard of the Austrian advance from the Inn. It was only in the following night that he discovered that it was a column of four army corps, with two more on its left rear.

However, union of the army, in place of the dispersion brought about by Berthier, was the supreme necessity in any case. Napoleon had, as he again and again repeats, always intended union on the Lech, and the Danube down to Ingolstadt, in the circumstances which had actually occurred. It was too late now to do this. The period of union must be shortened by a movement from both wings towards a central point, which entailed abandoning the Lech as a line of defence. The general ideas were that, whilst the Bavarians held the " column of Landshut " in front on the Abens, Davout should move on Neustadt and Geisenfeld, and Masséna

on Pfaffenhofen.   The centre of this new position would
be Ingolstadt, and Napoleon reckoned on having Davout
at Neustadt and Masséna at Pfaffenhofen by the evening
of the 18th.   With the army, on the 19th, in three
masses about Pfaffenhofen (Masséna and Oudinot),
Ingolstadt (Vandamme, Demont, Rouyer, Nansouty), and
Geisenfeld (Davout), with the Bavarians covering a front
of only 16 or 17 miles, the French would be in a position
to move against the Austrians between the Isar and the
Danube.[1]

By 10 A.M. on the 17th, Napoleon had made up his
mind as to Davout.   He was to fall back with all his
troops on Ingolstadt, whilst Lefebvre was to detain (tenir en
respect) the " corps de Landshut " and protect his movement.   The Emperor would hardly have written this
had he known the " column of Landshut " was of several
army corps, and not of one only.   Nor would he have
told Davout to take an opportunity of " falling on " that
column if he could do so without going more than half
a day's march out of his way.   In this same letter to
Davout, it is asked " which is the Austrian corps d'armée
which has debouched from Landshut ? "

After the general order to Davout to fall back on
Ingolstadt comes a remarkable sentence — " Friant's
division should equally retire on Ingolstadt ; he [Friant]
can, however, keep posts of observation on the Altmühl,
considering the Altmühl as a great bridge head, fifteen
miles from Ingolstadt."   As for Davout, he was to pass
by Neustadt where he should be on the evening of the
18th, and the Emperor could there give him fresh orders.
If there were no fresh orders, he should proceed by
Geisenfeld to within $7\frac{1}{2}$ miles of Ingolstadt "without
ever passing on to the left bank."   Clearly, in order to be
able to carry out these orders at all on the 18th, Davout
would require to receive them in the night of the 17th-

[1] *Bonnal*, 114.

18th at latest, and also to be concentrated on the right
bank in Ratisbon itself or outside it. The orders reached
him only at 8 A.M. on the 18th, when Morand was still
on the Regen, where he had been fighting with Klenau.
St Sulpice also was on the left bank, and Friant towards
Hemau, 20 miles off. In fact, when Napoleon issued
his orders of 10 A.M. on the 17th he was not rightly
informed of Davout's exact positions. General Bonnal[1]
argues that Napoleon's intention was that Friant should
march direct from Hemau to Kelheim, Abensberg, and
Neustadt, where he would rejoin Davout, marching by
the 'chaussée' from Ratisbon to Abensberg, on the
evening of the 18th. Though Davout was far superior
to Berthier in intelligence, the Emperor's letter deceived
even him. He understood that Friant was to march
with the rest of the corps, by the right bank, from
Ratisbon. Therefore, he must be waited for, otherwise the Austrians on the Regen would cut him off.
Accordingly, Davout replied that he could not be ready
to march till the morning of the 19th, twenty-four hours
later than the Emperor intended. That he should have
read the orders as he did seems by no means unnatural.
If Napoleon meant, as he almost certainly did, that
Friant was to march direct to Kelheim,[2] he was apparently thinking faster than he dictated, with the result,
that his orders were too elliptical even for Davout's
comprehension. The next orders (11 A.M.) were to
Lefebvre who was to unite his three divisions, with
Wrede's as advance guard, and contain the "column of
Landshut," or even co-operate in its defeat if Davout
attacked it. Yet another proof that Napoleon entirely
underestimated its strength. It was only at noon that
preliminary orders were sent to Masséna, and they only

[1] Pp. 115, 116.
[2] Unless he did so it would have been clearly impossible for him to reach
Neustadt on the evening of the 18th.

directed him to hold himself in readiness, with four days' supply of food, to march as soon as the closer approach of the enemy disclosed his intentions.

At 1 P.M., a fuller order was sent in which the precautions necessary for this march on the 18th were communicated.   They are thus summed up by General Bonnal[1]—

(1) To prepare four days' supply of bread, and the same of biscuit.

(2) To prepare Augsburg to withstand a siege.

(3) To let no one into or out of Augsburg, so as to keep the enemy in ignorance of the movement.

(4) To intercept the Munich road by cavalry.

(5) To leave all "impedimenta" at Augsburg.

(6) To place Augsburg in a state of siege.

Masséna was to make preparations so that by 4 A.M. on the 18th all his columns could be beyond Friedberg, a village four miles east of Augsburg on the eastern side of the Lech valley.   He was also to reconnoitre towards Dachau on the Munich road, to make sure the Austrians were not there.

Obviously, if he was to carry out these orders Masséna's duty was at once to concentrate on Augsburg the divisions which were at considerable distances west and south of it.[2]   He received the 1 P.M. letter about 7 P.M., and he could not possibly comply with Napoleon's orders, though he might have saved time by immediate orders to concentrate.   But, as General Bonnal says,[3] Massena was no longer the Massena of Zurich, Rivoli, and Genoa.   He failed to take these measures, and merely ordered the 1st, 2nd and 3rd divisions to hold themselves in readiness to march.   When, therefore, he received, at 2.30 A.M. on the 18th, the Emperor's full orders of 7 P.M. on the 17th, he was entirely unable to comply with them.   Those orders required him, during

[1] P. 119.   [2] *Vide supra*, p. 90.   [3] P. 122.

the 18th, to have Oudinot's two, and his own four
divisions echeloned with the head at Pfaffenhofen and the
tail at Aichach. Those orders were hardly possible of
execution anyhow ; they were rendered still more out of
the question by Masséna's neglect to concentrate at once
on Augsburg during the night of the 17th-18th.
Thus, owing to the impossibility of Davout or Masséna
marching up to time, the Emperor's projected union
of the army, on the 18th, on the line Pfaffenhofen-
Geisenfeld-Ingolstadt could not be carried out before
the 19th.

We must now see what was happening at the Archduke
Charles' headquarters.

General Bonnal [1] says Napoleon had too much respect
for Charles' talents to believe him capable of merely
seeking to join Bellegarde and Kolowrat by Kelheim,
when Davout stood at Ratisbon, marked out as an easy
prey. Nevertheless, that was Charles' plan on the 17th ;
for Binder v. Krieglstein [2] quotes the Archduke's letter
of that date to Bellegarde, in which he says that Davout
was still on the left bank ; that yesterday (16th) the
Bavarian division from Landshut was retreating on the
Danube. The French army being widely dispersed, he
(Charles) had decided, if possible, to break through its
centre between Ingolstadt and Ratisbon, to cross the
Danube and march on Eichstädt. Bellegarde should
march on Neumarkt, Kolowrat on Beilngries. Everything standing in their way was to be vigorously attacked
and driven back. Hiller was ordered to Pfaffenhofen
there to watch, in conjunction with Jelacic from Munich,
the French advance from the Lech, and to guard
the rest of the army against it.

These orders resulted in the positions already described [3] on the evening of the 17th. It was intended
that the corps from Landshut should be at Pfeffenhausen

[1] P. 128.   [2] Vol. i. p. 169.   [3] *Vide supra*, p. 89.

on the 18th, and Siegenburg on the 19th, a very slow rate of progression.[1]

During the night of the 17th-18th, Napoleon received the following items of information from the special officers whom he had despatched to reconnoitre immediately after his arrival at Donauwörth.

1. Charles with three army corps, estimated at 80,000 men, had marched on the 16th from Landshut towards Pfeffenhausen and Rottenburg.

2. A column of the strength of a corps had debouched, on the 17th, from Moosburg and Freising. This was correct and referred to Hiller.

3. A corps of 12,000 (Jelacic) had reached Munich on the 17th. This was practically correct.

Napoleon's inference is shown in his orders of 4 A.M. to Lefebvre. " It appears that the Archduke Charles, with three corps d'armée, is marching in the direction Landshut to Ratisbon ; you should, therefore, manœuvre on his left flank to delay his march on Ratisbon, to maintain your communication with the Duke of Auerstädt, and to make a diversion which will occupy a number of men equal to your own."

General Bonnal[2] says that during the night of the 17th-18th the Archduke, hearing that Napoleon was at Donauwörth and Davout at Ratisbon, resolved to march on the latter place. As will be shown presently, this is not absolutely correct, and Charles did not change his plans till about 11 A.M. on the 18th. The discrepancy is not very material. It is clear that Napoleon inferred correctly what his adversary's eventual move would be.

His views of the situation generally are clearly stated in his letter, to Masséna, of the morning of the 18th, or can be easily inferred from it.

---

[1] Landshut to Pfeffenhausen 12½ miles, Pfeffenhausen to Siegenburg 9 miles. That made two 9 mile marches as Charles was about 3 miles in front of Landshut.

[2] P. 132.

G

He believed that the Archduke would be marching on Ratisbon by the two roads through Rohr and Eckmühl, fending off the Bavarians by a strong flank guard on the left. Meanwhile, Davout, leaving Ratisbon in the morning, would have slipped by and got to Neustadt by evening. The Emperor still hoped that Oudinot's two divisions, and three of Masséna's[1] would be near Pfaffenhofen by the same evening. As for the Bavarians, they would act in concert with Davout, and there would be nothing decisive on the side of the Bavarians always yielding ground, if they could not actually stop the Austrian flank guard moving towards Neustadt.

Next day (19th) he hoped to advance from Pfaffenhofen with such of Oudinot's and Masséna's corps as had reached there, with Vandamme's Wurtembergers, Nansouty's cuirassiers, and anything else available. With these Masséna would fall either on the rear of Charles, or on the column which had debouched from Moosberg and Freising. "Everything leads to the belief that between the 18th, 19th, and 20th all the affairs of Germany will be decided." Davout could probably hold his own well against the Austrian advance (flank) guard, but the Emperor considered Charles was lost if only Masséna and Oudinot, with five divisions,[2] could debouch from Pfaffenhofen before daybreak on the 19th.

The idea was[3] that on the 19th Davout and the Bavarians would drive back the Austrian flank guard from the Abens on Langquaid or Rohr. Masséna, meanwhile, advancing from Pfaffenhofen on Au and Pfeffenhausen, would meet, and drive back on Landshut or Rottenburg the column (Hiller) advancing from Moosburg. After that, the whole army would be ready to march against Charles on the Great Laber, and drive

---

[1] He recognised that Boudet's arrival in time was out of the question.
[2] Boudet was too far off to be up in time.
[3] *Bonnal*, p. 136.

him into the angle of the Danube of which the apex is
Ratisbon. The stone bridge there would have been
destroyed by a detachment left behind by Davout, and
Charles, to avoid a disaster, would have to cross as best
he might on temporary bridges, losing his baggage, his
sick, and his supplies.

The Emperor appeals, through Masséna, to his troops
to do what is required, and he ends his letter with the
postscript, written in his own almost illegible hand—
" Activité, activité, vitesse !   Je me recommande à vous."
In that there is all the breathless hurry of the orders of
the 13th October 1806, just before the battle of Jena.
Napoleon was destined to be disappointed in his hopes as
to both Davout and Masséna.   By the evening of the
18th, Oudinot had only reached Schrobenhausen.[1]
Masséna had half his corps about Aichach, the other
half only just reaching Augsburg.

Rouyer had replaced Vandamme at Donauwörth, the
latter reached Ingolstadt ; Demont, with Nansouty in
front of him, was on the road from Ingolstadt to
Neustadt.   The Bavarians were concentrated between the
Abens and the Danube, about Neustadt, Mühlhausen, and
Abensberg.   In the evening they had driven back the
advanced Austrian posts on the left flank of the Abens, and
held Abensberg, Biburg and the Siegenburg bridge, or rather
the stream where it had been before the Austrians burnt
it.   There remains Davout.   On the morning of the
18th he reported to Berthier, at 8 A.M., that he had just
received his orders.[2]   Friant being still 20 miles from
Ratisbon, and St Sulpice 12½, they could not be on the
right bank before 8 P.M.[3]   Davout could not, therefore,
reach Neustadt till the evening of the 19th, instead of

---

[1] He was obliged to go round by Schrobenhausen because he found the
road direct from Aichach to be impracticable for artillery.

[2] The Emperor's had not arrived.

[3] Davout's reading of his orders has already been discussed, *supra*, p. 94.

the 18th. In this and a subsequent letter he refers to
Austrian attacks on the village of Reinhausen on the
Regen. The second occurred just as Morand was
marching off to cross the Danube on the 18th. There
had also been a cavalry skirmish on the Straubing road,
17 miles out from Ratisbon. Austrian cavalry had also
been seen south of Eckmühl.

On the evening of the 18th, Davout had all his four
infantry divisions, Montbrun's light, and St Sulpice's
heavy cavalry on the right bank outside Ratisbon.
Only the 65th regiment, under Col. Coutard, was left
behind, to keep off Kolowrat as long as possible.
Davout does not appear to have given any instructions
for blowing up the stone bridge, which is a very solid
structure with piers prolonged up stream to guard it
against floating ice. Savary says he was told to order
destruction of the bridge if Davout was forced to
evacuate Ratisbon ; but Savary did not reach Davout till
the afternoon of the 19th, and, anyhow, Coutard could
probably not have effectually destroyed so solid a
structure.[1] Friant had left on the Altmühl a battalion
and four squadrons to guard the passages at Riedenburg,
Dietfurt, and Beilngries against Kolowrat.

During the early part of the night (18th-19th)
Davout's divisions were posted outside Ratisbon thus—
Friant astride of the Neustadt and Landshut roads ;
Gudin at Burgweinting on the Landshut road ; Morand
(less the 65th and a battalion of the 30th) and St
Hilaire about Grass on the Neustadt road. Davout
drew out very carefully the routes of march for his
columns next day, and had them marked on maps.

The main road from Ratisbon to Abensberg was a

---

[1] On the 11th April St Hilaire had written to Davout regarding the
Ratisbon bridge—" I have the honour to call your Excellency's attention to
the fact that the bridge of Ratisbon over the Danube is a stone bridge, very
fine and very solid, and that I have neither the materials nor the workmen to
blow it up in part." *Saski*, ii. 110.

good 'chaussée.' Passing over the low hills two or three miles south of Ratisbon it descends to the bank of the Danube at Abbach where, for half a mile or so, it is shut in against the river by the hills on the east. Then it passes across an open plain, and is again closed in by precipitous hills until it reaches Saal, where it turns inland, away from the river. The defile ending at Saal is a dangerous one, with only just room now-a-days for the railway and the road. To guard this defile its head near Saal was occupied in the night of the 18th-19th by a battalion of the 30th (Morand's division). This chaussée was assigned to the baggage and reserve ammunition column.

All the other roads to Abensberg, east of this, were mere village tracks, unmetalled and difficult in wet weather such as there then was. The routes of the remaining columns were thus fixed—

(1) Morand, followed by St Hilaire. Ober-Isling, Hohen-Gebraching, Seedorf, Peising, Teugen, Buchofen, Abensberg.

(2) Gudin, followed by Friant. Burgweinting, Hink-ofen, Weillohe.

(3) Montbrun, with two battalions of light infantry and about 3000 light cavalry, to move on the left flank.

(4) St Sulpice in rear of the right column of infantry. Elaborate orders are given for advance and flank guards, guides, and other matters. The march was to begin at 5 A.M. Half-an-hour interval between divisions.

On this day (18th) the Austrian columns from Landshut had already started on their march to Pfeffen-hausen, as decided by Charles on the previous day. The Archduke was on his way to Pfeffenhausen when he received an important letter from Rosenberg (IV. corps) dated Essenbach 5.30 A.M.[1] It probably reached

[1] *B. K.*, i. 180.

him about 6.30 or 7 A.M. It contained a despatch from Vecsey, of the previous day, reporting the skirmish with Montbrun on the Straubing road; also that he had heard artillery and infantry fire on the Regen, and seen a village burning there. Moreover, he had gleaned from a prisoner that Davout, on the night of the 16th, had 30,000 infantry and four light cavalry regiments on the right bank, in Ratisbon. Rosenberg suggested that, if Davout remained there, the Archduke should make him smart for it. Charles resolved to march against Davout, as Napoleon anticipated he would. His former plan of crossing the Danube had evidently been based, as he stated, on the assumption that Davout would remain on the north bank of the Danube, that he would be driven west by Kolowrat and Bellegarde, and that Charles, crossing the Danube at Kelheim, would complete his destruction.

With Davout on the south bank the situation was altered. For Charles to cross at Kelheim would be merely to strike a blow in the air, allowing Davout to pass, across his communications with Landshut, to join Napoleon. Hiller would almost certainly be destroyed. The plan now resolved on was for Kolowrat to press Davout from the north, whilst Charles advanced against him from the south. Charles' orders did not issue from Pfeffenhausen till 11 A.M., to the following effect—

III. and IV. corps to move to Rohr with advance guards up to Schierling, Thann, and Abensberg.

V. corps to Ludmansdorf, watching up to the Abens. Of this corps Lindenau's division was to be transferred to the I. Reserve corps, which was to take post between Rottenburg and Rohr.

II. Reserve corps to be under the commander of the V. corps (Archduke Louis), at Pfeffenhausen.

Vecsey to push towards Ratisbon.

Jelacic to remain at Munich.[1]

Hiller was to go as quickly as possible to Au, there to safeguard the left flank of Archduke Louis (V. corps and II. Reserve) who, in turn, would be the flank guard of the other corps.

Kolowrat was to annoy as much as possible the corps of Davout, whom Charles hoped to attack on the 19th.

Headquarters were fixed at the post-house at Rohr,[2] where a council of war was summoned to meet in the night.

The positions of the corps at night were these—

IV. corps—beyond Rohr, with advance guard in Langquaid.

III. corps—Rohr—advance guard Scheuern and Bachel.

I. Reserve corps—Eulenbach.

II. Reserve corps—about Pfeffenhausen.

Hiller still at Moosburg (but promised to be in Au early next morning), with a detachment under Schaibler at Pfaffenhofen. He had received a reinforcement of four Viennese volunteer landwehr battalions.

V. corps (less Lindenau's division) at Ludmansdorf, with advanced guard, under Radetzky, at Siegenburg, and two battalions and two squadrons at Mainburg waiting for Hiller.[3]

---

[1] Hiller had called him up to Freising so he had to return.

[2] A tablet is to be seen in the wall of the post-house at Rohr (right-hand wall in photograph at p. 102) bearing in German the following inscription :—

"This house was in 1809 honoured

by

On the 18th April,	On the 20th April,
the Archduke Charles	the Emperor Napoleon
coming from the	coming from the
East	West

with their presence."

A whole history suggested in a few words !

[3] One of Lindenau's battalions had to be left behind as, being full of un-trained recruits, it was useless.

Bellegarde promised to be at Neumarkt [1] on the 21st. The position this night was indeed a dangerous one for the French. There was every reason to suppose that, on the 19th, the Archduke, with his 65,500 [2] men, marching on Ratisbon, would meet and crush Davout, whilst his flank was protected from Lefebvre and Vandamme by the V. and II. Reserve corps, themselves protected by Hiller. [3] The three last-named corps might well beat Lefebvre and contain Oudinot, who could only reach Pfaffenhofen on the morning of the 19th, whilst Masséna was a march behind him.

After disposing of Davout and Lefebvre, Charles would be able to turn back on Masséna, leaving Bellegarde, Kollowrat, and Vecsey to dispose of the remnants of Davout and the Bavarians. That is the view of the situation taken by General Bonnal. [4] Strategically he considers the situation would have been desperate, but for the superior spirit of the French army, its general excellence, and the greater activity of its leaders, above all of Napoleon.

Charles' position was far more favourable than had

---

[1] South of Nurnberg. Neumarkt and Neustadt are common names and the places bearing them must not be confused.

[2] In round numbers—

III. corps (including Thierry, Pfanzelter, etc.)	= 25,500
IV. corps	= 15,000
Grenadiers . . .	= 10,000
I. Reserve corps plus Lindenau's division	= 15,000
	65,500

[3]
V. corps less Lindenau's division .	= 16,700
II. Reserve corps	= 5,300
VI. corps	= 23,500
	45,500

Vecsey's brigade is left out of consideration, though it would be in a position to help Charles' attack on Davout.

[4] Pp. 139-140.

been that of Bonaparte in 1796, or than that which the Emperor held afterwards on the 15th June 1815. It may be said that Charles had quite a day's march the advantage over either of those situations. He proved himself incapable of taking advantage of his central position.

Fifty-seven years later, another Austrian general, Benedek, was in a somewhat similar position but failed much more egregiously. Perhaps von Moltke, who had made a special study of the 1809 campaign in 1859, relied largely on Austrian incapacity to make full use of a central position.[1]

[1] Cf. *The Campaign in Bohemia*, by Lt.-Col. G. J. R. Glünicke, p. 62.

CHAPTER VI

THE BATTLE OF THANN

BEFORE describing the events of the five days 19th-23rd April it will be as well to note rather more fully the nature of the country in which they occurred.

The country between the Neustadt-Munich road, the Isar and the Danube contains the whole area. The Danube and the Isar require no further description. The Abens, which rises about Au and reaches the Danube at Neustadt, after a turn at right angles at Abensberg, is an insignificant stream, not more than 10 or 12 yards broad even at Abensberg. But it is not generally fordable, and, with its marshy valley, was an obstacle, especially in wet weather. On the left bank, opposite Siegenburg, and for some distance in either direction, is the Dürrenbuch pine forest.

The Great Laber, rising south-west of Pfeffenhausen, flows generally parallel to the Danube above Ratisbon, and reaches the great river some distance above Straubing. Its importance as an obstruction lies more in its marshy valley than in itself; for, even so far down as Eckmühl,[1] an active man with a leaping-pole would hardly anywhere be stopped by it in dry weather such as prevailed when the author saw it in September 1907. The Little Laber flows parallel to the Great, between

---

[1] The name of this place is Eggmühl in German ; but it is so much better known in military history by its Gallicised name that the latter is used throughout this book.

it and the Isar.   It is of little importance in this campaign.

The Pfatterbach, starting from near Dinzling, flows in a curve north-eastwards to the Danube above the mouth of the Great Laber.   Its valley in parts, especially about Thalmassing, is narrower and steeper than those of the other streams.

Another smaller brook, the Fekingbach, rises near the same point and flows past Hausen to the Danube at Saal.   It is quite small, but, like all the other streams, when swollen by heavy rain might be a serious hindrance.

The country south of Ratisbon is an undulating plain for three or four miles, when it rises into the hilly, wooded country which is the general characteristic, except in the valleys of the small streams which are disproportionately wide and absolutely flat.   The valley of the Great Laber at Eckmühl is perhaps a mile wide.

A great belt of pine forest covers the hills from Abbach to Saal, and stretches across to the Great Laber beyond Eckmühl.

The valley and its sides about Teugen are bare, but the forest covers the hills on either side.

Again, at Eckmühl there is a belt of bare low hills, on the left bank of the valley, a mile or a mile-and-a-half broad.

About Rohr, opposite Abensberg, opposite Langquaid, and between the two Labers, were more considerable blocks of forest.   The hills, though fairly steep in places, are rarely precipitous.

In 1809 there were in this area only the following ' chaussées ' :—

(1) Ratisbon to Abensberg and Neustadt, which has already been described.

(2) Abensberg to Landshut, running through the hilly country by Pfeffenhausen.

(3) Abensberg to Straubing, by Bachel and Langquaid.

(4) Ratisbon to Straubing.

Some of the other main roads, such as Bachel-Rohr-Ergolding, and Landshut-Eckmühl-Ratisbon, were fairly good, though, being unmetalled, they were difficult for artillery in wet weather. The majority of the other communications, notably those by which Davout's troops had to march, were mere tracks leading from one village to another. Many of them are just the same now, and, on the whole, the face of the country seems to have changed very little in the last century. Maps of 1809 show very few woods which have now disappeared. There are more metalled roads and a few railways, but the general aspect of the country seems to have changed so slightly that it is possible to follow every detail with the Bavarian staff map, part of which is reproduced in this volume.

It will be convenient to deal first with the Archduke Charles' general plans for the 19th.

During the night of the 18th-19th he received the following information :—

(1) In the evening (9 P.M.) Wukassowich wrote that there were strong bodies of Bavarians and French in Abensberg and Biburg.

(2) A false report that Davout had marched to Neustadt on the 18th.

(3) At 3 A.M. Wukassowich despatched to Charles, Lefebvre's letter of 4 P.M. on the 18th,[1] the bearer of which had been captured by a patrol. In it Lefebvre informed Davout that he had one division at Siegenburg-Biburg, and the other two behind at Neustadt. Also that he would support Davout by attacking the Austrian left flank as they marched to Ratisbon.

(4) Still more precious a find was that part of Davout's orders which laid down the composition of his columns for the 19th, and the precise routes by which they were

---

[1] Sent in duplicate by Lefebvre. The other copy apparently got through.

to march.[1] How this came to be captured is not clear, but undoubtedly Charles had it some time during the night.

The council of war assembled at Rohr at 1 A.M. We need not follow its discussions, or state the orders first issued. The final orders, issued about 5 A.M., were—III. corps by Bachel, Grossmüss, Hausen, Teugen, guarding towards Abbach and Peising. IV. corps by Langquaid and Dinzling to Weillohe, followed by the grenadiers of the I. Reserve corps.[2] The rest of the I. Reserve,[3] with Lindenau's division (transferred from V. corps) under Liechtenstein (to whom Vecsey was also subordinated) by Langquaid, Leierndorf, Schierling, Ober-Sanding, Thalmassing, Gebelkofen, on Ratisbon.

The Commander-in-Chief would be with the IV. corps. The V. and VI. corps had already been ordered to draw near the Abens and occupy the enemy there, preventing him from sending reinforcements along the Ratisbon road.

As an additional precaution, General Thierry, from the III. corps, with 6000 men and $1\frac{1}{2}$ batteries, was sent to the heights of Kirchdorf to watch the enemy beyond the Abens, and to form a link with the V. corps. The advance began at 6 A.M.

Meanwhile, Davout's corps had started from its positions south of Ratisbon at the hours and by the roads noted in the orders of which the Archduke had acquired a copy. Davout's strength[4] on leaving Ratisbon was :—

---

[1] *B. K.*, p. 190. The capture of these orders is not mentioned by Von Angeli, but B. K. positively asserts it, and, in a note, refers to " Operations Journal der Armee," an Austrian official document. The order in which the items of information came in cannot be stated definitely.

[2] 12 battalions—at least 10,000 men.

[3] 36 squadrons. Lindenau's division in numbers compensated for the 12 battalions of grenadiers.

[4] *Saski*, ii. p. 255 n. This was the total strength of his corps, but as Binder v. Krieglstein (i. 200) shows, after deducting Coutard's 65th and other detachments, Davout really had only 37,400 infantry and 7500 cavalry (total 44,900) on the march from Ratisbon.

	Infantry.	Cavalry.	Total.
(1) Flank guard column of Montbrun	1,930	3,370	5,300
(2) *Right combatant column—*			
Morand's division . .	7,800	—	7,800
St Hilaire's	10,800	—	10,800
Jacquinot's cavalry . .	—	1,000	1,000
(3) *Left combatant column—*			
Gudin's division . . .	9,150	—	9,150
Friant's	10,300	—	10,300
St Sulpice's cuirassiers . .	—	3,500	3,500
	39,980	7,870	47,850

Montbrun was the first to come into serious collision
with the enemy. He was engaged during nearly the
whole day with the very superior forces of the Austrian
central column in an action, more or less distinct from
that of Davout's main body, which will be described
later.

Stutterheim, with the advance guard of the Austrian
IV. corps, was at Langquaid overnight, and, as soon as
the corps began to come up, he moved forward. About
9 A.M., he found the edge of the wood east of Schneidhart occupied by the enemy's infantry, an advance guard
of Gudin's division (the 12th and 21st regiments) under
Petit. Stutterheim was unable to drive them out of the
wood after a long struggle. Meanwhile, the main body
of the IV. corps arrived on the heights between Grub
and Hellring. With it was the Archduke Charles, who
remained there with the 12 battalions of the I. Reserve
corps, under Rohan, which had, as already noted, been
attached to this column.

Charles now ordered Rosenberg, who had altogether
16 battalions and 15 squadrons, to attack the wood
north of Gschwend, whilst the Archduke himself remained
where he was with the 12 grenadier battalions. The
result of Rosenberg's attack was to cause the retreat of

Petit from the woods, which he had so far held against Stutterheim.

But Rosenberg had already shed one battalion and one squadron, left behind with the grenadiers. He was then, as he advanced on Dinzling, further deprived of Stutterheim, with one battalion and four squadrons left at Schneidhart. That reduced Rosenberg to 14 battalions and 10 squadrons for the attack on Dinzling, say 15,000 men—still about three times Montbrun's force, of which less than 2000 were infantry. About 10.30, Rosenberg was deploying, outside the wood through which he had passed, south-west of Dinzling. His advanced cavalry (3 squadrons) sent news that the enemy was at Dinzling with a large force of infantry and cavalry, of which the exact strength could not be estimated. Once more, Rosenberg proceeded to fritter away detachments. He left in rear five battalions to guard his communications with Schneidhart, and one on the height east of Moosholz. Thus, instead of his original 16 battalions and 15 squadrons, he now had only 8 battalions and 10 squadrons, still nearly double Montbrun. Meanwhile, the French commander, afraid of being cut off from Friant in the direction of Saalhaupt, stormed with his infantry the wooded heights near Moosholz, and deployed Pajol's cavalry brigade against the Austrians in the open ground to the east. The fight in the Moosholz woods was long undecided. Eventually, 18 Austrian guns coming into action forced the French infantry, who had no artillery, to retire to the western border of the woods between Moosholz and Saalhaupt, where they threatened the left flank of Rosenberg's advance.

In front of Dinzling there were, meanwhile, several fights between Pajol and the Austrian cavalry, in which the French generally had the upper hand. When Rosenberg, moving slowly forward with his right, reached Dinzling, there was a severe fight, which ended in the evening with the retreat of Montbrun, in perfect order and unpursued, to a position in front of Peising.

Rosenberg was quite satisfied with his performance, and held that he had " defeated the enemy's left wing and effected his object." [1]   Binder von Krieglstein rightly holds that Rosenberg's action was a " series of half-measures and intermissions."   The result was that 3000 French cavalry and 2000 infantry held in check an immensely superior force during the whole day, and retired, practically uninjured and unmolested, in the evening.

Whilst Montbrun was fighting his plucky action about Dinzling, there was proceeding a more important battle on his right.   Napoleon has chosen to call it the action of Thann, and as such it will probably be always known, though, as a matter of fact, no shot was fired, no sabre drawn within a mile and a half of that village.   The " battle of Hausen-Teugen " would have been more appropriate.   The right infantry column and the left, with which latter was Davout himself, had marched from their posts south of Ratisbon up to about 9 o'clock without encountering the enemy.   At that hour, Gudin's advance guard, at the head of the left column, consisting of the 12th and 21st infantry of Petit's brigade, was in the woods on the Saalhaupt-Schneidhart road.   Its fight with Stutterheim, and its retirement when Rosenberg advanced, have already been described.   The musketry fire of this fight reached Davout's ears as he rode with Gudin's main body, then about Saalhaupt.   At the same time, Morand's division, at the head of the right column, was descending on Teugen from Peising.   These two columns were never out of sight of one another.   As Morand reached Teugen, Gudin was marching down the valley from Saalhaupt.   Friant's division was not yet in

[1] *B. K.*, p. 197.   The above account of Montbrun's action is mainly drawn from B. K. and Saski.

sight.   It had been delayed by the wretched state of the
tracks, soaked with rain, and already cut up by the
previous passage of Gudin.   St Hilaire seems to have
been able to follow more closely on Morand's heels.
Davout was now aware that he was in presence of strong
Austrian forces, and he heard the first shots announcing
the meeting of his skirmishers, between Teugen and
Hausen, with those of the Austrians.   His first thought
was for his baggage and ammunition column in the defile
between Saal and Abbach.   He at once hurried off
Morand and Gudin by the cross track from Teugen to
the Danube at the mouth of the defile.   The road by
which they moved has already been alluded to as un-
rideable, for the most part, on a bicycle even now.   It was
described as being in 1809 "frightful defiles, which the
rain had rendered almost impracticable."[1]   As the rear
of Gudin's division passed out of Teugen it was fired
upon by Austrian sharpshooters who, under cover of the
long tongue of wood stretching down past the farm of
Roith, had penetrated into the Teugen valley.   A few
companies of voltigeurs sufficed to contain them for the
moment, but it was evident that the Austrians were
advancing in great force, and that Davout must fight if
he was to save himself from being driven into the Danube
behind him.

Before continuing the description of the battle between
Teugen and Hausen, we must briefly narrate the movement of the III. Austrian corps, which was now attacking Davout's main body.   The fighting strength of the
corps had already been reduced from 23,725 bayonets to
18,573, by the detachment of Thierry's brigade.   It was
now reduced by another 1000 or 1200 men [2] whom
Hohenzollern detached at Bachel to further guard his
left, and to connect him with Thierry, thus leaving him-

---

[1] Berthezène's Memoirs, quoted *Saski*, ii. 258 n.
[2] The weak brigade of Pfanzelter.

H

self little over 17,000 men. With these he pushed on, after starting at 6 A.M., to Bache. and Thann (Herrnwahl-thann on the map). At the latter place he heard the sound of the IV. corps in action on the right. The woods north of Hausen were occupied by French skirmishers who apparently spread right down to Hausen. Hohenzollern halted on the ridge between Thann and Hausen, sending forward (about 11 A.M.) Kaiser's brigade to clear Hausen and the woods beyond, on the ridge between it and Teugen. Crossing the valley and moving up the hill past Saladorf, Kaiser's two regiments drove the French skirmishers before them. The Austrians, clearing the woods on either side of the road, passed over the crest in the centre of the sort of horse-shoe formed by the woods here, the toe being towards Hausen.[1] From the highest point, in the centre of the horse-shoe, they could see the valley about Voxbrünn, but they could not see Teugen itself. Even the top of the church tower is invisible, being shut out by the Buch Berg which rises steeply from the village, and makes a screen two-thirds of the way down the slope.[2] On their right and left were the broad woods covering the ridge, cut into by the sort of horse-shoe already alluded to. The left side of this stretched far down to the Buch Berg in the narrow tongue of wood by which Kaiser's skirmishers descended against Gudin's rear.

St Hilaire had now reached Teugen. The first regiment sent against the Austrians was the 3rd of the line which advanced up the slope in a cloud of skirmishers, as there was no time to form for attack. Suffering from the fire of the enemy in the woods on their flanks, out of breath with the climb, which is very steep from Teugen

---

[1] The road (now metalled) passes through a gap of about 100 yards in the wood. The only difference in 1809 was that this gap was closed by woods perhaps 100 yards in depth.

[2] This from the author's own observation.

up the Buch Berg, the regiment was driven back in disorder, to rally half way down the hill.[1] This attack had
given time for the formation of the 57th, known in the
army as the " Terrible," which, marching steadily up the
Buch Berg (where it was defiladed from the enemy's fire),
deployed at the top under fire from the Austrian masses
farther up, and from their artillery on the Hausner Berg.
The attack of the 57th allowed the 3rd to rally and take
its place on the right of the 57th.

As soon as he had thus started the fight at Teugen,
Davout galloped off to look after Morand and Gudin at
Post Saal. He intended to bring them back against the
Austrian left flank and rear, up the Feking brook. As
he was arranging this, he received from St Hilaire an
urgent call for help. Leaving his proposed movement
by Feking to his two divisional generals, he hurried back
to Teugen, whither he also ordered back Petit with two
regiments.[2] Meanwhile, the enemy, attacking the 57th
in front, had sought to turn its right through the long
tongue of wood. But Davout held a battalion of the 3rd
in reserve which he sent along the outside of the tongue
and then turned into it, cutting off the skirmishers in it
and compelling their surrender. This movement was
repeated several times. The 57th and the 3rd eventually
got well into the wood, of which they held all the
northern parts, whilst the Austrians were still in the
southern, to which they had been driven in disorder.
The 57th was on the summit of the ridge, with its right
resting on the wood in which was the 3rd. The
Austrians had made several attempts to recover their
lost position, without success. A regiment of cavalry

---

[1] That is behind the Buch Berg.

[2] Davout's own account (*Saski*, ii. 256) seems to show Petit was brought
back from Saal. It seems, however, more probable (*B. K.*, i. 203) that Petit,
who had been fighting Stutterheim, as already mentioned, and had fallen
back on Saalhaupt as Montbrun retired, was on his way after Gudin through
Teugen when he got orders to stop and support St Hilaire's right.

had even essayed a charge on the left of the 57th, in most unfavourable ground. The French had no artillery up, except two guns and a howitzer. Both sides were more or less exhausted, and there was a pause whilst reinforcements came up. So far, nearly 6000 Austrians, with all the advantages of ground and wood, had failed to stop 4000 French, and had been driven from their position.

The Austrians were now reinforced by the following :—

(1) Alois Liechtenstein's Brigade of 4309 infantry.

(2) Wukassowich with 1665.

(3) A heavy battery on the heights between Hausen and Buch.

In reserve, behind Hausen, was Bieber's brigade of 4681.

The attacking force (irrespective of this reserve) now counted some 12,000 bayonets, with 68 guns. The French had also been collecting troops with greater rapidity. Of Petit's two regiments, one was thrown into the line on the right of the 3rd, the other behind it in reserve.

St Hilaire's other regiments were also coming up. The 10th marched through Teugen, whilst the 72nd and 105th remained just south of the village, ready to join in as required. Now, too, 30 guns coming up were, with much difficulty, got up the hill to the crest of the heights, whence they opened fire with effect on the Austrians in the southern half of the woods. Where these guns came from is a little doubtful. St Hilaire's A.D.C., Boudin de Roville, says that, by some unaccountable mistake, all but three guns had been left behind at their post of the previous evening and had to be hurried up.[1] Thus, St Hilaire had about 10,000 men and 30 guns in line when the fight recommenced, between noon and 1 P.M.

Friant also was now coming up to Saalhaupt, and saw the 7th[2] coming out of the woods beyond the valley.

[1] *Saski*, ii. 257-258.   [2] These were Montbrun's infantry.

He ordered Gilly, with the 15th light infantry, to clear
the woods opposite Saalhaupt, which was done right up
to the crest of the heights. Friant, meanwhile, was
moving towards Teugen. Guiton's cuirassier brigade
remained on a hillock to support Gilly, who was short of
one battalion left on the Altmühl as Friant marched to
Ratisbon on the 18th. The 48th, under Barbanègre,
pushed up the heights between Gilly's right and St
Hilaire's left. Its right was in the open, the left in the
woods, supporting with columns the 108th, which was
in front of it, almost entirely dissolved into skirmishers.
Every battalion that Friant had was sent up the hill, even
one of the 111th left behind to guard the reserve park
had to be called up by Gilly, who was hard pressed on
his left, apparently by Rosenberg's people. St Hilaire's
renewed attack was begun with 10,000 men, but by 2
o'clock there were quite 20,000 in line, and 5000 in
reserve. No detailed account of the confused fighting in
the forest is possible. Bravely led by their officers and
fighting gallantly, the Austrians were driven gradually
back through the wood. Petit, on the French right, was
first through the wood, followed by the artillery, which
was able to open on the Austrian left on the open slopes
on the Hausen side of the ridge.

Hohenzollern now sent his reserve brigade (Bieber),
from Hausen, into the fight, except one battalion kept
as a last reserve. With magnificent courage, the
Austrians once more breasted 'the hill north of Hausen,
and, for the moment, even succeeded in driving the
French back into the woods. It was 3 o'clock when
Hohenzollern wrote to the Archduke, still with the
grenadiers at Grub, that he could hope for nothing
better than to hold on in the wood, unless he were
reinforced. As he was writing, Davout, throwing his
whole force into the effort, drove the Austrians finally
out of the wood. Hohenzollern had to add to his letter

that he could not even hold in the wood, and must take up a position on the slopes of Hausen. He now had only 17,000 against 25,000 French. Here the battle practically ended, for the French stopped at the outer edge of the wood, and only carried on an artillery duel with the superior Austrian artillery beyond the Hausen valley at Buch.

Charles all this time had been standing with nearly 12,000 men on the heights of Grub. He called his force a general reserve, but he had done nothing with it, though he was less than two miles from Hohenzollern's fighting line. Even when he received that general's urgent call for help, he waited an hour before he decided to send one battalion of grenadiers, who did nothing beyond making a feeble attack on the woods, which had no effect.

As the grenadiers marched, about 5 P.M., the thunderstorm, which had been threatening all day, burst with fury over the battlefield, plunging it in darkness and deluging it with such a drenching rain that even the French soldiers sought shelter from it in the woods. The grenadiers soon lost heart and retired. Towards evening, a French column appeared on Hohenzollern's left. It was the 17th regiment, of Morand's division, sent forward from Mitter-Fecking to make a diversion in favour of St Hilaire. Fired upon by the Austrian guns from the heights of Buch, it disappeared in the woods with a loss of 13 killed and 29 wounded.[1]

The losses in this battle, in which the Austrian III. corps was badly beaten, are calculated by Binder von Krieglstein [2] thus :—

Austrians—Killed and wounded, 2995 ; prisoners, 166 ; missing, 685. Total, 3846.

---

[1] It seems to have been driven off with little difficulty. No doubt there was little anxiety to advance, as the battle was practically over.

[2] *B. K.*, i. 206-207. He does it, for the French, by a comparison of the present states of the 15th and the 20th April.

French (including Montbrun's force), 4376. This is perhaps rather below the mark.

St Hilaire, Friant, Petit, and Guiton (cuirassiers) bivouacked on the field of battle.

Morand, Gudin, and the rest of the cavalry about Reising on the Ratisbon-Abensberg road. There they were in communication with Lefebvre and the Bavarians.

During all this fighting, the Austrian right column, at least 15,000 strong, had been marching, without meeting any enemy, on Ratisbon. It covered 12½ miles of fairly good road, and bivouacked between Eckmühl and Hohenberg, whence Liechtenstein wrote that it was impossible to go farther that night. He mentions hearing artillery from the direction of Ratisbon, but makes no mention of all the uproar at Hausen and Dinzling. Seeing that he was within 1¾ miles of Grub at noon, it is impossible that he could have failed to hear it, whatever the direction of the wind. Probably he did not mention it as he knew it came from where Charles was in person. What he had heard towards Ratisbon was an attack on Stadt-am-Hof.[1] This was made, early on the 19th, by Kollowrat. Instead of doing his business properly, that general used a single battalion, which was badly beaten by Coutard's 2000 men of the 65th. The effect was to stop for the whole day a corps of over 20,000 men. Davout, in reply to Coutard's messages, had urged him to hold out to the death. The 65th were already short of ammunition and had to use the cartridges of Austrian prisoners or dead.[2]

Having completed the history of the battle between Davout's corps and the III. and IV. Austrian corps, we must turn to events on the Abens, and those in which

---

[1] The suburb of Ratisbon on the left bank of the Danube.
[2] Davout tried to send Coutard a supply next morning, but it was found impossible to get it through.

the V. and VI. corps were concerned. It will be remembered that Thierry's [1] brigade had been detached,
when the rest of Charles' columns marched to meet
Davout, to guard the left flank and form a link with the
V. corps. Later on, Pfanzelter had been left at Bachel
to form another link with Thierry.

Thierry marched at 6 A.M. for Kirchdorf, with six
battalions, six squadrons and three half batteries—
altogether 5152 bayonets, 700 sabres and 10 guns.
The three heavy guns had soon to be left behind on
account of the state of the roads. About 8 A.M. he
received an order from the commander-in-chief to leave a
strong reserve at Bruckhof, a detachment in the wood to
the right of Gaden to watch the Ratisbon road, and
others on the Kirchdorf heights to cover the march of
the III. corps against attack from Biburg and Abensberg.
If he was attacked by superior forces, he was to fall
back towards the V. corps on the Rohr-Rottenburg
road. The next order (9 A.M.) came from Hohenzollern,
requiring Thierry to occupy the Kirchdorf heights and
watch to the right Abensberg, and left Ratisbon (*sic*).[2]
From the heights above Kirchdorf, on the road to
Abensberg, Thierry saw large camps in the broad valley
near Biburg and Abensberg, and infantry and cavalry
moving northwards in the Ratisbon direction.[3] These
he felt it his duty to stop.

Leaving a battalion and a few dragoons in Kirchdorf,[4]
he started with the rest of the brigade by Bruckhof for
Arnhofen on the Abensberg-Ratisbon road. On the

---

[1] The written orders were for the detachment of Kaiser's brigade, which
fought at Hausen; but Thierry being thought more capable was sub-
stituted. *B. K.*, i. 193.

[2] Possibly "Regensburg" (the German name of Ratisbon) was a mistake
for Siegenburg, which would be on the left when Abensberg was on the
right, looking from the Kirchdorf heights.

[3] These were probably a part of the 1st Bavarian division, on the march
from Mühlhausen to Abensberg.

[4] The village is in a hollow, shut out from view of the Abens valley.

way he left 3 more battalions, 2 guns, and 7 sections of dragoons, so that he had left with himself only 2 battalions, 6 squadrons, and half a battery—less than half his brigade.

We must look for a moment at the position on the French side of the valley. Lefebvre's last orders had directed him to take a good position, " so as to contain a number of troops at least equal to your own. If the enemy weakens in front of you, follow him ; if he dares to resist, overthrow him." From what he learnt from Austrian deserters, Lefebvre, at 9 o'clock, believed he was about to be attacked by 120,000 men, and sent to Napoleon to beg for help. His view was confirmed by Wrede's hearing an Austrian regimental band. At this hour Wrede was at Abensberg, the Crown Prince of Bavaria on the march from Mühlhausen to Abensberg, and Deroy between Neustadt and the Abens, towards Siegenburg.

To return to Thierry : from Bruckhof to Arnhofen rising ground or woods shut out the view of the Abens valley. When Thierry came near Arnhofen, about 10 A.M., he saw a few Bavarian pickets, and then a cavalry regiment. On these he fired with his guns from the hollow[1] south of Arnhofen. Bavarian artillery replied from the Galgenberg, and infantry began to appear (6 companies), of whom part moved on Arnhofen and prepared to attack the wood.

Thierry sent forward his dragoons against the Bavarian cavalry, who, being double his strength,[2] and the ground being cut up by dykes, soon brought the Austrian attack to a standstill. Thierry now called up two of the three battalions left at Bruckhof, and all the cavalry. By the time they came up, the enemy also had large reinforce-

---

[1] Hesse Lohe on the inset to map iii., which is a reproduction of the Bavarian staff map.

[2] Another regiment had now joined the first one seen.

ments, and Lefebvre sent forward the whole of the Crown Prince's division, with a regiment of Wrede's from Biburg on its right. Half of Deroy's division was either with them or in reserve. The attack was general on the woods from Arnhofen to Bruckhof, and round Thierry's left flank there. The fight was long and against desperate odds on the part of the Austrians. A Bavarian battery, pushed forward half a mile along the Bachel road, was presently firing on their rear, and, by 4 P.M., the whole Austrian brigade was streaming back in confusion into the marshy woods north of Offenstetten.

Meanwhile, Bianchi's brigade, from the V. corps, had arrived at Perka, where Wrede attacked it with one infantry regiment. This fight soon became a mere cannonade.

In the midst of all this confusion, there broke the thunderstorm which had ended the battle at Hausen. Here also both sides sought shelter in the woods.[1]

Thierry had appealed in vain for reinforcements to Charles, to Archduke Louis of the V. corps, and to Pfanzelter at Bachel. He got none, except Bianchi's feeble attack.

That night, the Bavarians bivouacked where they were in the woods.

Thierry, calling a council of war at Offenstetten, had settled to retreat on Rohr when there arrived a staff officer with promises of help from the V. corps, and desiring Thierry to hold on. He decided to spend the night at Offenstetten.

To complete the story of this eventful 19th April, there remain the doings of the V. and VI. Austrian corps, and of Masséna and Oudinot on the French side.

[1] The violence of this storm must have been something phenomenal, for no one could suppose that the ardour of the troops would be quenched by any ordinary rain. It must, however, be remembered that, in those days, muskets became useless if the priming were damped. Compare the Katzbach und Dresden in 1813.

The palm for the slowest marching on this day must be awarded to the Archduke Louis' command, the combined V. and remains of the II. Reserve corps.

Lindenau's division, it will be remembered, had been taken from the V. to be given to Liechtenstein, and the II. Reserve had now only 6 squadrons, besides 5 battalions of grenadiers. Also 2 battalions and 2 squadrons from the V. corps had been detached to Mainburg to wait for Hiller and the VI. corps. The strength of Louis' column then was:—

	Infantry and Artillery.	Cavalry.	Total.
V. Corps . .	14,000	2,760	16,760
II. Reserve . .	4,500	800	5,300
	18,500	3,560	22,060

Receiving his orders, Louis started about 6 A.M. from Ludmansdorf. By 10, he was at Schweinbach on his road to Siegenburg. Less than two miles in four hours! Here he got Charles' orders of 6.45 A.M., telling him Lefebvre would probably attack him, that he, with Thierry on one side and Hiller on the other, must act together. If compelled to fall back, they should do so on Landshut, Hiller taking command of the whole.

Louis, who was only 25 years old and without experience in war, placed his troops, facing Siegenburg, across the Neustadt-Landshut chaussée between Ummelsdorf and Perka. Radetzky's advance guard[1] was towards Siegenburg. Reports of Thierry's fight came in, and it was said there were 16,000 Bavarians at Siegenburg, of whom some were moving on Abensberg. It was noon, so that in 6 hours the corps had covered less than $4\frac{1}{2}$ miles!

[1] Two battalions and eight squadrons.

Then Louis, thinking he would do some reconnoitring himself, rode forward with his staff to the heights in front of Perka. Thence he saw hostile infantry in front of the Dürrenbuch forest, others marching to Thierry's fight, which was now raging, and 2000 cavalry in the plain. He sent off to ascertain what Thierry was doing, and appears to have sat doing nothing till 4 P.M., when he heard that Thierry was falling back in terrible difficulties. Then he sent off Bianchi with his brigade. That officer, as we know, managed to do nothing, being stopped by the threat of a single Bavarian regiment, though he had 6000 men, and appears to have been joined by the battalion which Thierry had left at Bruckhof, and which was cut off by the Bavarian advance on Thierry's left.

By the main body of Louis' column nothing was done, beyond some firing with heavy artillery at the enemy, who were almost out of range.

About 5 P.M., it was resolved to do something, so General Schustekh was ordered, with 4 squadrons, to Rohr to support Thierry! Truly valuable aid!

At 7 P.M., Louis received a letter, dated 3.30 P.M., from Charles at Grub, by which he (Louis) was ordered to march, at nightfall, viâ Rohr and Langquaid, so as to be ready to support Charles against the expected renewal of Davout's attack in the morning. Under the circumstances, that was impossible, and for the night the V. corps and the other troops united to it, stood thus :—

Thierry at Offenstetten.

Bianchi between Kirchdorf and Bruckhof.

Reuss on the heights opposite Siegenburg.

Kienmayer (infantry of II. Reserve corps) on heights of Ludmansdorf.

Schustekh (4 squadrons) at Kloster Rohr.[1]

---

[1] Kloster Rohr is the old abbey, practically part of Rohr, at the lowest part on the south.

Mesko, called in from Mainburg, on the march to join the corps.

The Bavarians opposite them had the Prince Royal, and part of Deroy's division, in front of Abensberg. All the rest at Biburg. Vandamme's Wurtembergers had their cavalry near Abensberg; infantry near Neustadt, with light brigade at Mühlhausen, behind Wrede's Bavarians.

When Hiller left Moosburg with the VI. corps at 5 A.M. on the 19th, Jelacic was, as before, at Munich, and Major Schaibler had been since the previous evening at Pfaffenhofen, with $1\frac{1}{3}$ battalions and 3 squadrons. When Hiller reached Au, about noon, he found two letters. The first was the Archduke Charles', of 11 A.M. on the 18th, ordering concentration on Rohr, and requiring Hiller to march on Mainburg to protect the left of the V. corps.[1] The other was a note from Major Schaibler saying he had been attacked by 6000 French at Pfaffenhofen, and driven back towards Au. Nordmann's advance guard was ordered to receive Schaibler.

At 3 P.M., Hiller got Charles' orders of 6.45 A.M.[2] directing his immediate march on Pfeffenhausen.

His orders were (1) Schaibler to fall back, at dusk, on Mainburg, (2) Nordmann, when he had received Schaibler, to follow the corps to Mainburg, (3) Hohenfeld's brigade to wait at Au till joined by Nordmann, and then to march to Mainburg.

It was late at night when Hiller's troops reached Mainburg. They had marched a long 18 miles, a heavy march for Austrian troops, and were very tired.

But the interest of the 19th on this side centres in Napoleon's orders to Masséna.

At 4 A.M., Oudinot fell upon Schaibler's little force

---

[1] Note that this despatch reached Hiller 25 hours after issue !

[2] $8\frac{1}{4}$ hours covering $21\frac{1}{2}$ miles ! It was a counterpart of the orders to Louis.

with Colbert's light cavalry and Claparède's division of infantry. The Austrian force is greatly exaggerated in the French accounts.[1] The affair was a petty one with a loss of about 100 on either side.

Of this little action Napoleon, at Ingolstadt, had information from Masséna in time to enable him to date his reply at noon. In it he speaks with contempt of Schaibler's Austrians as "that scum which you beat this morning."[2] General Bonnal severely condemns the pride which led Napoleon to thus despise his enemy. In justice to the Emperor, it must be said that his information was that there were 4000 Austrians at Pfaffenhofen. Had he known there were only 1200 or 1300, he would perhaps not have spoken of their defeat by a whole infantry division and a light cavalry brigade in these terms.

The Emperor explains his movements thus : " You see that by this manœuvre I am refusing my left, wishing to advance my right which you form, and which, from to-day, begins to come on the scene." He directs Masséna to push Oudinot on Freising and Au, and to find out what is happening at Munich. "From Freising and Au, according to the news I receive to-day, I shall direct you on Landshut ; and, then, Prince Charles would find he had lost his line of operation, his protection, which is the Isar, and would be attacked on his left."

A postcript to the letter finally fixed the disposition of Masséna's divisions thus : One of Oudinot's on the Au to Neustadt road, the other on that to Freising. Masséna's own four divisions at Pfaffenhofen, for the present, ready to march on whichever of the three directions (Neustadt, Au, or Freising) might be necessary. If the left (Davout and the Bavarians) were too heavily engaged, it might be necessary to march on Neustadt,

---

[1] Even General Bonnal (p. 161) talks of 6 battalions and 6 squadrons, which is about four times the actual strength.

[2] "Cette canaille que vous avez battue ce matin."

but Napoleon's *desire* is clearly indicated to march Masséna on Landshut.

Now, on these orders General Bonnal bases a severe indictment of Napoleon.   He admits the absolute correctness of the Emperor's orders up to noon of the 19th. They aimed at uniting the army so as to be able to manœuvre against the left of Charles in his march on Ratisbon, and to seek a decisive battle.   With two divisions of Oudinot and Masséna at Geisenfeld, and four at Au, he would have been united, so that, whilst his left detained the Austrians, his right could attain their flank and rear.   But now, before he has even completed his union in two great masses within supporting distance of one another, he proposes to again separate them and send Masséna off to Landshut.

The critic attributes this to the Emperor's preconceived idea of marching, as he had done in 1805, to Vienna by the right bank of the Danube.   " This idea dominated him to such a degree that he sacrificed the primary advantage of beating the Austrian army to the secondary one of seizing a bridge on the Isar, and cutting, at Landshut, the communications of the Archduke Charles." [1]   If the latter should refuse battle, on finding his communications cut, he could still retire to Bohemia by Straubing, and between that place and Ratisbon, to say nothing of retreat by Ratisbon itself, as actually happened.   If, too, Charles should hear in good time of Masséna's separation, he would have the opportunity of falling on Napoleon's left (Davout and Lefebvre) with the whole of his army.

The conclusions General Bonnal arrives at are that Napoleon's view was obscured by a cloud of pride, which led him to overestimate his own strength, and to underestimate that of the enemy ; that he was beginning to look upon moral influences, not merely as a preponderant factor, but as taking the place of material forces.   He

[1] *Bonnal*, p. 164.

was "drawing from the arsenal of the so-called scientific (savantes) manœuvres of the 18th century a problematic means of inducing the retreat of his adversary without fighting, by the menace of an imaginary danger." In fact, he was losing sight, for the moment, of his own leading principle that battle is everything in war, to be sought with all possible available forces, and that secondary objects follow in the wake of the destruction of the enemy's army. Practically, General Bonnal holds that, but for this lapse from his own principles, this attempt to "hunt two hares at the same time," the war might have been ended in Bavaria, without all the time spent in the march to Vienna, or all the blood shed on the plain of Essling and Wagram.[1]

There will be more to be said, later, on this subject, but there seems strong reason to believe in this theory of the French general who has gone so deeply into the strategy and "military psychology" of the man whom he agrees with others in styling the "great master of war."

In accordance with Napoleon's orders, Oudinot's divisions bivouacked, on the night of the 19th, each with a brigade of cavalry in front, Tharreau on the road to Geisenfeld, Claparède on that to Freising. Three of Masséna's divisions, and Marulaz's light cavalry, were at Pfaffenhofen, but Boudet was still behind at Schrobenhausen.

[1] For the argument in full see *Bonnal*, pp. 163-165.

CHAPTER VII

ABENSBERG

IN his letter of the 17th, Napoleon had told Davout that the 18th would be a day of reunion ; on the 19th the army would be in a position to dispose of the enemy between the Danube and the Isar, perhaps even as far as the Inn. Everything had been put off by 24 hours, owing to the impossibility of Davout and Masséna reaching the prescribed points at the time contemplated. The Emperor, before he had even completed the union of the army, was now again to some extent dispersing it. Though he meant to send a large part of Masséna's command on the Isar and Landshut by Freising and Moosburg, he still thought he might require reinforcements for his centre. Orders were, therefore, issued to Masséna, through Berthier, at midnight of the 19th-20th, to manœuvre with two objects. He was to reinforce the centre by marching Oudinot, by Geisenfeld and Neustadt, or by the left bank of the Abens, to Abensberg ; the rest of his force on Landshut. Berthier seems to have forgotten the fact that, under previous orders, one of Oudinot's divisions should have been a march out on the road from Au to Freising. The result with an Austrian general would, perhaps, have been a literal compliance with the order, and a countermarch of Claparède's division back to Au and on to Abensberg. But Masséna took the reasonable course ; he left Claparède in the Landshut direction, and sent to the centre Tharreau of Oudinot's corps, who was already on the way, substituting for Claparède the division of Boudet which, at Schrobenhausen, was nearest to Neustadt. Oudinot himself was with Claparède; he was to join Tharreau and Boudet as soon as possible. He was only able to do so on the morning of the 21st. Berthier again wrote to Masséna, at 3 A.M. on the 20th, repeating the orders about Oudinot, and telling Masséna his own rôle was to secure for the French a bridge over the Isar, and to turn the Austrian flank by Moosburg when, on their retreat to Landshut, they should attempt to defend the Landshut passage. The Emperor was now attempting, not so much to compel a general action, as to induce the Austrians to fall back over the Isar and the Inn, hoping to break them up during the long retreat to Vienna.[1]

At 6.30 A.M. Napoleon writes to Masséna that all reports point to the Austrians being in retreat as fast as their legs would carry them, though, on the previous day, they had only been engaged with two French and one Bavarian division.[2] (Not a very likely thing certainly, and not true in fact.) He himself was about to attack them, if they still stood, or to pursue them hotly, if they were in retreat.

We have now come to a very important, and often misunderstood, part of the campaign. Many writers, including Sir Edward Hamley, have held that Napoleon deliberately set out to beat the Austrian left wing only, and to drive it away from the rest of the army, to repeat, in fact, the manœuvres of 1796 in the Riviera. As a matter of fact he did separate the Austrian left, and, when he came to publish his account of his operations, a few days later, he implied that he had done so deliberately. But his correspondence, as distinguished from his bulletins, gives him away. It is perfectly clear that, on the morning of the 20th, he thought he was

---

[1] *Bonnal*, 170.　　　　　　　[2] Two in reality.

about to drive, not a wing but the whole of the Archduke's army across the Isar back towards Vienna.

During the 20th, Masséna's command did not fire
a shot, and it is only necessary to note their unopposed
march. Marulaz's light cavalry was by evening between
Langenbach and Moosburg, on the left bank of the
Isar; Claparède, behind him, was between Freising and
Langenbach, Carra St Cyr near Freising; Legrand,
Espagne's cuirassiers, and the artillery park between
Unter-Bruck and Freising. Molitor, who only got off
from Pfaffenhofen at 11 A.M., found the bridge over the
Ampère at Unter-Bruck on fire, and was delayed thereby
for 12 hours.[1]

From Masséna's unopposed march we pass to what
Napoleon, followed by most historians, calls the Battle
of Abensberg. Bonnal calls it more appropriately a
"great battue." The reports of the events of the 19th
led Napoleon to the conclusion that Davout's two divisions
had checked the main body of the Archduke, whilst the
Bavarians had been attacking a strong flank guard. In
a very modified degree that was correct, but on two
important points the Emperor was completely wrong.
In the first place he seems to have believed[2] that what
the Bavarians had attacked on the 19th was really the
column which he knew had passed the Isar at Moosburg
and Freising, and believed to have then been used as a
flank guard. Secondly, he believed that the events of
the 19th had induced Charles to give up his movement
on Ratisbon, and either to be in full retreat on Landshut,
or else to be standing between him (Napoleon) and that
place.

Let us see what the Austrians really were doing.

---

[1] There were two columns of march, Marulaz, Claparède, Carra St Cyr by
Paunzhausen; and Legrand, Espagne, artillery park, and Molitor by Unter-
Bruck. It is not clear how the bridge at Unter-Bruck came to be fired
after the passage of the artillery park.

[2] *Bonnal*, 162.

The Archduke had already, on the evening of the 19th, ordered Hohenzollern to fall back with the III. corps [1] on Leierndorf, and Louis to move up to the support of the right wing. At 7.30 A.M. on the 20th, Charles writes to Louis expressing his intention of reaching Ratisbon that day, or at least of uniting with Kolowrat. If he could not even do that, he would fall back behind the Laber to unite with Louis. A large force of the enemy had gone to Kelheim or Abensberg, thus endangering Louis' flank. He (Louis) must, therefore, fall back behind the Laber at Rottenburg, whilst Hiller took post also behind it at Pfeffenhausen. Louis was to pass on this order to Hiller.

That is sufficient, for the present, to show that Charles' intentions were not at all what Napoleon thought.

The Emperor's idea now was to fall on the left flank and rear of the Austrians with Morand's and Gudin's divisions, the Bavarians, Wurtembergers, and Demont's division. He could even, perhaps, utilise Tharreau's and Boudet's divisions, which were on the march towards Abensberg.

At 3 A.M., Lefebvre was ordered to second Davout by a prompt advance with the Bavarians and Wurtembergers.[2] Morand, Gudin, and St Sulpice were directed to move on Bachel, on the left of the Bavarians. Vandamme was ordered to Siegenburg,[3] on the right of the Bavarians, Demont from Vohburg to Abensberg, in support of the Bavarians.

---

[1] Except Thierry's and Pfanzelter's detached brigades.

[2] Saski, p. 284, says orders were sent out to Davout during the night, to contain the Austrians in front of him, but the text of the orders is not given.

[3] Vandamme was so notoriously violent and insubordinate that the Emperor seems to have thought it necessary to write personally to him, and, moreover, to add that he (Napoleon) would personally direct operations. If Vandamme had been put too markedly under Lefebvre there would perhaps have been trouble.

Davout's report of the battle of the 19th only reached Napoleon at 6 A.M. on the 20th. The Emperor believed Davout had gained another Auerstädt, and this, added to his contempt for the enemy,[1] led him to suppose Davout would again press Charles southwards, whilst the Emperor's attack from Abensberg would drive him to Landshut, there to fall into the clutches of Masséna on the 21st.

On the night of the 19th there had arrived, in all haste from Spain, Marshal Lannes, Duke of Montebello. For him Oudinot's corps had been destined from the first, but, in order to give so trusty a lieutenant an immediate command, the Emperor gave him the two divisions of Morand and Gudin, with Nansonty's and St Sulpice's [2] cuirassier divisions. Napoleon and Lannes set out together from Vohburg.[3] When the Emperor reached Abensburg, he proceeded, about 8.30 A.M., to the slight elevation still known as the " Napoleonshohe," where the Kirchdorf road separates from that to Bachel about three-quarters of a mile out of Abensberg. Employing the Crown Prince of Bavaria as his interpreter, he harangued the Bavarians in the terms which he so well knew how to choose. He told them that their fight of this day would be a Bavarian battle, in which no French would take part. After an expression of his belief in Bavarian valour, he concluded, " *We are going to Vienna*, where we shall know how to punish Austria for the harm she has done to your country." The idea of the direct march on Vienna was ever in his mind.

It was 10 o'clock when the thunder of artillery from the direction of Bachel announced the arrival there of

[1] *Bonnal*, 176.

[2] One of St Sulpice's brigades was left to guard the defile at Saal.

[3] The Emperor's horses had only reached Strasburg on the 15th so he was riding chargers belonging to the King of Bavaria. His staff were mounted on cumbrous troopers taken from Nansouty's cuirassiers (*Castellane's Journal*).

Morand's division of Lannes' provisional corps. The Crown Prince's division now led the attack, followed, as reserve, by that of Deroy.

The 1st brigade followed the Abensberg-Langquaid road on the right, making for Offenstetten, whilst the 2nd moved from farther north on See. At the same time, the Wurtemberg light brigade (Hügel) started from Bruckhof on the Kirchdorf road. Altogether there were 11 battalions in front line, of which only two were Wurtembergers.[1]

Opposed to them was Thierry, who had now only $3\frac{1}{3}$ battalions. On Thierry's left was Bianchi, who now had $2\frac{2}{3}$ of Thierry's battalions, cut off the previous day, besides 6 of his own. On Thierry's right rear was Pfanzelter with one battalion. Behind Pfanzelter, at Rohr, was Schustekh, with 4 squadrons, and $1\frac{1}{3}$ battalions. The $14\frac{1}{3}$ battalions thus accounted for were, however, considerably scattered, and partially demoralised by defeat on the previous day.

Thierry, hearing of movements of French troops from Ratisbon to Abensberg, was under the impression the French must be retreating. Riding forward, however, he came upon the advancing Bavarians, and heard firing on his left, where the light troops were falling back before Hügel's Wurtembergers. He had already resolved on retreat when he found himself compelled by the Bavarian attack to fall back on the heights east of Offenstetten. There he attempted to stand, but, being attacked in front by the 1st brigade, on his left by the Wurtembergers towards Sallingberg, and threatened on his right towards Scheuern by the 2nd brigade, he fell back, in some disorder, through the wood in front of Scheuern. He endeavoured to reach Bachel, where he expected to find Pfanzelter. When, however, he got out of the wood he learnt that, instead of Pfanzelter, Jacquinot's light

---

[1] Hügel's other two battalions joined Wrede's right later in the day.

cavalry, followed by Nansouty's cuirassiers,[1] was at
Bachel, whence they had forced Pfanzelter to fall back on
Rohr and Langquaid. Jacquinot promptly attacked,
with the result that most of Thierry's infantry scattered
through the woods, and the rest fled in wild confusion,
pursued by the French cavalry nearly to Rohr. When
Schustekh's presence stopped the pursuit for the moment,
Thierry could only collect 3 companies of infantry and
half a squadron of cavalry out of his force. The time
was about 1 P.M., and there was now a great breach in
the Austrian line, extending as far as Rohr. Schustekh
led forward his four squadrons of hussars to try and
cover the retreat of the baggage and the remnants
of Thierry's brigade, but he was attacked by an overwhelming force, driven back, and, in a moment, the
whole of his and Thierry's men were in the wildest flight
towards Rottenburg. The scenes of confusion and
slaughter were terrible as the stream of Austrians rushed
along with the pursuing French cavalry in their midst.
It was not till he had reached Gieseltshausen, a little
short of Rottenburg, that Schustekh could report, about
5 P.M., the disaster which had befallen him and Thierry.
An attempt to stay the flight had been made at
Eulenbach, with the result of the capture of Thierry
himself and several thousand men. The pursuing force
had consisted of Jacquinot's light cavalry, part of
Nansouty's and St Sulpice's cuirassiers, four of Morand's
infantry regiments, and, later on, Zandt's Bavarian
cavalry brigade. The Bavarian infantry, with which was
Napoleon, went no further than Sallingberg and Scheuern.
Gudin had had a small skirmish with Pfanzelter, at 9 A.M.,
to the north of Bachel, and, when that General fell back,
had pressed on to the Great Laber, and bivouacked
between Adelshausen and Leithenhausen. At Rottenburg Schustekh met the head of the VI. corps. It is

[1] Both of Lannes' command.

difficult to say what were the losses of Thierry and Schustekh on this day, but Binder von Krieglstein puts the prisoners alone at between 3000 and 4000.[1] The Bavarian losses were insignificant, and Deroy's division was not engaged at all. It bivouacked at Bachel, the Crown Prince about two-thirds of the way from Bachel to Rohr.

It is not quite certain where Napoleon was during the day. Local tradition says he was most of the day on the heights west of Bachel, warming himself by a great bonfire and awaiting the result.[2] Here, at 4 P.M., he heard of Austrian cavalry at Thann, against which he sent Nansouty with Sandewitz's cavalry brigade (Bavarians), and two of Gudin's battalions, to occupy Thann and get into communication with Davout. One of the battalions got as far as Langquaid. At Bachel, at 8 P.M., Napoleon received two letters from Davout which he answered, and then moved on to Rohr, where he occupied the post house, in which two nights before had been the headquarters of the Archduke Charles. These letters from Davout will be dealt with later.

Whilst the 1st and 3rd Bavarian divisions and Lannes' troops were disposing of Thierry, Pfanzelter, and Schustekh, Wrede did not commence operations till 2 P.M. against the Austrian V. corps. That corps had been rejoined, early on the 20th, by Mesko's detachment from Mainburg, and it was from it that there were sent to Schustekh the 8 companies which shared the disaster at Bachel. The V. corps had received a reinforcement of 3 battalions of Vienna volunteer landwehr, but they were so exhausted that they could not proceed beyond Pfeffenhausen. Louis actually had, to face Wrede and Vandamme, at least 18,000 infantry. He strengthened Bianchi, at Kirchdorf, with an infantry regiment, and

---

[1] *B. K.*, i. 241.
[2] The day was raw and rainy, as had been the 19th.

called up five battalions, from Ludmansdorf, to the
heights of Siegenburg.   Thus he proposed to await
Hiller's arrival, after which, as he wrote to his brother
Charles, he would march by Rohr to support the right
wing.

Hiller, meanwhile, left Mainburg at daybreak to march
viâ Ober Hornbach.   He left Nordmann's advance guard,
towards Nandlstadt, to hold back Masséna, but the
Austrian soon had to retreat on Moosburg.   Hiller had
18,000 bayonets with him, and the head of his column
was at Ober Hornbach at 8 A.M., where a halt was called,
whilst Hiller and his staff rode forward to meet the
Archduke Louis and ascertain his position.   After a
short interview at Birgwang, Hiller went on alone to the
heights of Siegenburg, whence he saw active preparations, on the French side, for crossing the Abens.[1]   But
the great danger was from the north, whence came the
sounds of Thierry's action, gradually going farther east,
and thus leaving exposed the right flank of the V. corps.
Hiller returned to Louis, who seems to have accepted his
position as Hiller's subordinate[2] by no means loyally.
He also seems to have made up his mind for a retreat
on Pfeffenhausen.   He had done nothing to help Thierry
and Schustekh.   Hiller now (12 noon) resolved to carry
his own corps to their help.   Returning to Hornbach,
he set Hofmeister's and Weissenwolf's brigades in motion,
and himself rode forward as far as Pattendorf, where he
encountered the stream of fugitives, and heard of the
disaster of Thierry and Schustekh.

Returning to Rottenburg, he found Hofmeister's
brigade arriving there.   This was towards 7 P.M.   As
for Hiller, Binder v. Krieglstein remarks, " Heaven
knows where he had been riding about so long." [3]   The

---

[1] The bridge at Siegenburg had been destroyed by the Austrians on the
17th.

[2] Archduke Charles' orders, *supra*, p. 123.

[3] *B. K.*, i. 247.

four squadrons of light cavalry sent forward into the Laber valley met French horsemen yelling "Vive l'Empereur" and waving their helmets, a sure sign, in those days,[1] that Napoleon was in the neighbourhood. From Rottenburg Hiller appears to have sent a single regiment to attack the French about Ober-Buch, threatening his left flank. It was beaten off with heavy loss. At 11 P.M. Hiller had his corps assembled at Turkenfeld, under orders to retreat on Landshut.

We must now return to the Archduke Louis, who was left awaiting the attack of Wrede and Vandamme. His large forces and numerous artillery prevented Vandamme from crossing at Siegenburg, so he went round by Abensberg. Wrede had already issued by Biburg, about 2 P.M. The Bavarian commander advanced with some 10,000 men (besides 6500 in reserve) against the heights from Horlbach to Siegenburg, where he was opposed by at least 16,000 Austrians, whose commanders, however, had already made up their minds to retreat. Indeed, in the existing conditions, they could hardly do anything else. After capturing the heights of Horlbach from Bianchi, Wrede leant to his right as Bianchi fell back on the heights south of Kirchdorf, where he rallied on two battalions under Reuss. He continued to fall back between 2 and 3 P.M. Radetzky's right-hand battalion was driven from the heights of Perka by the 7th Bavarian infantry, whilst his other battalion encountered, in Siegenburg, the two battalions of Hügel's Wurtembergers which had not gone with the Crown Prince. Outnumbered by nearly two to one, Radetzky also fell back, covering the retreat of Bianchi to Birgwang. Vandamme, now up in the midst of the Bavarians, sent Minucci (Bavarian), with 5 or 6 battalions, southwards against

---

[1] In his final struggles in France Napoleon, knowing the terror of his own name, would have his troops told to shout "Vive l'Empereur" when he was not really present.

Radetzky, who was driven by them and Hügel's men to Birgwang. It is difficult, and perhaps not of much interest, to follow this confused pursuit over hill and dale. The Wurtembergers did not follow, but camped on either side of Siegenburg. At Schweinbach Wrede proposed to stop and spend the night. The Archduke Louis had long ago decided to retreat, and with the V. and II. Reserve corps, had betaken himself to Pfeffenhausen, leaving Radetzky, with 4 battalions and an Uhlan regiment, as rearguard at Ludmansdorf. But Napoleon had sent other orders for Wrede, requiring him to reach Pfeffenhausen that night. Just as both he and Radetzky had settled down for the night, each believing the fighting to be over for the day, Wrede got his orders, and had to set out again in the pitch dark about 10 P.M. Though Radetzky had been reinforced by a fifth battalion, he was forced back to Pfeffenhausen, where he fired the bridge over the Laber. It was after midnight, and he found the V., VI., and II. Reserve corps had, under Hiller's orders, proceeded on their retreat to Landshut. Everything with them was in the wildest confusion. The road was choked with fugitives, waggons, and bridge trains. Men in thousands threw their arms away, and the panic was almost as great as that of the Prussians after Jena and Auerstädt.

The whole of the Austrian left wing, some 42,000 in all, had been driven back in full retreat, with a loss of 2710 killed and wounded, besides about 4000 prisoners. The enemy had numbered 55,000, but had not actually employed more than 25,000, a number about equal to that of the Austrians who came into action.

We have still to deal with events in the direction of Davout and the Austrian right wing.

Davout now only had under his command the divisions of St Hilaire and Friant, with Montbrun's advance guard of two battalions and light cavalry. He made, during this day, no movement of any importance, but busied himself in clearing up and providing for his wounded of the previous day.

In a letter dated 4.30 P.M., he gives his positions, namely, St Hilaire on the ridge between Teugen and Feking, in and behind which village there appeared to be 6000 Austrian infantry and 300 cavalry. Friant had his right resting on Teugen, his left towards Peising, and saw, on the edges of the woods in front of him, 12,000 Austrian infantry and 600 cavalry, whilst the smoke rising from the woods seemed to indicate large hostile forces in them. Montbrun, at Peising, reported 18,000 men in his front, but Davout believed they included many of the same troops as Friant saw. "This morning," he writes, "the enemy has made on our front a very considerable movement from his left towards his right. Since 8 o'clock he is in the same position, with the exception of a continuation of his movement, which appears to be being made on Ratisbon."

Then follows a curious sentence in which Davout says he has no news of Morand and Gudin since the morning, or of what is happening on his right. Apparently, then, he had not been informed of the transfer of a large part of his corps to Lannes. In this connection it is noticeable that, when Lannes sent Gudin orders in the morning, the latter promised obedience conditionally on his receiving no commands from Davout. In addition to Davout's report of the Austrian movement on Ratisbon, Napoleon had a report to the same effect from the force which he had sent, at 4 P.M. under Nansouty, to Thann. In replying to Davout he says he wants to know what has become of the Archduke Charles. Some reports said he was marching on Ratisbon, others that he was retiring by Eckmühl on Landshut, others that he was still in front of Davout. He asks for Davout's opinion, and the latter is told that, in the absence of orders, his rôle is to attack and destroy the enemy wherever he meets him. Herein Napoleon shows that, though he ought to have seen that the main Austrian force was in front of Davout, he was allowing his preconceived idea of its retreat on Landshut to dominate him.   He greatly exaggerates the result of the operations in the centre, speaks of them as a " second Jena," and multiplies the number of prisoners by three.   To Oudinot he put the number at 20,000, five times the actual.

The movements of the Austrian right on this day require consideration.   There appear to be few written orders by the Austrian Commander-in-chief, but over-night Hohenzollern with the III. corps had been ordered to Leierndorf in the Laber valley, and Louis had been directed to close to the right.   At 7.30 A.M. on the 20th, Charles writes to Louis that he will endeavour to reach Ratisbon that day, or at least to unite with Kolowrat.   Failing that he would meet Louis behind the Laber.[1]   According to orders Hohenzollern marched, on the 20th, to Leierndorf where, receiving no further orders, he camped.   He had left a rearguard at Hausen,[2] and a connecting link at Dietenhofen.   This rearguard fell back, about 3 P.M., before a reconnaissance by Montbrun.   Soon after noon, Pfanzelter came in, report-ing the catastrophe to Thierry, the sound of whose fight had been heard.   Pfanzelter was posted at Langquaid. During the day the III. corps suffered from hunger.

The IV. corps remained about Dinzling.   Hearing the sound of Thierry's fight, Rosenberg, about noon, strengthened his advanced troops.   It was only then that he discovered that Charles had carried off the Grenadiers from Schneidhart and reattached them to the I. Reserve corps.

---

[1] *Vide supra*, p. 132.

[2] This is no doubt the force St Hilaire reported, and against which Napoleon sent Nansouty from Bachel.

Liechtenstein, with the right column, set out for Ratisbon, which he had been ordered to reach on the 19th. He had with him the I. Reserve corps, Lindenau's division of the V. corps, and Vecsey's brigade (II. corps). He advanced with a flank guard on his left, and another of 12 squadrons on his right, in which latter direction there could be no possible danger.

On reaching Ratisbon, he found it still occupied by Coutard with the 65th French infantry. That officer, as already related, had had a severe fight on the previous day with Kolowrat for the suburb of Stadt-am-Hof, had beaten off the Austrians and taken nearly 400 prisoners and a standard. But he was running short of ammunition, as he reported to Davout. The latter endeavoured to send him a supply on the morning of the 20th, and begged him to hold out to the last; for Davout had at last, on the evening of the 19th, met Savary, who told him of the Emperor's orders for the destruction of the Ratisbon bridge. Trobriand, who took Davout's orders to Coutard on the evening of the 19th, got to Ratisbon and back safely. He was then sent with the ammunition, but was attacked beyond Abbach, lost his ammunition, and only just succeeded, thanks to a good horse, in saving himself and getting through again to Ratisbon, where he repeated the orders to Coutard to blow up the bridge. But Coutard, having neither tools, nor powder, nor engineers, could not obey. The bridge is very solid, with great masonry ice-fenders projecting upstream.[1]

Without ammunition, with half his regiment *hors de combat*,[2] surrounded by Kolowrat on the north, and Liechtenstein on the south, Coutard had no option but to

---

[1] Presumably the bridge was in 1809 as it now is. The ice-fenders project so far, and the waterway between them is so narrow, that it would be easy to double the width of the bridge, at any rate for infantry, by throwing planks across from fender to fender.

[2] The 65th was 2087 strong when left. 1822 men surrendered; so that the loss in killed alone must have been 265.

surrender, about 6 P.M. on the 20th, in reply to the Austrian summons.[1]

It is a curious fact that it appears to be impossible to trace with certainty the personal movements of the Archduke Charles during a great part of this important day. At 6 A.M. he was with Rosenberg at Dinzling. At 7.30 he wrote the letter, already mentioned, to Louis. After that he wrote, from Hausen, to the Austrian Emperor, a letter expressing his views of the situation. He says that, being informed that the French had fixed themselves in Ratisbon, he had left the VI. corps on the Isar about Moosburg. He himself, with the III., IV., V., I., and II. Reserve, had marched for the Danube towards Kelheim and Ratisbon. He had made a forced march from the Isar, across the Great Laber, to Eckmühl, Rohr, and Rottenburg. Napoleon, who, according to prisoners, had reached the army the same day, had attacked him, but he (Charles) had held the battlefield. Nevertheless, Napoleon had attained his end by protecting the defiles of Abbach and Saal, at the expense of heavy losses to the large forces employed against the III. corps. In conclusion, he expresses his intention of awaiting in battle order the enemy's further movements.

At 11 A.M. Charles was still at Hausen, but from that

[1] Ratisbon, in 1809, was quite indefensible by a small force against a double attack. The ramparts on the south side were in bad condition to begin upon, as was shown on the 23rd April. Moreover, the hills on the left bank rise almost precipitously above Stadt-am-Hof. From their summit, 250 to 300 feet above the river, the range was but 900 yards to the centre of the bridge, and about 1800 to the extreme southern portion of the ramparts. Defence would only have been possible by an extensive occupation of the plateau above Stadt-am-Hof, for which a large force would be necessary. It has been suggested (*B. K.*, i. 325) that if Davout had been left in Ratisbon with his 50,000 men, instead of being marched on Abensberg, he might have held out against the whole Austrian army, attacking him on both banks, until Napoleon, with the rest of the army, could fall on the rear of the Austrians on the south. It seems doubtful if this would have been possible, unless the plateau above Stadt-am-Hof, and perhaps even that on the left bank of the Regen, had been extensively fortified, and held by forces larger than Davout could spare.

hour till 6.30 P.M., when he was at Alt-Egloffsheim, there is no sign of his whereabouts. The fact that for all these hours no order of the Archduke is traceable requires explanation. Even if the reports of Thierry, Schustekh, and Pfanzelter did not reach him direct, still Charles had information, through the III. and IV. corps, of what was happening. Yet he issued no order. Two explanations of this apathy are given. According to the first he was so impressed with the political importance of an early capture of Ratisbon, the ancient meeting-place of the Imperial Diet, and now of that of the Rhenish Confederation, that he neglected everything else for it. The theory does not seem a very probable one, especially as Charles was not occupied issuing orders to Liechten-stein, and had plenty of time to consider the difficulties of his centre and left.

The other explanation is put forward by Hormayr,[1] who, according to Binder v. Krieglstein, is generally well informed. It is that Charles was seized on this day with one of the epileptic attacks to which he was subject, that for several hours he locked himself in his quarters and would see no one. The German writer is inclined to accept this as the more probable, especially as it explains a complete apathy which was foreign to the Archduke's nature, though it must be admitted that he was sometimes wanting, in a lesser degree, in energy.

Kolowrat himself rode over to inform Charles of the capture of Ratisbon. He was ordered to march at once on Hemau. Bellegarde also was marching southwards, through Neumarkt, to the Altmühl, and his advance guard had driven in a small French post from Wappersdorf.[2]

The positions on the night of the 20th-21st have been given for most of the opposing forces. The French divisions of Tharreau and Boudet had reached Neustadt with Colbert's cavalry. Oudinot only joined them next

Kaiser Franz und Metternich.   [2] South of Neumarkt.

morning ; meanwhile, a letter from Berthier (opened by Tharreau) ordered them to move on Pfeffenhausen. Demont had joined the Bavarians at Grossmüss. Rouyer had marched from Donauwörth to Ingolstadt. Colonel Guyon (left by Friant on the 18th) guarded the passages of the Altmühl, from Beilngries to Kelheim, with $1\frac{1}{4}$ battalions.

K

CHAPTER VIII

OPERATIONS OF THE 21ST APRIL

(1) THE CAPTURE OF LANDSHUT

"YESTERDAY and the day before were another Jena. The Duke of Rivoli must have arrived at Landshut at 3 P.M.[1] You have nothing in front of you but a screen of three infantry regiments." Thus wrote Napoleon to Davout, at 5 A.M. on the 21st. Yet he had more than 9 hours earlier received Davout's report, of 4.30 on the 20th, pointing to an Austrian movement in the direction of Ratisbon. He had probably also received the report of Colonel Montmarie, to the same effect, from Thann. Nevertheless, he was determined to follow the Austrian left towards Landshut, and to believe that Charles was retreating behind the Laber, either on Landshut or on Straubing. The letter went on to say that Lefebvre[2] was being sent, with Deroy's Bavarians, Demont's Frenchmen, and St Germain's cuirassier brigade, to destroy this rearguard (of three infantry regiments) which was covering the enemy's parks and wounded, and to sweep up everything in the course of the day. Davout was to support it, if necessary, and the division of Boudet, at Neustadt, was placed at his disposal.

---

[1] He was not there till later than that on the 21st.

[2] Orders of 4.30 A.M. had directed Lefebvre, with Deroy, Prince Royal, and Demont, to march on Rottenburg. They were cancelled by those of 5 A.M., and only the Prince Royal division went to Rottenburg, where it stayed.

146

" Here is what you have to do ; the Duke of Danzig is going to pursue the parks, the transport, and even Prince Charles, if he takes the direction of the Isar and moves on Landshut by Eckmühl, or if he goes to Straubing." When Davout's rear was cleared, and he had gathered up the stragglers and baggage, he was to march on Ratisbon,[1] to attack Bellegarde and Kolowrat,[2] to drive them against the Bohemian mountains, and to clear the left bank of the Danube of everything but débris.

That was the frame of mind in which Napoleon decided to throw the greater part of his army on Landshut, against what he still persisted in thinking of as the Austrian army. In reality it was but the beaten V., VI., and II. Reserve corps. He announced Landshut as his own destination.

Leaving Davout for the present, we will first describe what happened on the roads from Rottenburg and Pfeffenhausen to Landshut, and at the latter place.

It was 2 A.M. when Wrede, with one weary battalion, came in front of Pfeffenhausen. The burning bridge over the Laber threw a lurid light on the scene, enabling Wrede to see that there were troops on the hills beyond. He heard the roar and rattle of the waggons in their flight to Landshut, and the cries of the panic-stricken drivers. Presently, he came across a pile of 500 abandoned knapsacks, and he rightly judged that there was nothing in Pfeffenhausen which could stop even his single battalion. He boldly pushed it through the stream.[3] The few Austrians left in the place fell back on Radetzky's rearguard on the heights above. Radetzky,

---

[1] Napoleon was still unaware of Coutard's surrender.

[2] The Emperor says Klenau. He was Kolowrat's advance guard commander. The mention of Bellegarde and Klenau as what Davout had to dispose of, is one more proof of Napoleon's insistence that Charles had given up his move on Ratisbon and was retreating over the Isar.

[3] Fording it apparently. It is quite small here, not far from its source.

seeing that Wrede threatened an advance, himself retreated, leaving only a small extreme rearguard, under
Hardegg, to watch Pfeffenhausen. Wrede could ask no
more of his exhausted battalion, and stopped in Pfeffenhausen, whilst Radetzky's strong rearguard retreated to
Furth and Arth.

By 3 A.M. four more of Wrede's battalions had arrived,
as well as Hügel's Wurtemberg brigade, which had been
sent after the Bavarians by Napoleon's orders. Hügel
now attacked Radetzky's extreme rearguard on the
heights, driving them back to their main body. At
4 A.M. Napoleon issued orders to Wrede to push on to
Landshut, which may have reached him about 6.

Leaving behind, for some rest, the exhausted battalion
which had taken Pfeffenhausen, the Bavarian general
marched again, frequently having little combats with the
retreating Austrians in the grey of the morning. In the
later of these there joined some of Lannes' cuirassiers,
from the Rottenburg road, who had set their hearts on
the capture of Radetzky. The latter thought it advisable
to retire to Pfettrach.

Meanwhile, the head of the V. Austrian corps had
reached the broad valley of the Isar at Altdorf by
4 A.M.; the II. Reserve corps had already passed
through Landshut and crowned the heights beyond.
The head of the VI. corps was just arriving from the
direction of Unter Glaim. It had abandoned Rottenburg in the night, and continued its retreat on Landshut,
making only one threat of resistance at Turkenfeld. On
the dead-level plain which forms the valley of the Isar,
there was a frightful scene of confusion. Waggons,
pontoons, and all the impedimenta of an army were
hurrying along the Landshut road. There were double
lines of them at first, and then, beyond the junction of
the roads from Pfeffenhausen and Rottenburg, the lines
were four and five abreast. Terrified and demoralised

drivers, aiming at the fancied security of the farther
bank of the Isar, jostled one another and flogged horses
which were exhausted by the rapid retreat over roads
rendered worse than ever by the rain, and by the previous passage of hundreds of vehicles and guns.   The
streets of Landshut were equally blocked.   Hiller saw
that, if his troops were to have any chance of escape,
they must gain time for this rabble to get clear of the
roads in the valley.   He posted three regiments and the
brigade of Hohenfeld (VI. corps) on the right of Altdorf,
whilst Radetzky, with advanced troops, stood across the
Pfeffenhausen road at Aich.   The VI. corps had been
pursued by Lannes' cavalry, but, so far, there were but
few of the French infantry available, and the Bavarians
on the Pfeffenhausen road were almost worn out.

At 6 A.M. there were moving on Landshut, from Pfeffenhausen and Rottenburg, some 40,000 French, Bavarian,
and Wurtemberg infantry, and 9000 cavalry.   In rear
marched Tharreau with nearly 7000 more infantry from
Neustadt.   At the same time, Masséna was advancing
down the Isar with 36,000 infantry and 5000 cavalry.
Altogether, including Tharreau, over 80,000 bayonets
and 14,000 sabres were closing in on Landshut and the
36,000 infantry, and perhaps 3000 cavalry, still under
Hiller's command.

About 9 A.M. Radetzky again fell back on Altdorf,
without seriously resisting the attack of Wrede.   About
this hour Napoleon, with Lannes' cavalry and Morand's
leading troops, reached Ergolding, just as the rear of the
VI. corps left it in disorder.   Hiller now collected 32
squadrons, which he placed under Vincent with orders
to hold on to the left bank of the Isar as long as
possible.   Against them Napoleon brought 46 squadrons
of cuirassiers, and French and Bavarian light cavalry.
The cavalry was now under Bessières, who, as well as
Lauriston, an artillery general, had just arrived from

Spain. For a moment, the bravery of the Austrian cavalry seemed to afford some hope, but the French cavalry soon bore them down, and drove them across the river, some escaping by the bridges, others swimming their horses over.

Meanwhile, Radetzky and the infantry at Altdorf, had retreated into the suburbs of St Nicholas and Seligenthal, on the left bank opposite Landshut. Their place on the heights was at once taken by French artillery, brought up by Lauriston, who was able to use his guns with effect on the Austrians in the battle raging at his feet. Wrede's cavalry also joined in.

It was about 11 A.M. when the French cavalry, flushed with victory, rode wildly against the suburbs. Though these were held by infantry, nothing could withstand the fury of the French attack, made as it was with the knowledge that the Emperor himself was watching it.

The Austrians streamed out in wild flight towards the bridges and the town, and it was only at the left branch of the Isar that the pursuit was momentarily arrested, about noon. It was now about time for the effect of Masséna's advance to be felt beyond the Isar. It was the knowledge of his advance which had decided Hiller to make no serious attempt to defend Landshut, but to fall back to Vilsbiburg. With Masséna on the right bank above Landshut, the defence was manifestly impossible against the double attack of greatly superior forces.

Masséna's troops started at 4 A.M. on the 21st. The order of march had been laid down overnight, over Becker's signature as usual. Marulaz's light cavalry to reconnoitre in front. Claparède to follow, and to repair the Moosburg bridge at once, if damaged. Then were to follow the Baden and Darmstadt cavalry, the divisions of Legrand, Carra St Cyr,[1] Molitor, Espagne's cuirassiers,

---

[1] For some reason not explained, Carra St Cyr marched in front of Legrand.

the parks, etc., in rear. " The marshal will give, during the day, his orders for ulterior operations." Subsequent orders, of the 21st, directed (1) Ficatier's brigade of Claparède's division and the Baden cavalry to march by the *left* bank; (2) Legrand to stop half-way between Kronwinkel and Landshut; (3) Molitor, the parks, etc., to stop at Moosburg.

Legrand was told that Claparède and Carra St Cyr were marching to seize Landshut, but there does not appear to have been any order to those two generals for such action. Under the final clause of the original orders, just quoted, they would expect to receive orders from Masséna personally. That was all right if Masséna had been, where he ought to have been, with his advance guard, as Napoleon had told him a few days before he should be.[1] But he was not there. He left Freising so late that he only reached Moosburg at 11 A.M., and then he stayed there and only caught up Claparède about 5 P.M., when it was too late.

The march, as ordered, was faithfully carried out. Marulaz with his leading troops reached Moosburg just as Nordmann's men set fire to the bridge as they retreated over it. The French cavalry, dismounting under fire from the right bank, threw the burning straw into the river, and saved the passage. Nordmann[2] fell back along the right bank to Landshut, harassed on the way by Marulaz. The last-named commander, with the 23rd chasseurs, got within a mile of Landshut, saw a large force on the hills south of it, and heard the fight proceeding on the farther side of the Isar. Judging it imprudent to expose his cavalry in the now narrow space between the hills and the river, he fell back as far as the opener valley at Hofham. Here he was joined,

---

[1] Berthier to Masséna—Donauwörth, 17th April; 7 P.M.

[2] It will be remembered that Nordmann had been left near Nandlstadt on the 20th, and had been forced to retreat on Moosburg.

about 2 P.M., by Coehorn's brigade, of Claparède's division.

According to Binder v. Krieglstein, Marulaz and Coehorn were going to make an immediate attack, when Claparède came up and stopped it. If so, he did it because he was ignorant of the wishes of his still absent chief, who had given no instructions. Claparède, the man who a few days later made the desperate attack at Ebelsdorf, was the last man to be deterred by want of personal determination, or a desire to economise troops. The result of Masséna's absence was that Marulaz, Claparède, and Carra St Cyr were still standing within sight of Landshut and the retreating Austrians, doing nothing when the marshal came up, about 5 P.M., and ordered an advance. It was too late to stop the Austrian retreat. When Marulaz and Coehorn entered Landshut, it had already been taken from across the river, and Masséna's men, beyond the alarm which they created in the mind of Hiller expecting an immediate attack on his flank and line of retreat, took practically no part in the events of the day. In the evening Marulaz's division was put under Bessières for the pursuit towards the Inn. The other divisions bivouacked for the night; Claparède and St Cyr at Hofham, Legrand and Espagne at Kronwinkel, Molitor, etc., at Moosburg.

We must now return to the French on the west of the Isar whom we left just after the capture of the suburbs beyond the left branch of the river. Then began a fusillade across the river between Morand's troops and two Austrian regiments in the island. Napoleon soon got tired of this and called up his aide-de-camp Mouton, him on whose monument at Phalsbourg is inscribed the Emperor's little joke, "mon Mouton est un lion." Him Napoleon sent, at the head of the grenadiers of the 17th of the line, to take the bridges.

The first bridge appears to have been crossed with com-

parative ease, and the island was occupied.   Then came
the more difficult crossing to the mainland.   A deadly fire
was poured on the grenadiers from windows, a church,
and the tower defending the bridge.   It was useless
replying in the same terms, so Mouton, again placing
himself at the head of his grenadiers, thundered at them,
in a voice more leonine than sheepish, the order " No
firing! march!"   Rushing across the already burning
bridge at their head, Mouton got the gate broken in with
axes, and found himself inside a town still full of enemies.
There was, however, ample support following him over
the bridge, the fire of which had been extinguished.
The time was towards 5 P.M., just when Masséna was
reaching his advance guard at Hofham.

Hiller now sent the Archduke Louis to lead the
retreating corps to Neumarkt, whilst he for some time
defended himself with the rearguard in the houses of
Landshut.   Three grenadier battalions of the II. Reserve
corps, under Kienmayer on the heights south of the
town, showed face against Masséna.   Presently, all these
fell back on the road to Neumarkt.   There was still a
terrible confusion, drivers raising sudden panics, and
waggons crowding the road to such an extent that the
troops often had to take to the fields and woods.   It was
after midnight when Hiller at last reached Neumarkt,
leaving seven squadrons on the Vils to cover the
retreat.

Binder v. Krieglstein estimates the Austrian losses
on this day at about 9000, of whom two-thirds were
prisoners or missing.   They also lost large quantities of
waggons and guns, as well as a bridge train.

Here it will be as well to anticipate somewhat by
stating what became of Hiller on the following day.   He
reached Neumarkt at 2 A.M. on the 22nd ; at 5 A.M. he
again started towards the Inn which he reached, at Neu-
oetting, late that evening, having in 36 hours of flight

covered the distance which the army had taken 7 days to cover in the advance. The losses of the 19th-22nd in the V. and VI. corps alone were 12,140 men, 11 guns, and 328 waggons.[1] Adding the losses of the II. Reserve corps, which are not ascertainable, and deducting the whole from the 42,000 men whom Hiller commanded on the 19th, it is not probable that he had more than 27,000 or 28,000 men, at the most, on the evening of the 22nd. Bessières' pursuit had not been very vigorous, which may be partially accounted for by the fact of his weakness till Molitor should come up, and that general had not passed Vilsbiburg on the 22nd. That evening Marulaz was at Rohrbach, Wrede at Neumarkt, with advanced troops at Rohrbach and Eggenfelden.

Bessières reported from Neumarkt that the Archduke Charles had begun his retreat, on the evening of the 21st, by Dingolfing on Neumarkt. His belief in this false news may perhaps have rendered him unwilling to press forward too fast.

(2) DAVOUT'S BATTLE OF THE 21ST APRIL

Whilst the Austrian left wing had been thus defeated and driven back in flight, rather than in mere retreat, the centre also, under the Archduke Charles, had been engaged with Davout and Lefebvre.

Kolowrat, whom Charles had, on the 20th, ordered off to Hemau, was recalled early on the 21st. Leaving one battalion in Ratisbon he was to take post to the south on the Ober-Isling road. Vecsey, from Liechtenstein's command, was ordered towards Abbach, to reconnoitre towards Peising. Lindenau's division, between Wölkering and Hinkofen. Cuirassiers of I. Reserve corps to occupy Weinting, Gebelkofen, etc. Grenadiers to Köfering. The IV. corps was to take position "behind Dinzling,"

---

[1] *B. K.*, i. 309.

covering the Eckmühl-Egloffsheim road, with advanced posts on Weillohe. III. corps "behind Unter Laichling, with outposts, Leierndorf to Dinzling." Until the Arch-duke Louis should come into line, this corps (III.) was to leave a brigade, on the heights of Lindach, to cover Eckmühl, and to send a reconnoitring detachment on Langquaid. Louis was written to that the army would be, on the 21st-22nd, between the Great Laber and Ratisbon. He was, therefore, to hurry to Eckmühl, as were Schustekh, Thierry, and Pfanzelter. Hiller was to cover the roads to Landshut. Bellegarde, beyond the Danube, was to hurry to Hemau.

These orders make no mention of any intention to attack, and can only be supposed to indicate an intention to reassemble the army for future operations.

Before the orders even reached the corps, the position of affairs had been changed by Davout's and Lefebvre's advance.

At 2.30 A.M., Davout had replied to Napoleon's letter of 9 P.M. of the 20th. He said : (1) that he was now in touch with the Bavarians by Hausen and Thann ; (2) that the Austrians in front of him, whom he estimated at 15,000 to 20,000,[1] had gone towards Schierling ; (3) those in front of Montbrun [2] had not moved ; (4) com-munication with Ratisbon was cut ; (5) he would march at once on Langquaid.

On Davout's left flank was Montbrun with a detach-ment about Abbach and himself at Peising. He reported strong Austrian forces in front of Abbach. Fearing an attempt to break through to Abensberg along the Danube, Montbrun asked for infantry and guns.

In sending on (at 7.30 A.M.) this report, Davout wrote to the Emperor : (1) that the Austrian army of Bohemia had debouched by Ratisbon ; (2) that Coutard and the 65th were prisoners ; (3) that Charles and the Bohemian

---

[1] Hohenzollern's III. corps.   [2] Rosenberg's IV. corps.

army had united ; (4) that Montbrun was very weak on the Neustadt road ; (5) that St Hilaire and Friant were attacked by Hohenzollern. All this information, except item (4), had been gleaned from the Austrians themselves under the following circumstances.[1]

Davout, in accordance with his promise, had set out for Langquaid at 5 A.M. He himself rode with Piré's advance guard from Hausen. Behind him was St Hilaire, also starting from Hausen. Friant, starting from Teugen, had first crossed the field of battle of the 19th to Hausen, and then followed about a mile in rear of St Hilaire.

About the same hour, Hohenzollern had set out from Leierndorf, where most of his corps stood on the right bank of the Laber, with Wukassowich's outposts on the left bank. First he went to Langquaid, where Pfanzelter had been left the night before. Then he moved up with his escort[2] to the heights north-west of Ober-Leierndorf.[3] The wood on his right was already in the hands of French skirmishers, and below him was Piré's advance guard coming from Hausen. The time may have been 7 o'clock, or a little later. Piré himself now rode forward with a flag of truce, on the pretext of an extravagant demand for surrender. He was met by Staff-Lieutenant Hundt, who seems to have been simple enough to give him the important information just mentioned in Davout's

---

[1] It is extremely difficult to follow this day's fighting. Even General Bonnal seems not to have got it quite correctly. The following account is based on that of Binder v. Krieglstein and the documents published in *Saski*, ii. p. 300, etc. The report extracted from the " Archives of the Prince of Eckmühl " (*Saski*, p. 311) is particularly difficult to follow ; for the third part of it (p. 313) gives the impression that Päring was taken late in the evening, which was certainly not the case. It is difficult to avoid the suspicion that " Päring " (five lines from bottom of p. 313) is a misprint, especially as in other places names are omitted, apparently because illegible in the original.

[2] He had with him two troops of hussars and a horse battery. *B. K.*, i. 270.

[3] Probably that marked 455, in the open south-west of Grub.

letter. The demand for surrender was, of course, refused, as Piré no doubt anticipated, and he rode back to Davout, who, with his staff, was waiting in sight of Hohenzollern, and on whom the horse-artillery battery now opened.

Davout at once attacked, sending the 3rd infantry into the woods on Hohenzollern's right, and the 10th [1] against the Austrian centre and left. Hohenzollern, still having no orders, and no notion of the general plan, resolved on retirement to Schierling, covered by Wukassowich.

Just as Davout advanced, Lefebvre's leading troops reached Langquaid. That Marshal had, under Napoleon's orders, left Bachel at 5 A.M., or soon after, with Deroy's Bavarians, followed by Demont's small French division, and St Germain's cuirassier brigade.[2] Minucci's squadron of dragoons [3] promptly charged by the level valley on Lefebvre's right of Langquaid, whilst the infantry took the village, without much difficulty, driving out Pfanzelter's people. Then Deroy, keeping to the left bank of the stream, moved on Leierndorf.

This support on his right enabled Davout to bear to his left with Friant's division, whilst St Hilaire pushed on straight in the direction of Unter-Laichling.

As Hohenzollern was moving with his main body on Schierling, he suddenly saw troops of the IV. corps falling back rapidly from the direction of Dinzling, apparently on Schierling also. At 8 A.M., he received a note from Rosenberg, who said superior hostile forces in his front compelled him to fall back on Eckmühl " or still more to the right." He would endeavour to unite with the III. corps. Hohenzollern, reaching Schierling, took

---

[1] Both regiments of Lorencez's brigade, St Hilaire's division.

[2] Lefebvre's first orders (4.30 A.M.) were to march with Deroy, etc., and the Crown Prince to Rottenburg. These were cancelled half an hour later. The Crown Prince was ordered to Rottenburg, Lefebvre and the rest to Langquaid, to support Davout.

[3] Lefebvre's escort.

up a position on the right bank of the Laber, with his right in Schierling, his left towards Mannsdorf, and the deep bed of the Allersdorf brook covering his front. His heavy artillery was sent to the rear. Wukassowich, with the rearguard, was slowly falling back. In the distance, the grenadiers (of I. Reserve corps) were to be seen at Eckmühl. In this position Hohenzollern hoped to be able to await the arrival of Rosenberg on his right.

The last-named general had, during the night, been alarmed at Dinzling by reports of a French advance. He, therefore, brought Stutterheim's advance guard, west of Päring, up to a strength of 3 battalions, 6 squadrons, and 1 horse battery. At 6 A.M., Stutterheim's outposts warned him of Friant's start from Teugen. Thereupon, Rosenberg occupied Päring with 6 battalions and some cavalry, with orders to cover the retreat, if necessary, of the rest of the corps from Dinzling on Laichling.

After St Hilaire's affair with Hohenzollern, Friant had been directed to the left on Päring. Simultaneously St Hilaire had moved forward, with Lefebvre on his right. Deroy was much annoyed at Leierndorf by an Austrian battery beyond the Laber which fired the village and partly destroyed the bridge. This battery was presently silenced by the Bavarian guns, and compelled to fall back on Hohenzollern's position. Demont following Deroy, restored the Leierndorf bridge and crossed, with one brigade, to the right bank, where he remained all day without any fighting. Deroy pushed on towards Schierling.

Friant was soon engaged in a very hot action with Stutterheim's rearguard at Päring. He first drove Stutterheim back on Päring itself. Then he sent the 111th,[1] supported by the 33rd, to the left to turn Päring, which, at the same time, was stormed in front by the 108th, who took 400 prisoners. Stutterheim and the

[1] The 111th had only two battalions, the 1st having been left on the Altmühl.

rest of the force in Päring fell back on Laichling, whilst,
under cover of the fight at Päring, the rest of Rosenberg's corps had moved from Dinzling in the same
direction. Rosenberg had just received the Archduke's
order to cover the Eckmühl-Ratisbon road, and considered he could do it best on the line of the two
Laichlings.

It was about 11 A.M. when Päring was taken, and at
this hour Deroy had already taken Schierling. His
first attack with one battalion had been beaten back,
but a second with two battalions had been successful,
notwithstanding that they were charged on their left
by Stutterheim's cavalry. Schierling was, according to
Lefebvre, several times during the day attacked by the
Austrians without success. Deroy advanced no farther.
Demont remained at Leierndorf, with one brigade on
either side of the Laber.

Meanwhile, Hohenzollern had left his position on the
right bank, under verbal orders from the Archduke
Charles, who had reached the IV. corps about an hour
earlier. He was to take the place of the grenadiers at
Eckmühl. Leaving Wukassowich to hold on at Schierling as long as possible, he had gone at the double to
Eckmühl. On the way he got Charles' early morning
orders, prescribing a position at Unter-Laichling. At
the same time, he received a third order, under which he
was to destroy the bridges at Leierndorf and Schierling
(which was no longer possible), to take post on the
heights of Unter-Laichling, and to detach a brigade to the
heights of Lindach, beyond the Laber, as a link with
the V. corps![1] He sent Wukassowich to Lindach. As
he marched out of Eckmühl, he received yet more orders
which had the result of splitting his corps up all over the
place, and leaving him and his staff almost alone, without

[1] The V. corps, as we know, was about Landshut in full retreat to
the Inn.

any troops. Kaiser's brigade was taken by the Archduke Maximilian and placed behind Rosenberg towards Unter-Laichling, another brigade went along the Ratisbon road, and Bieber's went with Wukassowich to Lindach and Buchhausen.

When Charles reached the retreating IV. corps, at 9 A.M., he issued the following orders, in addition to those to Hohenzollern :—

(1) Liechtenstein to unite Vecsey and Lindenau towards Wölkering, to reconnoitre towards Abbach and to threaten Davout's left towards Weillohe and Luckenpoint. Two cuirassier regiments were also sent to Wölkering.

(2) Six battalions of grenadiers and a cuirassier regiment between Hohenberg and Mooshof, behind two battalions " Archduke Charles " infantry.[1]

(3) The other six battalions of grenadiers, two cuirassier regiments and the remaining battalion " Archduke Charles," under Siegenthal, between Alt- and Neu-Egloffsheim.

All these measures were of a purely defensive nature, and, as Binder v. Krieglstein points out, there is no glimmer in them of an offensive movement, notwithstanding the fact that Charles had available in this direction about 50,000 infantry and 6000 cavalry, against Davout's and Lefebvre's 30,000 bayonets and 5500 sabres.

We now return to Davout who, having taken Päring, was now moving against the IV. corps in its position about Unter- and Ober-Laichling. Rosenberg stood with Stutterheim on his extreme left on the Vorberg. In and behind Unter-Laichling, and extending as far as Ober-Laichling, was Sommariva's division as centre, whilst Hohenlohe formed the right, extending up to and

---

[1] Of Lindenau's division. "Heaven knows how they got there." *B. K.,* i. 275.

into the woods beyond the Mitterberg.[1]   The bank of
the valley on Rosenberg's side rises about 120 feet above
Unter-Laichling, whilst on Davout's side it is not quite
so high.   The IV. corps had scarcely got into position
when St Hilaire's guns reached the height marked 437.9,
about 1200 yards west of Unter-Laichling, whence they
could fire on the Austrian position.

Davout says he at once attacked and took Unter-
Laichling with a battalion of the "Terrible" 57th and
a voltigeur company of the 10th, assisted by some
Bavarian infantry on the right in the valley of the
Laber.   Binder v. Krieglstein says the attack was beaten
off, and, on the whole, that seems probable; for after
that Davout kept three out of St Hilaire's five regiments
(the 57th, 72nd, and 105th) in column on the heights
west of Unter-Laichling.   He could hardly, therefore,
have held the village, as these regiments did little or no
fighting.[2]

All the real hard fighting was done in the woods on
Davout's left.   Through these woods, much cut up by
ravines and rocks, Friant pushed forward.   Such wood
fighting is generally so confused, and between such
scattered troops, as to be impossible of subsequent
description.   All that can be said of it on this occasion
is that Davout kept endeavouring to turn the Austrian

---

[1] The Mitterberg north of Ober Laichling.

[2] It is difficult to get at the truth regarding this attack on Unter-Laichling.
Berthezène, then colonel of the 10th, does not mention it, and, as the 10th
had to take it on the 22nd, it is clear Davout did not hold possession of it
on the 21st for long.   Indeed, when one looks at the place, it is clear it
could not be held long whilst the Austrians remained in force, with artillery,
on the bank above.   If it was taken on the 21st, it must have been either
re-taken by the Austrians, or evacuated by the French of their own accord.
B. v. Krieglstein does not quote the authority for his account.   It is a
curious fact, raising suspicion of more confusion, that the account from the
"Archives of the Prince of Eckmühl" gives the number of the prisoners
taken in Unter-Laichling as 400, precisely the number Friant says were taken
in Päring.

L

right through the woods, and, as Friant got forward, Rosenberg kept sending more and more reinforcements from his left to his right, until he had 11 battalions in the latter direction. Davout's turning force was generally the 111th and 33rd regiments. Towards evening, they had gone so far to the left, in the endeavour to outflank the Austrian right, that Ober-Sanding was taken. This was done by Compans, Davout's Chief of Staff, with the 48th, backed by Friant's six guns firing from the edge of the woods on the heights above Ober-Sanding. Compans was sent by Davout in consequence of the death of the brigadier-general Hervo, who was shot down by some Austrians cut off in the wood fighting. Just after Compans started, an Austrian column suddenly appeared in front of Davout from some broken ground in which it had been concealed. Davout himself turned a howitzer on them, and, receiving them with it and infantry fire at close quarters, succeeded in repulsing them, though he was, for the moment, forced back into the wood.

Just as Compans and the 48th got into Ober-Sanding, the Archduke Charles arrived with his own regiment, whilst the grenadiers and two cuirassier regiments appeared on the heights to the east. The "Archduke Charles" regiment, somewhere between 5 and 6 P.M., drove Compans out of Ober-Sanding at the point of the bayonet. Then, however, they were charged in right flank by some companies of the 108th, which Compans had sent still farther northwards, and compelled to retire again. The fight in the woods now gradually flickered out as darkness descended on the scene, though there were little skirmishes here and there until well into the night.

In Davout's centre and on his right the battle had been confined for 5 or 6 hours to an artillery duel, which exhausted the French ammunition.   Davout's park, which had been ordered up from Neustadt on the 20th, only arrived with its head at Langquaid at 2 A.M. on the 22nd.

For the night, Rosenberg collected his corps between the Mitterberg and the Vorberg, whilst Davout still held all the positions he had won.   Bavarians at Schierling and Friant's extreme left (48th and 33rd) thrown back, facing north, with its front covered by "abattis."   Davout gives his losses at about 1500 killed and wounded, more than two-thirds of them in Friant's division. The Bavarians probably did not lose more than 150.

The Austrians admit about 3000 killed and wounded, and a "very few" prisoners.   The latter item does not at all agree with Davout, who claims to have taken at least 1500.

The Archduke Charles, out of all the 56,000 men he had available, seems hardly to have engaged seriously more than 17,000.

Whilst Davout was fighting, almost for existence, on the right, Montbrun on his left was not engaged beyond perhaps a few skirmishes.   He appears to have been reinforced by the 15th light infantry from Friant's division.   All day long his detachment at Abbach was threatened, but not attacked, by superior forces.   At first, whilst Rosenberg was still at Dinzling, Montbrun dared not advance.   When Dinzling was evacuated, he moved into it, and from there to Abbach watched the country towards Ratisbon.

Boudet's division, at Neustadt, had been placed at Davout's disposal and ordered to Abensberg.   Davout could not call Boudet up to himself; for, during the day, he heard that his posts on the Altmühl had been forced to retire.   He had to utilise part of Boudet's force to support them and eventually to order Boudet back to

Ingolstadt. Tharreau's division was on the march to Landshut, and had reached Schweinbach, when Oudinot received orders from headquarters placing him, with Tharreau's infantry and Colbert's cavalry, at Davout's disposal. It was, however, too late for him to be of any use that day to Davout. He spent the night at Schweinbach.

Napoleon was perpetually urging his marshals to send him fuller and more frequent information. Davout on the 20th April must have satisfied his craving for news, for the marshal, between 7.30 A.M. and 11 P.M., sent no less than six reports. The first four forwarded despatches from Montbrun, and dwelt on the danger of an Austrian advance on Abensberg by the Danube. They also described the progress of Davout's battle, and again and again emphasised the strength of the Austrians, and the fact that their whole main army was opposed to him. At 7 P.M., Davout sent Piré to Napoleon to personally explain the situation. At 11 P.M., he again wrote to the Emperor. He had won the day, no doubt, but his ammunition was exhausted, and he was faced by "la presque totalité" of the Archduke's army, extending in a great semicircle from Lindach beyond the Laber to Abbach on the Danube. At most he could only keep the positions he had won, and the Austrians showed no signs of retreating. Even the Emperor was beginning to admit that he had failed to compel a general retreat of the Austrians on the Inn. When he had got Landshut he wrote that he had only overthrown 12,000 to 15,000 of the enemy. He still professed to think Davout strong enough, but told him he could send for Tharreau, and even for the Crown Prince of Bavaria from Rottenburg. Still, General Bonnal holds that, up to 2 A.M. on the 22nd, Napoleon's pride forced him to a false view of the real state of affairs, and a belief that the greater part of the

Austrian army was in front of himself retreating to the Inn.[1]

At 2 A.M. arrived Piré, and what he had to say at last compelled the Emperor to admit the truth of what Davout had been urging on him ever since the 19th, the presence of the main body of the Austrians opposite the French left.

About 6 P.M. the Archduke had issued fresh orders for the assembly of his troops thus—

(1) Grenadiers in wood of Mooshof, and at Neu-Egloffsheim.

(2) III. corps on heights in front of Alt-Egloffsheim.

(3) Wukassowich about Lindach, guarding the Straubing road.

(4) IV. corps on heights of Laichling.

(5) Lindenau's division at Gebelkofen.

(6) Vecsey across the road to Abbach, at Weillohe and Luckenpoint.

A staff officer was sent to see to the restoration of all bridges over the Danube, from Ratisbon to the mouth of the Isar.

Once more these orders point rather to an intention to retreat next day than to a vigorous offensive. Yet the idea of a general attack seems to have been present to Charles, for he says, writing to his brother the Emperor at 10 P.M., "To-morrow I shall draw to me the II. corps and unite it with the III., IV. and I. Reserve corps for a general attack."

The position, then, in the first half of the night of the 21st-22nd was this—

Davout and Lefebvre stood, as already noted, with less than 35,000 men, against more than 50,000

---

[1] *Bonnal*, p. 226, where also will be found an interesting calculation of times of march to and through Landshut which should have shown the Emperor that he could not have been following a column of anything like 50,000 men.

Austrians, who were to be joined during the night by Kolowrat's corps of 20,000, which had been sent to Hemau on the 20th, and at once recalled thence.

In the direction of Landshut was Napoleon with 60,000 or 70,000. Bessières was pursuing the defeated Austrian left wing with cavalry towards Neumarkt and the Inn. Tharreau was at Schweinbach, under Oudinot ; Boudet near Abensberg, with orders to go to Ingolstadt and support the detachment between the Danube and the Altmühl. The Crown Prince's Bavarians at Rottenburg.

At 7.30 P.M., Napoleon had ordered St Sulpice, with his cuirassiers, a Wurtemberg cavalry regiment, and Hügel's Wurtemberg light brigade, to march on Essenbach and Ergoldsbach, clearing off small stray hostile forces supposed to be in that direction.

CHAPTER IX

ECKMÜHL AND RATISBON

(1) THE BATTLE OF ECKMÜHL

PIRÉ, despatched by Davout at 7 P.M. on the 21st, covered the 37 miles[1] of dangerous, crowded road which separated him from the Emperor in 7 hours, and was shown into Napoleon's quarters at 2 A.M. A few minutes' conversation sufficed to tear from the Emperor's eyes the scales which he had allowed to dim the natural clearness of his vision. Though Davout had persistently, since the evening of the 19th, represented to his master that his corps was opposed to overwhelming forces, in fact the greater part of the Austrian army, Napoleon had refused to set aside his own preconceived notion that the inevitable result of his own manœuvre on Landshut must be the retreat of the Archduke Charles on the Isar and the Inn. Yet, even now, he had not entirely divested himself of this preconceived idea ; for he still writes of Eckmühl as on the rear of the Austrian army, thereby plainly showing that he expected the Archduke to retreat eastwards over the Isar, and not northwards, through Ratisbon, to Bohemia. If Charles would, by retreating through Ratisbon, find himself cut from his 30,000 remaining men of the left wing, he would be more than compensated by his union with 50,000 undefeated troops of the corps of Kolowrat and Bellegarde.

[1] This is the distance as calculated by Bonnal. Piré had to make a detour.

However, it was at last clear to Napoleon that he had driven towards the Inn, through Landshut, a comparatively small portion of the enemy. For the pursuit of this wing he at present considered Bessières' cavalry (Marulaz), supported by Wrede's Bavarian division, to be sufficient. Molitor, the rearmost of Masséna's divisions, could stop at Landshut, ready, if necessary, to follow Bessières and Wrede.

To Davout the Emperor wrote still fondly hugging the notion that Charles would retreat in obedience to the threat of Landshut, and was only holding on still in order to get his artillery clear away. If, however, he still held out during the 22nd, Napoleon could fall on his *rear* at Eckmühl with 25,000 men. Davout, if he found it impossible to hold his present position, could fall back as he thought best, always provided he covered the line from Landshut, by Rottenburg, to Rohr, forming the lateral line of communication for the reunion of the army. This was at 2.30 A.M. At 4 A.M., a duplicate of this letter was sent; but to this was added an important postscript in which it was said that the Emperor had decided to reach Eckmühl at noon, followed by 40,000 men. He would be in a position to attack by 3 P.M.

Between 2.30 and 4 A.M., the following orders had been issued for the march on Eckmühl—

(1) Vandamme to start at once for Ergoldsbach, preceded by his cavalry and light infantry brigade (Hügel).

(2) Gudin, leaving Ergolding at 4 A.M., to reach Ergoldsbach at 9.

(3) Morand, starting from near Landshut, to reach Martinshain at 9, immediately in rear of Gudin.

(4) Masséna, with three divisions and Espagne's cuirassiers, to march from opposite Landshut, at 6 A.M., behind Morand, leaving the 4th division (Molitor) in Landshut.

All this long column, of six divisions of infantry,

besides cavalry and artillery, had to march on the single
road to Eckmühl, and General Bonnal, by a simple
calculation,[1] shows that the last of Masséna's three
divisions, with the hours given, could not leave Landshut
till 11 A.M., and could not reach Eckmühl till 8 P.M. The
head of Gudin's division could only arrive at 2 P.M. From
Landshut to Eckmühl is about 24 miles, and the road
passes over the watershed between the Isar and the Little
Laber, and then over that between the two Labers.

Other orders issued were—

(1) Wrede to follow Bessières.

(2) Rouyer and Boudet at Ingolstadt to defend the
Altmühl. In very unexpected circumstances they were
to cut the other bridges, holding only Ingolstadt.

(3) To Bessières, informing him of Wrede's and other
movements.

Lannes received his orders, the same as had already
been sent direct to Morand and Gudin, and was told to
pick up St Sulpice at Essenbach. He ought also to have
picked up Jacquinot's brigade of light cavalry, but, having
no orders to do so, he left it at Ergolding.[2]

Having recorded the orders of Napoleon for the rescue
of Davout and Lefebvre, and for the destruction of the
Archduke Charles, which he now constantly lays down
as his objective, we must return to Davout and his
opponents.

At 6 A.M. on the 22nd, Kolowrat's corps, after its
weary and useless promenade to Hemau and back,
reached Ober-Isling with 19,000 infantry and 2000
cavalry.[3]

Charles had now made up his mind to crush Davout.
He should have done so 24 or 36 hours earlier, when the

---

[1] *Bonnal*, p. 241.

[2] Bonnal (p. 233) quotes this as an instance of the dependence of even a
marshal like Lannes on detailed orders from Napoleon, and his unwillingness
to rectify an oversight of the Emperor.

[3] 2000 infantry and 300 cavalry were still behind.

Emperor had separated himself so far from his left that he would have been powerless to save Davout.

At 8 A.M., the Austrian commander-in-chief issued orders. The first column, consisting of Kolowrat's tired corps, followed by the nearest portion of Vecsey's brigade, was to seize Abbach. The 2nd column, consisting of the rest of Vecsey's brigade, Lindenau's division, and four squadrons, all under Liechtenstein, was to march on Peising. The third column (Hohenzollern) of St Julien's division (III. corps), and the regiment 'Archduke Charles' as advance guard, also to attack towards Peising. Thus there were 41 battalions detailed to attack Davout's left flank from the north.

Whilst this attack was in progress, it was to be covered by the rest of the army. The IV. corps to hold on where it was, but, if forced back, to retire on the line Hohenberg-Sanding and Haus Neu-Egloffsheim, on the left of the 3rd column. Wukassowich, at Buchhausen, and Bieber at Lindach, were put under Rosenberg's orders. Two regiments of cuirassiers were to be at Thalmassing, the rest at Köfering. Rohan's position, with the grenadiers, is not stated, probably because Charles meant to be with them in person. The whole force is estimated at not less than 66,000 infantry and 8000 cavalry.[1] The attack was ordered to begin between noon and 1 P.M. At 2 A.M., Stutterheim had reported that Napoleon was about to attack the left flank with the Bavarians and Wurtembergers. That was regarded at Austrian headquarters as a mere " blind."

The early morning, like that of Jena, had been obscured by a thick fog, which only cleared off about 8 o'clock.

Davout was not in a position to renew the attack

---

[1] *B. K.*, i. 287. Angeli, following Stutterheim, puts them as high as 72,000 infantry, and 8400 cavalry.

against forces he knew to be so vastly superior to his
own, and he must have been thankful that he was left
in peace.   Nothing had happened up to 12 o'clock,
beyond the slow preparations of the Austrian army for
attack.   At that hour Wukassowich reported, from
Buchhausen, that the enemy was on the Landshut road,
threatening to attack the left flank of the IV. corps.
A later report said that, Bieber having been withdrawn
to Eckmühl, Wukassowich was unable to defend himself
with only two weak battalions and a couple of sections
of hussars.

Wurtemberg cavalry now came along the road, and
skirmished with Wukassowich's hussars ; presently, an
infantry attack on Buchhausen sent him hurrying back
to Eckmühl, where he was still fired on by Wurtemberg
batteries.

Rosenberg, fearing this attack from the south, threw
back his left wing on to the Bettelberg, and placed
Bieber still farther to the east, stretching up to the
heights of Rogging.   His right, holding Unter-Laichling
in front, stretched along the line of heights, through
Ober-Laichling, towards Ober-Sanding.   A battery of
16 guns was placed on the heights north of Kraxenhof.

About 2 P.M., there being evident symptoms of an
approaching attack from the west by Davout and
Lefebvre, Rosenberg twice asked for reinforcements, but
says he got no answer.

Napoleon had now reached the field.   Accompanied
by Masséna and his staff, he turned to his left at
Buchhausen and reached the heights of Lindach.   What
he saw thence cannot be better described than in the
words of Pelet, which are just as applicable to the
country now as in 1809, except for the railway bridge
on the right.

" We perceived, through its whole breadth, this battlefield rising gently in an amphitheatre.   The summits of

the hills were crowned with fine forests ; the valleys opened before us, bare enough, but cultivated and separated from one another by hills of slightly marked feature. There was the valley of Eckmühl (running from south to north), up which wound the Ratisbon road, and there was that of the two Laichlings, separated from one another by a small wood. . . . At our feet we saw the Laber, flowing from the large village of Schierling on the left through green and damp pasturages. We could follow the twistings of its bed, planted with willows and poplars, in the bottom of a valley $2\frac{1}{2}$ miles [1] broad, adorned by fine villages, cut up by little canals and shady roads, and having sides sloping gently up. On our right, the heights rose to the wooded hills of Roking,[2] dominating the neighbourhood and apparently destined to play a great part in the battle."

Koch tells a story of how Napoleon, gazing on the white-coated Austrians beyond the valley, seized Masséna by the arm and rapidly sketched out his plans. Davout would attack Laichling, whilst the Emperor turned the Austrian left by Eckmühl, and drove them on Ratisbon. " Either the archduke will fight a second battle in front of that place, in which case the war will be ended under its walls ; or he will repass the Danube, and then we shall go direct to Vienna." If this story is true it goes to confirm General Bonnal's theory that the Emperor meant to reach Vienna, even if in doing so he had to forgo, for the present, the decisive battle which is the true object of war, and victory in which would lay Vienna at his feet.

From the postmaster at Buchhausen Napoleon ascertained that there was a ford at the Schnitzelmühle, 300 yards or so above the Eckmühl bridge.

---

[1] This is an exaggeration, the breadth from foot to foot of the hills cannot exceed a mile.

[2] Rogging.

The Emperor's orders were issued at once. Lefebvre and Davout were to drive Rosenberg back on to the Ratisbon road, Vandamme, with Hügel's brigade, to attack Eckmühl and push along the road ; Lannes to break off to the east to Rogging and Pfelkofen, and on by Gailsbach and Triftelfing.

Davout had already begun to move.[1] His attack began soon after 2 P.M., at which hour also began the attack on Eckmühl, and the advance of Lannes on Rogging.

The archduke, meanwhile, instead of going to the front, had stayed at Thalmassing where he received Rosenberg's report of the French column on the road from Landshut. Charles' own columns had done nothing, beyond some reconnoitring towards Abbach by the II. corps. He now at once, without riding forward to satisfy himself, abandoned the idea of attacking Davout. Kolowrat was ordered back to Ober-Isling ; Liechtenstein to Gebelkofen-Thalmassing ; Hohenzollern to Thalmassing-Sanding ; Rohan was put under Hohenzollern ; and Rosenberg was ordered to extricate himself from the fight as best he might, the intention evidently being for him to fall back northwards. To Bellegarde, now at Hemau, urgent orders of recall were sent. Practically, Rosenberg's corps was a strong rearguard, covering the retreat of the army on Ratisbon, though Charles does not appear to have meant that general to offer so much resistance as he actually did.

It was just after 2 P.M. when Hügel's light brigade reached the bridge of Eckmühl, at which they found one of Wukassowich's battalions. The other was in the village and château of Eckmühl. In 1809 the village was surrounded by a dilapidated wall, which has now disappeared. Round the château was an earthen rampart, which is still to be seen. As an advanced post

[1] Lefebvre was under Davout's orders.

in a field of battle, both were capable of a long defence. One of Hügel's battalions, after being twice beaten off, captured the passage of the river, followed its defenders across the 200 yards of open ground to Eckmühl, and took both village and château, with 300 prisoners in the latter. Wukassowich had retired on to the hills to the north when the bridge was lost. The affair was over by 2.30 P.M. At this hour, the position was this—Gudin's division had just reached the Laber, followed by Morand, at the Stangelmühle. From Schierling (right bank) to the heights of Lindach were some 20 squadrons of Bavarian and Wurtemberg light cavalry, and on their right two brigades of cuirassiers, waiting for the opening of the Eckmühl bridge, and suffering some loss from the Austrian battery behind Kraxenhof. That battery the French guns were unable to silence, on account of the range (between 2000 and 3000 paces). Nansouty was just coming up by the Landshut road, and Masséna's leading troops were behind his cuirassiers. In Eckmühl were the Wurtemberg infantry. Farther to the left, Sendewitz's cavalry, in front of Deroy's infantry, filled the space between Davout's right and the stream. Behind Deroy was Demont, who had a battalion and a squadron on the right bank of the Laber. Behind him again was the Bavarian Crown Prince, just arriving from Rottenburg.

On Deroy's left, on the wooded heights north and north-east of Schierling, was St Hilaire's division, with his right brigade (Lorencez) opposite Unter-Laichling, whilst de Stabenrath's brigade extended on the left to the Laimberg. Thence Friant took up the line, as far as the wood marked on the map Faul Leithe. Piré's cavalry was distributed amongst these two divisions. Montbrun, with Pajol's brigade, was gone towards Dinzling, in which direction he was engaged all day in small attacks on the Austrian outposts.

Over against this great semi-circle of French, Rosen-berg was posted thus—

(1) Bieber's brigade (III. corps) from Rogging heights to the Weinberg, just east of the modern railway bridge.

(2) North of Kraxenhof the Czartoriski regiment, the "Vincent" chevaux legers,[1] and the Stipsics hussars,[1] besides what was left of Wukassowich.

(3) On the Bettelberg was the 16-gun battery.

(4) Six battalions were on the Vor-, Hinter-, and Fuchs-bergs, and holding Unter-, and Ober-Laichling. Of the remaining six, four were on the Mitterberg and in the Oberholz[2] beyond, two in reserve.

Soon after 2.30, Gudin, on the French right, crossed the Laber at Stangelmühle, attacked Bieber and Wukasso-wich, and effected a firm lodgment with his skirmishers in the woods north-east of Eckmühl. Thence they refused to be driven by repeated Austrian attacks, and they held firm for two hours, whilst the rest of Gudin's and Morand's divisions got across the stream.

The French cavalry, now busily crossing the Eckmühl bridge, and the Schnitzelmühle ford, still suffered severely from the enemy's battery on the Bettelberg. A gallant attempt was now made by Sendewitz's Bavarian cavalry to storm this battery. They managed to get forward unnoticed as far as the southern foot of the Vorberg, and then made a dash up the slope for the flank of the battery. Met in front with a heavy fire of case, and then charged in flank from Kraxenhof by 4 Austrian squadrons, the gallant Bavarians were heavily defeated and driven back up the valley.

At the same time, St Hilaire's attack started, supported by Deroy on his right. The 10th light infantry, under Berthezène, supported by the 105th, had no great

---

[1] Eight squadrons each.

[2] The detached wood on the east of the valley opposite the Mitterholz.

difficulty in capturing Unter-Laichling, where they took several hundred prisoners. The little hanging wood on the steep slope above Unter-Laichling was less easy, and cost more in men to take; but, presently, the French were just emerging from it driving the Austrians before them on to the Hinter-berg, when Stutterheim, with four squadrons of hussars, attacked them in the nick of time and brought them to a standstill and to a long musketry fire, at the wood and Heu Kurbe, with the two Austrian infantry regiments. Deroy's attack on the Vorberg also, being insufficiently supported by artillery, came to a standstill. Only Lorencez's brigade had been employed by St Hilaire, and it was too weak, until Friant on the left afforded the necessary support.

The last-named general took his artillery, the six guns which had done so well the previous day, on to the Laimberg, whence he could command Ober-Laichling and the slopes beyond. Hence he sent forward the 33rd, with the 48th on its left. Through the great wood on his left (Leibholz and Mitterholz) advanced the 108th and 111th, whilst the 15th light infantry stood in reserve behind the centre of the division. The Austrian fire was heavy and earthworks had been thrown up at Ober-Laichling. The attack in that direction was at a standstill when one battalion of the 48th dashing forward stormed many of the works and almost reached the crest of the hill. The other two battalions, and the 33rd following on, held firm on the ground thus conquered. Simultaneously, the 108th and 111th attacked the three Austrian regiments occupying the Oberholz. Here the Austrians made but a poor fight, and were quickly driven out to Ober-Sanding, thus uncovering the right flank of the troops at Ober-Laichling. St Hilaire had now brought up more troops which stormed the heights above Unter-Laichling, and between it and Ober-Laichling. Deroy was also getting well on to the

Vorberg when, once more, the intrepid Stutterheim charged with four squadrons of chevaux legers, and drove back the French skirmishers, just as they were approaching the 16-gun battery.

The French cavalry was now coming into action, under the eyes of the Emperor as he watched the battle from the heights of Deggenbach. The Wurtemberg cavalry (less two regiments sent to Davout) deployed in the Kleine Au, after crossing the Eckmühl bridge, and turning to the left. On their right, across the Ratisbon road, were four regiments of St Sulpice's cuirassiers.

Sendewitz's Bavarian cavalry, on St Sulpice's left, was now again to the fore, burning to retrieve its defeated attempt to take the great battery. He had on his right and left the two Wurtemberg regiments sent to Davout, and, still farther on his right, St Sulpice's 5th cuirassier regiment, in all 20 squadrons, which now (3.30 P.M.) galloped forward against the Bettelberg. Against these the Austrians had 16 squadrons (including the four with which Stutterheim returned from his successful attack on the infantry) of light cavalry, and 6 squadrons of cuirassiers, 22 in all. Notwithstanding the attacks of these, the case shot of the battery, and the adverse slope of the hill, the allied squadrons pressed forward against the battery, near which was Rosenberg with his staff. Advantage might possibly have been taken of the confused cavalry fight on the slope to withdraw the battery, but this was not done. Presently the Austrian squadrons were overpowered and fled in wild confusion, leaving the greater part of the guns to fall into the hands of the victors. Now, at last, only just in time, Rosenberg ordered a general retreat. He was attacked on three sides, his centre was broken, and his retreat by the Ratisbon Road almost cut off. For two hours he had held on bravely against immensely superior forces. It is true that only 30 battalions actually attacked his

M

22⅔, but there were 38 more behind them. His orders were for Bieber to retire on Hohenberg, the rest of the infantry, through Sanding to Egloffsheim. Rosenberg himself would cover the retreat on the Ratisbon Road. Napoleon had, as already described, placed his great body of cavalry in readiness to pursue, and the infantry also followed up the beaten Austrians. Under this pressure their orderly retreat soon degenerated into a panic-stricken flight. Seeing that in less than an hour the main body was between Neu- and Alt-Egloffsheim, some four miles from the field of battle, the rapidity of the flight can be judged.

In order to understand the remaining events of this day, we must, for the moment, leave the hopelessly defeated IV. corps, and hark back to the other Austrian corps.

The II. corps, in accordance with the Archduke's midday orders, retired to Isling, practically unmolested.

The 2nd column (Liechtenstein), consisting of Lindenau's division, Vecsey's brigade, and four squadrons of cuirassiers, took position, to form a rallying point for the IV. corps, on the heights between Gebelkofen and Thalmassing, leaving Vecsey at Weillohe to show a front to Montbrun. The Archduke Charles himself was at the castle of Alt-Egloffsheim, whence he sent Schneller's cuirassier brigade (12 squadrons, II. Reserve corps) to occupy the defile on the Ratisbon road, where it passes through woods at Hagelstadt. Rohan, with the grenadiers, was directed to Hohenberg, which stands on the highest point of the road between Eckmühl and Ratisbon.

The III. corps (Hohenzollern) was, according to the morning disposition, the nearest to Rosenberg's. It now consisted of only 14 battalions and 4 squadrons.[1]

---

[1] From the original corps deduct the brigades of Wukassowich and Bieber, made over to the IV., and add the regiment "Archduke Charles," and four squadrons of hussars, made over to Hohenzollern.

Hohenzollern had ridden forward to the heights south-
east of Luckenpoint, whither his corps was following,
when the firing in Rosenberg's direction became lively,
and, at the same time, Montbrun's outposts were visible
on the right. After some discussion with his Chief of
Staff, Hohenzollern was advancing, when he received the
orders consequent on Rosenberg's report of Napoleon's
advance. Hohenzollern was to take post between Thalmassing and Sanding, with an outpost on his right at
Luckenpoint. At the last-named place the regiment
"Archduke Charles" was left. Kaiser's brigade was
posted on the heights on the right bank of the Pfatterbach, at the places marked "Auf der Höhe" and "Auf der
Wöhrt." Alois Liechtenstein's brigade, and the "super-
fluous" artillery, remained on the left bank of the
Pfatterbach. Several bridges were thrown over the
Pfatterbach, and its affluent the Sandbach.

All these arrangements were complete about 5 P.M.,
some time after Rosenberg's retreat had begun. They
had not been long finished when a new order came to
Hohenzollern. He was now to send one of his brigades
to Rohan, to take post in the woods behind Neu-
Egloffsheim, as a support for the IV. corps. He sent
Kaiser's brigade. Rohan was at this time between
Sanding and Hohenberg. Hohenzollern's remaining
troops were to stand on the heights behind Egloffsheim.

Friant's division of Davout's corps was now rapidly
pushing forward, through the two Sandings, on Neu-
Egloffsheim. Against him advanced Mayer, with Kaiser's
brigade, and the 4 squadrons of hussars also charged
several times. Friant admits that they greatly hampered
him, by compelling him to form squares. All across
Hohenzollern's front streamed the fugitives of the IV.
corps, with Friant behind them, and, at the same time,
Montbrun was attacking the "Archduke Charles" regiment at Luckenpoint. Then occurred a curious incident,

namely, the disorderly retreat of all but two battalions [1]
of Rohan's grenadiers, who had apparently been broken,
somewhere between Hohenberg and Neu-Egloffsheim, by
the fugitives of the IV. corps.

Hohenzollern now decided to retreat to Köfering. On
his way he had to halt to let the stream of fugitives cross
his line. It was nearly dark when he saw, on the right
bank of the Pfatterbach, heavy masses of cavalry, which
he presently made out to be French cuirassiers, marching
on Alt-Egloffsheim.

Napoleon had sent his cavalry in pursuit by the east
of the Ratisbon road. In front of them fled Bieber's
brigade, also Rosenberg's cavalry and part of his infantry,
on the road by Hohenberg and Hagelstadt. The first
serious stand was made in front of Alt-Egloffsheim,
where was Schneller's cuirassier brigade of 12 squadrons,
to whom were joined 16 squadrons of the IV. corps, and
4 other squadrons of hussars, 32 squadrons in all. There
were available, at the same time, four regiments of cuirassiers (24 squadrons), under John Liechtenstein, between
Gebelkofen and Thalmassing, but these quietly marched
on Traubling, at the very moment when Hohenzollern
was compelled to turn more to the west, in order to avoid
the French cuirassiers between Hagelstadt and Alt-
Egloffsheim. The Archduke Charles appears to have
been in the neighbourhood, yet he took no measures for
adding these 24 squadrons to those at Alt-Egloffsheim.
Had he done so, he would, with four squadrons of hussars
who were with Hohenzollern, have been able to oppose
60 squadrons to a number certainly not greater, and
certainly more tired by a long march, on the side of the
allies. The latter had 6 squadrons of Wurtemberg light
cavalry on their right front, 24 squadrons of Nansouty's
cuirassiers on the left rear of these, 16 squadrons of
St Sulpice's cuirassiers behind Nansouty, $10\frac{1}{2}$, or perhaps

[1] These two will be heard of presently.

14½, squadrons of Bavarian light cavalry as reserve—altogether 56½ or 60½ squadrons.

The scene which was about to be enacted under the pale light of the rising moon, about 7 P.M. on this 22nd April, was perhaps one of the most dramatic and awe-inspiring in modern war.   There cannot have been less than 13,000 to 15,000 cavalry engaged.   To view the stage on which it was enacted, stand on the Rochusberg in the midst of Nansouty's horse artillery, busy firing on the Austrian cavalry line in front of Alt-Egloffsheim, and stretching north-eastwards beyond it. Behind the spectator are the great woods stretching to the Pfatterbach ; on his right front, beyond the road, the moonbeams glint from the cuirasses and arms of three French regiments, deployed on a line running north-eastwards.   At the distance behind them of a squadron's front, stand two more regiments of cuirassiers, the two lines together forming the French first line.   Behind these are two columns of St Sulpice's cuirassiers, two regiments in each of them, forming the second line.   Altogether, nearly 6000 of the splendid heavy cavalry which Murat or Bessières would have loved to lead, a duty which, in their absence, fell to Nansouty.[1]

To the right of this central mass, the Wurtemberg light cavalry is deploying, whilst, closer at hand, the Bavarian horsemen are continuing the line across the road close up to the spectator's feet.   Let him look now to the left to see the Austrians deploying, they also with their cuirassiers in two lines in the centre, but with a front of only one regiment, opposed to the three of Nansouty.   The light cavalry are on the flanks of the cuirassiers.   Now the two opposing lines advance.   Were

---

[1] Nansouty had a very good opinion of his own value. On one occasion when the Emperor censured him, he replied : " It is not Your Majesty at any rate who can teach me how to lead cavalry." Thoumas, *Les grands Cavaliers de l'Empire*—Nansouty.

it not for the din of the guns, it would be possible to hear the frequent order, " Close ! Cuirassiers close up ! " as the heavy Norman and Flemish horses move forward at a walk. The Austrians, less fatigued than the French, are already trotting, and about to break into a charge. Now only 100 yards separate the opposing fronts, when the carbineers in Nansouty's centre halt. At the same moment the cuirassiers receive the order, "Trot ! March ! " The halt is only for a moment whilst the carbineers can fire a volley in the faces of the Austrians, and then, drawing their sabres, join in the line which is now trotting forward in a semicircle, with the outer regiments threatening the Austrian cuirassiers' flanks. At the trot still, the French line meets the Austrian galloping horsemen in a fearful crash which drives each front line back on its supports. Each penetrates the other, whilst the light cavalry meet on either flank. The shock is followed by an indescribable melée of individual combats, the Austrians generally employing the edge, the French the point of the sword ; the French protected in front and back by their double cuirass, the Austrians open to attack in rear, since they have no back-piece. The fight could last only for a few moments, for there were five French regiments of heavy cavalry against only two Austrian.[1]

Before St Sulpice's four regiments could throw in their weight, the Austrians were in the wildest flight back, past Alt-Egloffsheim, to Köfering, followed by and intermingled with the pursuing French. St Sulpice still trotted steadily in rear, until he came upon the two battalions of Rohan's grenadiers which had not joined in the flight of the rest.[2] These two battalions, formed in squares, endeavoured to stop the pursuit, but St Sulpice's

---

[1] The general slope of the country is downwards in favour of the French, but, as it is undulating, it would only be possible to say which side it favoured if the exact point of collision were known.

[2] *Vide supra*, p. 180.

ponderous columns, not dissolved by the shock of collision
as was the case with Nansouty's lines, literally rode over
them, breaking them in pieces.[1]   The Archduke Charles
himself was at Köfering at this time and escaped with
the utmost difficulty.

At Nieder Traubling the French cavalry were too exhausted to continue the pursuit, for they had already, for
the most part, marched over 30 miles, besides fighting,
and that was about as much as could be expected from
heavy horses carrying steel-clad men.

During this fight Hohenzollern had reached the heights
"Auf der Platte," west of Köfering, and thence he witnessed the preparations for the great cavalry battle.   With
him was Lederer's brigade of two cuirassier regiments, and
a horse battery.   The guns he sent forward at a gallop
to in front of Köfering, under protection of the cuirassiers, who ought to have been in the cavalry fight.   At
the same time, Kaiser's brigade was attacked, in rear and
right flank, by Friant.   To clear for himself a way,
Hohenzollern ordered Lederer to attack the French
cavalry at Alt-Egloffsheim.   At the same time, the commander of the III. corps marched his infantry over the
brook at a point (Kumpfmühle) west of Köfering.   Very
soon, Lederer's cuirassiers went streaming back to
Köfering with the rest of the cavalry, themselves riding
over one of the grenadier battalions.   Five of their six
guns had been lost.   Hohenzollern was now alone with
his staff near Köfering, as his infantry had gone on to
Traubling.   Another battery had lost its way and was
captured by the French cavalry, and, finally, an attack
by Friant at Gebelkofen ended in Hohenzollern's rear-

---

[1] The above account of this memorable charge is based on the account,
published in 1829, by Count v. Bismarck, an officer who was present, as a
captain of Wurtemberg cavalry.   Unfortunately there is no official record
traceable of the operations of Nansouty's division.   This is the best authority
obtainable, but, though based on the observation of an eye-witness, it must
be accepted with care as a record of details.

most regiment being ridden over by its own beaten cavalry.

About 9 P.M., the fighting was over for the night. Napoleon, at that hour, after inspecting the Wurtemberg cavalry, sent them along the Straubing road in pursuit of the Austrian baggage, which, however, had got away. He undertook no further pursuit of the Austrians that night, on the ground of the exhaustion of the French troops. He himself fixed his headquarters in Alt-Egloffshiem. The exact positions of the French army cannot be given in detail. It was mainly in two masses, one between Alt-Egloffsheim and Köfering, and back along the road as far as Eckmühl and Buchhausen, the other between the roads from Ratisbon to Landshut, and to Ingolstadt. Friant was in front of Ober-Sanding, St Hilaire behind it, Montbrun at Dinzling and Luckenpoint, Tharreau far behind at Langquaid.

The Austrian positions were :—II. corps at Ober-Isling, I. Reserve corps astride of the Ratisbon to Landshut road at Ober-Traubling, III. and IV. corps retreating, covered by the I. Reserve, on Burgweinting, and Bellegarde (I. corps) was at Hemau, where he received, late in the evening, his orders to hurry to Ratisbon.[1]

Of the 74,000 men who might have been brought into this day's battle on the Austrian side, Binder von Krieglstein calculates that 30,000 infantry and 2000 cavalry practically did no fighting at all. Add to these 9000 grenadiers who were not engaged till after the retreat had commenced. That leaves only about 33,000 really engaged. The losses are difficult to calculate, but are put by the same authority at little short of 10,000, of whom only about 4000 were killed or wounded, the rest being prisoners or missing. The III. and IV. corps lost at least 33 guns.

On the French side, leaving out Tharreau and Colbert,

---

[1] *Vide supra*, p. 173.

who could only march as far as Langquaid by evening,
Napoleon had about 96,000 men. But the whole of
Masséna's three divisions, owing to the length of their
march and the lateness of their start, could not arrive in
time to take a part in the battle. A great part of the two
Bavarian divisions were also not engaged, and Montbrun
had very little to do. That left only about 53,000 infantry, and, as Morand did little, and Gudin's losses were
slight, it follows that less than 50,000 infantry, and, at the
most, 10,000 cavalry, were seriously engaged. The French
losses are almost impossible to reckon with any accuracy,
but it is not probable that they were more than 3000
for the whole army.

(2) THE STORM OF RATISBON

During the night after Eckmühl the Archduke Charles,
who had betaken himself to Ratisbon after his escape
from the French cavalry, was suffering from a despondency
which was by no means warranted by his position.   It is
true he had suffered a series of reverses, but he had not
been decisively defeated as Napoleon chose to represent.
He had lost touch with his left wing, but, on the other
hand, he had gained it with the I. and II. corps, neither
of which had suffered any demoralisation by defeat.   His
part of the army had lost its communications with Vienna
by the right bank of the Danube, but those by the left
bank were as yet untouched, and the road by Bohemia
was not even, at present, in danger.

Early on the morning of the 23rd, he wrote to the
Emperor Francis that he had hoped to hold out in front
of Ratisbon, but the enemy's cavalry had attacked and
defeated his own, and even part of his infantry.   Under
these circumstances, with half his army gone, there was
nothing left but to cross the Danube, and retire into
Bohemia. He would be lucky if he did that after

yesterday's battle. His army had fought well but had lost heavily, especially in officers, and many guns had been lost on the 22nd. As far as he could make out, Louis was separated and had lost heavily in retreating over the Isar. From the army little more could be expected against Napoleon, who was daily acquiring more strength. There was, perhaps, still opportunity for negotiations; but, once the French had crossed the frontier, there was nothing to be looked for but the fate of Prussia. He advised the Emperor to leave Schärding, and not to rely on him—altogether a very dismal letter! During the night of the 22nd-23rd, the Austrian baggage was hurried through Ratisbon across the river. The stone bridge, being clearly insufficient for the rapid retreat of a great army, a pontoon bridge was constructed opposite Weichs, below the lower end of the island opposite Ratisbon.[1] At 4 A.M. the troops were collected in two masses, the II. corps on the road to Abbach, the III. and IV. on that to Straubing. At 5 A.M. began the retreat of the III. and IV. corps. "For greater security" only one gate of the city was left open, and that the most westerly, the Jacob's Thor. No written orders for the retreat are traceable. These corps were followed by Lindenau's division, whilst the cavalry of the I. Reserve, still 4600 strong, covered them between the Abbach and Straubing roads, and a battalion held Burgweinting. Charles still had some idea of holding out to the south of Ratisbon, and a staff officer was deputed to search out a good defensive position, which would certainly be difficult to find on the plain there.

At 8 A.M. Stutterheim's outposts were still somewhere on the Pfatterbach; Vecsey was with the main body of

---

[1] General Bonnal (p. 264) is in error in supposing the pontoon bridge was above the stone one. See *B. K.*, i. 314. A note, based on the Bavarian archives, says there was another bridge, inside the walls, to the lower part of the island.

the Austrian cavalry; the III. and IV. corps were retiring in very poor plight after their rough handling of the day before. The positions of the II. corps and the I. Reserve corps, at this hour, are doubtful.

We must now return to Napoleon, who, with Berthier, Masséna, Lefebvre, and Lannes, spent the night in the château of Alt-Egloffsheim. At 3 A.M. the following orders were issued :—

(1) Masséna, with his three infantry divisions, and Espagne's cuirassiers, to march on Straubing, to endeavour to seize any boat bridge the enemy might have constructed there, and to hunt up the enemy's stragglers, baggage, etc., on both banks.

(2) Bessières to pass the Inn and the Salzach at once, and seize Brannau, calling up Molitor to the assistance of Wrede and the cavalry.

The orders for the advance on Ratisbon appear to have been given verbally, and are not forthcoming. What they were must be judged by their execution.

The cavalry reserve, apparently, left Köfering about 5 A.M., followed by Gudin and Morand. Behind Morand were Vandamme's Wurtembergers, behind them Deroy's Bavarians and Demont's French. All moved on Egglfing and Ober-Isling. Montbrun marched from Peising to Abbach, and thence along the high road. Friant, followed by St Hilaire, marched by Thalmassing, Hinkofen, and Grass to the ground, beyond the Abbach road, on the west of Ratisbon. Between them and Gudin, Lefebvre came into position, with Deroy and Demont, about noon. It was 9 A.M. when the French cavalry began to come into contact with Stutterheim at Burgweinting. He had fallen back to that place as they advanced. The cuirassiers promptly attacked Stutterheim, to whose support the Archduke, in the neighbourhood at the moment, sent one of Klenau's uhlan regiments.

It appears from the Austrian "Operations Journal"[1] that it was only at this juncture that it was finally decided to carry the whole army across the Danube.

It would appear that the III. and IV. corps had already gone over, probably by the pontoon bridge, which would be nearest them, and to reach which they would not require to enter the city.[2] The infantry and artillery of the I. Reserve were to cross by the pontoon bridge and post guns on the left bank for its protection. The II. corps was to pass through the town over the stone bridge. General Fölseis was to occupy the southern part of Ratisbon with 5 battalions, and post one in Stadt-am-Hof. South of Ratisbon were the cavalry, supported by a few infantry. The latter soon had to retire.

Of cavalry there were certainly 56 squadrons actually engaged. Whether Schneller's 12 squadrons fought is not certain, but it is known that 24 of dragoons, belonging to the II. corps, crossed the river, though they might very well have joined the rest against the French. Of the 56 squadrons 24 were cuirassiers, the other 32 light cavalry. Against them came Nansouty and St Sulpice with 40 squadrons of cuirassiers, besides 20 of light cavalry of Montbrun's division. There were no allied cavalry. In numerical strength there was not very much to choose between the two forces.

During two hours there raged, all over the plain from Burgweinting to Prüll, a whirlwind of charging and struggling cavalry, certainly not less than 13,000 or 14,000. Description of this confused fighting there is none, and none worthy of confidence is possible. Probably the fortunes varied in different parts of the field, until, finally, the trend of the whole mass was

---

[1] *B. K.*, i. 312.

[2] As only the Jacob's Thor was open, it is impossible to suppose these corps would have been marched right across to the west of the town and then back to the centre to reach the stone bridge.

towards the north and the outskirts of Ratisbon. The Austrian cavalry made its way into Ratisbon and over the bridge.

It was only as the south-east side of Ratisbon was cleared of the enemy, about noon, that the French became aware of the existence of the pontoon bridge, over which the artillery of the II. corps and I. Reserve corps was still passing. The French horse artillery began firing on it, but there was as yet no infantry available to attack it. Almost before the last of their people were over, the Austrian engineers cut loose the bridge instead of withdrawing it. The current swung it backwards on to the right bank, where the whole of the pontoons fell into the hands of the French.

There still remained on the right bank of the Danube Mayer's brigade of four battalions, and Fölseis' five battalions on the southern walls of Ratisbon. The rest of the Austrian army had attained safety beyond the river.

At midday, there was marching against Ratisbon a great semi-circle of French and allied troops. On the right was Lannes, in the centre Lefebvre (Deroy), on the left Davout and Montbrun. Napoleon commenced his preparations for the assault. About one o'clock the Archduke Charles issued orders for the next five days! Naturally, orders which looked so far ahead, when in contact with a victorious enemy, turned out largely impracticable of execution. To begin upon, the proposed march northwards could not be begun, in daylight, with the enemy in great force threatening a 'coup de main' on Ratisbon, and the army requiring reorganisation. Fölseis was ordered to hold out in Ratisbon till 6 P.M., then to leave 300 men in the place, who could surrender next morning, and to rejoin the II. corps.

Soon after 1 P.M., Gudin, attempting an assault, was beaten off. The walls of the place were old but still serviceable, and there was a broad and deep ditch in front of them with a masonry counterscarp. The French field guns were quite unable to make a breach. The place was perhaps less defensible than was Lübeck in 1806; for the latter had impassable wet ditches, whilst Ratisbon had not. Moreover, Ratisbon being no longer a fortress, houses had begun to grow up in the ditch, and one of these with its back against the escarpment was destroyed by artillery fire, forming more or less of a ramp which would be serviceable once a descent had been made into the ditch. Finally, Davout, who knew the place well, was able to point out a postern, near the Straubing gate, which might be forced, and would allow of an entrance.

From 1 P.M. till about 5, the French were busy making fascines and collecting ladders from the neighbouring farms. A bold and successful escalade was then carried out by Lannes, whose operations were facilitated by the opening of the postern. By 7 P.M. the whole place, with its garrison of 9 battalions, was in the hands of the French. It is disputed whether the French succeeded, as they allege, in capturing Stadt am Hof. Very possibly, as in the case of the village of Schloditten at Eylau, they got into it, but, finding it dangerous to hold during the night, evacuated it.

The losses on this day were not heavy on the French side, probably 1000 killed and wounded would be a liberal allowance. On the Austrian side Binder v. Krieglstein thinks the total losses may have been about 8000, but many of these were stragglers who rejoined next day, and a goodly proportion were prisoners, picked up here and there.[1]

It was during the interval between Gudin's abortive attack and the successful storming that Napoleon, reconnoitring in front of the walls, was struck by a

---

[1] Napoleon claimed 8000 prisoners as captured in Ratisbon alone.

spent ball on the right foot. The wound was a mere bruise which was dressed there and then, and did not prevent the Emperor from remounting. That was the only time he was ever wounded in 20 years of almost constant war.[1] The rumour of his being wounded soon got about, and on all sides there were the most frantic demonstrations of regret and devotion from the men who, after all, were but the instruments of Napoleon's personal ambition. Probably no general ever inspired such feelings of personal devotion as Napoleon. General Bonnal[2] justly remarks, " The old soldiers of the Grande Armée had these sentiments (of confidence and love) so deeply rooted in them that, later, the disasters of Moscow, of Leipzig, and of Waterloo detracted nothing from the character of infallibility attributed to the Emperor, and the men always laid the blame of failure to the account of treason."

All the same, slight as the wound was, it seems to have upset Napoleon somewhat, for Berthier tells Masséna that his master is too " fatigued " to issue orders which will bear delay. Generally, it seemed as if fatigue was unknown to this man of iron.

Masséna, at 9 P.M., reported that he had reached Straubing at noon, without fighting, and was busy repairing the bridges.[3] He also sent out parties up and down the river to pick up Austrian stragglers.

Bessières was again in touch with the Austrian rear-guard at Neumarkt and sent Wrede on as far as Erharting.

Hiller on this day passed the Inn, leaving a strong

[1] Las Cases in the Memorial de Ste Helène says the Emperor avowed that he had often been wounded but had succeeded in concealing the fact. The truth of this statement is more than doubtful.

[2] P. 266.

[3] At Straubing there were two bridges, one from the town to an island in the Danube, the other from the island to the left bank. Both had been cut by Wrede when he evacuated Straubing on the 11th April.

rearguard on the left bank, and taking position himself
between Mühldorf and Neu-Oetting. He wrote, at 11
A.M., to the Archduke Charles, of whose retreat he was
unaware, that he would advance on Neumarkt on the
24th and endeavour to rejoin the main army. In the
afternoon, however, when Wrede deployed at Erharting,
only 4 or 5 miles west of the Inn, Hiller decided to
attack him next morning, a decision which he communicated to the Austrian Emperor at Schärding,
where the latter was awaiting results. The force
blockading Passau was ordered to guard the passages of
the Inn at Braunau and Marktl. On this day, Jelacic
left Munich and reached Ebersperg on his road to the Inn.

The Emperor Francis, knowing nothing of Charles'
movements, ordered Hiller to rejoin the main army,
which of course was quite out of the question.

The Austrian army was hopelessly separated into two
parts. "This result, neither planned nor sought by
Napoleon, had come about of itself in the course of
events. It was the inevitable result of the difference
of energy and force between the two armies on the
theatre of war."[1] This verdict of the German critic
is practically the same as that of General Bonnal.
Napoleon in the first bulletin, which he composed at
Ratisbon, of course represents matters very differently.
According to him, the separation of the left wing of the
Austrian army had been designed by himself from the
beginning. The bulletin is full of exaggeration, mis-
statements, and deliberate misrepresentations. As history
it is worthless. The Emperor does not even trouble to
be accurate in unimportant details. For instance, he
says he harangued the Bavarians and Wurtembergers
before Abensberg, though the latter were far away on his
right. Again, he halves the strength of Coutard's
regiment and everywhere enormously exaggerates the

[1] *B. K.*, i. 308.

number of prisoners taken.   The first bulletin claims
50,000 prisoners as the result of the operations from the
19th to the 23rd April.   General Bonnal[1] has taken
the trouble to collate the numbers in the reports of each
day, with the result that the Emperor's 50,000 are
reduced to 18,000.

[1] P. 274.

CHAPTER X

THE STRATEGY AND TACTICS OF THE RÁTISBON CAMPAIGN

WE have perhaps dealt almost sufficiently fully in the course of the narrative with the strategy and tactics of this campaign up to the storming of Ratisbon on the 23rd April. But it is always well, when one has mastered the details of a campaign, to cast a glance back on it as a whole.

Napoleon, at St Helena, writing with the object of proving his own military infallibility, said : " The battle of Abensberg, the manœuvre of Landshut, and the battle of Eckmühl are the boldest, the most brilliant, the ablest manœuvres of Napoleon."

The verdict of modern military criticism is not quite so favourable as this. Whilst admitting to the full the brilliancy and soundness of many of the Emperor's orders and movements, it points out that there were others far short of the standard of excellence exhibited in 1806. All are agreed that nothing could be better than his orders for the strategical deployment of his army on the defensive, according to the date on which the Austrians might commence their advance over the Bavarian frontier. Unfortunately, the orders fell for execution to a man who was more or less of a machine, capable only of carrying out hard and fast directions, incapable of appreciating the principles which inspired them. We have sufficiently explained how Berthier's poverty of comprehension and imagination resulted in the pitiable confusion of his mind, and the dispersal of the army of a commander with whom concentration was the alpha and omega of his military creed.

There is equally but one view as to the general excellence of Napoleon's measures for the remedy of the almost desperate situation in which his Chief of Staff had involved him on the 17th April. The blot on them was the miscalculation of 24 hours as to the arrival of Davout and Masséna within supporting distance of one another and of the centre.

As for Davout, his flank march by the right bank of the Danube was, on the face of it, dangerous. It was based on the Emperor's misapprehension of the strength of the Austrian "column of Landshut" which, till some time in the night of the 17th-18th, he believed to be merely an advance guard of a single corps, instead of, as it really was, the main body of the Austrian army. Had he known that when he issued his orders to Davout on the 17th, he would perhaps have hesitated. Nevertheless, there was really but a very small risk if the march from Ratisbon to Abensberg had been carried out on the 18th, as Napoleon intended. He was not very clear as to the exact position of Friant, though he probably did not intend that general to move round by Ratisbon ; for Napoleon knew he was still a long way from there. Everything, his separate mention of Friant, and his order to him to leave detachments on the Altmühl, treating it as a great bridgehead to Ingolstadt, points to his intention that Friant should march across the Altmühl to the Danube, not that he should leave it on his right, sending detachments off in that direction to the passages of the river. At Neustadt or Kelheim Friant would cross the Danube and join Davout who, meanwhile, would have marched by the right bank. If, however, as we believe, that was Napoleon's intention, his orders were far from clear, and Davout, who was certainly not wanting in intelligence, misunderstood them.

In the case of Masséna, the Emperor was again misinformed as to the state of dispersion of his corps. The Masséna of former days would have done something to expedite the concentration, but nothing could have enabled the corps to be at Pfaffenhofen on the evening of the 18th.

When, at last, Davout was able to start his march on the morning of the 19th his position differed widely from what it would have been on the 18th. The Archduke Charles was already marching against him, and few generals have ever had such an opportunity of cutting off one-third of the enemy's army as Charles had on the 19th. With Lefebvre's letter of the 18th before him, as well as Davout's own orders for the march, he had every information he could desire. Yet he failed to destroy, or even seriously to injure Davout. Instead of keeping to his left, so as to meet the head of the marshal's columns, he sent nothing further west than Thann and he spread his army over much too broad a front. Liechtenstein, marching down the valley of the great Laber, must inevitably pass outside even Montbrun's flanking column. At noon he was within a couple of miles of Rosenberg's battle, yet Charles took no measures to call him in to fall on the flank and rear of Davout with the 15,000 men he had.

Rosenberg was allowed to fritter away his battalions, till he ended by meeting Montbrun with only half his available force.

Hohenzollern, too, detatched too many flank guards and had only 17,000 men left to fight between Hausen and Teugen. Finally, Charles himself stood all the day idle with at least 10,000 grenadiers, besides some of Rosenberg's troops, on the heights of Grub. From those heights one can look right down on the slope above

Saladorf in front of Hausen. Davout with 30,000 men (St Hilaire, Friant, Petit, and Montbrun) might have been opposed by more than 50,000 Austrians,[1] whereas he only met Hohenzollern's 17,000 and half of Rosenberg's men.

Davout's own conduct of the battle on the ridge was excellent, and the way in which Montbrun, with 2000 infantry and 3000 cavalry, kept at bay far superior numbers till evening was beyond all praise. Davout's action in sending Morand and Gudin to Saal, where they did nothing, is not so easy of explanation. It is true he was anxious about his baggage column in the defile, and he is said to have intended bringing the infantry divisions back up the Feking brook against the left flank of Hohenzollern. Nevertheless, one cannot help suspecting that he felt his position to be a desperate one, and that he had better try and save at least these two divisions by hurrying them through the still remaining gap to join Napoleon and Lefebvre.

General Bonnal was apparently unaware of the fact that Davout's orders had fallen into Charles's hands,[2] but, even without that, he considers Davout's situation on the morning of the 19th as strategically almost desperate. Yet, even if Charles had brought the whole of his available forces against Davout, it is not certain that the tactical superiority of the French, especially in a wooded close country, in which the genius of the French soldier shone, would not have retrieved the strategical situation.

In urging Liechtenstein on to Ratisbon, Charles was hankering after supposed moral advantages, which would

[1] Hohenzollern 17,000; Rosenberg 13,000; Grenadiers 10,000; Liechtenstein 15,000.

[2] Binder v. Krieglstein's book, which shows this, was not published till the year after the "Manœuvre de Landshut," and the fact of the capture of the orders is not mentioned by Von Angeli. On the other hand, Binder v. Krieglstein does not appear to have read Bonnal's book. He neither refers to it, nor mentions it in his bibliography.

have been much more surely gained by driving Davout into the Danube. The Archduke must have known that Davout could have left little, if anything, in Ratisbon, and that the place, bombarded by Kolowrat's artillery on the heights above Stadt am Hof, could not hold out more than a few hours.

Why did not Davout, after his success on the 19th, move the rest of his corps, after Morand and Gudin, towards Abensberg? General Bonnal finds the answer in the wretched condition of the roads, the fatigue of the men, and the necessity for collecting and caring for the wounded.

Napoleon's designs were perfect up till noon on the 19th. He calculated on having for the 20th Davout at Neustadt, Lefebvre at Geisenfeld, Masséna and Oudinot at Pfaffenhofen. If Davout and Lefebvre were attacked the Austrians would have their left and rear exposed to Masséna and Oudinot; if the attack were on Lefebvre and Masséna, Davout would be within striking distance of the enemy's right flank.[1] At noon on the 19th, the Emperor, at Ingolstadt, had not heard the guns at Hausen. He was nearly 30 miles away and the intervening woods and hills would deaden the sound. It was now that he began to fall away, and to indicate his intention of sending at least a large part of Masséna's force to Landshut, to threaten Charles' communications with the Inn. That idea was, General Bonnal holds, dictated by the dominating desire to move direct on Vienna and to keep Charles in front of him on that line. Thus he wanted, by manœuvring, to bind Charles to that line of retreat. It was no part of his programme to drive the Austrians to the north of the Danube, whither he had no intention of following them. To do so would be to abandon for the time the advance on Vienna. With his forces in the positions hitherto contemplated, the union

[1] See diagrams at pp. 126-127 of *Bonnal*.

of the whole army within striking distance would be complete ; now the Emperor was himself going again to disperse it, by sending Masséna in a direction from which he would not be able to take part in a battle on the Abens. He was even exposing Masséna to the risk of Charles' turning back against him, and, behind the screen of the Isar, defeating him before the Emperor could succour him.

When he heard of Davout's success, the Emperor's view was this. Charles would be driven back by Davout, on the 20th, towards the south, or at least checked in his northward advance. Then the attack of Napoleon's column on his left from Abensberg would compel him to retreat on Landshut, where he would find Masséna ready to complete his destruction. Here the Emperor's undue optimism again appears. He thinks of the hard-fought battle at Hausen as a second Auerstädt, and he writes of Masséna being at Landshut at 3 P.M. on the 20th, more than 24 hours before he actually reached it. He contemplated the prospect of the whole Austrian army standing in the angle between himself and Davout, attacked in front and left flank and driven on Landshut. He never allowed for Charles' actual movement from left to right to the eastward of Davout and then northwards to Ratisbon.

He decided, therefore, to push forward on the 20th with Lefebvre, Vandamme, Morand, Gudin, and the cuirassiers, from the Abens towards Landshut, calling up two of Masséna's divisions, and sending the other four by Freising and Moosburg on Landshut. Davout, he seems to have presumed, would move southwards ; therefore, he sent him no orders, and Davout, who knew the Austrians were doing something quite different from what the Emperor expected, spent the day without serious action.

As Napoleon drove the Austrians before him with ease on the road to Landshut, he was under the impression, though the slight resistance should have shown him otherwise, that he was driving the greater part of the Austrian army into the cul-de-sac of which the farther end would be closed by Masséna. He refused to believe Davout's reports indicating a movement on Ratisbon, and, even on the 21st, he assured Davout that he had nothing in front of him but a weak screen of three regiments. Davout knew better, but it was only at 2 A.M. on the 22nd that Piré's arrival at last convinced the Emperor that he had been employing the greater part of his own army in defeating less than one-third of what Charles commanded on the two banks of the Danube, which were now united for the Austrians by the surrender of Ratisbon.

By the evening of the 21st, Napoleon had driven the remains of Hiller's 42,000 men through Landshut towards the Inn. But Masséna had failed him, and left the end of the cul-de-sac open at Landshut. The Austrian left wing was driven away from the rest, but the Emperor is romancing when, in the first bulletin, he sets out that that had been his object in the advance from the Abens. His excessive optimism is again apparent when he compares Abensberg to Jena, and multiplies the number of prisoners taken by three or more.

Once he is disillusioned by Piré, at 2 A.M. on the 22nd, he returns to the true faith and acts with immense energy. Now he is all for making an end of the Archduke on the 22nd, and so bringing the war to a conclusion. But it was too late now ; he had missed his chance of decisive battle, though he had been fortunate enough, owing to Davout's excellent conduct on the 21st, to escape a disaster to his left.

Charles, too, had again missed his opportunity of destroying Davout on the 21st, for he had shown no symptoms of the offensive, and had sent Kolowrat from Ratisbon on a useless tramp to Hemau and back, instead of keeping him to help in crushing Davout, for which purpose Bellegarde might also have been called up. What Charles' motive for sending Kolowrat to Hemau was is far from clear. When he decided to fall on Davout with over 70,000 men on the 22nd, it was too late, and the scheme was abandoned the moment the appearance of the head of Napoleon's column from Landshut was signalled. The attack on Davout was given up, though Charles failed to ride forward, as he should have done, to Eckmühl to see for himself the position of affairs.

The battle of Eckmühl, so much vaunted by Napoleon, was in reality nothing more than a rearguard action, fought by Rosenberg with the IV. corps against a greatly superior enemy attacking him from west, south, and east. In only telling Rosenberg to get out of his position as best he could, Charles failed in his duty, a failure due perhaps to a natural tendency to indolence.

Count Yorck von Wartenburg,[1] who has little fault to find with Napoleon's earlier movements, condemns his failure to pursue Charles in the night of the 22nd, during which the Austrians got the greater part of their army ready to cross the Danube at Ratisbon. Lannes is said to have counselled pursuit ; the other marshals held that the troops were too fatigued. Lannes' corps had marched 22 miles from Ergolding to Eckmühl, and, by the route it followed, it would be another 17 miles on to Ratisbon. The cuirassiers' horses were so done up that they could not charge at more than a trot. Davout and Lefebvre, it is true, had not covered much ground, but they had had much fighting, both on the 22nd and the 21st. Masséna's men, owing to the length of the column on a single road, were behind, and had had more marching than even Lannes. Finally, the Emperor had only fought two Austrian corps,[2] and the

---

[1] *Napoleon as a General*, ii. 57.
[2] The IV., supported later by the III.

probabilities were in favour of those behind them being able to offer a strenuous resistance. Moreover, Ratisbon itself was a serious obstacle, and, even if the pursuit were carried up to its walls, that would not have prevented the Austrian passage of the stone bridge, or the throwing of a pontoon bridge. On the whole, it would seem hardly justifiable to accuse Napoleon of want of energy in not pursuing in the night after Eckmühl.

But the case is different when we come to his refusal to follow Charles across the river on the 24th, except with Davout's corps, which observed rather than pursued the enemy. On this question there are diversities of opinion. Jomini, in his *Life of Napoleon*,[1] puts into the Emperor's mouth the following defence of his action. " Some have blamed me for not having, on the contrary, pursued the then scattered army of the Archduke Charles. I was deterred from this by several reasons ; first, the woody chain of the Böhmerwald mountains offered to the enemy positions of great advantage ; secondly, the Archduke Charles had written me a letter showing a desire on his part to treat. By pursuing Hiller I might complete his ruin and dictate a more advantageous peace at Vienna. On the other hand, attacking the enemy in the mountains of Bohemia, Hiller, with the Archduke John and Chasteler coming from Italy and the Tyrol, might collect 80,000 fresh troops on the Danube, at the instant when the Archduke Charles, reinforced by the landwehr of Bohemia, would charge me in front."

To this it may be replied that the difficulties of the country were not in the least likely to stop French troops ; on the contrary, the country was one in which the tactical advantage would be all with the French, just as it was in the wooded country south of Ratisbon. The Archduke's letter was certainly meant as a feeler

[1] Vol. iii. p. 43. Translated by Halleck.

regarding peace negotiations, but it did not reach Napoleon till the 1st May, when his army was already far on its way to Vienna, and he himself on the Salzach. As for Hiller, the Emperor had plenty of troops to keep him on the move towards Vienna, without interfering with the pursuit of the main Austrian army. Chasteler had but a small force, still many days' march from the theatre of operations, and, on the 22nd, the Archduke John was marching on the Adige and Verona, after defeating the Viceroy of Italy at Sacile.

It was the very absence of serious pursuit which enabled Charles to gather in the Bohemian landwehr. Had he been hard pressed, the very fluid landwehr battalions would probably have broken up without joining him.

Charles we shall see had made up his mind, if pursued, to fight at Cham on the Bavarian side of the frontier. He had 90,000 men, but only two of his corps were untouched and he had to reorganise his army. The idea of fighting at all was only a council of despair, a less desperate alternative than to allow his army to disperse in the difficult and ill-provisioned Bohemian mountains. A letter from Grünne to the Prince de Ligne, written after the war was over, deals with this question from the Austrian point of view. It is given in full by Saski,[1] but we must confine ourselves to a summary and a few quotations. Grünne almost commences by speaking of "the mistake which, in my opinion, Napoleon made in not having followed us after the battle of Ratisbon." He says the army was retreating sore stricken, having lost two-thirds of its artillery, with execrable roads behind it, and these covered with stragglers. The troops were bivouacking in snow and mud, supplies no longer arriving. "I ask if that army, even reinforced by Bellegarde's corps, could have resisted

[1] iii. 331 n.

the victorious Napoleon, if he had pursued it 'l'epeé dans les reins'? He would have thrown it into the forests of Bohemia, where it would have disbanded for want of supplies; the landwehr, which afterwards furnished 60,000 men, would not have formed, our depots of recruits would have dispersed, and in a fortnight Napoleon would have become master of, and disposed of all our resources." He goes on to affirm that Napoleon, in conversation with Wimpffen, admitted his error, adding that he had believed it impossible for the Austrian army to rise, like the Phœnix, from its ashes.

Yorck von Wartenburg, on the other hand, concurring with Jomini, considers that, once Charles had been allowed to escape after Eckmühl, it was too late to pursue him, that he would be able to offer serious resistance in the Bohemian forests, and that a direct march on Vienna was the only way for the Emperor to reach the capital before the Austrians.

General Bonnal's opinion is decided, and, as we venture to think, beyond doubt correct. He holds that Napoleon, after first losing his chance on the 20th April of compelling Charles to a battle in unfavourable circumstances, again lost it on the 26th, by not following him to Cham. He desired a decisive battle, no doubt, but his predetermined movement on Vienna put it off till the 5th-6th July. He twice relinquished the substantial chance of battle for the shadowy possibilities of a strategic manœuvre. "But," says Bonnal, "every strategic manœuvre aiming at great results without recourse to battle is deceptive, when one has before one an energetic enemy; it retards the decision of the war, and, as a consequence, necessitates much greater sacrifices than those it would have been wise to accept at once." [1]

The Austrians had, since 1805, vastly improved in every way, an improvement for which Napoleon's over-

[1] *Bonnal*, 351.

weening pride did not suffer him to make allowance.
Still, the French infantry, and their allies following in
their footsteps, had to a great extent maintained their
tactical supremacy, though the gap between them and
the Austrians had been sensibly diminished. In Davout's
battle of the 19th April, and again on the 21st, Austrians
were pitted against the very pick of the French divisions,
and that largely in wood fighting, where the French were
sure to show to the best. Some of Davout's battalions
were entirely broken up into groups of skirmishers.
That would have been contrary to the Austrian drill-
books, which laid down hard and fast rules as to the
proportion of skirmishers to the battalion, and the time
for their withdrawal on the main body. Probably no
Austrian battalion could have stood the strain of this
breaking up into skirmishers without entirely going to
pieces. There were constant instances in the "battue"
of Abensberg where defeat resulted almost at once in
panic flight, without any attempt to rally. Later on, we
shall see Austrian troops, and those not all of the same
excellence as the men of the Ratisbon campaign, fighting
on open ground better suited to their system. Then, as
might be expected, the French superiority to a great
extent disappeared.

In marching capacity there was still no comparison
possible between the two armies. The Austrians took
7 days to cover unopposed the 63 miles from the Inn
to the Isar. In the 4 days from the 19th to the 22nd
April the divisions of Morand and Gudin covered no less
than 81 miles, and that included some fighting on the
march to Landshut, and in the capture of that place,
besides a good deal of marching straight across a rain-
soaked country. The French infantry soldier of 1809
carried less weight on his back than his successor of
to-day,[1] and his burden and accoutrements appear to

----

[1] *Bonnal*, 356.

have been distributed so as to cause him the minimum of fatigue and discomfort.

Regarding the artillery, it is well to remember that the field batteries had attained very little mobility, and that it was only the horse artillery which could move faster than a walk, or a very slow trot for a short distance. The limbers and guns had no seats on them, and the ammunition waggons, having tops in the form of a roof, could equally not be used to carry the men.

In numbers the Austrian guns were superior to the French, and during all the earlier part of the battle above Teugen Davout had but three pieces to oppose to the Austrian guns on the crest.

CHAPTER XI

ON THE MARCH TO VIENNA

(1) The Archduke Charles' Retreat through Bohemia

AT whatever period we hold Napoleon to have originally made up his mind to march to Vienna by the right bank of the Danube, there can be no doubt that he had done so by the 23rd April, when he drove the Archduke Charles across the river at Ratisbon. He had already, on the morning of that day, ordered Masséna to Straubing, and the Crown Prince of Bavaria to Landshut. In the evening, orders were sent to Masséna to move on Passau, and to Lefebvre to go with Deroy's and Demont's divisions to Landshut. Early on the morning of the 24th, orders issued for the movement of all the remaining troops at Ratisbon, excepting only Davout's corps (the 3rd) and St Sulpice's cuirassiers, on Landshut.

There was now a reconstitution of the 2nd and 3rd corps, the formation of which had hitherto varied. To Davout were given his old three divisions of infantry, Morand's, Friant's, and Gudin's, together with Montbrun's light cavalry and St Sulpice's cuirassiers. The last-named, as a matter of fact, went to Landshut, not with Davout.

To Lannes were given the divisions of St Hilaire, Tharreau (now commanded by Oudinot), and Claparède, with Colbert's light cavalry. Claparède, being with

Masséna at present, was only to join Lannes on the Inn.

Vandamme, with the Wurtembergers, was to go at once to Eckmühl, whence he could go on, if necessary, to Landshut.

Thus, on the morning of the 24th, five divisions of infantry (St Hilaire, Deroy, Demont, Oudinot, Vandamme), Nansouty's cuirassiers, and three brigades of light cavalry were on the way to Landshut. By evening these were echeloned from Eckmühl (Vandamme) to Landshut (Lefebvre). Lannes was between Vandamme and Lefebvre, and the latter had found the Crown Prince's division at Landshut.

Meanwhile, the Archduke Charles was retreating on Cham. His corps were in the following positions on the evening of the 23rd :—The I. corps (Bellegarde) was marching from Hemau to Ratisbon on the 23rd when he received fresh orders, at Etterzhausen, directing him on Burglengenfeld.

Of the III. corps, St Julien's division was still short of the Regen on the road by Kürn to Cham. The rest of the corps, and the I. Reserve, were at Nittenau ; the IV. at Kürn. It was only after dark that the II. corps retired from the heights above Stadt am Hof to the neighbourhood of Regenstauf.

On the 24th, the III. and I. Reserve corps reached Cham ; the I., Schwandorf and Schwarzenfeld ; the IV., Bruck ; the II., Nittenau and Kürn. On the 25th, the Archduke took up a strong position on the line Rotz-Cham, between the Schwarzach and the Regen.

To Davout and Montbrun[1] had been confided, on the morning of the 24th, the task of pursuing the

---

[1] Montbrun, replaced under Davout's orders on the 24th, had 5 cavalry regiments and one of infantry. The 13th light infantry had taken the place of the two battalions of the 7th, which had had much fighting.

Austrian main army, and of cutting off its baggage,
stragglers, etc. Their operations could hardly be called
a pursuit. They amounted rather to a cautious following and observation of the enemy, who was immensely
superior to them in force. The Archduke reported on
the 27th that he had only 50,000 men at Cham, but he
really had the following :—

I. corps	28,000
II. „	20,000
III. „	13,000
IV. „	15,000
I. Reserve	12,000
Mayer's brigade (V. corps)	4,000
	92,000

The fact was that great numbers of stragglers and
" missing" men had rejoined by that date.

There would be no advantage in going into details of
Davout's so-called pursuit, which will be summarised very
briefly. On the 25th Davout was, with his main body,
at Regenstauf, whilst Montbrun and Gudin moved on
Kürn and Nittenau, at which latter place they drove a
rearguard (4 battalions, 10 squadrons) of the Austrian
II. corps over the Regen, but were stopped by the
burning of the bridge.

There now ensued a rather curious correspondence
between Davout and Napoleon. The marshal forwarded
a report from Montbrun in which that general indicated
the direction of the Austrian retreat as Bruck, Rötz,
Pilsen, that is north-eastwards into Bohemia. Notwithstanding what Montbrun said, Davout held that the
greater part of the Austrian army was making for Cham,
intending thence to return to the Danube at Passau.
To that view the Emperor replied that Masséna ought
to be at Passau to-day (26th), and that such a flank

o

march as Davout supposed would be very hazardous. He was clearly inclined to agree with Montbrun rather than with the corps commander. Nevertheless, he had got Boudet, who had been marched up from Ingolstadt on the 24th, at Straubing, and he would be kept there till matters were clearer. Rouyer, with the contingents of the minor States, and Dupas were under orders for Ratisbon.

General Bonnal [1] thinks this is evidence that Napoleon was led to discredit Davout's view because it was not in accordance with his preconceived idea of Charles' intention to retreat through Bohemia. This seems rather far-fetched, and, as a matter of fact, both Davout and Montbrun were partially right. Davout was right in supposing the Archduke to be concentrating at Cham, whilst Montbrun was right in his estimate of the Austrians' eventual destination. The correspondence continued during the 26th, but, by the afternoon of that day, Davout had almost come round to the view that Charles was bound for Pilsen. He was still rather puzzled as to the movements of Bellegarde with the I. corps. On the evening of the 26th, Davout's corps stood thus—Montbrun between Nittenau and Bruck; Gudin and corps headquarters at Nittenau; Friant at Kürn; Morand at Regenstauf. It was on the 26th that Napoleon at last began to admit, inferentially, that the operations of the 19th-23rd had not been quite the second Jena which he had represented them to be. He now says that there must be a great battle before Vienna is reached, and, on the 27th, he indicates the battlefield as somewhere between Passau and the capital. In other words, he expects the Archduke to recross the Danube somewhere below Passau, to rejoin his left wing, and to stand with the re-united army for the defence of Vienna somewhere between that city and Passau.

[1] P. 321.

For that battle he wants every man available, and he writes, through Davout, to Bernadotte to move on Ratisbon and to place himself between it and Bohemia, so as to watch the latter country, whilst maintaining his communications with the main army through Ratisbon. Bernadotte had evacuated Dresden on the 16th April, after sending off the Royal family into security on the Rhine, and sending the contents of the arsenal down the Elbe. On the 20th, he was, with the Saxon army, at Gera ; on the 26th, he wrote from Rudolstadt (near Saalfeld of 1806 fame) that he would now, as ordered on the 24th, march on Bohemia, and hoped to be at Plauen next evening. It will be some time before we find him taking an active part in the operations.

If Davout was still not quite satisfied as to the Austrian movements on the north bank, Napoleon was quite so by the morning of the 26th, when he felt it safe to leave Ratisbon for Landshut.

Davout's orders were clear : the moment the enemy had drawn off to Bohemia, he was to march on Passau, leaving Dupas at Ratisbon until Bernadotte's arrival.

On the 27th, Davout feeling certain that the Austrians were concentrating on Cham, moved his corps more to the right, so as to interpose it between that place and Ratisbon. In the evening he had Pajol at Bruck, and Montbrun at Falkenstein, with outposts in a semicircle in front of them. On Montbrun's right was a Wurtemberg cavalry regiment, sent by Boudet, from Straubing, across the Danube. Davout's three infantry divisions were posted thus : Gudin at Kürn, on the road to Nittenau, with a detachment at that place. On Gudin's right was Friant, at and behind Süssenbach, on the road to Cham. Morand formed the reserve to these two, at Gonersdorf, the junction of the two roads.

Charles had taken up his position about Cham,

with the intention of there offering a defensive battle, if Napoleon followed him. It was soon, however, apparent that the Emperor had no intention of following the Archduke on the north bank of the Danube, but was going direct to Vienna by the south side. Charles, it is true, had over 90,000 men, but they had been considerably demoralised by the events before Ratisbon. For this and other reasons, he abandoned the idea of a renewed offensive at this period, and had made up his mind, after reorganising his army at Cham, to march into Bohemia, retreating *viâ* Budweis to Vienna. On the 24th April, he wrote to Hiller to make for Linz, there to cross the Danube and unite with himself for a fresh offensive.

Having restored order to some extent in his army, and collected all the available horses for his transport and artillery, he started on his retreat on the 28th April. As this retreat was quite unmolested, and as Charles does not appear again on the stage of active operations till the third week in May, it will be convenient at once to indicate his line of march, before returning to events on the right bank of the Danube.

On the 29th, his headquarters were at Klattau, with the II. and I. Reserve corps. Bellegarde, with the I., was marching by Bischofsteinitz farther north, the IV. corps more to the south. Klenau, with a composite division of 9 battalions, 1 squadron, and 1 battery, was sweeping still farther south, by Eisenstein to Winterburg, as a flank guard to block the passes leading from the Danube into Bohemia. Stutterheim, with 2 cavalry regiments, and a horse battery, was making forced marches by Klattau, Budweis, and Freystadt to Linz, there to hold the bridge till Hiller's arrival.

The Archduke now (29th) wrote to Hiller that he hoped to reach Budweis on the 4th May, thence to make for the Danube at Linz, Krems, or Vienna as might be

practicable. Hiller was therefore to retire accordingly,
letting his chief know what he could do.

On the 2nd May, Charles, becoming alarmed about a
possible attack from Saxony on Bohemia, decided to
leave a whole army corps to oppose it on the western
Bohemian frontier. For this purpose, Kolowrat was
given 23 battalions, and 15 squadrons, besides 23
Bohemian landwehr battalions, the latter in very bad
condition and of very little value. This corps was now
called the III., and the old III. became, henceforth, the
II. Kolowrat marched back to Pilsen, almost exactly in
the reverse direction to that by which he had reached
Sedlitz where he turned. The rest of the army continued
as before. By the 6th May, the whole army (except
Kolowrat at Pilsen) was resting at and to the north and
south of Budweis, including Klenau and Stutterheim.
The march, averaging about 12½ miles per diem, had
been rapid for the Austrians.

Charles' intentions at this time seem to have been
rather doubtful. On the 3rd May, he wrote to his
brother John : " In a few days it must be certain whether
the enemy means to follow and attack me, or to march
on Vienna by the Danube ; in the first case, I shall fight
at Budweis ; in the second, I shall seek to operate
against the enemy's communications across the Danube."
That seems clear enough, but is very different from what
had been written to Hiller two days earlier. Briefly,
Hiller had been told (1st May) that if he was attacked
before the 7th or 8th by such superior forces that he
could not halt, he was to cross at Linz, and rejoin the
main army north of the river. If, however, he had been
driven beyond Linz by the 7th or 8th May, he was to
fall back fighting, and delaying the enemy as much as
possible, across the Traun and the Enns. Whether he
crossed at Linz or at Mauthausen, he was to leave 8000
or 10,000 men on the right bank, to destroy the bridges

on the road to Vienna as they retired. Hiller was to carry over all boats and bridging material on the Danube to the left bank as he passed. Binder von Krieglstein [1] remarks that, if this order is somewhat deficient in clearness, it, at any rate, indicates that Charles was quite prepared to hear that Hiller had not been able to cross at Linz. That despatch Charles seems to have forgotten ; for, when he heard that Hiller had fallen back over the Traun, he expressed his astonishment, and even complained to the Emperor Francis of Hiller's disobedience to orders. Charles himself had reached Budweis on the 3rd, and here the Emperor rejoined the army. Charles wrote to Hiller to cross at Mauthausen without delay, but that officer replied that it was now impossible for him to cross short of Krems. To that Charles replied that he would leave Budweis on the 6th, and join Hiller about the 13th or 14th, near Krems. The boat bridges at Mauthausen and Krems [2] were to be withdrawn for later use, not burnt. He was to leave sufficient troops at Krems to prevent a restoration of the bridge, and to support these by himself encamping, concealed from the enemy's view from across the river. It was hoped Hiller could hold out till Charles' arrival.

From this it seemed beyond doubt clear that the Archduke meant to unite with Hiller north of the river. Yet, at the same time, he wrote to his brother Maximilian that he proposed to cross the Danube on the 13th or 14th, in order to cover Vienna ; if that was not possible he would march by the left bank to the capital. The two letters defy all attempts to reconcile them with one another.

Charles now called back Kolowrat from Pilsen, with orders to guard the march of the main army from any

---

[1] *B. K.*, ii. 11.
[2] The Mauthausen one had already been burnt by the Bavarians, whilst Hiller had himself burnt that at Linz.

enterprises of the enemy from Passau.   Though he knew the French were pursuing Hiller, he was thus going to waste a whole army corps in guarding against a most improbable movement in his rear.

The Archduke only got off again on the 7th, instead of the 6th.   On this date he again changed his Quartermaster-General, dismissing Prohaska, and appointing Wimpffen.

He was constantly troubled with fears of a French crossing to the north bank as he marched, and took excessive precautions against it by detachments, thus disseminating his forces.   At Gratzen, on the 8th, he heard from Hiller that the enemy appeared to intend crossing between Krems and Vienna, to attack the army on its march to the capital.   This made him change his plans again.   Hiller was now told on no account to allow himself to be driven from the Danube, but to fall back by it on Vienna.   If he was forced to cross it, he was to make for Gfüll.   To Archduke Maximilian, now Governor of Vienna, Charles wrote that he expected to join Hiller north of Krems, to leave the VI. corps there, and with the rest, to march to the north of Vienna, somewhere about Stockerau.   Unless there should be a battle about Zwettel, he hoped to reach Vienna on the 17th or 18th, to cross the river there, and meet the enemy.   Therefore, at all costs, Vienna must be held till that date.   If Maximilian were forced out of it, the bridges must be removed and the north bank held.   On the 8th May, from headquarters at Weitra, Charles sent orders to Kolowrat to leave only detachments to watch the Bohemian forest, and, with the mass of his corps, to move on Linz or Mauthausen, to cross there and attack the French communications. The enemy was to be deceived by the spreading of a report that the main army was going to cross at Krem in order to operate on the enemy's rear.

On the 9th, Hiller reported the French were on the Traisen, nearer to Vienna than Charles. An attack on the French from the line Krems-Tulln now seemed to Charles no longer feasible. Therefore, Hiller was ordered to leave 8000 men at Krems, to hurry back with the rest by the left bank, and to occupy a position between Krems and Vienna. He was to oppose any attempt of the enemy to cross, and to act in concert with Maximilian. Should the French succeed in passing the river, Hiller was to fall back on Gaunersdorf. Should the enemy pass before Hiller had taken up his position between Krems and Vienna, he was to open his communication with Vienna by force, and, in the last resort, to retreat to Maissau.

On the 10th Charles was at Zwettel, when he heard of Napoleon's arrival before Vienna. He had now only to hasten on to the north side of Vienna. Marching by Neu-Polla (11th), Horn and Molt (12th), Wetzdorf (13th), he reached Göllersdorf on the 14th, and halted there on the 15th. During the night of the 15th-16th, he marched to between Stockerau and Korneuberg, where, on the western slopes of the Bisamberg, he at last rejoined Hiller.[1]

(2) NAPOLEON'S ADVANCE TO THE TRAUN

Having somewhat anticipated events by describing briefly the march of the Austrian main army, which led up to the final struggle at Vienna, we must now follow the movements, on a parallel line, of the French army. In doing so it is not proposed to weary the reader with a detailed description of the movements of every small body or detachment, or with any full account of the operations against the revolted Tyrolese. The latter, with the history of Andreas Hofer, have been the subject

---

[1] For above account of Charles' retreat, see *B. K.*, ii. ch. i.

of more than one volume.   Nor do the operations of the
French and Austrian armies of Italy come within the
scope of this volume, until they reach the plains of
Hungary.   They will, in due course, be so far summarised as is necessary to the understanding of the parts
these forces played near Vienna.

We have already given the movements towards
Landshut, effected under Napoleon's orders, up to the
evening of the 24th.   At 4 P.M. on that day the
Emperor sent orders to Lefebvre to march with the
Crown Prince's division to Munich, which it was supposed had been evacuated by Jelacic.   If that general
was still there, Deroy would support the Crown Prince,
and endeavour to capture the Austrians.   Once the
Crown Prince was in Munich, all three Bavarian divisions
would make for Mühldorf and Burghausen.

Meanwhile, about noon on the 23rd, the Austrians
under Hiller (V., VI., and II. Reserve corps) were between
Neu-Oetting and Mühldorf, with rearguards on the left
bank of the Inn at Winhöring, Eggenfelden, and near
Mühldorf.   The brigade (Dedowich) blockading Passau
on the right bank of the Danube had come in to Braunau
and Marktl, and, though belonging to the IV. corps, had
been put under Hiller.   Hiller, including Jelacic's division
at Munich, now had about 35,000 men, say 25,000
without Jelacic.   Seeing that the French pursuit on the
22nd and 23rd had not been very vigorous, Hiller
plucked up courage for an offensive return.   He wrote
to the Emperor Francis that he hoped to be back on the
Isar, in touch with the Archduke Charles at Dingolfing,
by the 25th.   A letter from the Emperor crossed this,
in which Hiller was ordered to prevent the enemy from
falling on Charles' left flank.   At 11 A.M. Hiller wrote
to Charles that he would try, next day, to get back to
Neumarkt, nearer the main army, of the defeat and
retreat of which he was still entirely ignorant.

He had burnt the bridge over the Inn at Mühldorf, but appears to have had the means of re-passage by a pontoon bridge. He now sent forward his rearguards to cover his passage to the left bank, and directed Jelacic to relieve the pressure by an advance from Munich, where he still was on the 23rd, towards Landshut. Meanwhile, Bessières, reaching Neumarkt with Wrede's division on the 22nd, had called up Molitor. Marulaz alone, supported by one battalion, moved towards the Inn on the 23rd. Late that evening his 3rd Chasseurs, attacked at Erharting by Hiller's advance guard, were driven back in disorder on the 19th Chasseurs and the supporting battalion. The whole then fell back on Neumarkt, where Wrede held the heights to the south-east above the low-lying town.

About midnight, Bessières received Napoleon's order of the 23rd,[1] directing him at once to push over the Inn and the Salzach. That he could no longer do at present. Molitor was still at Vilsbiburg which he had reached, by a night march, on the morning of the 23rd. Bessières at once sent for him and ordered Wrede to advance next morning.

Hiller also, as we know, was advancing with 40 battalions and as many squadrons. Against these Bessières had, for the moment, nothing but Wrede's 10 battalions and 8 squadrons with, at the most, 20 squadrons of Marulaz's light cavalry. The attack fell on Wrede just as he began to move on the 24th. Hiller advanced in three columns, of which the right (12 battalions 9 squadrons) came directly against Wrede, whilst Radetzky with his advance guard felt to the right towards the Isar at Landau.

The fight began by the repulse of Marulaz by the Austrian central column. About 8 A.M., the right

---

[1] *Vide supra*, p. 187.

column attacked Wrede's position. The battle raged till noon with varying fortune. Then Bessières perceived that he was being outflanked on both sides. By 1 o'clock, he found himself compelled to retire before Hiller's great superiority.

Molitor [1] was now up and sent two regiments over the Rott to cover Wrede's retreat, whilst the rest of the division remained in reserve on the left bank. The Austrians continued to push forward, inflicting considerable loss on the retiring Bavarians at the passage of the Rott. By 3 P.M. Neumarkt was lost, and Bessières fell back in good order on Vilsbiburg. Hiller did not follow beyond the Rott. The losses appear to have been approximately: Austrians, 776 killed and wounded, 122 prisoners [2]; Wrede alone lost 586 killed and wounded. Bessières mentions a loss of 200 cavalry and a few of Molitor's men.

General Bonnal [3] blames Bessières for allowing himself to be frightened into retreat when, by a bold offensive with Wrede and Molitor, he would probably have forced Hiller to retreat. That, says the critic, is an instance of the small value of most of Napoleon's marshals when not acting under his immediate command. On the other hand, it must be remembered that Bessières was very largely outnumbered, and had no reason to suppose that there was anything to support him.

He is certainly right when, in reporting his retirement, he surmises that Hiller would not have recrossed the Inn had he known of Charles' defeat. He *did* hear of it in the night of the 24th-25th from the Emperor, who had received Charles' despondent letter of the 23rd. Thereupon he promptly withdrew to his old quarters at Neu-Oetting, with the II. Reserve at Marktl, and three rearguards west of the Inn.

---

[1] *B. K.*, ii. 24. Bessières says *all* Molitor's division was in reserve. Molitor himself says he only kept two regiments in reserve.

[2] According to Bavarian accounts, 407.   [3] P. 310.

Jelacic had occupied Munich on the 16th and remained there till the 23rd when, hearing of the Archduke's misfortunes, he hastily left, at 8 P.M., for Wasserburg. At Steinhöring, on the evening of the 24th, he heard of Hiller's success against Bessières, whereupon he began to move again on Munich. Whilst on his way, he got an order from Hiller to fall back on Salzburg and defend the line of the Salzach between Burghausen and Salzburg. He reached Wasserburg on the 27th.

Napoleon was still at Ratisbon when the news of the affair at Neumarkt reached him from Bessières on the 25th. Writing to Masséna at 5 P.M., the Emperor says Lannes is under orders to march next morning with 25,000 men to support Bessières. Masséna should do what he could to help and to compel Hiller's retreat.

On the 26th, Napoleon proceeded in person to Landshut, where he arrived about 2 P.M. Lannes reached Vilsbiburg in the evening, and found Bessières had already begun to advance again, as Hiller had retreated. The Austrians had passed both the Inn and the Salzach, reaching Burghausen with the V. and VI., Braunau with the II. Reserve corps ; rearguard at Neu-Oetting.

At 9.30 P.M. (26th), Lefebvre wrote that he had heard during the previous night of Jelacic's fresh advance on Munich. He had, therefore, sent the Crown Prince to the Bavarian capital, whilst he himself, with Deroy, prepared to fall on Jelacic's rear. Then, when the Austrians once more fell back, Lefebvre with his two divisions was advancing by Ebersberg to the Inn. As for Wrede, Lefebvre had told Lannes that he could keep him till they both got to the Inn. At that moment Wrede was at Mühldorf. Masséna had reached Passau at 1 P.M., had captured the passage over the Inn, after a sharp fight in which he took 400 prisoners, and was busy repairing the bridge for the passage of the cavalry and artillery. Legrand had gone to Schärding, had dis-

persed the enemy beyond the Inn with a few cannon
shots, and hoped to restore the bridge very shortly.
On the 27th, the Imperial Guard, which had been left
behind owing to the early outbreak of war, was beginning
to arrive. There were already 2900 of them at
Landshut, and another 5400 at Augsburg, or between it
and Landshut.

At 6 A.M. on this day, the Emperor writes to Lannes
that Masséna's movement has apparently drawn Hiller
towards Passau and the Danube ; therefore, Lannes must
pass the Inn and the Salzach, so as to create a diversion
in favour of Masséna.

To Lefebvre orders were sent to press on to Salzburg,
at the same time taking measures for the relief of the
Bavarian fortress of Kufstein, which was besieged by an
Austrian detachment. Wrede, at 6 A.M. on the 27th,
passed the Inn at Mühldorf, which place Napoleon
reached at 4 P.M. Masséna was across the Inn at
Passau, marching by the Linz road[1] to join Legrand at
Schärding. He was also reconnoitring towards Linz
and Braunau, thus threatening the retreat of Hiller who
had taken up what he called a " central position " in the
neighbourhood of Altheim.

At this period, the Emperor Francis was exercising an
unfortunate influence on the Austrian command south of
the Danube. His interference was no doubt encouraged
by the separation of the two wings of the Austrian army
at a time when the Emperor[2] was in easy communication
with Hiller, while Charles was not. Hiller also was only
too ready to avoid taking orders from Charles. Resistance by Hiller to the overwhelming forces opposed to
him could lead to little but disaster to himself, and his
best course, the one which Charles wanted him to follow,

---

[1] The road leaves the Danube at Passau turning south, as far as Schärding,
along the right bank of the Inn.
[2] He had to leave Schärding on the 25th and went to Linz.

was to make his way to Linz as quickly as possible, burning all bridges behind him, and then making quite secure his passage to the left bank at Linz itself. He had lost two days by his return to Neumarkt, which practically resulted in nothing. In this movement he had been encouraged by the Emperor. Now again he proposed a fresh offensive against Masséna on the 27th. For the command he selected Schustekh who, though a brave old man, was no general. Then Hiller gave him only some 10,000 men whom it would take many hours to collect. Among them was the blockading force under Dedowich which had retired from before the south side of Passau. Dedowich, however, did not stop, but fell back to Ried, and, thereupon, Schustekh, having failed to get his force together, gave up his operation as impracticable. If Hiller was going to attempt anything against Masséna, he should have attacked him with his whole force; but he would have done much better to continue his retreat. Masséna would probably have defeated his whole force, and the marshal lost a great opportunity of making an end of Hiller by a march southwards. Instead of that, he did nothing but write rather querulous letters to Berthier. Truly the Duke of Rivoli was no longer the Masséna of Rivoli, Zurich and Genoa. Hiller was now afraid of being driven far south towards Ischl, and he moreover received this day (28th) Charles' letter of 24th, indicating Linz or Budweis as the point of reunion. He therefore,[1] as he wrote to Charles, proposed to march by Ried, Haag, Lambach, and Wels to Linz where he would complete the fortifications, throw a bridge below the town, and generally make every preparation to hold out till the arrival of the main army. If Masséna's advance prevented his getting to Linz, he would go by Wels to Mauthausen, cross the Danube there, and march back

---

[1] See *Angeli*, iv. 210, etc.

to Linz by the north bank, the Linz bridge being meanwhile destroyed.

We need not follow Hiller's march to Linz which he was able to reach, as he hoped, on the 2nd May. As usual, he wasted an excessive portion of his force in scattered rearguards which were here and there defeated by the enemy's advance guards. Otherwise, there was nothing remarkable in Hiller's march. Napoleon on this day ordered everything in rear to be hurried up for the advance south of the Danube. He wrote to Berthier, "give orders for everything which is at Augsburg destined for the army, infantry, cavalry, artillery, to be directed to Braunau, and everything arriving at Landshut, Munich, and Augsburg to follow the same direction." He had already ordered the advance of all troops on the Danube above Ratisbon, excepting a small detachment to guard the bridgehead at Ingolstadt.

The time had now arrived when the advanced base of the army could be moved forward from the Lech to the Inn at and below Braunau and to Passau, which latter place had been carefully prepared before the outbreak of war, and had been held until Masséna's arrival relieved it.

By 7 P.M. this evening, Lefebvre, in pursuit of Jelacic, had reached Wasserburg, where he was repairing the bridge burnt by Jelacic. This was not so difficult as the repair of the bridge over the Salzach at Burghausen, which had been very thoroughly burnt by the enemy, and could not be restored till the 30th April. Up till that date, fortunately for Hiller, the Emperor, with Lannes' corps, was unable to cross the Salzach. The river was over 100 yards wide and in full flood, consequent on the wet weather which still continued.

On the 29th, Napoleon had plenty to occupy him during his enforced stay on the left bank of the Salzach, for he had received a good deal of bad news.

In the first place he had heard of Eugène Beauharnais' defeat at Sacile, and his retreat behind the Adige before the Archduke John's army of Italy. Then there was a deal of trouble in the Tyrol, which had broken out into revolt against the Bavarians, to whose domination the mountaineers had been, against their wish, transferred after Austerlitz. The revolt had commenced at the same time as the Austrian advance. Space will not allow of any attempt to deal at length with this popular rising, the tragedy of its eventual suppression, or the execution of Andreas Hofer—in February 1810.[1] The Vorarlberg was with the Tyrol, and in the latter was a considerable nucleus of regular troops under Chasteler, to say nothing of Jelacic's division which was going in that direction. All this was a cause of anxiety for the French right flank. Therefore, Napoleon issues special instructions to Lefebvre, whom he assumes to be at Salzburg.[2] In the first place he was to ascertain whether Chasteler, who had advanced from Italy by Brixen, had retired. If not, Lefebvre's forward movement (he was to make out he had 40,000 men) would probably compel him to do so. As soon as Kufstein was relieved, Lefebvre was to form a column, composed of the relieving force and the garrison, to watch the Tyrol. He was, by proclamations of Hiller's danger, to try and expedite that general's retreat. Wrede was to be sent to Strasswaldchen.

[1] Would Hofer have received quite so much hero-worship as has fallen to his lot but for Napoleon's blunder in having him shot, and thereby conferring on him the crown of martyrdom? One is accustomed to associate him with the organisation of military measures, and active command in the field. It will perhaps surprise others, as it did the author, to read in the introduction to Hall's translation of *Hormayr's Life of Hofer* that he was never at the front in action, but generally at some tavern in the rear. It seems disappointing to be expected to believe this of the man whom his enemies sometimes represented as leading his peasants with a rosary in one hand and a flagon of beer in the other.

[2] Delay at the broken bridge of Wasserburg prevented his getting there till the 30th. Wrede arrived before him, on the afternoon of the 29th, and took Salzburg after a slight resistance by Jelacic.

Lefebvre himself was to thoroughly fortify Salzburg, utilising the guns of Kufstein, so that with his main body he might take up his position there in safety, ready to support either Wrede or the Tyrol column. A provisional government was to be formed, and the militia was to be disbanded with many threats of the consequences of re-assembly.

From Germany, too, the Emperor kept getting news of insurrectionary movements. On the 29th, he heard of the plot of Baron Dornberg, the commandant of the chasseurs of the guard of Jerome, King of Westphalia. On the 9th April, the Emperor had given to Jerome the command of the 10th corps, consisting of his own Westphalian troops, of those at Hamburg, and of the garrisons of Küstrin and Stettin, requiring him to maintain order from Hamburg to the Main. On the 12th April, Jerome was again warned to watch Dresden, Hanover, and Hamburg. Now (29th April) the Emperor considered it necessary to have more troops on his left rear, not only to keep order in Germany, but also to oppose any Austrian raid on his communications. He, therefore, constituted the "Corps of Observation of the Elbe," to the command of which he appointed Kellermann. He expected to arrange for nearly 14,000 men in the direction of Hanau, using for the purpose three of the six provisional regiments of dragoons forming at Strasburg, four fourth battalions at Paris, and the provisional demi-brigades forming at Mayence, Metz, and Sedan. Two batteries were to be organised at Metz. Kellermann was to represent his corps as 50,000 strong, and even Jerome was told it was 20,000. Kellermann would hold it concentrated, ready to answer a summons from Jerome. On this 29th April, Davout was nearly satisfied that Charles was gone to Bohemia. His own troops had penetrated as far as Rötz and Cham, and now he had arranged for Morand to reach Plättling and Friant

P

Straubing on the 30th. Gudin was still kept back with Montbrun. Boudet had left Straubing and was with Masséna. As for Masséna, he was still waiting on the Inn, merely reconnoitring towards Linz. On the 30th, Davout, at last quite satisfied about Charles, was moving with Gudin to Straubing where, still cautious, he remarked that he would be able to move against Charles in the unlikely event of the Austrian's retracing his steps. Montbrun was left to move to Passau by the north bank, watching the issues from Bohemia. Bernadotte was understood to be at Neumarkt.[1] As soon as he reached the level of Ratisbon, it would be safe to bring Rouyer and Dupas to Straubing.

This afternoon, Bessières, now at last across the Salzach, was ordered to march by Ried on Linz.

Lannes was to restore the Braunau bridge, if possible, and also march to Ried.

Masséna to advance on Linz and try to surprise the bridge.

Walther, with the Guard, to move from Oetting to Braunau.

To Lefebvre Napoleon wrote that Jelacic with 8000 men was on his way to Radstadt. Lefebvre with 10,000 [2] was to follow, to drive him as far away as possible, and try to get news of Chasteler. Vandamme was censured for delay in his march to Braunau.

On the 1st May, Napoleon issues a long order regarding his new base at Passau. In it he provides for the defence of the place and its *tête de pont* on the left bank of the Danube, for provisions, and for the guidance of the battalion of sailors to be quartered there and to patrol the river. In a subsequent letter, he mentions that there are 12,000 of the Guard at Braunau.

[1] The Neumarkt north-west of Ratisbon of course.

[2] In a letter which crossed this Lefebvre explained that he had only 8000 or 9000 men between his two divisions, but would get in some stragglers when he got to Salzburg, where Wrede already was.

On this day there is a quantity of correspondence between the Emperor, Davout, and Masséna. Napoleon had just received from Davout a letter written by the Archduke Charles and delivered to Montbrun's outposts. It proposed an exchange of prisoners, but was really meant as a feeler as to the possibility of peace negotiations. The terms are fulsomely flattering,[1] and, considering the person to whom it was addressed, it is hardly surprising to find Napoleon saying of it: " I will answer it when I have time. Meanwhile, keep the ' parlementaire.' It will be sufficient to answer eight days hence. Those people are as vile in adversity as they are haughty on the least gleam of prosperity."

In later letters Napoleon says he will be at Linz and on the Traun next day. The bridge at Linz was burnt and the Austrians hoped to unite by Mauthausen, where, however, they might be anticipated. The Emperor of Austria was at Sternberg yesterday, and Prince Louis behind the Enns.[2] Davout must hurry up. Dupas, now marching on Ratisbon, would form the garrison at Passau. In Ratisbon nothing was to be left except a regiment or two of cavalry, to guard against raids, till Bernadotte was up. Dupas and Rouyer should close in on Passau when

---

[1] " Sire,

" Your Majesty has announced to me your arrival by cannon shots, without leaving me time to compliment you. I had scarcely heard of your presence when the losses I sustained caused me to realise it painfully. You have taken many men from me ; my troops, on their side, have taken from you several thousands of prisoners, at points where you did not command in person. I propose to your Majesty an exchange, man for man and rank for rank, and, if this proposal meets your wishes, I beg you to inform me of your intentions regarding the place where the exchange should be made.

" I feel flattered, Sire, at measuring swords with the greatest captain of the age. I should be truly happy if Fortune had chosen me to assure to my country a durable peace ; but, whatever may be the chances of war or of peace, I beg your Majesty to believe that my ambition leads me always towards you, and that I shall hold myself equally honoured, Sire, whether it is with the sword or with the olive branch in my hand that I meet you."

[2] This was incorrect as regards Louis.

Davout left it. Davout himself must be able to reach Linz by the 4th or 5th if required.

At 10 P.M., Davout sends correspondence with Dupas, showing that the latter had been ordered by Bernadotte to Baireuth ! ! Morand was due at Passau on the 1st, with Friant close behind. Gudin could only arrive there on the 2nd. Davout himself would be there on the night of 2nd, or early morning of 3rd. He still wanted to wait at Straubing for Montbrun's reports about Charles. Montbrun, moving by the left bank, would rejoin Davout at Passau with the greater part of his division ; the rest would still watch the issues from Bohemia, furnishing information to Bernadotte.

The correspondence with Masséna begins with the latter's report that provisions were scarce, especially owing to the burning of Schärding. No enemy worth mention was near. He hopes to be at Efferding on the 2nd, and Linz next day.

Berthier replies, at 2 P.M., that headquarters will be to-night at Ried and to-morrow (2nd) probably at Lambach. Masséna is to hurry to Linz, and, if possible, seize the bridge over the Traun. If the enemy proposed defending the line of the Traun, he would doubtless do so at Ebelsberg,[1] where the right bank commanded the left ; but he would be driven out, since the Emperor, crossing at Lambach, where the advantage of the bank was the other way, would come up on Hiller's left flank. Charles could not reach Linz before the 7th, so he would probably seek a junction with Hiller at Krems.[2]

Masséna, at 5.30 P.M., forwards a report of a small fight with Schustekh's rearguard near Neumarkt.[3]

[1] Generally written Ebersberg in the French accounts and despatches.

[2] The French staff calculated that from Cham to Krems was only one or two marches farther than from Cham to Linz. The French, on the other hand, would have to march 55 miles from Linz to St Polten, and another 18 to Krems. *Saski*, iii. 106, n. 2.

[3] On the road to Wels. Not to be confused with the many other places of the same name in these parts.

Late in the evening of the 1st, Lefebvre reports a brush between Jelacic and the brigade sent after him, which had resulted in the Austrians being driven over the Lammer. As for the idea of sending 10,000 men,[1] he could only muster 4572 bayonets at Salzburg, after deducting one brigade sent to Kufstein, another after Jelacic, and 2500 stragglers. Jelacic appeared to be going to defend a fort at Lueg.

Early on the 2nd, Masséna marched for Efferding, with Carra St Cyr's division leading, followed by Legrand, Claparède, and Boudet. About 8 A.M., St Cyr's advance guard, under Trenqualye, came upon an Austrian rearguard which it drove back on Efferding, and, being reinforced by St Cyr with infantry and artillery, drove it through the town. After passing Raffelding bridge, Bianchi's brigade was met, and eventually driven back as far as Alkoven, where it took post with its right on the Danube and left on the heights south of the road.

Bessières, arriving at Wels, wrote that he found the bridge broken, though it could easily be repaired. From the same place, Lannes wrote that Hiller had gone by the left bank of the Traun to Linz, that he was said to be marching by Krumau and Budweis to rejoin Charles. He added that sappers (of whom he appears to have had none) were required to repair the bridge at Wels, and concluded : " In case Your Majesty wishes me to pass here, I beg you will give orders to the divisions of St Hilaire, Molitor, and Demont. General Oudinot's division is here."

Vandamme, reporting his arrival at Riedau, was ordered to press on to Wels. Wrede writes, from Frankenmarkt, that the Lambach bridge was burnt. He received orders, late at night, to hold fast at Voikla-brück, communicating with Lefebvre on his right and

[1] *Supra*, p. 226.

" ourselves here." Napoleon had reached Lambach between 3 and 4 P.M.

Lefebvre, writing at 3 P.M. from Salzburg, gives an account of the fort at Lueg and of his own arrangements for turning it. Chasteler is reported to be near Innsbruck, for the purpose of leading the Tyrolese insurgents. To this Berthier replied that Lefebvre is to be left for some time at Salzburg, that he is to drive the enemy from Gölling, to refit, collect his stragglers, and keep the enemy several marches away from the right flank of the French army. Wrede can assist him if necessary. The Emperor attaches great importance to Salzburg, which must on no account be allowed again to fall into the enemy's hands.

Davout reports that he will be at Passau on the 3rd, Dupas probably on the 4th. Rouyer was also under orders to move up from Ratisbon, leaving there only one battalion, till Bernadotte should arrive. Davout adds a postscript in which he says that the 65th, which was taken by the Austrians at Ratisbon, has orders to retire to Augsburg if the Austrians should move on Ratisbon. The regiment had been released, apparently, on the parole of the officers promising for selves and men not to fight again till exchanged.

Bernadotte was at Wunsiedl, still several marches north of Ratisbon. He says there are reports that Prussia is arming, and notes that Schill had left Berlin on the 28th April on that gallant but desperate raid which was to end with his own death, in the streets of Stralsund, on the 31st May.

CHAPTER XII

THE BATTLE OF EBELSBERG AND THE CAPTURE OF VIENNA

NAPOLEON had at first credited Wrede's report that Hiller was gone behind the Enns; but, by the night of the 2nd-3rd May, he was enlightened by Bessières and Lannes as to the true direction of the Austrian retreat. Very early on the 3rd, Lannes again wrote from Wels saying he thought the Archduke Louis (that is Hiller) meant fighting at Linz to preserve his communication with Charles, but probably hoped that the French would not be ready before Charles arrived. At 5 A.M., the following orders were issued :—

(1) Bessières to march on Linz with his cavalry.

(2) Lannes to support him with infantry, if he heard a cannonade.

(3) Nansouty and St Sulpice to move on Wels.

The orders provided for Bessières' cavalry going to the Danube, and for the assembly at Wels, on the left bank of the Traun,[1] of three infantry divisions. Napoleon, leaving Lambach at 7 A.M., was at Wels by 9. At 1.30 P.M., he ordered Bessières to march on Enns, followed by Oudinot. At 2, he wrote to Masséna for news, having heard nothing from him. He appears, however, to have learnt that Hiller had given up the idea of holding Linz, for a knowledge of this is indicated by his order to

---

[1] Lannes promised to have the bridge there restored by 7 or 8 A.M., and had it done by the earlier hour.

Bessières, and by one of about the same hour to Lannes, ordering him to march on Steyer. To the latter is added a postscript saying that all the harm possible must be done to the enemy retreating from Linz. Before 3 P.M., he appears to have heard from Masséna, for that marshal is ordered to pursue on Enns and restore the bridge there. Masséna, meanwhile, had occupied Linz at 9 A.M., finding Hiller gone and the bridge over the Danube destroyed. His order of march had been (1) Trenqualye with an advance guard of three cavalry regiments, (2) Claparède, (3) Legrand, (4) Carra St Cyr, (5) Boudet.

Marulaz, who had bivouacked at Efferding, joined the advance guard with four more regiments of light cavalry abreast of Wilhöring, where he found Austrians barring the defile on the Linz road. The cavalry being beaten off, Marulaz had to give place to Claparède's infantry advance guard which pushed forward without difficulty into the suburb of Linz. As Marulaz debouched from it on the road to Enns, he again came under infantry fire from the woods on the near bank of the Traun which were held by the Austrians, whose main body now occupied a strong position on the farther (right) bank at Ebelsberg.[1]

On the Austrian side, in the night of the 2nd-3rd, the Emperor Francis left Linz to rejoin the army in Bohemia, though he knew Hiller was about to engage in a serious action. Before leaving, he gave written orders according to which Hiller was with his left wing to defend the Traun towards Lambach, whilst his right held Ebelsberg, endeavouring to delay the enemy's advance over the river. If he could not do this, he was to concentrate behind the Enns.

About 3 A.M., Hiller started his march across the Traun, the II. Reserve corps leading, followed by the

---

[1] Though the place is called Ebersberg in French accounts it is spelt as in the text in all German accounts and maps.

VI. and V. Bianchi's brigade was rearguard, and altogether, with Schustekh, Radetzky and Vincent, Hiller employed four out of his eight brigades as rearguards, besides a light cavalry regiment as support to Bianchi near the Ebelsberg bridge. Another cavalry regiment had been sent across the Danube, to keep in touch with Klenau and Stutterheim (of Charles' army) at Freystadt.

Let us now glance at the position which Hiller had decided to take up.

From Wels downwards the Traun flowed close under the heights on its right bank, whilst on the left bank was a level valley about three miles broad, through which it reached the Danube in several branches. It was 15 feet deep in the main stream, with a very rapid current flowing over a stony bed. It was nowhere fordable, unless in a very dry season. The heights on the right fell steeply to the river. The main stream at Ebelsberg was 500 paces broad, the islands in the valley were marshy, and the level plain covered with sodden meadows, ditches, and small woods. A little above Ebelsberg, the Krems flowed through a steep-sided valley into the Traun. The only approach, with the river swollen as it was by rain and melting snow, was over an embanked road and a wooden bridge of some 550 yards in length, and only 15 or 16 feet broad. This defile was easily commanded by artillery on the heights above. The bridge was closed by a tower with a gate only wide enough for one vehicle to pass at a time. Above the bridge on the north was the castle, which commanded a large part of the bridge. After the gate of the bridge was passed, there was still another gate across the road before it reached the heights, and narrow streets led up steeply into the town on the right.

It would be difficult to find a position better suited for defence under the circumstances, and with the arms of 1809. Napoleon had already indicated it as the place where the Austrians would probably fight, if they did so short of Vienna.[1]

Austrian retreats through defiles in 1809 were not exemplary, and in that leading into and through Ebelsberg the scenes of the retreat through Landshut were repeated. There was the same wild struggle of transport and artillery, drivers of ammunition waggons and ambulances all striving to outstrip one another in the race for the bridge, and for safety on the farther bank. It was almost impossible for the staff to restore order. At last, however, the troops were able to pass, protected by the rearguards of Radetzky and Vincent. Even Bianchi was over by 9 o'clock, but Radetzky and Vincent were still on the left bank, and Schustekh had not yet come up from the south-west.

Vincent had 6 battalions and a light cavalry regiment. He posted one battalion in the village of Klein München, the other 5 between it and Scharlinz, the cavalry regiment on his right, north of the Linz-Wels road.

Radetzky, with 2 battalions and 6 squadrons, was on Vincent's left, waiting to receive Schustekh. Hiller, as usual taking half measures, sent on the II. Reserve to Asten, two-thirds of the way from Ebelsberg to Enns. The V. and VI. corps he marched on to the heights beyond Ebelsberg, and there set them to cooking their food as if nothing was going to happen. Then it seems to have struck him that he ought to occupy the town and castle, so he sent a small force down, of which the chief constituents were three battalions of Vienna landwehr volunteers and three companies of the Lindenau regiment. The latter went to the castle, where Hiller took up his post, the rest were scattered about in a rather aimless way, and one battery was placed near the castle. No attempt at fortification seems to have been made.

[1] *Vide supra*, p. 228.

It is doubtful what it was that Marulaz had encountered in the defile of Wilhöring [1]; Binder von Krieglstein surmises it may have been one of Bianchi's battalions. The fire which met him from the woods beyond Linz was that of Vincent's men.

It was now 10 A.M. Marulaz drew up his French regiments across the road with his Germans in reserve. Opposed to him was the "Rosenberg" chevaux-légers regiment. The heavy fire from the woods north of Scharlinz necessitated an infantry attack which was made by Coehorn's brigade heading Claparède's division. As soon as Vincent saw this, he drew back to defend the northern side of Klein München. Just at this moment, Schustekh's rearguard began to arrive on Coehorn's right, marching from the south-west.

Here there is a considerable discrepancy between the Austrian and the French accounts. According to the former, Radetzky was attacked by Bessières with an overwhelming force, against which he made a brave stand whilst Schustekh's people got across the bridge. The French accounts, on the other hand, make no mention of this, though it is stated that Bessières arrived at this juncture from Wels. Instead, however, of the cuirassier divisions, which the Austrians represented him as having, he brought only one hussar and one chasseur regiment. The Austrians made a great deal of Radetzky's alleged action, and he received the cross of a Commander of the Theresa Order for his behaviour at Ebelsberg. Binder von Krieglstein's lengthy discussion of this story is scarcely worth following. He finally seems to be convinced that there is a deal of exaggeration in the Austrian account.

Coehorn's brigade now vigorously attacked Vincent (Brigade Hofmeister) in Klein München. The Austrian general sent back his cavalry regiment ("Rosenberg")

---

[1] *Supra*, p. 232.

over the river, and himself stood firm to cover the retreat of Schustekh and Radetzky. But Coehorn would not be denied. His men, breaking into Klein München after a short fire contest, attacked the Austrians in it with the bayonet, driving them out with heavy loss. Hofmeister, with what he could collect of his brigade, passed the first portion of the bridge over the mill stream, and again stood to fight at the entrance to the bridge over the main stream. Behind him on the bridge was great confusion amongst the fleeing troops, many of whom had already, in the struggle to get over, been knocked into the water by their comrades.

Hiller had given orders for preparations to fire the bridge the moment his men were over, and he now at last left his quarters in the castle to come to the front. Captain Simbschen of the staff was entrusted with the burning of the bridge, and he managed to be behind-hand.

Hofmeister's attempt to stop Coehorn on the left bank did not come to much. The French, headed by Claparède himself, opened a heavy fire on the Austrians, and just at that moment Bessières also came up with his two cavalry regiments. Hofmeister's men did not see any particular reason why they should be sacrificed when the rest of the army was safe over the river, and Vincent clinched the matter by ordering their retreat. To that they responded by making off in rapid flight across the bridge. The moment the French saw their opponents beginning to give ground, they rushed forward for the bridge with the bayonet, thus cutting off the Austrian wings on either side. Some of these troops, finding themselves unable to reach the bridge, tried to swim the Traun, in the waters of which many were drowned. Others fell, or were captured by the French. Claparède had got up some guns, and these opened fire on the Austrians endeavouring to fire the bridge. On the bridge itself there were frightful scenes of slaughter, for the French followed close on the heels of the fleeing Austrians, whilst the Austrian guns from beyond the river played on the crowd on the narrow footway, destroying friends as well as foes. Through the narrow gateway at the end of the bridge poured Austrians and French together into Ebelsberg, filling the little square below the castle.

The gallant Coehorn at once led his men to the left up the approach to the castle, driving before him a few Austrian infantry right up to the castle gate. Here the head of his column was met by a withering volley from the garrison, which compelled him to retreat hurriedly.

In the streets of Ebelsberg there commenced a fierce fight against the Austrians in the houses. Coehorn was weak in numbers and attacking at a great disadvantage up steep streets. It is probable that he was driven right back to the bridge tower, though many of his men held on to the houses near the river. Then arrived the other two brigades of Claparède's division, passing the bridge at the double in open order so as to avoid heavy loss from the Austrian guns, still playing on it from the castle heights. They restored the fight in the town, but the whole division was not sufficient to get through the place to the heights beyond, on which the Austrian main body was ready to meet them. Austrian troops swarmed in the town, and musketry fire was directed from every window and every roof upon Coehorn's men below. The castle, too, was still untaken, and it commanded a great part of the town and the bridge. The French had only got over two guns with their infantry, and these could not do much in this street fighting, whilst the Austrian battery on the castle hill could at least sweep the bridge.[1] Masséna had about 20 guns on the left bank of the Traun

---

[1] These two guns remained in the square till towards the close of the fight, when their commander, Moreton de Chabrillan, says he was told to get his ammunition out of the way, as the town was on fire and it might blow up.

above and below the bridge, but they could do little, seeing they were commanded by the enemy's batteries high above them within case-shot range. The Austrians certainly had not less guns than Masséna, though their number is not very certain.[1] From 10 A.M. till noon or later, Claparède's single division held out bravely against a vastly superior enemy, but could make little progress, and had failed to take the castle.

Where Hiller was and what he was doing at this time is not known. All that is certain is that he was not at the head of his troops in Ebelsberg after the French got over, and that he did nothing up to this time to bring in reinforcements from his troops on the heights, in order to destroy the isolated division of Claparède.

Masséna, seeing the necessity of reinforcing Claparède, had sent back to hurry up Legrand, who was some miles behind. It was a little after noon when Legrand arrived at the head of his division with Ledru, commanding the 1st brigade, consisting of the 26th regiment followed by the 18th. Masséna at once ordered the brigade across the bridge, one regiment to attack the castle, the other to turn to the right into the streets of the town. Crossing in open order the 26th lost but 5 or 6 men. Reforming in the square in sections, the regiment was sent up the narrow winding road, on its left, leading to the castle. There was only room on it for a front of 5 or 6 men.

Arriving at the top of this hollow road, the leading company was within 30 or 40 paces of the castle on its right. Silence reigned, not a man was to be seen; but as the regiment issued from the defile it was received with a volley, every shot of which told. The colonel (Pouget) alone was untouched.

The entrance to the castle was by a vaulted archway open at the outer end, but closed by a strong wooden gate at the inner end. Above was a window, closely

---

[1] *B. K.*, ii. 111-112.

barred with iron, and loopholes on either side. From all of these there poured a heavy fire, especially from the grated window. The losses of the besiegers, as they stood and returned the fire from the exposed space between the archway and the mouth of the hollow road, were fearful. Men crowded up to take part in the fight, which was directed by Pouget from the angle of the archway, whence he could see both his own men and the grated window. The French infantry fired as quickly as they could ; some even used the dead bodies of their comrades to raise them more on to a level with the window. Then Pouget sent for a well-known sportsman, Lieutenant Guyot, who, taking post within 5 yards of the window, poured in shots as fast as loaded muskets could be handed to him by the soldiers. Other picked marksmen joined him, and, at last, the Austrian fire began to fail. Sappers had now arrived and were at work breaking in the thick gate.

In the enthusiasm of the fight Colonel Baudinot and Sub-Lieutenant Gérard of the 2nd battalion had managed to get forward, though most of their battalion was blocked in the narrow road behind. These two intrepid men, followed by a few others as brave as themselves, managed to find a way by the cellar ventilators, whence they got into the castle. Between Gérard and a grenadier of the garrison, who entered a room on the first floor simultaneously, there was a desperate encounter, which was not interfered with by the entrance of a third visitor in the shape of an Austrian round shot. Just at this moment the gate was broken in, and the garrison, including, presumably, Gérard's grenadier, very soon surrendered as prisoners of war.[1]

Whilst the castle was being stormed by the 26th, or rather by the few leading companies which alone could find room, the 18th, followed by three Baden battalions,

[1] For this account of the storming of the castle, see *Saski*, iii. 136 n.

had completely cleared the Austrians out of Ebelsberg, driving them on to the slopes above. An attempt to follow on to the heights was not so successful, and was repulsed for the moment. Presently, however, the French and Baden troops began to get forward, the 26th issuing from the farther gate of the castle. The time was after 4 P.M., and the French were cut off alike from retreat, from reinforcements, and from their artillery by the town and the castle, now everywhere in flames.

Hiller, meanwhile, had chosen this moment to order a retreat, just when another serious effort would probably have driven Claparède's and Legrand's divisions back into the burning town. On the heights, not a thousand paces from the eastern side of Ebelsberg, he had whole regiments of infantry and cavalry, with many guns, absolutely doing nothing.

The French could do little in the way of pursuit, for they were weak in numbers and their hands were more than full with the task of quelling the flames which rendered Ebelsberg impossible of passage for cavalry and artillery. The whole place was on fire, nothing was undamaged, save the one thing the Austrians should have destroyed—the bridge.

Hiller, with the V. and VI. corps, started his retreat about 5 P.M. At Asten he picked up the II. Reserve, and the whole, except a rearguard of two cavalry regiments, Bianchi's brigade, and another battalion, reached Enns without further serious mishap. The rearguard was not followed beyond Asten by Marulaz's light cavalry.

In this desperate battle the French had in or opposite Ebelsberg the following forces :—Claparède's division of, at the highest estimate, 8400 men ; Legrand's of 10,000 (4000 French and 6000 Germans) ; Marulaz's cavalry, 2500 ; and Piré's two cavalry regiments, 1200—total, 22,100. The estimated strengths are those arrived at by Binder v. Krieglstein, but he admits they are very

high, and is clearly of opinion that they are excessive.
The French had 20 guns.

Hiller, on the other hand, had, at the very lowest
estimate, at Ebelsberg 22,000 men with 70 guns. This of
course does not include the II. Reserve corps which, with
4500 infantry and 800 cavalry was at Asten ; nor does
it include Nordmann's brigade of 3000 towards Lambach,
nor the dragoon regiment sent across the Danube from
Linz. On the whole, the French were, even in mere
numbers, distinctly inferior to their opponents.   But
they had many other disadvantages to contend against.
Hiller had all his men ready to hand, whilst Masséna
could not get up Legrand's division till after noon.
Hiller had, too, an immensely strong position which he
ought to have been able to hold.   In the action on the
left bank of the Traun, the French infantry of Coehorn's
brigade was only 4000 strong, against 12,000 Austrian
infantry.   Marulaz's cavalry (2500) was not very superior
in numbers to the Austrian (2000).   Even when
Claparède's whole division was up and in Ebelsberg, he
had little more than half the strength of the Austrians in
the place, into which they had been driven and followed by
a very inferior force.   Even when Legrand arrived, raising
the attacking force to 18,000, at a more than liberally high
estimate, the Austrians had been raised by reinforcements
to 16,000, and they had all the advantage of the slope of
ground, of the defence of houses, and of the castle.
The French cavalry, except a few of Marulaz's, were
unable to pass the bridge into the town, and, if they had
got there, would of course have been useless.   Of the
6000 Hessian and Baden troops in Legrand's division
only a small portion actually fought.   Yet the French
cleared the town and broke out at the farther side.
Hiller's conduct of the fight was as feeble as it could
possibly be.   He was content with a purely passive
defence, never attempting, by bringing down his men

Q

from the heights into the town, to destroy Claparède's division, as he ought to have been able easily to do during the two hours it was fighting alone. At least he should have been able to drive it back over the bridge, and complete the destruction of the only possible means of crossing this rapid and deep river.

Binder v. Krieglstein's verdict is that a man who could fail so hopelessly in such a position, who could rest content with a passive defensive when the least enterprise should have assured a serious check for Masséna, is not worthy of the name of a general. The condemnation seems hardly too strong. He had not the excuse of inferior troops, for Masséna justly says that the "enemy defended himself like a lion." That is true of the Austrian soldiery, but what could they do when they were so miserably handled by their commanders? The losses were naturally very heavy, though it is, as usual, difficult to say precisely what they were. French returns are often missing, and when they are given they are not often very reliable. Legrand alone gives his killed and wounded at 701, out of the 4000 French who were almost all that he engaged. The Baden brigade only lost 23 men. Masséna says he lost altogether 2800, of whom 1880 were killed. The proportion of killed to wounded is incredible. Even at that rate, Claparède must have lost 2100 (2800 − 700 Legrand) out of 8400—25 per cent. of his whole force.

The Austrians give their loss at about 2000 killed and wounded, 2200 prisoners. Masséna estimated his prisoners at 7000 or 8000. Probably the actual numbers were intermediate between these figures.[1] Masséna also says he took 2 guns and 2 flags, of which the Austrians make no mention.

Napoleon's letter of 3 P.M.[2] shows that, at that hour,

[1] Napoleon next day, writing to Lannes, put it at 4000.
[2] *Vide supra*, p. 232.

he was unaware of the action which had been proceeding
for the past five hours at Ebelsberg. He got his first
news soon after 3, and at once ordered Durosnel, with
the 9th hussars, to make for Ebelsberg by the right
bank of the Traun, followed by Nansouty.   Molitor,
who was on the march from Lambach to Kremsmünster,
was diverted to Ebelsberg, where he arrived, in company
with the Emperor, towards evening.   Masséna had,
meanwhile, gone back to Linz, thinking the Emperor
would go there. He was called up to Ebelsberg with
the whole of his corps.   Napoleon had evidently been
alarmed when he heard of the frontal attack on Ebelsberg ; for, next day, he wrote to Lannes : " As soon as
I knew that they had had the stupidity to attack by
force this famous position, and the only redoubtable one
on the Traun which it was necessary to take, I feared
some misfortune." Meanwhile, Lannes wrote, at 5.30
P.M. on the 3rd, that, on hearing from Berthier of the
passage at Ebelsberg, he had ordered Durosnel to Neu-
hofen with the 9th hussars, whilst Colbert with his other
two regiments moved on Steyer.   St Hilaire could not
do more than get to Kremsmünster this day (3rd), and
to Steyer next morning.   Lannes himself would be at
Kremsmünster, from which place he was writing, for the
night.   He was ordering Demont to march in the morning from Lambach on Steyer.   Vandamme, who was
wounded, was a few miles south-west of Wels, and,
hearing of Austrian infantry and cavalry in front of him,
was sending a large detachment after them.

Davout had Morand at St Willibald, Friant at Eisen-
bruck, Gudin at Passau, Dupas marching on Passau to
reach it next day.   Davout had orders to arrive at Linz
on the 5th with his whole corps, except Dupas and
Rouyer, who were to stop at Passau.   He also sends a
report of Montbrun regarding the troops flanking Charles
march on Budweis and Krems.   He adds : " He (Charles)

must be a long way off ; that is not surprising, as the roads in Bohemia are extremely bad."

Hiller, as we know, reached Enns on the night of the 3rd, and was greeted with two pieces of bad news. He heard that the enemy had already reached Steyer, which was not true. He also heard, and that *was* true, that the bridge at Mauthausen was no longer practicable. Two burning cargo boats had floated down against it in the afternoon, striking it with such force as to break it and compel the withdrawal of the remaining boats constituting it.[1] He accordingly decided not to attempt to hold the line of the Enns. Ordering the remains of the Mauthausen bridge to be floated down to Krems, he marched for Strengberg and Amstetten, with Reinwald's brigade and a hussar regiment, commanded by Schustekh, for rearguard. One battalion and one squadron were left behind at Ennsdorf.[2] These had orders to burn the bridge, and to hold the crossing for 36 hours. Nordmann was, with 2 battalions of regulars, one of newly arrived landwehr and a few hussars, in Steyer on the 3rd. He left on the morning of the 4th as Lannes approached. The bridge-burning at both Enns and Steyer was so effectually done as to cause serious delay to the French, and to give Heller a good start on his way to Krems. That was the point at which he must endeavour to cross to the left bank.

He was now ordered to make for Krems, and he was also relieved of the presence of the Austrian Emperor who had been at the bottom of the decision to retire from Linz behind the Traun. Probably Charles knew this quite well, but thought it wiser to throw the whole blame

---

[1] Saski (iii. 155 n.) merely says the boat bridge had been withdrawn, which seems to point to the burning boats having floated down by accident. Had they been despatched purposely it is hardly likely the French accounts would not have mentioned the fact.

[2] On the right bank of the Enns opposite the town of Enns. Hiller had received, at Enns, a reinforcement of 6 landwehr battalions.

on Hiller, and the Emperor was not man enough to own up that he had been interfering and leading Hiller astray.

We may leave Hiller for the moment to return to Napoleon, who, reaching Enns on the morning of the 4th, found himself as badly held up as he had been a few days before on the Salzach. Do what he would, it was only in the night of the 5th-6th that the restoration of the bridge over the Enns was completed, and it was only at the same time that some boats could be got up, with great difficulty, from the Danube, for another bridge for the artillery. Lannes, at Steyer, was able to construct a bridge of boats, but, with the left wing held fast at Enns, it was not safe for him to push on.

Napoleon's objective being Vienna, he wished to push Hiller on as fast as possible, so as to prevent his re-union with Charles at Krems. Whilst making all possible arrangements for this, he found himself forced to cast an anxious eye upon his ever-lengthening line of communications, and to guard, not only against the possibility of Charles turning back against that line, but also against dangers to it from the insurrection in the Tyrol and the Vorarlberg, as well as from small raids from Bohemia, and from popular outbreaks in Bavaria, Baden, or Wurtemberg. North Germany, too, was becoming more and more a source of anxiety to him. We will take the opportunity of the enforced halt at Enns to note, anticipating to some extent, the arrangements made by Napoleon to meet these dangers.

In the first place he created another reserve division, in addition to that which he now calls the " Corps of Observation of the Weser," [1] under Kellerman. The new division was to be under Beaumont, with its centre at Augsburg. It was to consist of Beaumont's 5 provisional regiments of dragoons, the Berg regiment of infantry, a

---

[1] This is what he formerly called the " Corps of Observation of the Elbe."

Wurtemberg regiment, several miscellaneous bodies drawn from Bavaria, and a couple of batteries. Altogether, Napoleon hoped to get together 6000 men. Beaumont could thus have three movable columns, each of 500 cavalry, 500 infantry, and 2 guns, with a central reserve of 3000 infantry, and 6 guns at Augsburg. His objects were to be, (1) to stop incursions from the Tyrol, (2) to prevent local insurrections in the allied States, (3) to prevent small raids from Bohemia, (4) to preserve Augsburg, before all things, and to retire into it if his columns were attacked in great force.

Davout, still nervous about Charles' movements, kept sending in reports that the Archduke was staying in Bohemia, sending only a detachment to Vienna. The marshal was puzzled by the flank guard (Klenau and Stutterheim) which Montbrun kept coming across on the north bank. He evidently still thought it possible Charles might break back against the communications of the French army. Napoleon's orders to him were to stop at Linz for the present, to restore the bridge and fortify a bridge-head on the north bank. When that was done, he could send a column to gather information about the movements in Bohemia. Dupas, at Passau, was to hurry on defensive works so that, in eight or ten days, he might be safe against all attack. He was to have detachments out towards Deggendorf, and small columns, of 400 or 500 men, moving up and down the Danube, to look out for raids, whilst the main body of the division was concentrated at Passau.

Vandamme was sent up to Linz to be in charge of the place and of the reorganisation of the government of the province. He was to be under Davout so long as that marshal was there. As, however, Vandamme was notoriously quarrelsome, and had already in previous campaigns fallen foul of Soult and Ney, the Emperor thought it well to give Davout a hint in the words, "traitez bien le général Vandamme, et ne vous disputez pas."

Vandamme lost no time on arrival at Linz, on the night of the 4th.[1] He summoned the Austrian commander[2] on the north bank to surrender the boats he had there. That demand being refused, Vandamme next morning bombarded the Austrians across the river, and then, sending a force across in boats, captured nearly the whole of the brigade.

Bernadotte was moving very slowly, and, so late as the 6th, was still at Rötz. Meanwhile, orders had gone to him to reach Passau on the 9th. If he found a detachment of the enemy there, inferior to himself and Dupas combined, they were to be attacked. If there were no movements against the communications, Bernadotte would probably be called up to Linz.

It is in his letter of the 6th that Bernadotte mentions that "the chief of brigands, Schill," has cut off communication with Wittenberg, and that Prussia is generally reported to be arming. He begs for French troops, as his Saxons were less in numbers than represented,[3] and were mostly recruits who could not march properly.

On the French right, too, Lefebvre was in difficulties, having constant small fights and having to report the repulse, on the road to Kufstein, of Vincenti (4 battalions, 3 squadrons, and 3 guns) by 7000 or 8000 insurgents, with a backing of Austrian troops. To his rescue 2 battalions were being sent.

This drew down a storm from headquarters.[4] It was ridiculous, the Emperor considered, to send only 2 battalions to Vincenti's assistance. Lefebvre should

[1] Davout's corps was still on the road from Passau.
[2] This was Richter, who, with a landwehr brigade, had blockaded Passau on the north. When he left it, he marched by the left bank to opposite Linz.
[3] He believed he had only 12,000 or 13,000.
[4] Berthier to Lefebvre, 6th May.

leave only a sufficient garrison in the citadel of Salzburg and march with all the rest to the relief of Kufstein, which was of great importance. If Jelacic's force towards Radstadt threatened trouble, Lefebvre could call up Wrede. Wrede was ordered back to Strasswaldchen in order to be at hand.

The bridge of boats at Enns being finished on the night of the 5th-6th, Bessières crossed, his advance guard (Colbert) coming up with the Austrian rearguard at Amstetten at 10 A.M. There was a sharp cavalry fight at Neumarkt on the Ybbs, where St Hilaire had also arrived,[1] and Colbert, pursuing the beaten enemy closely, managed to capture the bridge. The enemy were retiring on St Polten. Behind St Hilaire, Oudinot, Boudet, and Claparède were marching on Neumarkt.

At 8.30 P.M. on the 6th, orders were issued to Masséna to march next morning on Amstetten. Lannes, at the same hour, was ordered to move on Mölk, unless unforeseen circumstances forced him to take up a position short of it.

At 10 P.M. a letter went to Davout, informing him of the positions and giving him instructions. He had received 300,000 rations which he was to send down in boats along the Danube. The boats, in addition to carrying supplies, would be useful hereafter for a bridge. As for the bridge-head opposite Linz, the Emperor had constructed one in 1805. What was required was a sort of entrenched camp, in which 10,000 men could defend themselves against 30,000 or 40,000, with a *réduit*. This letter crossed one from Davout, in which he raised difficulties regarding a bridge-head, which he said would be commanded at musket-range from the heights above, the latter being too extensive for occupation. Hiller this evening reached Mölk, where he received Charles' order of the 4th and 5th, ordering him

---

[1] He had bivouacked at St Peter.

to join the main army by Krems. Thereupon, he issued
orders for his own march to Mautern on the 7th, whilst
Dedowich was to command the force retreating on
Vienna by the right bank. To him were assigned 21
battalions and 20 squadrons, making a trifle over 10,000
men. Nordmann's and Provenchère's [1] cavalry brigades
were already on the march to Vienna, making *détours*
to avoid contact with the French.

At 3 A.M. on the 7th, Hiller and Dedowich parted
company, the latter going by St Polten to Kapellen.
Hiller sent the infantry of the V. corps to Bergern,
whilst he, with the rest, went to Meidling and Göttweig.
Beyond some patrols, they saw nothing of the enemy.

Bessières was at Mölk by noon of the 7th, and reported that all accounts pointed to the enemy's intention
to stand and fight at St Polten ; this he qualified, at the
end of the despatch, by the remark that some said Hiller
was going over the Danube to meet Charles in Moravia.

Meanwhile, Napoleon had sent orders to Masséna to
start on the morning of the 8th for Mölk, and also to
send detachments to guard the Danube and stop all
boats not belonging to the army. To Davout the
Emperor wrote that he should send a division to Enns,
where the Guard was expected on the 7th. Charles
might be moving on Linz, but the Emperor believed
Krems to be his destination. Davout was, therefore, to
be ready to march the 64 miles to Mölk in two days.
Davout still thought Charles was barricading himself in
Bohemia. Bessières' report, just mentioned, rather
puzzled the Emperor, so, as usual in such cases,[2] he sent
Savary with 150 cavalry to clear up the situation towards

---

[1] This brigade belonged to Jelacic's division, but, as cavalry was useless
to him in the mountains, he had sent it back to Hiller on the 1st May.

[2] This had been done several times in the campaigns of 1806 and 1807.
It was on the night of the 7th-8th that Marbot carried out his famous reconnaissance across the Danube for the capture of prisoners. From them it was
ascertained, almost with certainty, that Hiller was across the river.

Mautern. By the afternoon of the 8th, the military detective was able to report, from near St Polten, that part of Hiller's force was across the Danube, whilst 15,000 men had been left to march on Vienna by the right bank. At 7 P.M. on the 8th, Savary was at the Abbey of Göttweig, whence he reported that he could see the Austrian bridge all ready for burning, whilst he was prevented from getting into Mautern by the presence of Austrian infantry. The monks told him they had seen great numbers passing the river and marching partly on Vienna, and partly towards Budweis. He also heard that Charles had been at Budweis four days previously, and would probably be at Vienna on the 10th. He describes the position at Mautern, and shows that it is as impossible for the Austrians as for the French to cross there in face even of an inferior force.

By the evening of the 8th, Napoleon's army had reached the following positions. Colbert with the point of the advance guard was near Sieghardtskirchen, whence he reported 10,000 men in front of him on the Vienna road. Bruyère and Marulaz at St Polten, Massena at Mölk, Guard at Neumarkt, the two cuirassier divisions behind it. Davout was, with Morand and Vandamme, at Linz, where he was constructing a strong *tête-de-pont* on the left bank with a triple line of works. Gudin was on the way to Mölk, which he was to reach on the 9th, followed by Friant.

Lefebvre reported that he was marching on Kufstein, with Wrede and Deroy, whilst the Crown Prince remained at Salzburg, which was safe from attack in so far as concerned the part on the left bank of the Salzach, and would shortly be on the right also. The Austrian general Chasteler, he had ascertained, was at Innsbruck.

By midnight, then, Napoleon knew that Hiller had crossed the Danube, leaving 10,000 men to retreat to

Vienna direct on the right bank.   There was nothing in
front to hinder the French march to the capital.

Hiller had started his crossing at 3 A.M. on the 8th,
with the baggage.   The combatant forces followed, and
were all over by noon, except Radetzky, left with a
strong rearguard in Mautern on the south bank.   In the
evening, after the appearance of Savary, Radetzky also
crossed, and safely swung the bridge of boats over to
the left bank.

That night the V. Corps was at Lengenfeld and
Stratzing, the VI. at Hadersdorf, the II. Reserve at
Langenlois.   Dedowich's column was at Sieghardtskirchen.

At 2 A.M. on the 9th, Napoleon writes to Bessières and
Savary that, as it is impossible to cross at Mautern, the
Austrians had better be forced, by an attack, to burn
their bridge.   St Hilaire could help if required.   At
6 A.M. Savary reported that Mautern had been evacuated and two arches of the bridge [1] destroyed, which
could be repaired in about four hours, but that would be
easier for the Austrians than for the French to do, as
the former were better supplied with wood.   Everything,
however, pointed to an Austrian retreat on Vienna.

The Emperor now ordered the supplies of food sent
down by boat to be taken off at Mölk and moved by
land to St Polten ; to send them further by water would
be to take them far north of the army's line.

The Archduke Maximilian had been appointed to the
command in Vienna, and a copy of his proclamation,
calling on the Viennese to offer a stubborn resistance,
fell into the hands of Bruyère at Traisen, who sent it to
the Emperor.   There is a perfect deluge of orders by
the Emperor on this day which we can only summarise
very briefly.

At 2 A.M. Masséna was ordered to echelon his

---

[1] It would appear that there was a permanent bridge at Mautern, as well as
one of boats.

divisions between St Polten and Mölk; the Emperor was at the former. Next morning Masséna would march on Vienna.

Davout was instructed as to his duties in watching the Danube; he was to reconnoitre towards Steyer, and to use his own discretion as to whether he would keep Morand at Linz, or send him on to Enns. Then, later, there were more instructions as to his action in case Charles operated on the rear. He was to instruct Vandamme clearly as to his duties at Linz. What was Dupas doing? Where was Bernadotte? He *ought* to be between Passau and Linz. The Emperor believed Charles was making for Vienna, but was still not certain. Davout's reiterated suspicions, that the Archduke was hanging back in Bohemia, rendered him still more uncertain. Davout had better stay at Linz himself for the present, and not press on his two leading divisions too fast, in case they were required back at Linz. These orders issued at 4 A.M. Later on, Napoleon, hearing that Charles was marching on Zwettel from Budweis, writes (6 P.M.) to Davout to concentrate on St Polten on the 10th, though the detention of Morand at Linz was still left to his discretion. If this was not necessary, Morand should be at St Polten in three days, whilst Davout himself should be there on the 10th with Gudin and Friant. Montbrun was to watch Mautern, supported, if necessary, by Gudin.

Lefebvre again comes in for strong language. He is told that, up to the present, "il n'a fait que de petits paquets"; the Emperor is much exercised on the subject of incursions from the Tyrol, threatening Augsburg and the communications. Both Bernadotte and Lefebvre are warned to be on the look-out for these, and the latter is directed to march on Innsbruck, if there were such incursions, leaving strong forces to garrison Salzburg and watch Radstadt. His business was to relieve Kufstein and overawe the Tyrolese, which in the last 4 or 5 days he had failed to do.

To Moulin, commanding at Augsburg, Napoleon conveyed approval of his action in detaining drafts on the way to the army, since there were rumours that Chasteler had 22,000 men.

To Beaumont orders were sent to hurry up the organisation of his reserve division. All this shows how extremely anxious the Emperor was about the safety of his rear. Bernadotte was ordered to approach Linz. He was at Straubing on this date (9th).

The only fighting this day was at Sieghardtskirchen, where Lannes arrived with Oudinot by 9 A.M. Finding Dedowich, who did not intend moving, Lannes promptly attacked and drove him back with some loss on Purkersdorf.

At night the following positions were held by the French : Oudinot at Sieghardtskirchen ; St Hilaire somewhere on the road from Mautern to Vienna ;[1] Claparède and Demont north-east of St Polten ; Legrand at St Polten ; St Cyr at Gerasdorf ; Boudet at Markersdorf ; Molitor and Gudin at Mölk ; Montbrun south-east of Mölk ; Friant a few miles behind Gudin ; and Morand at Linz. Bessières, with Espagne's cuirassiers and Jacquinot, was near Diendorf ; Piré at Traismauer, Colbert in front of Sieghardtskirchen.

Hiller, on the 9th, was resting peacefully in his positions of the previous night when he received an order from Maximilian from Vienna to march thither. But, as his orders from the Commander-in-chief were to join the main army with his three corps, he thought it best to take one of his usual half measures by sending the II. Reserve corps alone to Kirchberg. At 2 A.M. on the 10th, Lannes, as ordered overnight, started for

---

[1] His exact position is unknown. He turned towards Vienna when it was known his assistance was not required at Mautern.

Vienna, Oudinot's division leading, followed by St Hilaire and Claparède. Colbert's cavalry was in front of all. At 9 A.M. the head of the French army was, for the second time in less than four years, before the Austrian capital.

The city on the right bank of the Danube consisted of an outer portion of unfortified faubourgs, and of an inner portion with the small branch of the river behind it, separating it from the large island on which is the Prater and the suburb of Leopoldstadt. Round the southern side of this inner city there was a series of bastioned fronts, the site of which is now marked by the great semi-circle of boulevards known as the Ring. Between the bastioned enceinte and the faubourgs was a glacis or esplanade with a width of over 300 yards. The enceinte was insufficiently armed with 48 guns. The garrison consisted, according to von Angeli, of about 35,000 men, namely—

(1) 14 battalions of Austrian and Moravian land-wehr, and 6000 citizen militiamen—all under O'Reilly, who was in charge of the defence on the right bank.

(2) Dedowich's division of 8⅓ battalions of the line, 6 battalions of Austrian landwehr, and 6 of Viennese volunteers.

(3) Kienmayer's reserve of the grenadiers of the II. Reserve corps.

(4) Mesko's and Nordmann's brigade of 4 battalions and 5 squadrons which, though joining in the defence, did not strictly belong to the garrison.[1]

The divisions of St Hilaire and Claparède took post outside the faubourg of Mariahilf, whilst Oudinot marched into it and debouched on the esplanade. There the French were received with artillery fire. Lannes, having thus ascertained that resistance was to be expected, withdrew Oudinot's men into the shelter of the faubourg,

[1] *Angeli*, iv. 260.

and formed a line of posts round the inner city, with its flanks resting on the Danube. The day was spent in an exchange of artillery fire between the garrison and Lannes' troops.

Colbert, sent to watch the roads leading from Hungary, reported, in the course of the day, that it seemed probable that the Hungarians would not take an active part.

During the day, in accordance with orders of the previous evening, Masséna's leading division (Legrand) reached Purkersdorf, the others behind it. Marulaz was before Vienna by 3 P.M.,[1] and the Emperor took up his quarters, as in 1805, at the Palace of Schönbrünn. Thence he sent, through Berthier, a formal summons to the Archduke Maximilian to surrender. The bearer of Lannes' summons in the morning had not been returned. The Emperor's summons was rather of the nature of a lecture to Maximilian on his duties ; it was delivered only at 10 A.M. on the 11th, and was not replied to. Savary reported that the Austrians had burnt the bridge at Mautern.

Marulaz was now ordered to relieve Colbert in the watch towards Hungary. Davout had decided to leave Morand at Linz for the present, and Bernadotte wrote (on the 10th) that he hoped to reach Passau on the 11th or 12th. Masséna was ordered to send two divisions to Schönbrünn, to keep one at Purkersdorf, and one at Sieghardtskirchen. In the morning of the 11th, Napoleon reconnoitred Vienna and ordered preparations for its bombardment in the evening. He also ordered reconnaissances of favourable places for throwing a bridge both above and below the city. He then went with Boudet's division to reconnoitre a place of passage to the Prater island, the capture of which would turn the defence on the right bank. Across the narrow branch

---

[1] A march of 44 miles.

south of the island, towards its lower extremity, an
A.D.C. of Berthier swam with some men and brought
over boats and rafts, under protection of a heavy
fire from Boudet's artillery. A voltigeur company was
then ferried over and established itself in the pleasure
pavilion (Lusthaus), where it was attacked by two
Austrian battalions whom it beat off, with the help
of the artillery on the right bank. Meanwhile, the
bridge was pushed on.

The bombardment commenced at 9 P.M., some 1800
shells being fired into the city in four hours. Between
3 and 4 A.M. on the 12th, a fresh attack, by 5 Austrian
battalions under d'Aspre, was repulsed by the defenders
of the Lusthaus and Boudet's artillery. At 11 A.M.,
Boudet's division, followed by those of Legrand and
Carra St Cyr, crossing to the island, advanced on the
suburb of Leopoldstadt, right in rear of the inner
city. Marulaz, with the 14th chasseurs, led the advance,
whilst Molitor watched the Pressburg road. The first
of the French were fired on by artillery as they passed
into Leopoldstadt, but very soon afterwards the white
flag was hung out.

Maximilian was young and without experience in war ;
the bombardment and the capture by the French of the
Lusthaus on the previous day were enough for him.
He called a council of war in the night of the 11th-12th,
at which it was decided that Vienna must be evacuated
by a retreat to the left bank, and the bridges must be
burnt. D'Aspre's attack on the Lusthaus really covered
the evacuation, which was begun in the early morning,
Maximilian leading the way. O'Reilly was left behind
to capitulate with a few depôts. A great part of the
city militia, volunteers, etc., seem to have gone to their
homes.[1]

---

[1] See Schulmeister's report in " L'espionnage militaire sous Napoleon I.,"
p. 145.

Maximilian had got away with the best of his troops, but had left in Vienna with O'Reilly no less than 13 generals, 17 staff officers, and 163 captains and sub-alterns, with 2000 men. Nor had he made any attempt to carry off the heavy artillery, or to destroy the stores of food, ammunition, and arms. As many as 100 guns fell into the hands of the French when the capitulation was finally arranged, at 2 A.M. on the 13th. Also a treasure chest with 4½ million gulden (£450,000). On the 12th, there were still divergent views as to the Austrian movements north of the Danube. Napoleon agreed with Davout that Charles had gone to Moravia ; Vandamme asserted that he was marching on Brünn or Znaim. As we know, he was actually, on this date, 60 miles or more to the north-west of the capital.

Hiller, meanwhile, had remained at Krems till the night of the 9th-10th. At 2 A.M. on the latter day, orders had reached him from Charles directing him to leave about 8000 men at Krems, and, with the rest, to take up a position between that place and Vienna. If the French had already crossed the river, he would retire on Maissau towards Charles. These orders he carried out by sending the II. Reserve corps on to Am Spitz (on the north bank opposite Vienna), leaving Schustekh with 9000 men and 13 guns at Krems, and marching with the rest 28 miles to Korneuburg. He had two divisions at Lang-Enzersdorf, one at Jedlersee, and Radetzky, with one battalion and eight squadrons at Stockerau, making a link with Schustekh at Krems. From the II. Reserve Kienmayer was sent, with d'Aspre's brigade, as reserve to Vienna. When, on the 12th, Hiller heard of the approaching fall of the capital, he only thought of retirement towards the main army, without attempting to hinder the French from crossing. When he had got back his forward corps to Stammers-dorf, he stopped again, as the French had made no

R

attempt to cross, and he even kept his advance guard (Nordmann) at Am Spitz.

Napoleon was still getting bad news from the rear. Beaumont, at Augsburg, wrote that there were 3000 insurgents at Memmingen and Lindau, against whom he was marching ; but his force was less than the Emperor imagined, for Moulin, after all, had not stopped the drafts.[1]

[1] *Supra*, p. 253.

CHAPTER XIII

VIENNA

NAPOLEON, established at Vienna on the 13th May, had still before him the greater part of his task; for the Archduke Charles stood on the north bank, still some way from Vienna, with an army which, when united with Hiller, would number about 130,000 men. The destruction or defeat of that army was the true objective of the French, the substantial objective which the Emperor had abandoned temporarily for the shadowy advantage of the occupation of the enemy's capital. He had occupied it in 1805 without being able to exact peace before the crowning victory of Austerlitz; he had again taken it without being any nearer peace than he was in November 1805. His position, in 1809, was not so good as it was in 1805; for in the latter year he had succeeded in acquiring the passage of the river; whilst now the bridges had been burnt and a crossing was opposed by an army of unknown strength. What the Emperor required was a bridge-head on the left bank, by which he could debouch when it should suit him. He did not necessarily want to pass his whole army over at once, for then the Archduke might have crossed above him, severing his communications with France, and compelling him to fight for bare existence with his face towards home, as he himself had compelled the Prussians to fight at Jena in 1806. For once the taking of the initiative was not altogether desirable, though the

command of it was. The author once saw, on a High-
land mountain, a shepherd's dog meet a blue hare
coming down hill. The hare was just in time to stop
before he ran into the dog's jaws. Both sat down, facing
one another at 2 or 3 yards' distance, and for some time
neither moved. At last the hare made an attempt to
escape to one side, when the dog was on him in an
instant. If the dog had moved first the hare would have
escaped, to one side or the other. Napoleon was in the
position of the dog. If he crossed the Danube with his
whole army, whilst Charles was still at some distance
from Vienna, the latter would have had time to cross at
Krems, or higher up, and the Emperor would have found
himself, not with an escaping enemy before him, but
with one standing across his line of communications,
and using the supplies meant for the French army.
There was still that danger when Napoleon was at
Vienna and Charles north of Krems. The Emperor
had to take infinite precautions against a crossing in
his rear, and to keep back a large part of his army to
meet it. Here is what he afterwards said in his " Notes
sur l'art de la guerre " at St Helena.

"In the meantime, the Archduke Charles was approaching by the left bank of the Danube. The Emperor
resolved to anticipate him and pass on to that bank.
The position on the right bank was good only on condition of possessing a 'tête de pont' on the left bank,
because without that the enemy would be master of the
initiative. That consideration was of such importance
that Napoleon would have placed himself on the Enns,
if it had been impossible to establish a bridge-head on
the left bank. To pass a great river in face of such an
army seemed impossible, but the idea of moving to a
distance could not be entertained for fear the enemy,
who had two bridge trains, should move on Vienna."
The last words show the undue importance which the

Emperor still attached to possession of the capital, as compared with the paramount object of defeating the enemy's army.

On the 7th May, Napoleon had written to Davout : " I suppose that Prince Charles is taking the direction of Krems, where I hope you will arrive before him. I hope to have enough boats to throw a bridge there, and perhaps I shall then decide to manœuvre on both banks." On the evening of the 12th, he wrote to his step-son, Eugène Beauharnais : " It appears that whatever enemies are here are rallying in Moravia." In that view of the case he naturally thought of crossing the river, for the enemy would be too far north and east to be able to cross in his rear. He apparently expected only to find Hiller and the Vienna garrison near the river.

During the morning of the 13th, Bertrand had ascertained that it was hopeless to attempt to restore the Vienna bridges. There had been altogether four wooden bridges over the four branches of the Danube, and they were all burnt, or destroyed beyond repair.

The Emperor then wrote to Songis that he proposed throwing one bridge at Nussdorf above Vienna, where he had one in 1805, and one at the best place that could be found between Vienna and Pressburg.

Songis reported the same day to the following effect :—

(1) Between Fischamend and Orth the banks were so high and steep that, if a bridge were thrown, it would be very difficult to have access to it.

(2) The banks would be more suitable at Fischamend, where there was an island in the stream, but it would want 80 boats at least, as the river was 600 or 700 yards wide.

(3) Opposite Kaiser-Ebersdorf was the best place, as the river was narrower, and sand banks in its course would enable trestles to be used, thus economising boats.

(4) Songis recommended Nussdorf only, unless the

Emperor was determined to have a bridge below Vienna also. At Nussdorf, though the banks were high, there existed the abutments of a road on either side, which could be utilised.

The Emperor promptly decided for Kaiser-Ebersdorf, and ordered Masséna to employ all his sappers, pontoniers, and engineer officers, as well as Molitor's division, on the work. He thought 50 boats were available, and they ought to suffice.

To Lannes was confided the bridge at Nussdorf, a scheme which was never carried out. St Hilaire's division had moved to Nussdorf in the morning. The first thing to be done was to send a detachment to the left flank to protect the construction. The voltigeurs who went over found themselves, not on the mainland, but on an island separated from it by a channel which appeared at first not to be fordable, though it was afterwards found to be so, and to be crossed by a dyke. The voltigeurs were fired on, suffered some loss, and were compelled to return. There was also very little bridging material, and only three boats.

The Emperor now arriving, 700 or 800 men were passed over, but they were attacked by very superior forces which crossed the small arm by the dyke, or in boats. The French, notwithstanding the support of artillery on the right bank, were gradually driven to the extremity of the island, where 700 of them had to surrender.

The Emperor practically decided to give up the Nussdorf crossing, unless as a diversion, and to rely on Masséna's bridge at Kaiser-Ebersdorf. On this day (13th) Davout is censured for his and Vandamme's rash use of detachments, of 400 or more men, reconnoitring far from Linz beyond the river and along the left bank. Some of these, such as that of Major Ameil, were characterised rather by reckless daring than by conformity to the rules of war. Ameil's own account[1] of how he pushed down the left bank to opposite the mouth of the Ybbs, and then cut his way back, is as entertaining as Marbot. The Emperor, however, only remarked on it, "This man is a madman, to whom the chief command of an expedition should never be given."[2]

On the 14th, Napoleon threw out a cavalry screen to protect his operations from the south and east. Montbrun, with Jacquinot's and Piré's brigades, was sent to intercept the road leading from Pressburg to Italy, and to cover the country between the Neusiedl lake and the Danube. Marulaz to act as second line on the left; Colbert to cover from the lake westwards to Wiener-Neustadt; Nansouty, at Laxemberg, and Espagne, at Hinberg, would be in support of Montbrun south-east of Vienna. Bruyère, when he came up, was to go to Bruck on the Leitha, under Montbrun's command.

The news from Lefebvre was now better. After various small encounters with insurgents, he had come up with Chasteler at Wörgl, on the Inn, where he had inflicted a serious defeat on the Austrians, capturing over 600 prisoners and 11 guns. Deroy, meanwhile, had relieved Kufstein.[3]

Lauriston was now operating with the Baden brigade of the 4th corps (6000 men) towards Altenmarkt, where his principal duty, for the present, was to reconnoitre southwards and to suppress popular outbreaks. It was his arrival which enabled Bruyère to be sent to Montbrun.

Bernadotte was echeloned between Passau and Linz, in consequence of orders of the 12th. These orders the Emperor appears to have forgotten, for he writes (15th) assuming him to be at Linz where, including

---

[1] *Sakhi*, iii. 278 *n*.   [2] *Ibid.* 284.

[3] It is in the postscript to this report that Lefebvre complains of the absence of rewards for his division, and also of the jealousy of Wrede, with whom he finds it difficult to get on, even by pocketing his pride. *Saski*, iii. 276.

Vandamme, there should be about 26,000 infantry and 4000 cavalry. Bernadotte had suffered a good deal from contradictory orders from headquarters.

On the 16th May, the two portions of the Austrian army, which had been driven asunder on the 20th April, were at last reunited by the arrival of the Archduke Charles, with the exception of the III. corps under Kolowrat.

On the night of the 16th May the Austrian positions and strengths were these :—

	Infantry.	Cavalry.	Total.
I. corps about Flandorf .	23,947	1,013	24,960
II. „ „ Stetten. .	20,701	786	21,487
IV. „ „ Enzersfeld .	21,904	1,677	23,581
V. „ „ Strebersdorf .	14,529	754	15,283
VI. „ „ Stammersdorf	12,713	721	13,434
Reserve corps [1] Gross-Ebersdorf and Gross-Enzersdorf .	12,463	4,557	17,020
Schustekh at Krems . .	6,924	209	7,133
Klenau at Klosterneuburg .	8,749	2,269	11,018
	121,930	11,986	133,916

The advance guard of the VI. corps held Aspern, and a few companies were in the Lobau island.

On the side of the French, the work of bridge construction at Kaiser-Ebersdorf was carried on vigorously. Materials were collected at Vienna to be floated down, and the Emperor proposed sending the pontoons of the Prater bridge down and substituting boats for them. Bertrand, in indenting for materials, estimating that the width of river to be bridged was 853 yards,[2] and the length of bridge covered by each boat at 32 feet, required

---

[1] The I. and II. Reserve corps were now amalgamated under the command of Prince Liechtenstein. *B. K.*, ii. 179.

[2] The actual length was 825 yards, which was covered by 68 boats and pontoons and 9 rafts. The last bridge, beyond Lobau island, was in addition to these. It consisted of 15 Austrian pontoons and 3 trestles.

80 boats. The main stream at Ebersdorf flowed on the south side and was interrupted, first by a sandbank, and then by the island known as the Schneidergrund; so that there were three stretches of bridge. Then came another island, followed by a narrow stream, fordable when the river was low, and beyond it the great island of Lobau, covered in many parts with wood and intersected in places by water courses. Even beyond that, the left bank was only reached by the passage of another important branch of the Danube, rarely fordable, and from 120 to 180 yards wide. For the crossing of this final branch, the place which obviously suggested itself was the apex of the angle re-entrant towards Lobau. The ground in front of the bridge could there be swept for a considerable distance by a cross fire from the Lobau.

There were two great dangers to any bridge, the first of which consisted in the sudden rises of the Danube, which were apt to occur at this time of year when the snows in the upper basins of the great tributaries were melted suddenly by a few hot days. Napoleon had been warned, by Comeau and others, of the probability of such a rise, but does not appear quite to have believed in it.

Another great danger was from floating trees, boats, fire ships, or water-mills [1] sent down by the Austrians from the left bank. They had clearly studied the course of the currents with care, and had already, as Masséna reported, succeeded in breaking the bridge to the Prater. The point marked Am Spitz, seems to have been the one best suited for reaching the great bridge at Kaiser-Ebersdorf.

---

[1] These water-mills ("moulins"), of which we shall hear a good deal, are thus described at p. 228 of Le Général Curély. "These water mills are established on a kind of boat held fast by an anchor; they are moored in the current of the river which works them."

The arrangements for the passage are a remarkable example of the carelessness of which Napoleon was now beginning sometimes to be guilty, as well as of his contempt for the enemy, whom he, on more than one occasion, spoke of as " canaille." Something must also, no doubt, be attributed to his erroneous supposition that the greater part of the archduke's army had gone to Moravia, and that, if opposed at all in his crossing, he would only have to meet that part of the enemy which he had already driven before him from Landshut to Krems.

He disregarded the warnings given to him of the danger from freshets in the river, and he failed to note, when he heard of the breaking of the Prater bridge, how great was the danger from floating masses launched by the Austrians opposite Vienna. He trusted the fate of his army to a single bridge, unprotected either by stockades on the up-stream side, or by proper cruising boats catching the floating mills or fire ships.

He seems to have been unaware of the arrival of the whole of the Archduke's army on the Bisamberg. Popular risings were getting troublesome, and Vandamme had to be ordered with 6000 men to Steyer to deal with them.

Bertrand's report, on the 17th May, shows that the bridge was still far from completion. Fresh demonstrations were ordered at Nussdorf, with the object of deceiving the enemy. Probably they had little effect, for, from the heights of the Bisamberg, the Austrians commanded a fine view of Ebersdorf and the Lobau island.

The most important event of this day (17th) was an attempt by Kolowrat on the bridge-head opposite Linz. Kolowrat, it will be remembered, had been left behind by Charles, with a whole army corps, to guard Bohemia against attacks from Saxony, or Bavaria. Later, on the 8th May, Charles had added to his task that of threatening the French communications towards Linz. Kollowrat, therefore, leaving behind two line battalions and twelve of landwehr to guard against an inroad towards Egra, where there was really no danger, assembled the rest of his corps at Budweis on the 13th. On the 16th he was at Neumarkt,[1] and there decided on a general attack on the bridge head of Linz on the 17th. Two columns, under Sommariva and Wukassowich, were to attack it on either side, whilst a third, under St Julien, was to distract the enemy's attention from the point of attack by an advance on Mauthausen. A strong reserve was kept in hand.

Just as the two first columns were attacking about 2 P.M., news was received that the head of Bernadotte's corps had arrived at Linz from the direction of Passau. Thereupon, Kolowrat at once abandoned the idea of the attack and decided on retreat on Gallneukirchen. Bernadotte had reached Linz at 7 A.M. with the Saxon cavalry and an infantry brigade. Presently they were reinforced by the Wurtembergers, and Bernadotte in the afternoon crossed by the bridge. The Austrian column attacking the east side arrived first before the bridge head. Bernadotte at once fell on it and drove it back with considerable loss. Then he turned on the other column and served it in the same fashion.

The result was the retreat of Kolowrat on Freystadt. Bernadotte says he lost 400 or 500 men, and the Austrians show a loss of 883 and four guns. As for numbers, Binder v. Krieglstein thinks there were, at the outside, 10,000 Saxons and Wurtembergers, against more than 20,000 under the command of Kolowrat.

On the 18th May, the main Austrian army remained inactive, and all idea of the offensive appears to have been abandoned. The position assumed was a purely

---

[1] North of Linz.

defensive one, though there was ample opportunity for activity, especially in an occupation in force of the Lobau Island; for it is scarcely possible to suppose that the French preparations for throwing a bridge from Ebersdorf to Lobau can have escaped the attention of the Austrians. That operation would scarcely be feasible over so broad a river in the face of a strong Austrian force on the island, supported by another at Aspern and Essling, with communication by a bridge over the northern branch of the river. As it was, the preparations for the bridge continued uninterrupted, and in the evening Molitor, passing over to Lobau, cleared out the small Austrian garrison.

On the 15th, the Emperor appears to have been aware of the approach of Charles, for the arrival of strong columns of Austrians from the west on the Bisamberg was observed by Captain Galbois of the staff, and Davout's reports confirmed him. On that evening, Napoleon wrote to Davout, "The opinion of this country is that Prince Charles is seeking to give battle; therefore, keep your troops fresh, so as to be able to move when it may be necessary." On the 17th, he wrote to Lefebvre, "We hope to be able to debouch this evening [1] by the bridges which we have thrown over the Danube, so as to march and attack the Austrian army, which appears to be assembled on the left bank." To Eugène he wrote, later on the same day, "I hope to pass on the 18th or 19th, and to disperse the armies which are united between the Danube and Moravia." The bridge was actually commenced only on the night of the 18th-19th, after Molitor had occupied Lobau. Molitor had only 6 guns, which he disposed so as to sweep the approaches of the Mühlau on the north bank, from Lobau. This, however, was only on the 19th, for all he had done

---

[1] Note the optimism which led the Emperor to assume the bridges would be ready much sooner than was possible.

on the previous evening was to seize with part of his division the outer island, the Lobgrund, separated by a channel twenty feet broad from the main island. The rest of the division crossed on the 19th and had a two hours' fight to clear the island completely. The work of throwing the great bridge continued during the whole of the 19th and the succeeding night. Napoleon was at Ebersdorf in person on the 19th, issuing orders for the coming passage.

Marulaz was to leave Montbrun to guard the Pressburg road, and to be ready himself to pass. Lannes was to pass at 9 A.M. on the 20th, and Bessières was to be ready at Ebersdorf with Espagne, St Sulpice, and Nansouty. Lasalle had just arrived from Spain, and to this brilliant light-cavalry leader were given the brigades of Piré and Bruyère, who were also to be ready to cross.

The very large force of cavalry to be sent over at first is noteworthy, and seems to point to the Emperor's belief that he would not, at first, meet the main body of Charles' army, but only Hiller. The cavalry were all to be over before Lannes.

To Davout the orders were, (1) to send Pajol with two cavalry regiments to Tülln and Sieghardtskirchen, to assist Vandamme in repulsing any Austrian crossing in that direction; (2) to hold himself in readiness to march with his three infantry divisions, of which Friant's was to take post in order of battle between Schönbrünn and Vienna. It was uncertain what the enemy intended, and perhaps Davout would not move after all on the 20th.

Claparède, with two brigades, was to occupy Vienna, and to have one brigade at Nussdorf and Klosterneuburg.

Later orders, dated 19th at 8 P.M., to Davout altered all this. He was to reach Vienna on the 20th, Gudin going to Nussdorf. Morand was to be so placed as to cover the right bank of the Danube between Mölk and Vienna, to guard St Polten, and to arrive at Vienna when the enemy abandoned the left bank.

Vandamme, with headquarters at Enns, was to hold the Linz *tête de pont* with 2000 men, and to occupy Steyer. Orders to Bernadotte to enter Bohemia were not destined to be executed.

Early in the morning of the 20th, the Austrians attempted to throw troops across the Danube at Nussdorf. The attempt was easily frustrated and was, no doubt, merely intended as a diversion.

At midday, the two portions of the French bridge leading from Ebersdorf to Lobau were complete. Molitor reported that his outposts faced those of the Austrians on the opposite side of the northern branch of the river. The troops standing ready at Ebersdorf began to pass into the Lobau, Boudet first, then Legrand and Lasalle, followed by several trains of artillery. Napoleon himself went over and ordered the construction of the final bridge at the salient of the Mühlau. The work was protected by 200 voltigeurs sent across into the wood on the promontory. The bridge, begun at 3 P.M., was ready by 6.

In the evening, Molitor's division passed to the left bank and took post towards Aspern, which he occupied with a few companies. Already there had been a breakage of the second division of the great bridge, the part leading from the Schneidergrund to Lobau. This occurred about 5 P.M., when the bridge was struck by a large boat floated down by the Austrians. This was just when half of Marulaz's cavalry was over, and his division was cut in two for the night whilst the damage was being repaired.

Napoleon took up his quarters for the night at the Jägerhaus on the Lobau. During the night he observed camp fires only on the Bisamberg, a fact which led him to the belief that Charles did not contemplate an attack on the French, but would await them in a selected position.

The construction of a bridge head to protect the bridge over the Stadlau arm [1] was ordered.

The Emperor was quite wrong in his estimate of the Archduke's intentions. Charles had established on the Bisamberg an observatory with a semaphore telegraph from which, at noon, he received prompt news of the completion of the Ebersdorf bridge. About 3 P.M., he issued orders for the army to take up a new position.

The V. corps was to remain as it was at Strebersdorf, the others to reach the following positions — I. corps, heights north of Gerasdorf; VI. heights north of Stammersdorf; II. heights between the left of I. and the Russbach; IV. heights north of Deutsch-Wagram, astride of the Russbach. The grenadiers of the Reserve corps were to stand north of Seiring, whilst the cavalry, under Liechtenstein, were north of Aderklaa, with orders to support Klenau's advance guard if required; otherwise to keep together for the attack of the French cavalry. Headquarters Seiring, to move to Gerasdorf next morning.

To his army Charles issued an address in the following terms—

"To-morrow, or the following day, there will be a great battle. The result of it will, in all probability, decide the fate of the monarchy and of the freedom of every one of you. Between eternal disgrace on the one hand, and undying fame on the other, there is no middle way. I count on the bravery of the army, on the example and spirit of enterprise of the officers. Great rewards or great penalties must follow the result of the battle. Corps commanders must assemble their subordinate generals, and these their staff officers, to earnestly impress on them

[1] The arm separating Lobau from the left bank.

the absolute necessity in the present moment of victory
or death. But the lower ranks also must realise this
truth, and must display to the full their sense of honour,
their patriotism, and their attachment to their Sovereign.

" This decisive battle will be waged under the eyes of
our Emperor, and of the enslaved inhabitants of our
capital, who look for their enfranchisement to the bravery
of the army."

The order is a palpable imitation of Napoleon, but
somehow it seems to miss the electric fire, the touch of
personal appeal which characterised the heart-stirring
words of the Emperor, and the thrilling Trafalgar signal
of Nelson.

Napoleon would have spoken, not of a defensive action,
the idea of which pervades this proclamation, but of
driving the enemy headlong to destruction in the waters
of the Danube. Charles' notions clearly did not contemplate any such things; even Von Angeli can only
say that his idea was to let a sufficiently large number of
French reach the left bank to make their destruction
decisive of the fate of the whole army. The assertion
is not supported by proof. The generally defensive ideas
of the Archduke naturally dominated the whole of his
army.

There was no attempt on the part of the Austrian
commander to call up his outlying detachments to the
decisive point; on the contrary, the main army was
weakened by more detachments to the rear. Napoleon,
on the other hand, was hurrying up Davout, and ordering
Bernadotte to advance on Bohemia. The latter, however,
replied that, instead of the 30,000 men Napoleon credited
him with, he could bring less than 18,000 against the
20,000 or 25,000 which he believed Kolowrat to command. Lefebvre reported that he was in Innsbruck and,
certainly very prematurely, that the Tyrol was as good
as pacified, Chasleter gone to Carinthia, and Jelacic

contemplating an advance against the Crown Prince at Salzburg.

Lauriston had driven the enemy's detachment from a strong position on the Semmering Pass, where he was firmly established.

CHAPTER XIV

THE BATTLE OF ESSLING-ASPERN

(1) FIRST DAY—21ST MAY

ACCORDING to the memoirs of Lejeune, Napoleon was still in doubt, during the night of the 20th-21st, whether he would be opposed by the enemy's army or not. Then it was reported to him that the northern and north-western sky was illuminated with a glow which could only proceed from the camp-fires of a great army. Masséna, mounted on the church tower of Aspern, verified the report. Whether Napoleon was with Masséna as stated is uncertain, but it was in accordance with his usual custom to make a personal reconnaissance before a battle.

In the course of the night, the rest of Molitor's division, followed by Legrand, Boudet, and Espagne's cuirassiers, passed from Lobau on to the mainland, where the construction of a bridge head was already in progress. Marulaz got over about 2 A.M. The positions taken were these—Molitor was about the brick-kiln south of Aspern, having in the village only a few companies of the 67th. Legrand was on Molitor's left rear. Boudet was in the direction of Essling; the cavalry between the two villages, Lasalle in first, Espagne in second line. No

---

[1] The battle is generally known as "Essling" amongst French writers, whilst by German authors it is called "Aspern." We have used the double name here as representing both sides.

274

attempt was made to fortify the villages or the space between them.

Napoleon was on horseback about 4 A.M., consulting his marshals as to their views of the enemy's position. Lannes would have it that there was nothing in front but a rearguard of 6000 or 8000 men, which should be overthrown at once. Bessières, relying on the reports of his cavalry, said there was nothing within several miles. Masséna, on the contrary, supported by Mouton, was of opinion that the whole Austrian army was within a short distance. Berthier said nothing, and counted for nothing.

Binder v. Krieglstein naturally remarks on the extreme inefficiency of Napoleon's cavalry as a reconnoitring force, a fault which we have already seen in the campaigns of 1806 and 1807. Immense Austrian camps stood within a few miles of Aspern and Essling, and cavalry with any enterprise in the matter of reconnoitring should surely have discovered them. Napoleon himself tried to get forward from the Aspern-Essling line, but was stopped by the presence of the enemy's light cavalry, which had moved forward before daybreak. That does not show that at an earlier hour the French cavalry might not have got farther. As in 1806, the cavalry on either side was about equally inefficient in this matter. Yet, when on the march to Vienna, and in watching towards Hungary and to the south of Vienna, the French cavalry had done well enough.

The Austrians, on the other hand, were fully aware that the French army was crossing from Ebersdorf; they had seen the first accident to the bridge, and they must have known that the river was rising rapidly; it had risen 3 feet, or more, during the night.

At 9 A.M., Hiller, who had ridden forward to Stadt-Enzersdorf, reported the continued passage of the French, and their occupation of Aspern and Essling. At the same time Wimpffen reported French advancing on

Hirschstetten. At 10, the Archduke Charles assembled his corps-commanders to explain to them his orders for the attack, on which he had now resolved. It was to be made in five columns.

(1) The VI. corps, on the extreme right, to advance to the Danube about Jedlersdorf, and thence to move down along the river.

(2) I. corps, marching from Gerasdorf on Kagran, to join the left of the 1st column at Hirschstetten.

(3) II. corps (Hohenzollern) by Süssenbrünn and Breitenlee.

(4) The part of the IV. corps on the right bank of the Russbach, by Aderklaa and Raasdorf towards Essling.

(5) The other half of the IV. corps, starting from between Deutsch-Wagram and Baumersdorf, and passing east of Raasdorf, to endeavour to pass to the left of Stadt-Enzersdorf, having its extreme left covered by a hussar regiment.

The cavalry of the Reserve corps to halt south of the line Breitenlee-Neu-Wirtshaus within supporting distance of the 3rd and 4th columns.

The Grenadiers of the Reserve to take post north of Gerasdorf.

The V. corps was not to move, but to watch the Danube from Am Spitz to Krems. Klenau, who had hitherto acted as advance guard for the whole army, would now do so for the 4th and 5th columns. All movements to commence at noon. The general idea was "to drive the enemy entirely over the first (Stadlau) branch of the Danube, to destroy his bridges, and to occupy the bank opposite the Lobau with a large force of artillery."

The result of these orders would be to bring four Austrian infantry corps on to a front in a semi-circle in front of Aspern-Essling extending from Stadlau to

Enzersdorf, about 6¼ miles.   Of the five columns, three were destined for the attack of Aspern, leaving only two for the interval between it and Essling, and the attack on the latter.

It was Whitsunday, 21st May, and the wet weather which had characterised the earlier part of the campaign had given place to glorious summer weather, with a cloudless sky and a blazing sun which, at the head waters of the affluents of the Danube, rapidly melted the snow-fields and poured huge volumes of water into the great stream.   The clouds of dust raised by their columns almost concealed from the French the great circle of Austrians advancing, with bands playing, down the almost imperceptible slope to Aspern and Essling.

The front of the French position consisted of the two villages of Aspern on the west and Essling on the east, forming as it were two bastions.   The curtain connecting the two was a slight depression in the ground and a slightly embanked road ; the distance was a trifle over one mile.   There was very little, if any, defensive strength in this curtain, but it was different with the villages, of which Aspern was much the larger, boasting of several streets, whilst Essling had but one.   Both were solidly built in masonry, and were surrounded by a small earthen embankment to keep out high floods. Each of them had strong ' réduits ' in the form of specially substantial buildings.   In Essling the most notable was a great granary in the centre, and a walled enclosure farther west.   A farm and garden stretched southwards towards the Danube.   In Aspern the church and the cemetery at the western end formed a sort of citadel, from which the whole of the streets running east and west were enfiladed.

Just behind Aspern there flowed a very small branch of the Danube, of no serious importance as an obstacle, but enclosing a partially-wooded island, the Gemeinde-

Au, which was of great importance, as closing the French left flank between Aspern and the Danube. The right flank was more exposed ; for, between Essling and the Stadlau arm, there was a space of open ground.

Directly in rear of the curtain between the two villages was the salient of the Mühlau, at the extremity of which was the single bridge by which the French crossed from the Lobau. Just north of the bridge, a covering work had been begun, but was not yet in a defensible condition. In front of the work was a wood.

Northwards from the French front the ground, perfectly open and covered with green crops, stretched upwards in an almost imperceptible glacis-like slope to Breitenlee, behind which it fell again very gradually towards the north before rising once more towards the hills in the background. The slight ridge on the Breitenlee-Raasdorf line thus screened the Austrian advance from the French until that line was passed.

Aspern and Essling were about equi-distant from the bridge, but, on the whole, the French right flank was weaker than the left. One would have expected Napoleon to have at once set to work to fortify the two villages, the curtain between them, and the flanks between them and the river. That he did not do so would seem to point to the fact that, until the actual advance of the Austrians began, he did not expect to be opposed by a great army. Had he done so, he would hardly have neglected to strengthen this great ready-made bridge head. He had not even occupied Essling at all, and in Aspern there were only a few companies of Molitor's division.

He had, by 1 P.M., on the left bank of the Stadlau arm only three divisions of infantry (Molitor, Legrand, and Boudet), and two cavalry divisions (Lasalle and Espagne).

The Austrian attack broke first, from the north-west, on Aspern, taking the French by surprise. Meanwhile, a fresh misfortune had befallen the great bridge, in the section between the Schneidergrund and Lobau. A great boat had been floated down which, impinging on this part of the bridge, broke it, so that communication was interrupted for some hours. When Napoleon first heard of this, Pelet says he was inclined to withdraw into Lobau, leaving on the left bank a corps sufficiently strong to defend the peninsula (Mühlau) beyond the last bridge. However, subsequent reports decided him to hold on.

As soon as he was aware of the Austrian approach, Napoleon ordered Masséna to defend Aspern with Molitor's and Legrand's divisions, whilst Lannes defended Essling with only Boudet's.

The first attack was by Nordmann's advance guard (4 battalions, 8 squadrons) of Hiller's corps, which drove in the weak French outposts between Stadlau and Aspern about 2.30 P.M. The main body soon came up, marching with its right flank on the river, and its left (cavalry) just across the road from Hirschstetten to Aspern. Nordmann, with only three unsupported battalions, endeavoured to get into Aspern from the south-west. Molitor had as yet but one battalion in the village, but that, supported by the fire of another on the way, drove off Nordmann's feeble attack. Then there was a pause, during which Molitor and Masséna reached Aspern, near which, on the Austrian side, was Charles. A second attack was made in conjunction with the advance guard of the I. corps, which had now passed through Hirschstetten. It, like the first, was made with insufficient forces, and suffered the same fate at the hands of the 37th and 67th, which were all that had arrived of Molitor's division. The Austrians, it is true, got into the west side of the village, but Molitor, bringing forward his two regiments, drove them out again. Before a third attack could be made Molitor had got up his two other regiments.

Bellegarde had strengthened his attacking column by 3 battalions, and Hiller gave the command of the attack by the Gemeinde-Au to his chief of staff Esollich. This attack failed even more dismally than the others. Bellegarde's people were beaten off from the western side of Aspern, without getting into it at all, whilst Esollich's column was badly beaten and lost 700 men in a few minutes.

At this point, the third column also began to come up on the left of Bellegarde to the attack of Aspern, but did no more than bring part of the artillery of its advance guard into action against the village.

The time was now about 5 P.M. ; three columns of the Austrians had come more or less into the battle, and had made three rather feeble attacks on Aspern, without gaining any ground in the village. Indeed, at one time, when he only had the 37th and 67th, Molitor was moving out in pursuit of the repulsed columns when he was recalled to Aspern. The 4th and 5th Austrian columns had not yet appeared before Essling.

Though the attacks on Aspern had been beaten off, victory had only been achieved by Molitor with great exertions, and partly owing to the fact that the Austrians, though in greatly superior numbers in the third attack at any rate, had still not employed anything like the strength they might have, and had not attempted an attack from the north, but only from the west and south-west.

Now, at 5 P.M., Charles, realising the supreme importance of the capture of Aspern, ordered a "general storm," though exactly what he meant by that seems doubtful. Abandoning his own proper position as General-in-chief, he personally appealed to his troops and his generals to take Aspern at all costs, and himself led the attack with reckless personal bravery. He had three corps in front of Aspern, the VI. on the south-west,

the I. on the west and north-west, the II. on the north.
Molitor had but four regiments, of which he posted the
37th and 67th in the western part of Aspern, the 2nd
on their left, and the 16th partly in reserve in the
village, and partly in the Gemeinde-Au—altogether, 12
battalions.

Against them in the fourth attack were brought
4 battalions of the VI. corps, 12 battalions of the I.,
and a brigade of the II., though the latter appears to
have done little. Behind these, of course, there were
overwhelming numbers in support, but the Archduke
might very well have thrown many more battalions into
the actual attacking force. Whatever we may think of
the wisdom of Charles' exposure of himself in leading for
a short distance this new attack, his conduct reflects the
greatest credit on his courage. No doubt, he would have
been better employed in seeing that fresh troops were constantly poured up from the rear into the fight. As it
was, the force was strong enough to force its way into
Aspern against the troops of Molitor, exhausted by their
long fight of nearly four hours, absolutely without support. The fight raged in the village with almost un-
precedented fury. The French were driven from the
church and cemetery, which they could not recover ; but
every house was a small fortress, every cart, every tree,
every tombstone afforded shelter for a soldier. Every
possible weapon was seized upon for use in the desperate
hand-to-hand struggles which were carried on in the
village, as one side or the other gained some temporary
advantage. When bayonets and clubbed muskets failed,
men did one another to death with ploughshares, with
scythes, with hatchets, and with flails. The carnage in
the streets, in the houses, and in the church and cemetery
were appalling. Six times was the village taken and
retaken.

Legrand, who had now come up with the 18th

and 26th, towering in stature above the men he led, pushed forward to the cemetery, but was forced to retire from that point. At 6 P.M., Carra St Cyr arrived, but even then the French were unable to recover the whole of the village. Molitor's shattered regiments had been withdrawn, much against their commander's wish, when Legrand was ready to take their place. Swaying backwards and forwards the fight raged with the utmost fury far into the night before the opponents gradually ceased firing, the Austrians holding the western, the French the eastern part of the village. Masséna, throughout, was the soul of the defence, exposing himself freely in the hottest of the fire, generally under the trees in the church square.

Meanwhile, about 4 P.M., as the pressure on Aspern increased, Napoleon had filled the gap between it and Essling with his cavalry, which was all that he had available for the purpose. Espagne's cuirassiers were in front line on the right nearest to Essling, Lasalle's light cavalry, and that of Marulaz, who was now up, continued the line towards Aspern. The whole force numbered rather under 7000 sabres. The Austrian artillery was at this time pouring from its largely superior number of guns and howitzers a perfect deluge of shot and shell upon the defenders of Aspern, whilst the three corps of infantry were preparing to attack it again. The left of Hohenzollern's corps spread in front of part of the unguarded space to the east of Aspern. Marulaz, by the Emperor's orders, now, at a little after 4 P.M., charged this infantry and the Austrian artillery. The enemy, apparently, formed squares and delivered their fire as Marulaz's men swept through them, taking heavy toll of the French cavalry. Though the cavalry passed through the greater part of the infantry, they could gain no great success, and the heavy fire compelled them to retire. Simultaneously with Marulaz's charge, Lasalle's two brigades, and Espagne's cuirassiers, led by Bessières, charged the Austrian cavalry, which now protected the left of Hohenzollern. Here, too, though the French charged with reckless bravery, and, according to Pelet, broke through three lines of Austrian horsemen, their action failed to break the Austrian centre, and the charge ended in their retreat to the curtain between Aspern and Essling. It seems hopeless to attempt to describe in detail the charges which were made by the cavalry of either side in this part of the field. Bravely leading his cuirassiers into the midst of the Austrians, Espagne was cut down by an Austrian sabre, a very serious loss to the French cavalry.

Whilst Masséna was defending Aspern, the other bastion, Essling, was held by the single division of Boudet, with which Lannes was present in person. The division belonged of rights to Masséna, but had been put under Lannes for the day, as his own corps was not over the river. The Austrian columns had arrived in succession in front of Essling, the 4th and 5th columns having been delayed by the long circuit they had been compelled to make, in order to enable the 5th to get round to their left of Enzersdorf. It was 6 P.M. before Dedowich with the head of the 4th column began his attack against the east side of Essling. Napoleon at once sent against him Espagne's cuirassiers, who had already lost their commander. Their charge brought the Austrian infantry, commanded by a feeble general, to a standstill.

Rosenberg now took the lead and renewed the attack on Essling. The village, like Aspern, ran from east to west, but it had only a single street. Its points of support were a large barn near the eastern side, a walled enclosure on the north, and a farm and enclosure stretching south towards the Danube. Lannes had disposed Boudet's division with much care in the village. Of the

attacks no details are forthcoming, but Pelet says that
Essling had been half ruined by Rosenberg's artillery,
and was attacked three times during the evening, from
the north as well as the east and south-east. Of the
result there is no doubt. The attacks failed completely,
and the Austrians never succeeded, that evening, in
setting foot in Essling.

At 6 P.M., St Cyr's division had at last arrived. It
was used entirely in supporting the attempt to recover
the lost part of Aspern.

At 7 P.M. arrived Nansouty with St Germain's cuirassier brigade and part of St Sulpice's cuirassiers, though
how many of them, or what regiments they were, is
unknown.

With these reinforcements, Bessières was able to renew
his cavalry attacks from the space between Aspern and
Essling. As with the earlier cavalry action, it is impossible to arrive at details. All that seems clear is
that the French cavalry again broke through between
the enemy's infantry squares and partially defeated his
cavalry. Then Bessières was compelled to fall back,
still unbroken, on the position from which he had issued.

The French could do no more that night. They
were beset on both flanks by vastly superior forces.
Rosenberg had fallen back some distance from Essling,
but in Aspern the troops of both sides were still in close
contact, the Austrians holding the west end of the village
with the church and cemetery, whilst the eastern portion
was still in the hands of the French. A few hundred
yards west of the village stood the corps of Hiller and
Bellegarde. In the Gemeinde-Au, Hiller, employing only
Nordmann's four battalions, had never got forward
against the four companies of the French 67th, which
were all that could be sent to this vital point, so long as
it was not more seriously threatened. The day had
been oppressively hot and the fighting had come to an

end chiefly on account of the absolute exhaustion of the troops on both sides.

Charles took up his quarters at Breitenlee, whence he issued orders for the night. Ammunition, food, and forage were to be brought up or requisitioned. All were to be under arms before daybreak, and the cavalry were not to unsaddle at all. Reconnaissances were to endeavour to ascertain whether the French were re-passing the Stadlau arm, as Charles evidently suspected they might. He would himself be with the 2nd column before daybreak.

Napoleon, at the same time, was sending for all that could possibly be got over of his troops on the right bank at Ebersdorf.

Davout was also ordered to send up all the troops and ammunition possible, keeping back only enough to guard Vienna. Of his three divisions, Morand's was at St Polten and Mölk, Gudin's at Nussdorf, and Friant's in Vienna, whilst the light cavalry watched the Danube above Vienna. The sun set on this 21st May on the most serious check which Napoleon had so far experienced in his military career. He had scarcely held his ground, for he had lost half of Aspern. He was surrounded on three sides by an enemy overwhelmingly superior in numbers and artillery. There was little or no hope of Charles' retreating during the night as Bennigsen had retreated from Eylau, for the Austrian was amply supplied with food and ammunition, both of which the Russian had lacked. Napoleon's position, with the rising river behind him, with constant accidents to his bridges rendering it doubtful how long they would hold out, was one of extreme peril. Without reinforcements it would be impossible for his small force to hold out for long next day, and reinforcements, as well as supplies, depended entirely on the bridges which, independently of the bombardment of trees, boats, and floating mills launched against them by the Austrians, were weakened and threatened by the immense stream of the swollen Danube bearing down on them.

For the first three or four hours of the battle the French had had only—Moliter (6200 men), Boudet (5300), Espagne (2550), Lassalle (2380), Marulaz (1400). Altogether 11,500 infantry and 6330 cavalry. Legrand and, at 6 P.M., St Cyr had brought another 10,900 infantry, and, at 7 P.M., had arrived St Germain with 1500 cuirassiers and perhaps another 1200 of St Sulpice's. Thus, even at the close of the battle, the French had only what remained of 22,400 infantry and 9000 cavalry.

On the Austrian side, the Archduke, leaving out of account the V. corps, had on the field 100,000 infantry and 11,000 cavalry.[1] How many of these actually fought it is not possible to say precisely. It is only certain that the Grenadiers were not engaged.

Nor can it be said with any certainty how many of the French were not engaged. Carra St Cyr's division seems to have done little or no fighting (one of his regiments was left at the bridge head) and only two of Legrand's regiments appear to have taken part in the fighting in Aspern.

(2) SECOND DAY—22ND MAY

During the night of the 21st-22nd there was little or no rest for the troops of either side, especially for the French. In Aspern there was, as might be expected, where the opposing troops occupied adjoining streets and houses, a certain amount of desultory fighting all through the night.

[1] See *B. K.*, ii. 209-210, where it is shown that the Austrian accounts, putting the number at 75,000-80,000, are, as Pelet also says, quite unjustifiably low.

During the night, the passage from the right bank was effected by Lannes' corps, consisting of St Hilaire's division and those of Tharreau and Claparède, the two latter combined into a sort of subordinate corps under the name of "Oudinot's corps of grenadiers." Also some cavalry and artillery passed, all with great difficulty, owing to the precarious condition of the bridges. At 3 A.M., the French troops on the left bank were posted thus. Boudet still held Essling; on his left, in the space between Essling and Aspern, were St Hilaire, Tharreau, and Claparède in that order from right to left.

Aspern and its neighbourhood was held, in so far as the French held it at all, by the divisions of Legrand and Carra St Cyr, whilst Molitor's shattered regiments, probably reduced by at least one fourth of their strength, stood in reserve to the south. The cavalry was in several lines behind the infantry. As a general reserve, the Guard was drawn up in front of the wood on the Mühlau covering the bridge head.[1]

Demont's division arrived in Lobau at some time before the final breakdown of the bridges.

Charles appears to have given no orders overnight for the active renewal of the battle. He did, however, give instructions for the floating during the night of fireships and mills against the French bridges. At 3 A.M., when the French had only just got to their posts, the battle broke out afresh in the midst of a thick mist which now covered the shores of the Danube. Which side began is doubtful. The fighting in Aspern soon became as furious as it had been on the previous day. In the first half hour the French recaptured the whole village, except the church, which the Austrian garrison had fortified

---

[1] The Guard appears to have got over the divisions of Curial and Dorsenne, about 7800 strong. Nansouty's cuirassiers had only St Germain's brigade. The greater part, if not the whole of St Sulpice's division was over. At any rate, the whole division was in Lobau on the 24th, the bridges having broken on the 22nd.

during the night. At 3.30 A.M. Masséna launched against it the 18th and 26th of Legrand's division, with two regiments of St Cyr's on their right. The attack is admitted to have failed completely. Later on, however, probably about 5 A.M., Cosson's brigade of St Cyr's division at last forced the Austrians even from the church and cemetery, taking several hundred prisoners, and driving the rest on to the plain beyond and back on the VI. corps, which itself had fallen back some hundreds of yards from the village.

Molitor, meanwhile, in the Gemeinde-Au was defending his position energetically against some fractions of the VI. corps. The time was now 7 A.M. All this while the battle had been raging also at Essling, where the 4th and 5th columns, commanded respectively by Dedowich and Rosenberg, had advanced, the 4th from the north, the 5th from the east, against the village. At first the attack progressed favourably, and the Austrians effected a lodgment in the outskirts of the village. But against the great granary they completely failed, and neither Rosenberg nor Dedowich appears to have been a man to press home the attack as Masséna or Lannes would have done.[1]

At 7 A.M., then, the French had recaptured the whole of Aspern, and had beaten off the enemy's attack on Essling.

Napoleon, ever on the outlook for an opportunity to pass from the defensive to the offensive, had remarked the apparent weakness of the Austrian centre, whilst the energy of their attack was concentrated on the two flanks at Aspern and Essling. According to Pelet, it had been Napoleon's intention from the beginning of the day to break the Austrian centre, so soon as Davout should arrive to support the attack. If he could do this,

---

[1] The Austrian authorities say Napoleon had made a counter-attack with a strong force of cavalry; but it is not mentioned by the French writers.

the result would be the driving asunder of the Austrian army, partly to Bohemia, partly to Hungary. Davout was not up, and, as it happened, never would be that day ; but the Emperor saw an opportunity of carrying through the manœuvre even without him.

The attempt was entrusted to the impetuous Lannes, now engaged in his last battle for the man he had served so well, and who for him almost alone felt a real friendship. Lannes himself led St Hilaire's division on the right ; Tharreau's and Claparède's, on the left, under Oudinot, were in echelons slightly in rear. The cavalry were behind the intervals of the infantry, which were kept open enough to allow of their passage. The general direction of the march was on Breitenlee.

The ground over which this advance was made was swept by the fire of Austrian guns, enormously superior in number to those of the French ; for Napoleon never got more than 144 guns over even to Lobau on the 21st-22nd, whilst Charles commanded 300. Against the storm of shot, shell, grape, and musketry fire which burst upon them, Lannes' divisions made but slow progress. Their artillery, carried well forward, was almost destroyed by the Austrian fire. Still ground was gained, with the result that a gap was left between St Hilaire's right and Boudet in Essling. Through this gap the French cuirassiers executed several gallant charges, but could make little headway through the terrible rain of artillery fire. Then an Austrian cavalry regiment threatened the gap between the left of Lannes' line and Aspern. That was driven off by the 105th thrown back 'en potence.'

The French advance was made in close order, some battalions in column, others in square ; for with the troops of 1809, the French leaders dared not deploy as they did in 1805. Thus they lost much in front of fire, besides exposing themselves to awful loss from the

T

Austrian guns, which tore great lanes in their masses. The French artillery was so overwhelmed that they could cause comparatively little damage to the enemy who, however, equally with them, lost front of musketry fire by close formations.

Notwithstanding all the difficulties of the French, the Austrian infantry were already wavering when the Archduke Charles arrived amongst them. Now he again displayed the same brilliant personal valour as on the day before. However inconsistent they may be with modern ideas of the functions of a commander-in-chief, such acts of heroism as his cannot but reflect the highest honour on the man himself. Seizing the colours of the grenadier regiment Zach and raising them on high, he rode forward at the head of the regiment against the enemy.[1] He had quickly appreciated the extreme danger of the French advance against his weak centre, and adopted this desperate method of encouraging his flagging forces. The effect of his noble example was immense, and the French had very nearly reached the end of their tether. St Hilaire, a man whose great military worth was surpassed by the amiability of his character, whose friends throughout the army were innumerable, who was held in respect and affection by superiors and inferiors alike, had fallen, struck down by an Austrian grape shot.

In addition to himself hurrying up with the grenadiers, Charles had called up reinforcements to his centre from both his wings. The French advance came to a standstill and resolved itself into a musketry battle.

Then Napoleon made a desperate effort to break through by sending Bessières forward with the cavalry through the intervals of his infantry. What the strength of the cavalry was, or what regiments composed it, is

---

[1] It is this incident which is represented in Fernkorn's equestrian statue of the Archduke in front of the Hofburg at Vienna.

not to be discovered. The cuirassiers appear to have passed, as before, through the intervals of the Austrian infantry, and a few of them perhaps got even as far as Breitenlee. But Savary distinctly says they were driven back, immediately after they had passed through the Austrian infantry, by the cavalry which they then met.

Pelet and Lejeune would have us believe that victory was already almost within the grasp of Napoleon when the news of the breaking of his bridges compelled him to abandon the advance. Binder v. Krieglstein [1] shows that this is romance, and that the advance of Lannes' corps had really been brought to a standstill by the Austrian resistance, and by the failure of ammunition, which Savary says was already beginning to be felt. The force available was not sufficient to attain the desired end without the assistance of Davout, and, even if the bridge had remained intact, the Emperor would have been compelled to fall back on the Aspern-Essling line until Davout had time to cross and come up. He unwillingly gave up the attempt to break the centre, because Lannes could not carry it through, not because of the rupture of the bridge. Had he been so near victory as the French writers represent, he would have persevered.

It was about 9 A.M. when Bessières was sent forward, and perhaps half-an-hour later Napoleon must have ordered Lannes to fall back and take up a position for defence, with his right resting on Boudet at Essling, his left on Masséna at Aspern.

Exactly when Napoleon heard of the disaster to the bridge between the right bank and Lobau is not certain. The Austrian captain of engineers, posted about Am Spitz for the purpose, had been bombarding the bridges with a constant succession of floating trees, boats, and mills, some of which it was beyond the power of the ' pontonniers ' to catch before they struck the bridges.

[1] ii. 214-217.

Somewhere about 9 A.M., both branches of the bridge were broken by floating masses, just as Colbert's light cavalry was passing over, the men obliged by the shaky condition of the bridge, due to the great rise of the river, to lead their horses. Only one squadron had got over when the breach in the bridge forced the others to return to the right bank. By great efforts the breaches were repaired by the afternoon, but scarcely had this been completed when the bridge nearest Ebersdorf was again broken. Attempts were also made to break the bridge from Lobau to the Mühlau, but the current in the Stadlau arm was not sufficiently rapid, and when one great boat threatened to destroy the bridge, some of Molitor's men were able to swim out and bring it to shore before it reached its destination.

All hope of a renewal of the French offensive at a later hour was now gone. The only problem was how to get back, without utter defeat, into the great island.

The Archduke learnt, about 10 A.M., by a message from his observatory on the Bisamberg, of the rupture of the bridges. His orders are not traceable, but there can be no doubt from the subsequent course of events that they amounted to an order for the renewal of the attacks on the two villages of Aspern and Essling.

Hiller's corps now again attacked Aspern, driving the French from the western side, but coming to a standstill, about 10 o'clock, without succeeding in recapturing the whole village, the eastern portion of which the French still held.

It was probably after 11 A.M. when the attack was renewed on Essling, still held by Boudet. This time it was made with greater forces and greater energy than before. Dedowich, with the 4th column, fell upon the north side, Rosenberg, with Hohenlohe's division of the IV. corps and four battalions of Rohan's grenadiers, upon the east. Both attacks penetrated into the village, but all their efforts failed to overcome the obstinate defence of Lannes in the central stronghold of the granary.

It was now the turn of the centre, where Charles led the 2nd and 3rd columns and the grenadiers against the line between the two villages. Once more Bessières and the French cavalry sacrificed themselves in frequent charges against the advancing Austrians, whose cavalry was not at hand. The attack was brought to a standstill before it reached the French infantry line, and then ensued a fire fight in which the superior Austrian artillery again wrought havoc amongst the French, many of whose guns were already dismounted.

Charles, having failed to take Essling with 25 battalions, now sent d'Aspre against it with only 4 of grenadiers! This time the attack was on the north-western side, and so vigorous was it that Napoleon felt compelled to throw in part of his last reserve, the Imperial Guard. Mouton was sent, with two divisions of the 'tirailleurs' and fusiliers of the Young Guard, to the support of Boudet, who was on the point of being driven out of the granary. The Old Guard still remained in reserve near the bridge. The combat was as furious as ever, and, even with Mouton's assistance, head could scarcely be made against the now reinforced Austrians. Two more battalions of the Young Guard, under Rapp, were now sent in with orders to disengage the garrison of Essling, and then retire on a position between it and the Old Guard. Now, at last, the Austrians were again forced back, at about 3 P.M., and the French once more held the village so long contested.

The battle died away into a cannonade directed by the Austrians against the villages which they had, after 24 hours' of fighting, failed to take. From this artillery fire Napoleon suffered an irreparable loss; for Lannes was mortally wounded. It was between 3 and 4 P.M., just after the death at his side of his old friend and early instructor Pouzet, that Lannes was struck by a small round shot fired from the Enzersdorf direction and ricochetting from the ground. The marshal was sitting with his legs crossed over one another, when the shot shattered both knees. At first there were hopes of his recovery, and he lasted till the 31st May, when fever, consequent on the wounds and the amputations, carried off one who was certainly one of the most brilliant, and one of the most upright and honest of Napoleon's marshals.

As the French retired on the Aspern-Essling line, the Austrians made no attempt to follow, and the two armies remained where they were till night fell. The Austrians bivouacked on the field of battle. At nightfall Napoleon returned to the island of Lobau, leaving Masséna in charge of the operations for the retreat which was now necessary, though it could not be carried out by daylight.

At 11 P.M. it began. First of all the wounded were passed over, followed by the artillery, the Guard, the heavy cavalry, Molitor, Boudet, Claparède, the light cavalry, and the 'Tirailleurs' of the Guard, in the order named. Legrand, Tharreau, and, apparently, Demont, covered the retreat of the rest, which was conducted in perfect order. Any disorder would probably have proved fatal and resulted in the breaking of the bridge over the Stadlau arm, strained as it already was by the rise of the river. Almost the last to pass was Masséna.

At 3.30 the bridge was drawn over to the Lobau. All were over, except the voltigeurs of the 18th, who passed, with Pelleport their commander, at 4 A.M., in two large boats.

As for the pontoons of the bridge, Masséna had orders to put them on waggons and send them across the island to the main bridge, which was short by some 15 boats.

The little stream which separated the Lobau from the Lobgrund had risen so rapidly as to carry away the trestle bridge over it. Much of the lower portion of the islands was now under water.

Napoleon's first care was to call on Daru his Intendant-General for supplies of food, of which there was scarcely any in the Lobau. It was to be floated down from Vienna on boats, a difficult and perilous enterprise in the existing state of the river, in high flood and constantly carrying down the Austrian floating mills and boats aimed at the bridges.

Davout, sent for by the Emperor during the afternoon, had crossed in a small boat. After receiving Napoleon's instructions, he had returned in the same way to the two divisions (Friant's and Gudin's) which he had at Ebersdorf.

In the morning of the 22nd a great part of the population of Vienna had come out to watch the battle, becoming more and more excited as it progressed. Davout, utilising such of Nansouty's cuirassiers as were too late to pass on account of the breaking of the bridge, drove the people back to Vienna, into which he also sent some infantry to keep order.

Thus ended, on the evening of the 22nd May, this terrible two days' battle, the losses in which probably equalled in numbers those of Eylau in February 1807.

On the first day the French had available on the left bank approximately 22,000 infantry and 9000 cavalry, though the numbers were much smaller at first. The Austrians had 100,000 infantry and more than 11,000 cavalry.

What the losses of the first day were it is impossible to state separately.

On the second day the Austrians received no reinforcements, so that they began it with the same forces as the previous day, less the casualties. The French reinforcements, passed over in the night, brought up their total to somewhere about 50,000 or 55,000 infantry, and certainly not more than 12,000 cavalry. From these must be deducted the killed and badly wounded of the 21st. The Austrians on both days had about 300 guns, Napoleon never more than 144 in Lobau and on the left bank.

The Austrian returns show their losses on the two days as 4286 killed, 16,314 wounded, 837 prisoners, and 1903 missing. Total, 23,340, besides 2048 horses, 1 standard, and 6 guns. As usual, it is almost impossible to get at Napoleon's real losses. He put them, in his bulletin, at 1100 killed and 3000 wounded, which is as manifestly an under-estimate as the Austrian statement of them at 43,000 is excessive. Thiers says 15,000 or 16,000, and Thiers always understates French losses. Most of the heaviest fighting was in the two villages where, in such close combat, the losses would be fairly equal. In the centre, the probabilities are that, under the great superiority of the Austrian artillery, the French suffered most. It would certainly not be safe to take the French loss at less than the Austrian; possibly it was rather more, and, proportionately to the numbers on the field, it was of course much higher. Binder v. Krieglstein only hazards a guess that the French losses largely exceeded 20,000 but probably did not exceed 30,000. He is careful not to attribute any authority or exactness to this guess, and there we must leave it.

The Austrians captured 3 guns, 1 pair of colours, and 7 ammunition waggons.

The battle was distinctly a victory for the Austrians, but it was not a victory of the Napeolonic stamp, where the defeated side was practically destroyed. To Napoleon its great importance was in the blow which it inflicted on his prestige, the consequent encouragement which it afforded to his declared enemies all over Europe, and the temptation to desert him which it offered to his half-hearted allies, Russia in particular.

At 3 A.M. on the 23rd May, a small boat carried Napoleon and Berthier, across the still rising waters of the Danube, from the Lobau to Ebersdorf. A fierce thunderstorm was raging as the Emperor made the now perilous passage. The story goes that when he reached Ebersdorf he slept for thirty-six hours. Whatever be the truth of that, it is certain that he issued no orders on that date. Binder von Krieglstein thinks it quite possible that the tenth bulletin, bearing that date, may have been the handiwork of his staff. The bulletin is about as worthless as others from the point of view of history. It represents the breaking of the bridge as the sole cause of failure. The enemy were completely routed at that moment, they had lost 12,000 in killed alone, and nothing could have saved them but the necessity for caution on the part of the Emperor, on account of the severance of his communication with Davout. Fiction certainly, but Napoleon was bound to make the best to France and Europe of the desperate plight in which he found himself. He can hardly be seriously blamed for doing so. Meanwhile, the Austrians rested in their bivouacs till the afternoon of the 23rd, excepting the few who followed Masséna to the Mühlau, whence a few cannon shots from Lobau soon drove them. In the afternoon of the 23rd, they at last ventured to move forward, and bivouacked for the night in two lines, the first, consisting of the IV., V. and VI. corps and Klenau's advance guard, on the line Aspern-Essling; in second line the Reserve cavalry behind the VI., and the Grenadiers with the headquarters at Breitenlee.

In the course of the day Charles had heard, from his observatory on the Bisamberg, that the French were retiring to the right bank, but had been stopped by a fresh breakage of the main bridge.

Thinking, apparently, that he ought to do something bearing the appearance of activity, he ordered a night attack on the Lobau, for which he told off the IV. and VI. corps with Klenau. Hiller with the VI. was to cross into the Lobau through the Mühlau, whilst Rosenberg, with one infantry brigade and 200 cavalry, was to cross on the eastern side of Lobau, near the Uferhaus,[1] and attack the Schneidergrund. Rosenberg was given twenty pontoons, but there is nothing else traceable about means of passage. The attack was clearly a sham, and both generals, when they got to the Stadlau arm, finding it overflowed and impossible to cross with the means at their disposal, quietly retired. It was only on the morning of the 24th that Napoleon appeared to recover from the lethargy into which he had sunk after the severe blow which had been struck at his prestige by his repulse at Essling. He had erred in attempting the passage with insufficient means, and he was now determined to make his arrangements for the next attempt as perfect as patience and care could make them. It took him from the 24th May till the 4th July to complete them, and it seems that the clearest way to deal with the intervening six weeks will be to treat of them in two parts. First the operations carried out in the field at some distance from Ebersdorf and Lobau, and secondly, the actual preparations at those points for the passage which was to lead to the battle of Wagram. The Austrian operations will be treated similarly.

[1] Known by the French as the "Maison Blanche."

CHAPTER XV

OPERATIONS OF THE ARMIES OF ITALY, AND IN POLAND AND GERMANY

FRESH forces were now about to enter the main field of operations, in the shape of the Archduke John's army of Italy and the remains of the forces in the Tyrol on the one side, of the French army of Italy, under Eugène Beauharnais, and the corps of Marmont, from Dalmatia, on the other. This history of the campaign on the Danube can only deal very briefly with the operations in the south.[1]

When the war began on the 9th April the Archduke John had roughly the following forces :—

VIII. and IX. corps, west of Villach and west of Laibach	48,000
Part of the VIII., under Chasteler in the Tyrol	12,000
Stoichewich, towards Dalmatia . .	8,000
Reserve of Landwehr, Croatian Insurrection, etc.	32,000
	100,000

Eugène had about 63,000 men, but he was by no means concentrated. Expecting the Austrians, if they advanced at all, by Tarvis, he was surprised by their move-

---

[1] A fuller account of the Italian campaign is given in General D. Haig's "Cavalry Studies," to name an easily accessible book.

ment with the VIII. and IX. corps on Udine, and at
once fell back behind the Tagliamento and the Liveuza.
John was at Udine on the 13th April. On the 15th
Eugène's rearguard was caught and beaten at Pordenone.
Next day he rashly stood to fight at Sacile, in a bad
position, with the river behind him. He had only about
36,000 men against John's 45,000 ; for one infantry
division and Grouchy's dragoons were prevented by floods
from reaching him in time. He was badly beaten, with
a loss of 3000 men, and much heavier losses in the
retreat. He went straight back behind the Adige at
Verona. On the 26th April, he was facing the Austrians,
who had occupied the heights of Caldiero, but a short
way east of Verona.

Meanwhile, Chasteler had made himself master of the
Pusterthal, had joined Andreas Hofer at Innsbruck, and
was now threatening to descend on Eugène's flank and
rear by the Adige and Lake Garda.

John, holding the passage of the Adige with his left,
was actually nearer than Eugène to Mantua and the Po.
To deal with a situation like this required a Napoleon,
not an Eugène. The latter was saved by the news of
the Austrian misfortunes south of Ratisbon, which decided
John to retreat, just as Charles himself had been compelled by the news of Ulm, in 1805, to retreat before
Masséna, after the battle of Caldiero. What with losses
and detachments to watch Venice and other places, John
had only about 22,000 men on the Adige in the last
days of April. Eugène, on the 28th April, made an
unnecessary and useless attack on John at Caldiero,
which was repulsed.

Then John began his retirement on the Brenta and
the Piave, which latter he crossed on 6th May. Two
days later, Eugène, following in a somewhat leisurely
fashion, forced the passage. Thence John retired on
Sacile, and passed the Tagliamento on the 10th, followed,

next day, by Eugène who, on the 14th, was once more on the eastern frontier of Italy. John now himself moved by Pontebba, sending Gyulai towards Laibach. The forces under John's control, including Jelacic, now made over to him, stood thus :— [1]

Chasteler in the Tyrol . . .	8000
Albert Gyulai, in Carinthia, about Tarvis .	4000
The Ban of Croatia (Ignatius Gyulai) Laibach	8000
Main Army (Archduke John), Villach-Arnold-stein	10,000
Jelacic, Radstadt	7000
Stoichewich in Croatia, watching Marmont in Dalmatia	4000
	41,000

besides Landwehr, Croatians, etc.

John hoped by this wide dispersal to guard the whole frontier, and to determine Eugène's advance by the Laibach road, with the object of joining Marmont coming from Dalmatia with 10,000 men. As will be remembered, however, Lefebvre, under the persistent goad of Napoleon's orders, had beaten Chasteler at Wörgl, driving him back on Innsbruck. Chasteler had lost most of his infantry, and now commanded little more than insurgent peasantry. John, therefore, ordered him to follow the Drave down to Marburg, whilst Jelacic, marching by the valley of the Mur, directed his retreat from Radstadt on Graz. John himself remained at Villach till the 17th, reaching Klagenfurt next day. Here he received orders from the Emperor Francis to march on Salzburg, to join Jelacic, and with him to operate from the south against the French communications, in correspondence with Kollowrat's opera-

[1] *Angeli*, iv. 281. The estimate seems rather low.

tions from the north towards Linz. This was no longer possible, as Jelacic had left Radstadt, and Eugène's army, having forced the passes of Malborghetto and Prédil, had occupied Villach. Macdonald, also, a few days later (22nd) compelled the capitulation of the frontier forts of Prewald, and of the entrenched camp at Laibach.

This Italian campaign between Eugène and John is of very little interest; for neither of the commanders possessed any great military abilities, and the whole thing was a series of blunders on both sides. It was Eugène's first campaign in command, and he certainly had not his stepfather's genius for war. Napoleon wrote to him: "I am sorry to see you have no notion of what war is, or how to carry it on." He was more complimentary in his letters to Josephine about her son. As for the Archduke John, he was inefficient and insubordinate. It will be seen later that he was full of wild plans, and, by pressing them first on his brother Charles, and then on the Emperor, very much hindered the Austrian commander-in-chief, and, in the end, failed to put in an appearance at Wagram.

That Napoleon should have entrusted the chief command in Italy to one whom he knew to be a beginner is, perhaps, the best evidence of his complete realisation of what he so often laid down, that the decision in a war between Austria and France must lie in the valley of the Danube, not in that of the Po.

To the fact that Eugène commanded the army of Italy we are indebted for many of Napoleon's most instructive despatches, in which he lays down, for the instruction of the young commander, many general principles of the art of war. At this period, when he had no son, the Emperor, perhaps, thought to find a worthy successor in Josephine's son.

On the 26th April, Napoleon had received the news of

Eugène's defeat at Sacile 10 days earlier. He was alarmed lest a force from Italy should threaten his right flank, and he wrote to Lefebvre[1] to send strong parties along the road to Spital in Carinthia, in order to get news of events in Italy, and early warning of any hostile forces coming from that direction. Later news showed that the Archduke John was retreating before Eugène, and, as the French advanced on Vienna, it became necessary to guard against John, and to seek union with Eugène. As we know, the Emperor Francis had actually ordered John to co-operate with Kollowrat against the French communications; but Lefebvre's successes put that out of the question, and John set out to retreat on Hungary, hoping to be joined there by Chasteler and Jelacic from the Tyrol, and to find strong reinforcements of the Hungarian "Insurrection."

Jelacic's orders were to reach Graz by the 26th or 27th May, and there to hold the place till the arrival of John, marching by Klagenfurt and Marburg. Eugène, however, only sent in pursuit of John, Grouchy with the light cavalry, which would also form a link with Macdonald. He himself followed the direct road to Vienna by Leoben, with the result that, on the 25th, he came upon Jelacic, also marching on Leoben.

Jelacic, delayed by the artillery fire of Serras near St Michael, was kept there till Eugène came up with reinforcements. The Austrians were completely defeated in the engagement which followed, and Jelacic only succeeded in escaping with some 2000 out of the 7000 whom he commanded.

On the 26th May, Eugène had his headquarters at Leoben, with Durutte on the road to Graz, and Serras on that to Vienna. The light cavalry reached the Semmering pass, where they met some chasseurs from Lauriston's corps, detached from the main army to feel for Eugène. Lauriston himself went to meet Eugène next day at Bruck.[1]

Grouchy, leaving Pacthod at Mahremburg, reached Marburg at the same time as Macdonald, on the 30th May. The Archduke John, meanwhile, having arrived at Graz on the 24th, was in a most advantageous position, inasmuch as he was between the two wings of the French, and stronger than either of them singly. Thus, he might have crushed either Eugène or Macdonald before the other could come up. He proposed to stay where he was, to pick up the detached portions of his army between the 26th and 28th. Instead of reinforcements, he only received the shattered fugitives of Jelacic's division The same evening he set out on his march for Körmend on the Upper Raab, in anything but good order.

As soon as Napoleon heard of Eugène's junction with Lauriston, he sent orders to unite the army of Italy at Bruck, and to hold the Semmering pass, thus setting Lauriston free to draw nearer to Vienna at Wiener-Neustadt. Eugène was to arrange for the government of the conquered provinces, for the collection of provisions, and to communicate with Lefebvre, who was now marching on Vienna, the Tyrol being for the moment more or less subdued. On the 28th, Eugène received two long letters from his stepfather, who estimated Eugène's own column at 30,000 and Macdonald's at 15,000, which was a great deal too high. The two together probably did not exceed 30,000 men at this time. Napoleon explains that he has a screen of light cavalry to the south-east, Lasalle at Hinberg, with posts towards Pressburg; Montbrun at Oedenberg behind the Neusiedl lake, with posts towards Graz. Lauriston had been ordered to Oedenberg, to

[1] This is another very common place-name. Care must be taken not to confuse this Bruck (near Leoben) with Bruck on the Leitha, between Pressburg and Vienna.

push parties thence against the flank of the Archduke John, who was probably making for Raab. Klagenfurt was to be fortified as a supply store. The Emperor was, at the same time, writing to Murat at Naples, and to his sister Elisa, to send up reinforcements from Italy, a plain indication of how severely he felt himself pressed.

When the Archduke Charles heard, on the 30th, of Jelacic's disaster, and of his brother's march on Körmend, he naturally enough took a gloomy view of the situation. He at once wrote to John to do his best to stop the enemy from crossing the Raab, or at any rate the Marczal. He proposed, he said, uniting with John and the Hungarian "Insurrection" towards Pressburg and the two great islands of Schütt, formed by the separation of the Danube into three branches below Pressburg. On the 1st June, Charles, hearing that John had but 7000 men left, wrote that separate operations on the latter's part would be useless; he was, therefore, definitely ordered to march at once by the Schütt island to Pressburg. On this day (1st June), John had reached Körmend, whilst Eugène was moving on Wiener-Neustadt, Macdonald being left at Graz to reduce the citadel and look out for Chasteler, who was still not finally accounted for.

Charles sent orders, on the 2nd, to John to send definite information as to his strength and the direction of his march. To Joseph, Palatine of Hungary, orders were issued to assemble the Insurrection [1] and join John at Raab. John, at the same time, was writing that he still had 20,000 men resting at Körmend. and, therefore, he proposed to undertake something. He calmly proposed to reach the Danube at Pressburg, there to join the Insurrection, and then, as the left wing of the army, to attack the French between Vienna and Neustadt, that

[1] Only 20,000 of them had been got together so far.

U

is the greater part of Napoleon's army. Truly the project of a madman !

On the 3rd June, Napoleon wrote to Eugène that John was threatening Oedenberg. The Viceroy should, therefore, move thither, keeping in touch with Bruck, and a careful watch towards his right. If John were going to Raab, Eugène, with the co-operation of Lauriston and Montbrun, might inflict an injury on him.

On the 4th June, the Viceroy, now at Oedenberg, was informed that the Emperor was going to recall Lauriston to Ebersdorf, and that, the army of Italy being now in a country fertile in supplies, its commander should take measures to collect them, not only for himself, but also for the main army. John was still at Körmend doing nothing, beyond hatching more mad schemes of operations for submission to headquarters, notwithstanding the fact that he had received orders clear beyond doubt on the 1st. His latest idea was to march against Marmont and Macdonald, though he had been retreating before the latter for the last fortnight, and the former was still far away.

On the 6th June, Napoleon wrote a very important letter to Eugène. He had just heard that Colbert was, on the 5th, in contact with John. He says that, in order to raise Eugène (without Macdonald) to 30,000 men, he must have Baraguey d'Hilliers and the (Italian) Guard. Another 6000 would be provided by Lauriston, Montbrun, and Colbert, who were to be at his disposition. Half of these 36,000 were to be marched on Körmend, always subject to the tenor of fresh information as to John's movements. Then follows a disquisition, for Eugène's instruction, on the difference between operations in a mountainous country like Carinthia, and in the open plains of Hungary, where the enemy would have more liberty of movement.

Napoleon's views of the situation in front of Eugène are best stated in the Emperor's own words. " In the situation in which he finds himself, what ought the enemy to do? Ought he to abandon Styria, Carinthia, the corps of Gyulai, and all the south of Hungary, to uncover Pesth before the movements of Macdonald and Marmont, in order to pass to the left bank of the Danube? Or ought he, on the contrary, to serve as a nucleus for the assembly of the whole Hungarian Insurrection, to rally the troops which have fled before Marmont, to harass your line of communication from Graz to Laibach, and cover Pesth, which after all is the capital of Hungary? In this last case, it would be possible that the enemy might manœuvre on Körmend, behind the Raab, harass the communications from Graz to Laibach, and still hold himself in a position to cover Pesth. Then your movement on Raab would carry you away from him, and might even give him the idea (for he, unlike us, is at home and well informed) of attacking and overthrowing Macdonald. I think, therefore, that the wisest movement is first on Güns, then on Stein am Anger, then on Körmend, or from Güns on Sárvár, provided you have no fresh information. This evening you could march on Güns with Colbert's brigade, the seven regiments of Grouchy's division, a quantity of artillery (you should place your light guns, at least twelve, with your cavalry) and the divisions of Serras and Durutte. Baraguey d'Hilliers' corps can arrive this evening at Oedenberg, or even at Güns, or march to the intersection of the roads from Sárvár and Raab to Zinkendorf. According to the information you receive, you will be able to-morrow to combine the movement of your two columns on Sarvar, or on Körmend. General Montbrun should have been yesterday evening (5th) at Gols, and, as he should be united with General Lauriston, you cannot fail to have news.

As for me, it does not appear to me to be yet proved whether the enemy is retiring on Körmend or on Raab. I think he will remain in observation, and will act according to the manœuvres we make against him, always keeping open his retreat on Pesth, and that if he retires on Raab, it would be better to outflank him on his left than on his right, for by this means you would pass the river[1] towards Sárvár, and would throw him into the Danube; for, at Körmend and at Raab, he requires at least three days to cross the Danube; and, finally, by this manœuvre you protect General Macdonald and General Marmont, and can unite with them. As for the danger of his[2] marching on Pressburg, the Duke of Auerstädt is opposite to it. It will suffice, if you perceive this movement, that you press him vigorously. The sole precaution necessary would be to let General Montbrun fall back before him on Bruck (on the Leitha), whilst you pursue rapidly; but this combination appears to me extravagant." This " extravagant " idea had been proposed by John on the 2nd June.[3]

At last, on the 7th June, John having failed to get his schemes accepted by his brother, and having information of the Viceroy's presence at Güns, marched at night to Baltávár on the road east of the Raab from Körmend to Raab. The information which reached Napoleon from Eugène and Macdonald induced him to believe (2.30 P.M. on 7th June) that John was concentrating at St Gothard, west of Körmend. He, therefore, orders Macdonald (whose force he over-estimates at 15,000) to march with his whole corps against John, whilst Eugène was to arrange that Lauriston, Colbert, and Montbrun should also be up in time for the battle. Even Marmont might possibly join in on Macdonald's right, if it were true that he had arrived at Marburg. Macdonald was only to leave behind, at Graz, enough to blockade the

---

[1] The Raab. [2] *i.e.* the enemy's. [3] *Vide supra*, p. 305.

citadel, the fall of which must follow John's defeat. There are further instructions as to the fortification of Klagenfurt, and as to the necessity of Rusca, who commanded there, keeping a watch on the Tyrol, which was again ablaze.[1]

Late on the night of the 7th, Napoleon seems to doubt if John is marching against Macdonald, and infers that he is very weak, since he has not already attacked Macdonald. As a matter of fact, John was still at Baltávár all the 8th and 9th. On the latter day his rearguard came in contact with the advance-guard of Eugène, who had reached Sárvár. John marched, during the night of the 9th-10th, to Tuskevár. Napoleon was still in doubt as to whether the Archduke was making for Raab or Pesth; in either case, Sárvár was Eugène's best direction.

On the 10th, Eugène's advance guard was at Kis Czell, Montbrun at Papocz, Macdonald half way between Graz and Körmend. Napoleon was now aware that Chasteler had been before Klagenfurt, cutting the communications with Italy, which had been restored when Rusca had beaten off Chasteler's 4000 or 5000 landwehr and they had retired on Marburg, whence, however, there was some danger of their falling upon the force left by Macdonald to blockade the citadel of Graz.

On the 11th, John, retiring on Szalok, had a brush with the Viceroy's advance guard, and continued his retreat to Papa.

On the 12th, he reached Teth, and, during the ensuing night, marched to Raab. There he met the Hungarian Insurrection under the Palatine.

Napoleon's orders of the 11th directed Eugène, in the event of John's retirement on Pesth, to occupy Raab and cover the line from that place to the Platten lake.

[1] This letter (*Corr.* 15,310) contains a criticism of Eugène's pursuit of John, to which we shall return later.

Macdonald was at Körmend, but had left his heavy division (Broussier) at Graz.

When John reached Raab, at 9 A.M. on the 13th, he found the Hungarian Insurrection troops in a condition of extreme inefficiency. He also received an order from Charles requiring him to send some thousands of men to Pressburg, there to replace Bianchi's brigade, and, with the rest, to take post at Raab, to harass Eugène, and to separate him as far as possible from Napoleon. In the last resort, he was to reach the Marchfeld, by crossing, either at Raab or at Komorn, and marching up the north bank. Whilst John and the Palatine were discussing this order, Eugène's advance guard appeared in front of Szabadhegyi. The Insurrection cavalry were badly beaten and driven in, and the rest of the day passed in a desultory cannonade.

Napoleon, on this day, was still in ignorance of the real direction of John's retreat, and advised the capture of Raab, which would enable the adoption of a shorter line of communication between Eugène and himself, by Wieselburg. Gyulai and Chasteler must be kept away from John.

On the 14th June, the anniversary of Marengo and Friedland, Eugène fought his battle of Raab, which it pleased Napoleon to associate with the day, and to represent as a great victory. That was due no doubt to his personal affection for his stepson, and it is not in the least likely so much would have been made of the affair had it been the work of one of the marshals.

THE BATTLE OF RAAB[1]

The Pánsza brook, flowing from the south-east, joins the right bank of the Raab just above the fortress of the

---

[1] Colonel Saski's fourth volume, when it appears, may throw some light on the battle of Raab. At present it is difficult to arrive at a reliable account of it. Binder v. Krieglstein gives no details, evidently placing no great

same name. It is marshy and difficult to cross, and a short distance east of it is a slight elevation stretching from Szabadhegyi on the north, to the village and farm of Kis-Megyer. On this height the Archduke placed his infantry, which was partly composed of Hungarian 'Insurrection' troops of small value. They were intermingled with his regular troops, some 17,000 or 18,000 in number. On his right, in the space between Szabadhegyi and the embouchure of the brook, were about 1000 Insurrection cavalry which, shut in by the brook, were more or less paralysed. The bulk of his cavalry was on his left, in the open plain beyond the farm of Kis-Megyer, where they had good ground for manœuvring. In the Austrian line there were three strong points of support; on the right the village of Szabadhegyi; in the centre the village of Kis-Megyer; in front of the left, close down to the brook, the farm of Kis-Megyer. The last-named, with its loop-holed walls, formed a sort of small fortress projecting in front of the line, and was of great value. So long as it was untaken, the attack could not advance, as it would be taken in flank from the farm.

The Austrian front was well garnished with artillery, superior in strength to the French. What the numbers on either side were is very doubtful. Binder v. Krieglstein thinks they were probably about equal. Von Angeli gives Eugène's strength at 45,000, but includes Macdonald (8000), no part of whose corps was up in time to take part in the battle. Probably 35,000 on each side is as near as we can get. The greater part of John's cavalry was Hungarian, and some part of his infantry also belonged to the 'Insurrection.' The French were distinctly

reliance either on that of von Angeli or on the French histories. The following account, which must be taken for what it is worth, is based on, (1) Binder v. Krieglstein, (2) von Angeli, (3) Du Casse's biography of Eugène and the latter's correspondence, (4) Pelet, (5) Napoleon's criticisms in *corr.* 15,358.

superior in the quality of their troops, and it was only John's regulars, and the strength of his position, which enabled him to hold out for four hours.

Eugène rightly employed the greater part of his cavalry on his right, viz. Montbrun and Grouchy. Montbrun, about 11.30 A.M., drove the Austrian outposts over the brook, to cover the preparations for the infantry attack. When it began, about 2 P.M., he moved to the right with Grouchy to meet the Austrian cavalry of the left and threaten their line of retreat. The infantry attack was by divisions, each in two lines, in echelon by the right. Serras with the leading division attacked the farm, Durutte, in the centre, advanced on Kis-Megyer village, whilst Severoli's Italians attacked Szabadhegyi. To the left of him Sahuc's cavalry contained that of the Austrian right. On the extreme left, the Baden troops watched the fortress of Raab from the left bank of the river of the same name.

Pacthod's infantry division, Pully's dragoons, and the Italian Royal Guard were in reserve behind the centre.

Serras, soon finding himself under a very heavy fire from the farm and the ditches in its neighbourhood, could make no way. Whilst he was stopped, Durutte's 25th Light Infantry attacked Kis-Megyer village (three more battalions moving to the left of it), and Severoli commenced his attack on Szabadhegyi with his 1st brigade. The Austrians in that village not only beat off Severoli, but also drove back Durutte's three battalions. between it and Kis-Megyer.

During this fighting, Montbrun and Grouchy had attacked the Austrian cavalry of their left wing. The Hungarians, not being able to stand the fire of the French horse-batteries, broke, leaving nothing but two weak regiments of light cavalry, who were easily beaten by the French. This, so far, was the only French success; for

Serras was still held up before the farm, Durutte had been driven out of most of Kis-Megyer, and Severoli's troops were almost demoralised, till they were rallied by Eugène in person, and supported by Pacthod. With these reinforcements, aided by the threat against the Austrian rear by the victorious cavalry, the French and Italian Infantry were able to advance, though it cost Serras a deal of desperate fighting and heavy losses before he succeeded in storming the farm.

It was about 5 P.M. when John recognised that, with the loss of his three points of support, and the appearance of the French cavalry towards his line of retreat, he could no longer hold his position. Part of his right wing, chiefly Hungarians, got into the fortress of Raab. The rest of the army fell back on Gönyö, the Hungarians in disorder, covered by the regulars, who still maintained good order.

The Austrians lost, according to Von Angeli, altogether 6211 men, of whom 2406 were prisoners, and 1305 "missing."[1]   Also two guns and, according to Eugène, two sets of colours. The losses mainly fell, with the brunt of the fighting, on the regulars. Mesko, who, with a force chiefly consisting of 'Insurrection' cavalry, had broken out from Raab during the battle against the French rear, found his retreat cut off. According to Von Angeli, he succeeded in cutting his way across Eugène's communications, where he picked up several despatch bearers, and broke up a French escort convoying several hundred prisoners. He then moved up the left bank of the Raab, escaping from Marulaz's cavalry sent in pursuit, crossed the river at Vágh, and safely joined Chasteler beyond Kis-Czell.

In public, Napoleon had nothing but praise for Eugène's battle ; even in a despatch to his stepson he spoke of Raab as "a grand-daughter of Marengo and Friedland."

[1] These were chiefly the men who got into Raab.

The remark may pass for Marengo, but the relationship to the chef d'œuvre of Friedland was hardly so close.

The Emperor goes on to say: "Since you attacked in echelons by the right, why not have placed 25 guns at the head of your echelons? Artillery, like all other arms, should be united in mass if one wishes to obtain an important result." [1]

After his victory Eugène spent the night in front of Raab. John, who had retreated to Gönyö, crossed the Danube on the morning of the 15th, took position behind the Waag, and occupied Komorn. Here he met Wimpffen with an order from Charles requiring him to resume the offensive! Naturally, the order was incapable of execution.

The remainder of the independent operations of the French army of Italy are not of much interest. Eugène was required to besiege and take Raab, which he eventually did, though it was not till the 23rd that the place capitulated. The Army of Italy was now practically part of Napoleon's main army, in which it was formally incorporated on the 28th. John, after his defeat at Raab, had manœuvred about on the opposite side of the Danube in a rather aimless way, and, on the 23rd, had, under Charles' orders, reached Pressburg, and taken over the command there from Bianchi.

It will be remembered that John had left Stoichewich on the Dalmatian frontier with 8000 men against Marmont's corp of 10,500. At first, the Austrian offensive operations were successful here also. The weak French outposts were driven in and forced to take shelter under the guns of Zara,[2] and Stoichewich took up a position at Kürn. There he was harassed by Bosnian and Turkish bands, and was also alarmed for his retreat

---

[1] The operations of Eugène's army in Hungary were generally directed by Napoleon himself. For a discussion of his orders on advance guards, see Colonel Foch's *Principes de la Guerre*, p. 236, etc.

[2] Zara and a few other places here mentioned are beyond the southern limit of the general map.

by the reported advance of the French on Laibach. He resolved, therefore, to retire on Gospić.

Thereupon, Marmont advanced from Zara on the 14th May, and badly defeated the Austrians at Pribudić, capturing Stoichewich himself, on the 16th May. The remnants of the brigade, under Colonel Rebrowich, retreated on Gospić, eventually joining Gyulai (Ban of Croatia) about Agram. That general, in the beginning of June, commanded about 27,000 men, of whom only 10,000 were regulars, the rest being chiefly the Croatian and Slavonic 'Insurrections,' irregular troops. He now found himself between Macdonald marching by Cilly to Graz, and Marmont, who had reached Laibach by Fiume on the 3rd June. On the 8th June, Gyulai came into communication with Chasteler, who had succeeded in passing from the Tyrol to Klagenfurt, in front of which he remained two days, interrupting the communications of Eugène with Italy, and then escaping in front of Marmont, and behind Macdonald. No sooner were Gyulai and Chasteler united than they separated again, Chasteler marching to rejoin John, whilst Gyulai made a dash to relieve and reprovision the citadel of Graz, blockaded by Broussier, who had been left behind by Macdonald. Gyulai reached Marburg on the 15th, and, hearing of Marmont's arrival at Cilly on the 19th, marched westwards, compelling Marmont to make for Graz by Unter Drauburg. Satisfied that Marmont was making this détour, Gyulai took the shorter road by Ehrenhausen and Wildon, compelled Broussier to raise the blockade of the Graz citadel on the 24th, and re-provisioned the garrison on the 25th.[1] On that day and

---

[1] Napoleon was furious with Broussier, who fell back on Marmont, then sent two battalions of the 84th back, unsupported, to Graz, and exposed to the whole of Gyulai's corps. They fixed themselves in the cemetery and made a magnificent resistance till help reached them. The splendid fight of the 84th was acknowledged by Napoleon, who caused to be inscribed on their colours, in memory of it, the words 'un contre dix.'

the next there were engagements with the advance guard of Marmont, in which the Austrians took 3 guns, but lost 2000 men. On the 27th, Gyulai fell back to Gnas, south-east of Graz. On the 28th, Marmont set out in pursuit, after renewing the blockade of Graz. On the 29th, however, he received Napoleon's orders to hurry by forced marches to Vienna for the approaching battle on the Marchfeld.

A few words may now be devoted to indicating what had been going on meanwhile on the northern frontier of Austria, where Archduke Ferdinand, brother of the Empress, commanding the VII. corps, was opposed to Joseph Poniatowski with a very inferior force of Poles, and a few Saxons.

On the 17th April, Ferdinand crossed the Pilica, and, after defeating Poniatowski at Raszyn, arrived before Warsaw on the 22nd. Next day, Poniatowski agreed to evacuate Warsaw, which was quite indefensible by his small force. He passed to the right bank of the Vistula and awaited Russian support, whilst actively striving to raise his countrymen east of the Vistula, and even to the west, where Dombrowski was particularly energetic.

Ferdinand, disregarding Poniatowski, pushed forward, apparently more in the hope of raising trouble in Prussia than in that of himself achieving any military success. He failed to cross to the right bank of the Vistula, both at Thorn and at Plock, but his advance caused some alarm at Danzig, though he never got so far as that. On the 5th May, Russia declared war against Austria, but her hands were full with the wars against Sweden and Turkey. Moreover, her hostility against Austria was at best very half-hearted, and there were constant disputes between Gallitzin, the Russian commander, and Poniatowski. The Polish Prince persistently maintained that Russia was really favourable to Austria.

The operations were very complicated and of no

military interest, though there were some smart enterprises by the Poles, notably the escalade of Zamosz.
Eventually, the operations in his rear, and the threats of
the Russians, compelled Ferdinand to retreat. Cracow
fell into the hands of the Russians and the Poles, who
nearly came to blows over it. Just before Wagram, the
Emperor Francis had to write to the Archduke Charles
that the whole of Galicia was lost, and no arrangement
with Russia was possible. He even wanted Charles to
send 12,000 or 15,000 men to Ferdinand's assistance,
an arrangement which was prevented by the approach of
the battle of Wagram.

The results of the operations about Ratisbon had, for
the moment, quenched any hopes that may have been
entertained by the Prussian government of a general
rising against Napoleon. They were revived by
Napoleon's defeat at Essling, and there were many
negotiations between the court of Koenigsberg and the
Austrian emissary Steigentesch. These came to nothing,
and there was no official participation by Prussia in the
war. The time for revolt against Napoleon's domination was not yet come. Yet, there were several more or
less private enterprises which gave great trouble to the
French. The conspiracy of Dörnberg has already been
mentioned, as well as Schill's daring, and, for a time,
successful enterprise, which ended in his defeat at the
hands of the Dutch troops, and his death in the streets
of Stralsund. In June, the Duke of Brunswick-Oels [1]
marched through Lusatia with his " Black Brunswickers "
and joined the Austrian Am Ende, who was, with 6000
or 7000 men, at Dresden on the 12th June. With
Brunswick were Dörnberg, Katt, and other German
patriots. The Saxon Royal Family had to leave the
capital hurriedly, and Brunswick did his best to raise the
country against the French.

---

[1] It was this Duke of Brunswick who was afterwards killed at Quatre Bras.

Radivojewich, with some 6000 Austrians, marched by
Egra to Baireuth, which he reached on the 14th June,
threatening to invade Suabia and join the insurgents of
the Vorarlberg. It was such enterprises that Beaumont's
reserve was intended to meet. There were popular outbreaks at Mergentheim (25th June), at Stockach, and at
other places. These were suppressed by the King of
Wurtemberg. The revolts in the Tyrol and the Vorarlberg were in full blaze. All these operations are merely
referred to as showing the great dangers which threatened
Napoleon's long line of communications, dangers which
he might probably have escaped if, instead of marching
on Vienna, he had fallen on Charles at Cham and
destroyed him. We need only allude to the renewed
troubles in Spain, to the English landings in Southern
Italy, and, later, at Cuxhaven, and to the arrest of Pius
VII., all of which matters seriously added to the
Emperor's anxieties.

In the last days of June, matters began to improve as
Jerome advanced towards Saxony with some 15,000
men, and Junot took command of the " Corps of Observation of the Elbe" at Frankfurt (20th June). Jerome
drove back the enemy from Leipzig, whilst Junot did the
same with Radivojewich, who fell back on Bohemia. On
the 3rd July, however, Radivojewich was joined by
Kienmayer with reinforcements, raising the united force
to about 15,000. They found themselves between
Jerome and Junot, on the latter of whom they turned.
Jerome, instead of at once following Kienmayer, betook
himself to Dresden. He delayed much, and was
frightened by the approach of a fresh force under the
ex-Elector of Hesse. Consequently, when he arrived at
Hof on the 10th July, he found the Austrian cavalry
there. On the previous day Kienmayer had met Junot
at Gefrees, defeated him, and driven him back on
Baireuth and Amberg. Jerome then fell back on Schleiz

eventually concentrating the 10,000 men he now had at Erfurt. He was followed to his frontier by Brunswick, who thence rejoined Am Ende, now again at Dresden. On the 21st, the armistice of Znaim having been notified, Dresden was again evacuated, as well as the whole of Saxony and the Palatinate.

CHAPTER XVI

FROM ESSLING TO WAGRAM

WE now return to Napoleon and the Archduke Charles, facing one another on opposite banks of the Danube near Vienna.

The Emperor seems to have at least suffered from a prolonged fit of depression and inaction on the 23rd May, even if his alleged 36 hours' sleep is an exaggeration. It would be absurd to suppose that he did not realise what a severe blow his prestige had suffered by his defeat at Essling, and that the consequences, in Germany especially, might be very serious. It was all very well to represent the battle as a victory. The French might console themselves with the fact that they had made a magnificent stand against forces which were at no period of the battle less than double their own ; but that did not alter the fact that they had been defeated in a great battle. They had not even, as at Eylau, ended by holding the battle-field, or by gaining, as they had at Eylau, much ground. No such reverse had been suffered by a French army led by Napoleon, and, if the defeat was due to inferior forces, to lack of ammunition, and to the impossibility of bringing over reinforcements when the bridges were broken, these causes were to be attributed mainly to their general, who, despising his enemy, had incurred the risk.

Napoleon never in practice admitted a mistake on his own part, whatever in theory he held as to the fallibility of all generals, not even excepting himself. He never took the step from the abstract statement that the greatest general was he who made fewest mistakes, to the concrete admission that on any given occasion he himself had failed. But his subsequent conduct, the infinite care which he bestowed on taking every possible precaution against the failure of his next attempt, are a tacit admission that his preparations before Essling were insufficient. On the 24th, he woke up in earnest and began to issue orders in all directions. Lauriston was ordered to be on the look-out for the expected arrival of Eugène, whom Napoleon knew to be approaching. Vandamme was directed to bring up his whole force to St Polten, setting free Davout's 1st division to move to Vienna. Occupying Mölk and Mautern, Vandamme was to hold fast the enemy's forces at Krems, and to keep a sharp look-out to the south, towards Lilienfeld and Mariazell. Bernadotte, behind him, was to guard Linz in the north and Steyer in the south, and was to beware of venturing far towards Bohemia, or risking defeat by Kolowrat, whilst keeping that general as far away as possible. The Emperor indicated that possibly he might call Bernadotte to Vienna, replacing him by Lefebvre, now that the Tyrol was more or less subdued. To the French nation by his bulletin, and to his German allies by a letter to the Crown Prince of Bavaria, he misrepresented the retirement from Aspern-Essling as solely due to the breaking of the bridge. It is noticeable that he, at this time, speaks of himself as holding the left bank of the Danube, whereas the fact was that he only held the Lobau—on the left bank, it is true, of the main stream, but still separated from the mainland by the broad stream of the Stadlau arm. That was a detail which would naturally escape the notice of the average man, unacquainted with the topographical details of

x

the neighbourhood. The Emperor rearranged his cavalry so as to form a great screen around him south of the Danube. Montbrun was ordered towards Fischamend and Bruck on the Leitha ; Colbert to Wiener Neustadt ; Nansouty to Fischamend and Schwechat ; St Sulpice to the line Laxemburg-Neustadt ; the 3rd division of cuirassiers (now under Arrighi, vice Espagne killed) was between Laxemburg and Bruck on the Leitha. Thus the light cavalry was supported by 14 regiments of heavy.

The 24th was, as the 23rd had been, a day of anxiety in the Lobau ; for supplies were short and had to reach the island by boat. It was not till the morning of the 25th that the main bridge was once more passable. It was at once used for clearing the island of all but the garrison which was to hold it for the present, that is the 4th corps and the 23rd chasseurs under Masséna, to whom Napoleon confided this important command, under his own constant supervision from Ebersdorf, when he was not in the Lobau.

The wounded, who had been lying in great misery in the island for the past two days, were first sent over, then the empty or damaged ammunition waggons, then the Guard, 2nd corps, St Hilaire's division,[1] and Demont's. Napoleon himself returned to Ebersdorf, where he was assured by Bertrand that no further serious damage to the bridge was likely.

Meanwhile, the Archduke Charles had begun to find that, in the prevailing hot weather, it was no longer feasible to keep his army in the Aspern-Essling position, where the air reeked with the fetid odours from the ill-buried corpses of the thousands killed in the battle. He also saw that he would probably still be able, with his main body in a position to the north, to prevent a French crossing, now that so many of them, as he knew

---

[1] Now under Puthod and returned to the III. corps.

from his Bisamberg observatory, had repassed the river. He accordingly withdrew his headquarters to Markgrafneusiedl, and posted the I. II., and IV. corps behind the Russbach, between that place and the Helma Hof. Hiller and Klenau were ordered to remain at Aspern and Essling, to harass the enemy, to prevent a fresh crossing, to damage the bridge, and, if opportunity offered, to attack the Lobau. The latter opportunity was hardly likely to arise. The cavalry reserve was distributed amongst the villages of Pysdorf, Grosshofen, and Glinzendorf. The V. corps retained its old position, with orders to guard the islands opposite Nussdorf. No orders were issued to Schustekh towards Krems, but Kolowrat, who was north of Linz at Neumarkt, was ordered to spread in Germany the news of the victory at Essling. Charles and the Emperor believed they could bring about a popular rising in Germany.

Next day, and for many days after, the Austrians were busy entrenching. These operations, together with Napoleon's measures of a like character, and his preparation of bridges and other necessities for the new crossing, will form the subject of a separate section presently.

Napoleon had, during the battle of Essling, become painfully aware of his own inferiority in artillery, as compared with his enemy. His first operation was to redistribute his corps artillery, the reasons for which he does not give. The guns would now be distributed thus : 2nd corps (Oudinot), 48 ; 3rd corps (Davout), 60 ; 4th corps (Masséna), 66 ; cavalry reserve (Bessières), 26. Total 100, besides the Guard.

Then he set about supplying his infantry regiments with guns on the same principle that the Prussians employed in 1806. Apparently the French regiments had formerly had guns of this class ; for in one of his orders the Emperor writes : "Every day I am more convinced of the great harm which was done to our armies by taking away their regimental guns." The object of this allotment of regimental guns appears to have been to give confidence to his new soldiers; for, in his order of the 26th May, Napoleon says : "It is indifferent to a battalion whether it has 4-pounders or 3-pounders or 6-pounders."

To provide these guns, Napoleon utilised the Austrian light guns which he had captured in previous battles, or in the arsenals of Vienna. They were distributed thus : Oudinot and Masséna 24 each, and Davout 30—total, 78. His ultimate object was to give two guns to each regiment. Besides this measure, more artillery was summoned from France and the rear.

On the 26th, on the Austrian side Hiller, on the plea of sickness, resigned his command and was replaced by Klenau—probably no very great loss to Charles, to whom Hiller was bitterly opposed.[1] At this time the Emperor Francis urged on his brother the desirability of a resumption of the offensive, but Charles did not see his way to it. He certainly could not cross at the Lobau, and a crossing either higher up at Krems, or lower down at Pressburg would have the disadvantage of endangering his communications with Moravia and Bohemia, and the arsenals and other sources of supply which he had there, at Brünn and Olmütz. He sent orders to Kolowrat to leave a suitable force under Sommariva opposite Linz, and to bring the rest of his corps to the main army. Reuss, Hiller (Klenau), and Schustekh were to keep the enemy alarmed by demonstrations threatening a crossing ; but, as Binder v. Krieglstein points out, the orders were half-hearted, and Charles was really bent on sitting still on the defensive. Next day, Bianchi's brigade was sent down to hold the bridge head at Pressburg, but even this Binder v.

---

[1] Hiller appears to have resumed his command, which he again resigned, on the same plea, just before Wagram.

Krieglstein does not consider to have really indicated an intention to cross.

On the 27th, the VI. corps made a slight demonstration and floated down a few boats, which did no harm to the bridge. It had, however, been broken during the previous night. On the 28th, threats of Schustekh and Radetzky above Vienna did not even have the effect of imposing on Vandamme, now in charge of this section. On this latter date, the VI. corps made another demonstration and occupied Am Spitz. Kolowrat, leaving Sommariva's division at Freystadt, marched with his other two for the Marchfeld.

Napoleon having now (27th) heard of the arrival of Eugène's cavalry on the Semmering, issued a magniloquent proclamation to the Army of Italy. In his letter to Eugène he gives the positions of his cavalry screen thus. Lasalle at Hinberg, with posts towards Pressburg ; Montbrun at Oedenburg, with posts towards Graz ; Lauriston would now move eastwards towards Oedenburg, with his cavalry and two Baden regiments. At the same time the Emperor ordered the strengthening of the bridge-head opposite Linz, so that it might be defensible by 3000 men against 30,000.

On the 31st May, Napoleon was somewhat alarmed by Bianchi's movement to Pressburg ; for he ordered Davout to send a division there to seize the bridge-head which the enemy was constructing. He also wrote to Vandamme about a threatened crossing about Krems. He was to use floating mills against the enemy's bridge, if he made one, and, in case of the crossing being successful, Davout would march, and everything about Mölk would fall back on the Enns, whilst Bernadotte threatened the intruder's right flank.

Lefebvre was now ordered to join Vandamme.

By the 4th June, Bernadotte's Saxons were at St Polten, Dupas' division at Mautern, Davout had bombarded the bridge-head at Pressburg, but had not succeeded in taking it.

Bianchi writing that he was attacked, Charles sent another brigade to support him. Beyond this, getting up reinforcements, and fortifying opposite Lobau, the Archduke had been idle for several days past.

Napoleon also, finding the enemy had not yielded at Pressburg by the 6th, sent reinforcements in the shape of Puthod's (4th of 3rd corps) division. He calculated at this date that he ought to have, in the corps of Bernadotte, Masséna, Davout, Oudinot, the Guard, the Army of Italy, and the cavalry, from 155,000 to 160,000 men with 400 guns. This leaves out of consideration Macdonald, Marmont, Vandamme, and Lefebvre. The estimate, which Berthier was ordered to verify, appears to be decidedly too high.

Even after the 20th June, Napoleon was much exercised about three things: (1) the failure of Davout to clear Pressburg; (2) the continued resistance of Raab; (3) Marmont's very slow advance.[1] Raab surrendered on the 23rd, but Pressburg still held out. Davout was, therefore, to send a notice to the Austrians, in the islands about Pressburg, that if they would evacuate them, there should be no French crossing there; otherwise Pressburg would be shelled and burnt. There is a curious instruction that this notice was only to be signed by a general of brigade. The reasons for this appear to be that, Pressburg being an open town not actually defended by the enemy (who were in the islands and the bridge-head), it would hardly be in accordance with the usages of civilised warfare to shell it; also it might hereafter be desirable to disavow the promise not to cross if the islands were evacuated. A notice signed by Davout, or his Chief of

---

[1] He had been delayed at the crossing of the Drave, and only reached Graz on the 27th.

the Staff, could hardly be disavowed ; one signed by a
brigadier-general only would be on a different footing, as
regards those who could not prove that the order was
Napoleon's. The bombardment was duly carried out,
at intervals during several days, without producing the
desired effect.

From the 28th June, it became apparent, if only from
the increase in Napoleon's outturn of orders, that the day
of battle was approaching. He was still waiting for
Marmont, to whom he wrote that, whereas he ought to
have been at Graz on the 23rd or 24th, he was still not
there on the 27th. The Emperor was altogether dis-
satisfied with him, and with Broussier, who had allowed
himself to be frightened from Graz. " Marmont has
manœuvred badly enough ; Broussier still worse," were
the words he used to Eugène.

Next day (29th), Napoleon, writing to Davout before
Pressburg, said, " the concentration is general." Davout
would be relieved by one of Eugène's divisions on the 1st
or 2nd July, and should march on Ebersdorf on the 3rd ;
on the 5th, the enemy would be attacked. Everything was
to come up, except 1000 men to garrison Raab, and such
force as Davout might find necessary to contain Bianchi.[1]

Marmont (who had really reached Graz early on the
27th), and Broussier, were to come by forced marches
to Ebersdorf. Eugène was to leave Baraguay d'Hilliers,
with 4000 or 5000 men, opposite Pressburg, and himself
to reach Ebersdorf on the evening of the 4th. He and
Davout would come by Bruck on the Leitha ; it was a
little farther than by the Danube, but the march would
be beyond the observation of the enemy on the left bank.
Lefebvre was to despatch Wrede's division on the 1st,
and, if he could spare it, part of Deroy's. These must
reach Mölk early on the 3rd July, so as to be able to
march another 7 or 8 miles if required.

[1] Really John who had taken Bianchi's place.

Before proceeding to describe the final preparations for the crossing, it will now be well to see what, during the 6 or 7 weeks since Essling, had been done by the Austrians in the way of fortification, and by the French in the same matter, in preparation for throwing bridges, and in the collection of supplies in Lobau.

Let us begin with the Austrians. Charles began fortifying on the 25th May, and continued till he had completed what seemed to him a satisfactory entrenched position.

Beginning on the Austrian right, the south-west corner of Aspern was connected with the river by a line of trenches, with abbatis in front, running generally south-west from Aspern across the Gemeinde-Au with several redoubts (I. and II) and other small works in it. There was a small work (III.) at the south-east corner of Aspern, and another farther out to the south-east. The village itself does not seem to have contained any special works, though the houses, of course, must have been prepared for defence. From the centre of the eastern side there ran eastwards a continuous parapet along the road to Essling. In this were three redoubts, the first near Aspern, the other two dividing the distance to Essling into three more or less equal parts (Nos. IV., V., VI.). Work No. VII. was at the southern extremity of the farm and garden stretching south from Essling. No. VIII. was on the road Essling-Enzersdorf, about two-thirds of the way to the latter, and it was connected by a parapet with No. IX., which stood on the bank of the Stadlau arm, opposite the lower end of the Ile Espagne. The parapet continued, at right angles to that just mentioned, along the left bank to another redoubt, No. XIV., nearly due south of Enzersdorf and opposite the Ile Lannes. No. X. was in the south side of Enzersdorf, XI. outside it to the south-east, XII. between X. and XIV., XIII. at the eastern exit of Enzersdorf, and

XV. south-east of XI. There the field-works ended, except for redoubt No. XVI. built at the junction of the Stadlau arm with the main stream. Between the line XIV.-XV. and this No. XVI. there was an interval of two miles unprotected by any work.

Napoleon's work in the Lobau, or as it was now called the "Ile Napoleon," was of a much more ambitious and complete character.

The breaches in the main bridge, due to the Austrian mills and other floating masses sent down on the 22nd, were only repaired on the morning of the 25th, as has already been stated. The bridge was again broken by the ever-rising waters, and by more floating mills,[1] during the night of the 26th-27th, and it was only on the 28th that one branch was restored. The other could not be so till next day, or later.

The bridges for the new crossing were to be of a very different character from the single bridge which had served before Essling. The new bridges over the first two arms, that is from the right bank to the Schneidergrund, and from that to the Lobgrund, took about three weeks to complete. Over both branches there was a boat or pontoon bridge as before. A short way above this was a bridge laid on piers formed of piles. Each pier consisted of five piles of a diameter of about 12 inches set at a distance from one another (measured from centre to centre) of about 30 inches. The piles were tied together by two diagonal trusses and one horizontal one, the latter just below the mean level of the surface of the river. There were altogether 60 spans (41 on the first arm, 19 on the second) covering a length of 840 yards. The spans between the piers varied from 23 feet to 49. The driving was done by seven floating pile-drivers, the anchoring of which in the powerful stream was often a matter of great difficulty. The roadway of this bridge,

---

[1] Corr. 15,272. "13th bulletin."

which was intended for all arms, was 12 feet 1 inch wide
with a strong railing on either side. The headings of the
piers, on which the roadway rested, were 4 feet 3 inches
above mean water level. The Danube here was in
places 25 feet deep. Over the second arm (Schneidergrund to Lobgrund) there was, in addition to these two
bridges, a second pile bridge, about fifty yards above the
great one. It was much lighter, being intended only for
infantry. The roadway was only 5 feet 3 inches broad,
and it is said that the structure swayed so much under
the action of the stream that it was necessary to hold on
to the handrail in crossing.

To protect these bridges from mills and other objects
floating in the stream, there was a double stockade above
them, the centre of which was on a sandbank.

Besides this, the Emperor had for the protection of
the bridges, as well as for assisting in military operations,
a fleet of 10 gunboats and 10 smaller patrol boats. The
gunboats (Rivoli, Arcola, Montebello, etc.) carried from
25 to 50 men each, and from 1 to 4 guns. They were
manned by the sailors of the Guard, commanded by
Captain Baste of the now useless navy.

Small pile bridges connected the Lobgrund with the
Lobau.

Of the latter island the Emperor made a regular
entrenched camp, to serve as an advanced base for his
final crossing of the Stadlau arm and his operations
beyond. A complete network of good roads facilitated
movement in any direction in the island; at night the
roads were well lighted, and they were provided with
numerous direction posts. There were magazines of
every description, a large bakery, and a small arsenal
with wharves and wood stores. In order to provide a
look-out post, the Emperor sent for one of the platforms,
with a ladder leading to it, which he had observed in use
for pruning trees in the gardens of Vienna. Being self-

supporting, it could be so placed, in front of a tree for example, as not to draw the enemy's fire. It was set up in the south-eastern part of the island.

Of fortifications a regular system was constructed. The Prater island opposite Vienna was fortified so as to prevent Austrian enterprises in that direction. There was a redoubt with two guns on the Ile Massena, nearly south of the Austrian works on the Gemeinde-Au.

On the Lobau there were seven works near the right bank of the Stadlau arm, flanking the tête de pont on the Mühlau. Their fire prevented the Austrians from carrying out their apparent intention of occupying the tête de pont and converting it into a work opposing the French.

Of the islands in the Stadlau arm, the Austrians held the Ile Bessières till the 2nd July, and the Ile Pouzet till July 5th. The Iles Espagne, Lannes, and Alexandre were all held and strongly fortified by the French, and each of them was connected with the Lobau by a strong bridge. There were two batteries at the mouth of the Stadlau arm, opposite to the Austrian work No. XVI. Another series of works lined both banks of the small channel between the Lobgrund and the Lobau, covering the bridges across it and converting it into a bridge-head to the main bridge, and a réduit to the Lobau. On the right bank of the main stream, an extensive tête de pont covered the approach to the main bridges from the south. Finally, a battery was placed opposite the mouth of the Stadlau arm.

The artillery arming these works was as follows :— North front, 24 pieces ; north-east front, 73 ; on the right bank in the tête de pont, 4 ; in reserve, 28. Total, 129, of which 46 were 6-pounders, 26 12-pounders, 30 18-pounders, 10 heavy howitzers, and 17 12-inch mortars.

The channels between the islands occupied by the

French and the Lobau were utilised for the concealment of the boats, pontoons, and other materials for bridging. This was especially necessary on the east side, from which the Emperor wished to divert the attention of the Austrians, and which, as will be seen from the map, he left almost devoid of fortifications below the Ile Alexandre, except opposite the Austrian work No. XVI.

The bridges were generally of pontoons, sometimes of rafts. The greatest triumph in the way of bridge construction was the bridge across which the infantry of Masséna's corps was to pass. This Napoleon desired to have "swung" in a single piece across the Stadlau arm below the Ile Alexandre. The channel between that island and the Lobau was only about 13 or 14 yards across, and very winding. The bridge to be swung would require to be 178 yards in length, and was to have a roadway of 7 feet 3 inches. It was therefore constructed in the channel in four sections. These were fastened to one another by rope hinges, so that they might be able to turn round the corners of the channel as the whole thing was floated down to the broader arm below. The bridge was made with 14 captured Austrian pontoons. Infinite care was bestowed on the construction, indeed a French engineer criticised it as too great, seeing that only infantry was to use the bridge. He says, with a little more strengthening of the roadway, etc., it could have carried all arms. However, as is remarked by the author of the work from which this description is taken,[1] the responsibility was great, and too great care could scarcely be exercised. We may anticipate events by describing how this great bridge was actually swung in the night of the 4th-5th July. In the evening of the 4th it was floated bodily down, through the channel in which its sections were constructed, to a point some 300

[1] "Essai d'une instruction sur le passage des rivières, etc," par C. A. Haillot, Paris, 1835, vol. ii., pp. 196-199.

yards below the lower end of the Ile Alexandre. Lying along the right bank of the Stadlau arm, with its lower end at the point indicated, its sections were permanently attached to one another. One section of pontonniers was told off to attach the hawsers holding the lower end to two large trees as the bridge swung into position; another section was charged with pushing off the upper parts of the bridge into the current; another with steadying it by means of a hawser over 400 yards in length; others attended to anchoring the pontoons as they came into position; and yet another party was ready at the outer end with an extra section of one pontoon, in case the bridge should be too short. Another hawser and a windlass had already been taken over to the left bank by the first of the five armed boats which carried across 1500 of Boudet's men to protect the work.

At 11 P.M. Napoleon arrived to personally supervise the swinging of the bridge. Turning to Captain Heckmann, in charge of the operation, he said, " How long do you require for the swinging?" "A quarter of an hour, Sire." "I give you five minutes. Bertrand, your watch!" Everything moved with precision, and, according to Haillot, the bridge was in position, though not properly fixed, in four minutes.[1] So impatient was Napoleon, that he would not wait for the final touches, but ordered the infantry to cross at once. They were actually on the bridge when it was being finally secured.

It may be considered that Napoleon's passage of the Stadlau arm actually began on the 30th June, and continued till the morning of the 6th July. On the former day, at 6 P.M., the batteries commanding the ground in the Mühlau, in front of the old place of crossing, opened fire, with 36 guns, on the Austrian outposts.

Under cover of this fire, the construction of a pontoon bridge was commenced, and 800 of Legrand's men

---

[1] Meyerhofer Vedropolje says 8 minutes.

passed over by boat. The bridge was complete in $1\frac{1}{4}$ hours, and the rest of Legrand's division passing over it took post on the mainland, whilst the completion of the bridge-head was actively pressed on. Firing continued till 10.30 P.M., but Legrand does not appear to have encountered very serious resistance. On the 1st July, Napoleon, whose headquarters had hitherto, since the 5th June, been at Schönbrünn, transferred them to the south-western portion of the Ile Napoleon (Lobau), at a point about three-quarters of a mile north-west of the end of the main bridge.

All this time Charles had been doing nothing, and it was only on the 1st July that he awoke to the fact that Napoleon was now in deadly earnest. The Archduke, therefore, began to assemble his army on the ground on which he proposed to fight. By the morning of the 1st he had got it into the following positions :—IV. corps Rutzendorf-Pysdorf ; II. between Pysdorf and the Essling house ; I. on the right of the II. as far as Hirschstetten ; behind it the grenadiers in front of Süssenbrünn ; III. in front of Gerasdorf ; cavalry reserve about the Neu-Wirtshaus, where Charles himself arrived at 2 A.M. The III. corps had one brigade on the Bisamberg, and the IV. sent Riese's brigade to strengthen Nordmann in Gross Enzersdorf. Weiss' brigade was called in from the river March, with the exception of two landwehr regiments. The advanced troops (Nordmann, Hiller, and Riese) were to hold their entrenched position (Aspern-Essling-Enzersdorf) to the last, if seriously attacked. From the look-outs, on the Bisamberg and the church tower of Enzersdorf, came reports that great masses of troops were concentrating on the right bank near the approaches to the bridges, and that, though there was not yet any strengthening of the forces in the Lobau, the eastern part of the island was held in sensibly weaker force. From all this the Austrian staff concluded

that Napoleon was going to repeat his manœuvre of the
20th May, and cross to the Mühlau, where he already
held the bridge-head, and where alone he, at present,
had thrown a bridge. That would, naturally, have suited
the Austrians exactly, and it was, equally naturally, the
most unlikely thing for Napoleon to do; but the Austrians
seem never to have been able to get over the idea that
Napoleon would do a foolish act rather than a wise one.

At 11 A.M., Charles began to push forward to within
supporting distance of the fortified line held by the VI.
corps, an¹ by Nordmann's advance guard. The III.
corps stood about 1000 yards behind Aspern, the II. the
same distance behind Essling, each of them in two lines.
On the heights¹ behind the interval between these was
the cavalry reserve. The IV. corps was about Wittau ;
the I. at Breitenlee, with the grenadiers as reserve at
Raasdorf. Mayer's and Riese's brigades, and the Hesse-
Homburg hussars supported Nordmann at Enzersdorf.

Thus the Austrian army was in an excellent position
to meet a frontal attack by Napoleon on the strongly
fortified line Aspern-Enzersdorf. Was it likely he would
dash his head against such a position, in front of which
he had no room to deploy ? If he supported his attack
by a flank attack from the Ile Alexandre, the IV. corps
was ready to meet that. It never seems to have crossed
the Austrian mind at this time that the main attack
might be from the east side of Lobau. Yet Hiller had
called attention to the weakness of the left wing. The
main objection to an attack on it was the fact that, at
first, the bridges would lie on the flank, not to the rear
of the French passing and deploying with their front to
the north. There were divergences of opinion in the
Austrian headquarters. Charles himself seems to have
believed that Napoleon intended crossing elsewhere, and

¹ "Heights" in speaking of the Marchfeld is hardly the right term, for
few parts of the plain exceed 10 feet above the general level.

that the preparations in the Lobau were only a feint to
hold the Austrians there. Wimpffen, and probably
Grünne, believed in a renewed attempt from Lobau, in
which case they wanted to fight farther back. Charles
would seize the enemy's weak moment, during the
crossing; his advisers, puffed up since Essling with
unlimited self-confidence, believed they could beat
Napoleon after he had got over, and destroy him as he
retreated.

The result of these divergences of opinion in high
quarters was that no definite conclusion was arrived at.
There existed two opinions, and, as they had not been
brought definitely into discussion and finally decided for
or against, first one and then the other appeared to gain
ground. Charles' movements at 11 A.M. pointed to the
prevalence of Wimpffen's theory, that the enemy would
cross from the Lobau, whilst, on the other hand, the
method of meeting the attack, during the crossing, and
not in a rearward position, was Charles'. The fact that
practically nothing was done on the 1st by the French
in the direction of pushing their advance rather tended
to confirm Charles' theory that the movement at Lobau
was only a feint. On the other hand, the news from the
Bisamberg observatory, indicating a concentration of the
French forces in Lobau towards the west of the island,
pointed to a renewal of the attack in the old direction.
The change of views is reflected in two letters from
Charles to John. In the first, John is told that, if he
cannot hold the Pressburg tête de pont for 48 hours,
he should destroy it and withdraw the troops. That
would mean liberty to Napoleon to draw in Davout and
Eugène, whilst Charles would call in John for the great
battle on the Marchfeld. The second letter was dated
in the evening, though not despatched till next morning.
It directed John to keep the enemy employed at Pressburg as much as possible. Whilst the first letter indicated

a belief that the great battle would be on the Marchfeld, and therefore Pressburg would no longer be of importance, the second indicated a belief that the French operations on the Lobau were only a demonstration, which could appropriately be answered by an Austrian demonstration at Pressburg.[1] Another order to the VI. corps directed it, if the French began fortifying the bridge-head, to drive them out. The corps was not strong enough for the purpose.

Napoleon, meanwhile, had observed with the utmost satisfaction the deployment of the Austrian army as if to meet an attack on the old line, which was just what he wanted, as his intentions were very different.

At 2 P.M. he took another measure also calculated to confirm the Austrian idea of an attack on the fortified line, Aspern-Enzersdorf. Masséna was directed to seize the Ile Bessières, just below the Mühlau bridge, to unite it to the Lobau by a bridge, and place an 8-gun battery on it. The operation was carried out in the early morning of the 2nd, and the Austrian garrison of only 100 men was destroyed.

When Napoleon gave Masséna the order for this attack, he also ordered him to bring Oudinot's corps over at 9 P.M. on the 1st, into the south-eastern part of Lobau, Molitor moving farther north. Boudet was also to move from the south-west of Lobau to the neighbourhood of St Hilaire island, so as to make room for the Guard about the Emperor's headquarters.

Writing to Eugène, the Emperor remarks that he is glad that the Viceroy will be up by the 4th, and that Broussier and Marmont will also be so. At 3 A.M. on the 2nd July, six guns on the Prater island, opposite Vienna, began bombarding the Austrian posts near Stadlau, and 500 men crossed and occupied the Schierlinggrund. At daybreak there was commenced the

[1] *B. K.*, ii. 291.

Y

building of a trestle bridge about 50 yards above the pontoon bridge by which Legrand had crossed to the Mühlau. Troops were also massed in this direction, evidently with the intention of confirming the Austrian belief in a crossing at the old place. At 8 A.M. nine French batteries opened fire on the Austrian works, Nos. VII. to XII., and, by their superior weight of metal, soon silenced them. The fire slackened after 11 A.M., and ceased entirely by 3 P.M. It had seriously damaged Nos. VIII. and IX., and caused a loss of some 300 men to Nordmann's troops. The Austrian commander-in-chief was all day at Enzersdorf and inferred that Napoleon was demonstrating against that place, in order to divert attention from Aspern, his real point of attack. In the evening Charles returned to Breitenlee. The long range of the French guns induced him to move the II. and III. corps 1500 paces farther back, and to make their advance again dependent on his special orders. Some of the French shells had fallen amongst the II. corps, without doing much harm.

Charles still felt doubtful as to whether the whole thing was not merely a demonstration; but, not liking a battlefield within range of the French heavy guns, he began to abandon the idea of falling on the French in the act of crossing, and to come round to Wimpffen's and Grünne's project of fighting farther to the rear.

To add to his troubles, his brother the Emperor wrote that he had vainly endeavoured to come to an arrangement with Russia, and that her troops now occupied the whole of Galicia. Therefore, unless Charles was prepared to carry out something himself within 48 hours, he should send 12,000 or 15,000 men to reinforce Ferdinand. Stadion also began to interfere, to complain of Charles' inactivity, and to suggest detachments. John now wrote that he was more hopeful of holding the

Pressburg bridge-head, as the works had been strengthened and the French attacks had slackened.

Charles seems at this period to have fancied peace was
possible, and Napoleon was only too anxious to encourage the idea, so as to keep Charles quiet.   A letter
from Wimpffen regarding exchange of prisoners, including that of the garrison of Raab against the 65th,
captured at Ratisbon, received a civil reply.   Also,
Charles' remonstrances against the bombardment of
Pressburg had resulted in its stoppage.   Napoleon's
overbearing tone had certainly come down after Essling,
but it was absurd for any one who knew him, as Charles
should have done, to suppose that he would now seriously
negotiate on the eve of a decisive battle.   Evidently the
Austrians over-estimated the importance of their success
on the 21st-22nd May.   So hopeful did Charles seem
that the Emperor Francis actually sent him, on the 3rd,
a letter to be transmitted to Berthier, if there was a
chance of peace without further bloodshed.

The 2nd and 3rd July were mainly employed by
Napoleon in filling up his supplies of stores and ammunition on the Lobau.   After the evening of the 3rd, he required the main bridges for the passage of troops, and
could not afford to have them blocked with waggons or
non-combatants.   Everything that was useless for the
coming battle (lame horses, baggage, followers, women,
etc.) was sent back to the right bank.   The outlying
forces, Davout, Eugène, Marmont, were all hurrying
to Ebersdorf for the passage from the Lobau to the left
bank, which was fixed for the night of the 4th-5th.

During the 3rd, the following orders were issued for
the passage of troops from the right bank to the Lobau ;
it was to take place at night, so as not to attract the
enemy's attention.   The Guard were to begin passing at
8.30 and to move to the neighbourhood of the Emperor's
headquarters.   Bernadotte was to follow, at 11.30 P.M.,

and bivouack in front of the Guard, reaching his post before daybreak.

Davout was not to cross till the following night (4th-5th), when he was to come into position between Oudinot and Masséna, in the eastern part of the island, arriving there by midnight. The Emperor clearly desired to draw no attention to this side of the island till the last moment.

Eugène was not to cross till 1 A.M. on the 5th, and then to take post between the Guard and Bernadotte. The light cavalry of the various corps was to rejoin them, being careful to pass in the dark; the cavalry reserve (Bessières') was to be ready at Ebersdorf for the passage at 4 A.M. on the 5th. Marmont and Wrede would pass as soon as they arrived.

A general order required all cavalry to bring with them green fodder for the 4th and 5th, whilst rations of bread and brandy, sufficient for the 5th and 6th, were to be served out to the whole army.

Orders were also issued for the throwing of a raft bridge from the western end of Bessières island to the Mühlau, with a flêche as bridge-head, flanked by works on the island.[1] A battery of three mortars was also to be constructed opposite the Maison Blanche (Uferhaus), where the Austrians had a battery, and, during the 4th, more batteries were to be completed there, so that the position might be overwhelmed when required.

On the 3rd, very momentous decisions were come to on the Austrian side. Charles had, during the preceding night, finally decided not to fight a great battle, under any circumstances, close to the Danube, where he would be exposed to the fire of the French heavy batteries. If he had to retreat from such a position across the open

---

[1] This bridge was a small affair of only 20 yards or so. The Danube was low at this time. Napoleon in his 24th bulletin states that it was 13 feet below flood level, and only 4 feet above extreme low water.

Marchfeld, it would be difficult to prevent the retreat from degenerating into a rout before the pursuit of the great French cavalry force.   Wimpffen and Grünne had considered this danger, and they also appear to have, at last, had an inkling that the main crossing might be from the east side of the Lobau.   If that was to be met as it was in progress, it would have to be so in broken and wooded ground, in which the French infantry had already demonstrated their superiority in the battles in April. Besides, defeat there might end in the driving of the Austrians towards Hungary, thus depriving them of the resources they still had in Moravia and Bohemia.   All these objections it was thought would be absent if a double position were taken up on the Bisamberg and the line of the Russbach, both strong positions nearly at right angles to one another.   Charles, having hitherto not contemplated occupying them, nothing had been done to strengthen them artificially.   Moreover, the army was not really strong enough to occupy both, and, as the Bisamberg covered the road to Bohemia, and the Russbach that to Moravia, to occupy only one would mean losing the line to one of those provinces.   Could they both be held, the French, manœuvring in the angle, would be as it were in the jaws of a pair of pincers, as the Austrians were at Koniggratz in 1866.   So thought Wimpffen and Grünne, but Charles was still far from being convinced that he was wrong in supposing Napoleon really meant crossing elsewhere, and was only demonstrating in the Lobau.   The latest news from the Bisamberg observatory was reassuring.   It said that troops were still exercising at Ebersdorf, as they had been for the last six weeks, and there was no essential alteration in the condition of affairs in the Lobau.   Charles, therefore, decided to withdraw his army from positions on which he had no intention of fighting into his former camps, there to await the development of Napoleon's plans. If, after all, the French should attack from the Lobau, no definite plan of action was decided on, but Charles was beginning to acquiesce in the views of Wimpffen and Grünne, and he placed his army in a position suitable for carrying them into effect. At 9 A.M., orders were issued for the withdrawal of the second line. The I. corps was to move, at 10, to Deutsch Wagram ; the grenadiers, at noon, to Gerasdorf, and, later, to the south side of Seiring ; the IV., at 2 P.M., to Markgrafneusiedl. The troops in first line were to wait till nightfall, and then to move, III. corps to Hagenbrunn, II. to Parbasdorf (Baumersdorf), Reserve cavalry to Süssenbrünn, Breitenlee, Raasdorf and Aderklaa. Thus all returned to the positions they had held for six weeks. The VI. corps, Nordmann, the brigades of Meyer and Riese, and the Hesse-Homburg hussars were to remain in the advanced line, which was to be strengthened. If " unexpectedly " they were compelled to evacuate it, the VI. was to fall back on Stammersdorf, Nordmann on Glinzendorf, protected in their retreat by the Reserve cavalry. It is difficult to see what advantage there was in their fighting an action on this ground, on which they would not be supported by the main army, which was not to fight so far forward. The order was a compromise, due to the existence of two conflicting opinions at headquarters.

At noon on the 4th July, General Reynier took over command of the French troops who were to remain behind for the defence of the Lobau and the islands in the Stadlau arm. He had for this purpose a Baden regiment from Masséna's corps, two battalions from Oudinot's, two Saxon battalions from Bernadotte's, and the Neufchatel battalion. He received full instructions for their disposal, into which we need not enter.

Orders were also issued for the disposition of the flotilla. Two gunboats were to remain off Stadlau, two off Aspern, harassing the enemy with their fire and stopping fire-ships. The rest were to be on the right, protecting that flank. These orders were drafted, if not issued, on the 2nd, and, on the 4th, the earlier part of them, dealing with the actual passage, was re-issued with modifications, mostly verbal, to Oudinot and Masséna.

All day the French worked hard at the bridge-heads on the Mühlau, at first under a heavy fire from the artillery of the Austrian VI. corps, now commanded by Klenau, vice Hiller sick, and of some of the Austrian batteries, especially Nos. VII. and IX. This was silenced by the French heavy batteries by 12.30.

Meanwhile, Davout had reached Ebersdorf, and Berna-dotte's Saxons had crossed to the Lobau. As the latter movement was reported by the Bisamberg observatory, Bernadotte appears to have been late, and to have passed by daylight. A heavy thunderstorm, at 2 P.M., put a stop to observations.

This news finally convinced the Archduke that Napoleon was not merely demonstrating at Lobau. How completely Charles had been hitherto persuaded that nothing serious would happen here is shown by a series of orders which he drafted for the despatch of nine or ten landwehr battalions to Bohemia, to oppose Jerome's advance from Saxony. Such an order could only have been contemplated on the assumption that nothing serious would happen on the Marchfeld, and that there was a chance of peace. In consequence of the report from the observatory, the orders were not issued. Binder von Krieglstein says that it was only at noon that Charles fully realised that Napoleon really meant crossing at the Lobau. The orders then issued show that the opinions of Wimpffen and Grünne had gained the upper hand.

A heavy artillery fire was to be begun at 11 P.M. on

the Mühlau, in the hopes of disordering the masses of French there, and perhaps destroying the bridges. For this purpose, the VI. corps was reinforced by "some" (*sic* in the orders) 12-pounder batteries. Previous experience had shown that, at this range, the Austrian guns could do little harm.

At 5 P.M., Klenau (VI. corps) received orders which stated that Charles proposed to stand behind the Russbach. Klenau and Nordmann were to sacrifice a large proportion of their troops before yielding the advanced line. Fighting to the last, Klenau was to fall back on the V. corps, Nordmann on Glinzendof. At the same time, Reuss (V. corps) received orders which Binder von Krieglstein believes to have been pressed upon Charles in furtherance of Wimpffen's scheme of crushing the French between the two arms of a pair of pincers. If the enemy moved in the direction of the Bisamberg, Reuss, Klenau, and Kolowrat (III. corps) were to hold that position till Charles could fall on the enemy's rear. If, on the other hand, the French turned towards the Russbach, then the Bisamberg group of three corps was in its turn to fall on the enemy's rear.

In consequence of the view of the situation now accepted by Charles, fresh orders were sent to John at Pressburg, at 7 P.M. Clearly, looking to the constant stream of French troops from the east, very little could be left in front of the Pressburg bridge-head, whilst everything pointed to a great battle on the Marchfeld, which must decide the fate of "our House." John was, therefore, to leave Bianchi, with a very few troops and some guns, to hold the bridge-head, whilst, with all the rest, but without baggage or useless impedimenta, he marched to Marchegg on the right bank of the March, where he would be on the right flank of any French attempt against Charles' left, a movement which the latter feared.

John was to report his arrival at Marchegg, where further orders would be sent to him.

Charles was clearly right, now that he realised that Napoleon was in earnest, in calling in his detachments for the decisive battle. Binder v. Krieglstein defends him against the reproach, which has been levelled against him, of not having called in Schustekh from Krems. That general's force was largely composed of landwehr of small tactical value ; it was not desirable to denude the posts above Vienna ; and, finally, Schustekh was detaining a disproportionately large force of Vandamme's Wurtembergers. In the evening, Charles wrote to his Imperial brother, informing him of the French concentration, and the evident approach of a decisive battle opposite the Lobau.

We do not propose to give in full Napoleon's orders of the 2nd and 4th[1] for the actual passage of the Stadlau arm, and the deployment on the left bank. They were carried out with such precision that the record of their execution will sufficiently indicate them.

By 6 P.M. Napoleon had in the Lobau Oudinot's corps, in the south-east towards the mouth of the Stadlau channel. North of him was Masséna, towards the Ile Alexandre. Between the two was a considerable empty space, into which Davout was to move between 8 P.M. and midnight. Masséna was a division short, as it will be remembered that Legrand was on the left bank in the Mühlau.

Bernadotte, and, south of him, the Guard occupied the western side of the island. The cavalry reserve were already at Ebersdorf, and Eugène was beginning to arrive there with the army of Italy.

The Emperor's design, generally, was to cross to the left bank at and south of the Ile Alexandre, to push out

[1] Corr. 15,481 and 15,489.

his right beyond Wittau, so as to deploy on a line facing north, with its left resting on the Stadlau arm opposite the Ile Alexandre. Then, seizing Enzersdorf, he would wheel to the left on that village as a pivot, rolling the Austrians up from left to right. The crossing at the Mühlau was a feint, though, had Charles brought his army on to the eastern side of the salient formed by the Lobau, Napoleon would perhaps have elected to cross by the Mühlau and roll the Austrian right on its left.

There was no sign of the latter movement, at the prevention of which the Emperor's concentration of troops in the west of the Lobau on the previous days had been aimed with success. For the attainment of his first objective it was necessary that the advance should begin from the right, and Oudinot's corps stood on the right, at the mouth of the Stadlau arm. It would be natural to suppose, under these circumstances, that, when the first deployment was completed, Oudinot would find himself on the right of the line beyond Wittau. But the orders were otherwise ; for Oudinot was to be in the centre of the first line, with Masséna on his left, and Davout on his right. Davout was to cross between the two,[1] and a glance at the map will show that the consequence of this must be that, in order that Oudinot and Davout might take up their positions in the line as ordered, the two corps would cross one another beyond the Stadlau arm.

Here we must quote Jomini [2] :—

"The enemy had, it is true, determined to offer no serious opposition to the passage ; but Napoleon did not know that fact, and the merit of his dispositions is not at all diminished by it.

"Singularly enough, however, the chief of the staff, though he made ten copies of the famous decree, did not

[1] Or rather between Masséna's infantry and his cavalry and artillery.
[2] *Art of War*, p. 267. Translation, Philadelphia, 1875.

observe that, by mistake, the bridge of the centre had been assigned to Davout, who had the right wing, whilst the bridge on the right was assigned to Oudinot, who was in the centre. These two corps passed each other in the night, and, had it not been for the good sense of the men and their officers, a dreadful scene of confusion might have been the result. Thanks to the supineness of the enemy, the army escaped all disorder, except that arising from a few detachments following corps to which they did not belong. . . . The error doubtless originated with Napoleon while dictating his decree ; but should it not have been detected by a chief of the staff who made ten copies of the order, and whose duty it was to supervise the formation of the troops?" This matter will be further discussed in a concluding chapter.

The thunderstorm of the afternoon was succeeded, between 8 and 9 P.M., by another of greater violence. The night was pitch dark, and the rain, mixed with hail, came down in torrents, drenching the men to the skin and almost freezing them ; for, midsummer though it was, the hail brought with it a sudden and great lowering of the temperature. The storm, which lasted nearly all night, was really a great advantage to the French ; for Napoleon's arrangements were so perfect that they were not deranged by it, whilst the Austrians, having no definite plans, and no knowledge of the Emperor's design, were bewildered, and, in some cases, surprised.

At 8 P.M., Oudinot began embarking 1500 men of Conroux's brigade (Tharreau's division) on 5 large boats at the mouth of the Stadlau arm, opposite the Austrian work No. XVI. At 9, these boats began to pass, protected by the armed flotilla under Baste. They had almost reached the opposite shore, the Hanselgrund, at 9.30, when they were perceived in the darkness by the 1½ Austrian companies which held the work with three 3-pounder guns. They were quickly crushed by the fire of the gunboats, of the 6-pounder battery on the French side, and of the infantry behind the bullet-proof bulwarks which Napoleon had had erected on the transports.

The sound of this engagement was the signal for a furious bombardment by all the French batteries on the northern and north-eastern sides of the Lobau, which served still further to distract the attention of the Austrians from Oudinot and Masséna.

Tharreau, as soon as work No. XVI. was taken, passed the rest of his division across in boats, whilst the engineers were busy throwing a bridge, the materials for which had been collected at the spot. By 11.30, it was ready for the passage of the rest of Oudinot's corps.[1] Tharreau, meanwhile, according to orders, had occupied the whole of the Hanselgrund island, after driving out the Austrians and capturing their three guns, and was preparing to throw three bridges over the small Steinbügel arm, separating the Hanselgrund from the mainland.[2]

Baste, with the gunboats, occupied the Rohrwörth island a little lower down the main stream, and protected Oudinot's right.

Oudinot's orders were to send one division to Mühlleiten and another to the Maison Blanche (Ufer Haus), but Masséna's progress in the latter direction set free the whole of Oudinot's corps to move on Mühlleiten, which he proceeded to do.

Masséna, meanwhile, had begun his operations about 10 P.M. First, 1500 of Boudet's men and 10 guns were sent across from the lower end of the Ile Alexandre in 5 large boats. At the same time, the pontoon bridge was floated down and "swung" as has already been described.[3] Across

---

[1] Frère's (late Claparède's) division, Grandjean's (late St Hilaire's), the Portuguese legion, and Colbert's light cavalry.

[2] It was hardly an obstacle in the present low state of the river, but pontoons had been sent for bridging it.

[3] *Supra*, p. 332.

it passed the rest of Boudet's infantry, and that of Molitor and Carra St Cyr, whilst the boats carried over artillery and ammunition waggons until a bridge was available for them. The bridge was constructed with pontoons, also in readiness behind the island, and joined the lower end of Ile Alexandre to the opposite bank. Across it passed the artillery and cavalry (Lasalle and Marulaz) of Masséna's command.

Below this bridge, and above the infantry bridge, Davout, who was now arriving, threw a raft bridge, also ready prepared behind the island. It was complete at 2 A.M., an hour before that used by Masséna's cavalry. Across it passed in succession as they arrived the infantry divisions of Morand, Friant, Gudin, and Puthod, Montbrun's light cavalry, and the dragoon divisions of Grouchy and Pully.

As each bridge was thrown, work was commenced on a bridge-head for it on the left bank.

We must return to Oudinot passing by Mühlleiten to Hausen, where he found two Austrian battalions holding the castle of Sachsengang. It was morning before they were compelled by howitzer fire to surrender.

Another pontoon bridge was thrown from the upper part of the Ile Alexandre to the left bank. When day broke on the 5th July, the storm was over, and was succeeded by perfect summer weather. At that hour, Oudinot was at Mühlleiten and Hausen, Masséna in the Schuster meadows, and Davout was busy crossing and marching on Wittau.

The Austrians had done little or nothing to oppose the crossing ; indeed it was beyond their power to stop it. The VI. corps had, as ordered, begun, at 11 P.M., to bombard the Lobau, but did no harm, and the cannonade was over at 2 A.M. Nordmann had collected most of his troops in or behind Enzersdorf and the neighbouring works, and had sent a few detachments towards Hausen and the Hanselgrund, where they were easily brushed aside, or captured, by the immensely superior French forces. The Austrians in the line Aspern-Enzersdorf suffered heavily from the fire of the French batteries in the Lobau throughout the night.

CHAPTER XVII

THE BATTLE OF WAGRAM

BEFORE describing the progress of this, the greatest battle, in point of numbers engaged, that Napoleon had yet fought, let us get an idea of the numbers of the two armies. It seems safe for this purpose to accept the figures of Binder v. Krieglstein, which are worked out with great care, and are probably as near the truth as can be got. The French corps were the following :—

	Infantry.	Cavalry.	Guns.
Imperial Guard . . .	7,300	3,700	60
2nd corps (Oudinot) and Colbert's light cavalry . .	18,000	1,200	92
3rd corps (Davout), Montbrun's light cavalry, and the dragoon divisions Grouchy and Pully . .	30,000	4,800	98
4th corps (Masséna) and Lasalle's light cavalry . .	24,000	3,200	90
9th corps (Bernadotte's Saxons and Dupas' division) .	15,700	2,200	42
7th corps (Wrede's division)	4,800	1,000	36
Army of Italy (Eugène) .	22,000	1,200	100
11th corps (Marmont) . .	9,000	...	12
Cavalry Reserve (Bessières) .	...	6,000	24
	130,800	23,300	554

154,100

All of these were up on the 5th July, except Marmont and Wrede. Besides them, there were Reynier's troops in the Lobau, numbering some 6000 infantry, with 129 guns of position. When we add in artillerymen and engineers, it may be taken that Napoleon did not much exaggerate when he said he intended attacking with 180,000 men.

The Austrian forces were altogether :—

	Infantry.	Cavalry.	Guns.
Advance guard (Nordmann)	11,950	2,500	48
I. corps (Bellegarde) . .	20,900	800	68
II. corps (Hohenzollern) .	25,800	560	68
III. corps (Kolowrat) . .	17,000	740	58
IV. corps (Rosenberg) . .	17,900	800	60
V. corps (Reuss)[1] . .	7,550	800	32
VI. corps (Klenau) . .	16,200	1,400	64
Reserve corps (Liechtenstein)	11,200	8,800	48
Archduke John (Army of Italy)	11,000	2,200	34
	139,500	18,600	480

158,100

But of these the V. corps, the Archduke John, and 1800 men of the III. corps detached on the Bisamberg never came into the battle. Thus Charles' army which actually fought at Wagram numbered 119,150 infantry, 15,600 cavalry, 414 guns, or, including artillery and engineers, say 142,000. A great many of these were landwehr who had been collected during the seven weeks between Essling and Wagram. There were 31 such battalions out of a total of 175.

As Masséna reached the left bank, he posted his troops at right angles to it, with Boudet next the river, then Molitor and Carra St Cyr, to whom was

[1] Exclusive of Schustekh's detachment at Krems.

added, about 4 P.M., Legrand. The latter was withdrawn from the Mühlau, his place being taken by Reynier's troops, when the passage had been established on the east of the Lobau. Lasalle and Marulaz were on the right of the infantry. Masséna gradually pushed forward, and, by 5 A.M., had driven the Austrians into Enzersdorf.

Davout had also moved forward towards Wittau, and, as his cavalry was not yet over, Lasalle and Marulaz had helped in clearing out the Austrian detachments, until they were stopped at Rutzendorf by the infantry fire of a battalion from the IV. corps holding the village. By 8 A.M., Masséna was master of Enzersdorf, the pivot on which the Emperor meant to wheel his army to the left. The place was held by two battalions, but it was overwhelmed by artillery fire, and Masséna's aide-de-camp, St Croix, with the 46th, after a sharp fight in the streets and houses, captured the greater part of the garrison. About the same hour, Oudinot moved up into his place between Masséna and Davout, and the latter, having now got his own cavalry, sent it to his right flank to look out for the possible arrival of the Archduke John.

Masséna's advance had cut off the retreat of the Austrian detachment in the Ile Pouzet and it had to surrender. This island being in Napoleon's possession, he now ordered the construction of two more bridges, one at a point between the Iles Alexandre and Lannes, and one connecting the Ile Pouzet to the Lobau on the one side, and to the left bank near Enzersdorf on the other. The former was ready by 2 P.M., the latter not till 9 P.M.

We must now see what the Archduke Charles had been doing. It was only at 5 A.M. that he received news of the French crossing, though he had heard the cannonade during the night. Then he received

z

a report from Nordmann that strong French columns were marching against his left flank, and the Bisamberg observatory announced a constant stream of troops from the right bank into the Lobau.

Then, at last, orders were issued for the fortification of the Russbach position, so as to enable it to be held by a comparatively small force, whilst the rest of the army resumed the offensive. Charles still seemed to believe that there would be no serious battle on the 5th, but that the French would be satisfied with strengthening the position they had acquired on the left bank. Nordmann was told that probably the French sought to pass below Enzersdorf and establish themselves so as to be able, later, to advance against the village. At 5.30 A.M., Charles wrote to John that he had no intention of fighting near the Danube, where the French would have every advantage with their heavy artillery in a well-established position. John was ordered, after a three hours' rest at Marchegg, to join the left of his brother's army at Markgrafneusiedl. Liechtenstein, when Enzersdorf was taken, sent his seven light cavalry regiments to Pysdorf, two cuirassier regiments to the Neu-Wirtshaus, and four in reserve to Raasdorf.

Nordmann, though his prescribed line of retreat was seriously threatened by the advance of the French right, hoped to be able to attack their left from Essling as they advanced from Enzersdorf. He therefore posted an infantry brigade and a regiment of hussars there. He was, however, compelled by artillery fire, about 9 A.M., to abandon his work No. VIII. to the east of Essling.

There now ensued a long pause in the battle; for the passage of a great army, even with the numerous bridges available, was necessarily a slow matter. It was not till 2 P.M. that Bernadotte reached his place in line, and the

Guard was not up till 4 P.M. Eugène arrived at noon. Between 10 and 11 A.M., the first line had occupied a great arc extending from the Stadlau arm south-west of Enzersdorf to Kimmerleindorf. On the extreme left, next the Stadlau arm, was the cavalry of Lasalle and Marulaz, with Boudet on Marulaz's right, all facing north-west. The rest of Masséna's corps faced north, as did Oudinot's, and both were now in line. Davout, in columns of divisions between Rutzendorf and Kummerleindorf, faced north-east, whilst Grouchy's and Pully's dragoon divisions were massed in front of the last-named village.

As they came up, Bernadotte formed the 2nd line behind Masséna's centre and right, Eugène behind Oudinot, the Guard and the cavalry Reserve in the interval between them.

A letter from Charles to the Austrian Emperor, dated 9.30 A.M., shows that by that time he had again changed his views, and expected a general attack that day.

At 11 he betook himself to the left flank, but passed no orders, pending the return of Wimpffen who had ridden to Nordmann at Essling.

At noon, Napoleon sent the light cavalry forward towards Raasdorf, Pysdorf, and Glinzendorf, covered by a heavy artillery fire, and Davout seized Rutzendorf with an infantry detachment. The cavalry manœuvred towards Liechtenstein's left flank, whilst overwhelming him with the fire of their horse artillery. Charles seems to have contemplated a half-hearted measure, by pushing forward Liechtenstein, supported by Rosenberg if necessary, to relieve the pressure on Nordmann's left. It came to nothing, as Liechtenstein was already retreating when he got the order at 4 P.M.

It was 2 P.M. when Napoleon began his general advance with the first line, Eugène and Bernadotte, the Guard, and the cuirassiers being still on the march.

Davout took the direction of Glinzendorf and Markgraf-neusiedl, followed by Eugène ; Oudinot marched towards Parbasdorf (Baumersdorf), followed by Bernadotte (less the 1st Saxon division, left to guard the bridges till Marmont was up); Masséna leant to his left, keeping Boudet touching the Stadlau arm and compelling the Austrians to evacuate the Aspern-Essling line. The next division on the right was Molitor's, directed on the space between Hirschstetten and Breitenlee. In touch with Molitor's right was Carra St Cyr, and on his right again was Legrand moving on Süssenbrünn. The direction of march of Oudinot and Masséna necessarily resulted in a great gap between them, and this was filled by Eugène on the right and Bernadotte on the left moving into first line. The Guard on arrival took post in rear of Eugène. The general order of advance was artillery in 1st, cavalry in 2nd line, and infantry in rear.

Masséna wheeled to his left on Boudet, who stood still in the line of Austrian works between redoubts VIII. and IX., until the operation was completed, about 5 P.M.

Meanwhile, the commencement of the French advance threatened the retreat of Nordmann from Essling to Grosshofen. He had lost heavily and had scarcely a serviceable gun left. He commenced his retreat at once, passing back to the Russbach position without any serious fighting.

Klenau, though he had reported at 2 P.M. that he would soon be forced to retreat, did not commence his retirement till 5, when he fell back before Boudet on to the slopes of the Bisamberg, having the III. corps on his left and the grenadiers beyond that, at Gerasdorf.

Boudet halted north-west of Aspern, with detachments in front at Kagran and Leopoldau. The rest of Masséna's corps was at and beyond Breitenlee, with a strong detachment at Süssenbrünn. Part of St Cyr's division, however, had reinforced Boudet, so that St Cyr had only 5 Hessian battalions at Breitenlee. On the French right Davout had stormed Glinzendorf by 5 P.M., and the line to his left passed through Raasdorf.

Thus, at 5 P.M., when Masséna was facing west, the corps of Davout, Oudinot, and Eugène were facing the Russbach position, and Bernadotte was moving into the gap south of Aderklaa, between Eugène's left and Masséna's right. Behind the Russbach the Austrians stood thus :—I. corps with its right in Deutsch-Wagram ; II. on both sides of Parbasdorf (Baumersdorf) ; IV. with its left flank at Markgrafneusiedl ; Reserve cavalry and Nordmann in rear of IV. corps; Fröhlich's hussars, which had retired from Rutzendorf, at Ober-Siebenbrünn.

Charles now once more changed his plans and gave up Wimpffen's " pair of pincers " idea. He proposed to assemble his whole army on the position Wagram-Markgrafneusiedl. The order was drafted, but, the rapid march of events rendering its issue impossible, it was torn up. It was too late to carry out the idea, and Charles had no course left now but acceptance of Wimpffen's scheme.

As Bernadotte was advancing on Aderklaa, he found his left flank threatened by Roussel's [1] cuirassier brigade, retiring from Neu-Wirtshaus. Against it he sent his Saxon light cavalry. The cuirassiers committed the fatal mistake of standing still to receive the charge, with the natural result that they were defeated, and only escaped pursuit owing to the opportune support of Lederer's cuirassiers.

The Russbach position, which Charles was now holding with some 90,000 men, was an extremely strong one ; it might have been made much stronger had it been properly fortified. As it was, the works, ordered to be begun only at 5 A.M., had not made much progress. On the left bank of the stream, the plateau had a con-

[1] A French " emigré " in the Austrian service.

siderable command over the plain on the south. As the bank was turned back at right angles at Wagram on one side and Markgrafneusiedl on the other, the whole plateau formed as it were a sort of fortress with a good command on three sides of a square, the fourth resting on the hills about Bockflüss. The front and right flank were further protected by the stream in front of them. It was but a small obstacle, 3 yards wide and 2½ feet deep, easily passable by infantry, but its fringe of osier beds and willows made it almost proof against cavalry and artillery, except at the bridges, of which there were eight.

The Austrian right and left rested respectively on Wagram and Markgrafneusiedl, a front of nearly four miles. Almost in the centre of this front, the Austrians held the village of Parbasdorf (Baumersdorf), forming a great bastion projecting into the plain, and flanking attacks on either side of it against the front.

The Austrians were thus in two great groups, the left wing on the line Markgrafneusiedl-Wagram nearly 90,000 [1] strong, the right wing, of over 50,000,[2] having its left (the grenadiers) at Gerasdorf, thus leaving a gap of three miles between it and the I. corps at Wagram.

Napoleon had succeeded in passing to the left bank of the Danube with his whole army, except Marmont and Wrede, not yet up, and in deploying it with something like 110,000 men facing the Austrian left, whilst another 27,000 faced westwards. He had gained some successes, but had done nothing decisive. The Austrian cannonade from beyond the Russbach had informed him that that position was to be held determinedly, and

[1] Strength at commencement of battle: I. corps, 21,700; II., 26,360; IV. corps, 18,700; Nordmann's advance guard, 14,450; Reserve cavalry, 8800. Total, 90,010 with 256 guns.

[2] Inclusive of the V. corps—Initial strengths: III. corps, 17,740; V. corps, 8350; VI. corps, 17,600; Grenadiers (Reserve), 11,200. Total, 54,890 with 190 guns.

he was aware of the general position of Charles' right.
If he could carry the Russbach position on the 5th, he
would prevent the junction, during the night, of the
separated Austrian wings. That he resolved to attempt,
though the day was now fast declining. Though he
rode far to the front, the trees bordering the Russbach,
and the bank beyond, prevented him from ascertaining
the enemy's dispositions or strength with accuracy.

It was between 6 and 7 P.M., when he began to send
out orders for a general attack, almost too late, even on
a July night, to hope for decisive results. Besides, the
various French corps were by no means at equal distances
from their objective, a fact which caused the attack to
be disjointed and piecemeal ; for there was not enough
of daylight left to defer it till Davout on the right and
Bernadotte on the left had brought themselves on a level
with the centre.

It was about 6 P.M. when Oudinot received his orders.
A furious cannonade now broke out along the whole line,
which soon set Baumersdorf in flames. Frère's (late
Claparède's) division was sent against Baumersdorf, which
was strongly occupied by Hardegg with 10 Austrian
battalions. Notwithstanding the support of Tharreau's
division, Frère was unable to take the village. At 8 P.M.,
Oudinot sent in the " Terrible " 57th and the 10th light
infantry, both of Grandjean's (late St Hilaire's) division.
The 57th, breaking into the village, engaged in a
desperate combat in the streets and houses. But it
never succeeded in driving out Hardegg, or in getting
possession of the two bridges which were so essential for
the passage of cavalry and artillery. The 10th light
infantry, meanwhile, passed the stream and forced its
way on to the heights beyond. There, however, it was
attacked on all sides by Austrian infantry, and, finally,
was charged by hussars led by Hohenzollern himself.
Unsupported by either cavalry or artillery, or by other

infantry, the regiment was driven back across the Russbach. Austrian reinforcements poured into Baumersdorf ; the French were forced to evacuate such portion
of it as they held, and to retire half-way to Raasdorf.
Oudinot was thus driven off with heavy loss.

Eugène, meanwhile, advanced with Macdonald leading
Lamarque's division, supported by the divisions of Serras
and Durutte, and by Sahuc's light cavalry. On the
way, however, Dupas' division, of Bernadotte's corps,
joined the column and took the lead in it. Then he
turned to his left up the Russbach towards Wagram,
driving in the Austrian skirmishers as he passed, and
seeking a crossing. On his right, Macdonald advanced
direct against the heights, at first with 7, then with
11 battalions. As the French charged up the bank,
panic seized the opposing Austrian infantry of the first
line. Ranks were broken and the men streamed to the
rear, many prisoners and some standards falling into the
hands of the victorious French. But the second line held
fast, and the regiments of the first line on either side of
Macdonald's column formed against his flanks. Suffering from a heavy fire on both flanks and in front,
the French were compelled to fall back, losing many of the
prisoners just taken. Now reinforced by part of Durutte's
division and some of Sahuc's squadrons, which had
succeeded in crossing the stream, they once more
advanced to the attack. Three squadrons charging an
Austrian battalion captured its standard. The Austrian
line was in serious danger of being broken when Charles
himself arrived on the spot, and, with his usual in-
trepidity, rallied his regiments and led the counter-attack.
Hohenzollern also appeared on the French right with
his hussars, fresh from their success against Oudinot, and
charged the flank of Macdonald's column. Before the
superior forces now opposing them, Macdonald's men
yielded, gradually at first until, overcome by panic, they

fled in disorder across the Russbach, never stopping their flight till they were brought up by the Guard standing in reserve.

Whilst Macdonald was fighting on his right, Dupas had crossed the Russbach and pushed even into the easternmost houses of Wagram. But it was clear that he could not hold out on the left bank, especially as the two Saxon battalions attached to his division appear to have been fired on by mistake by their French comrades. One of them disappeared altogether, and only 43 men of the other were to be found.

The disorderly flight of the defeated troops of Eugène's command is notable evidence of the deterioration of many of Napoleon's young soldiers. No such panic is conceivable, under similar circumstances, in the armies of Austerlitz or Jena. It was well for the French that darkness prevented the Austrians from following up, or even appreciating their success. Bernadotte received his orders at 7 P.M., and it was only as the columns on his right were defeated that he led his troops forward by Aderklaa against Wagram. He was very weak, for he had not Dupas with him, and he had had to leave detachments behind for the protection of the bridges. He had but 10 battalions when he attacked Wagram, and it was already dark. The scene was lighted only by the burning houses of the village, and the confusion in the fighting was such that friends constantly fired on friends, this being due no doubt also partially to the fact that the combatants on both sides were mainly German-speaking. The Austrians had six battalions, of which two were in reserve on the flanks of the village, but joined in the defence from the commencement. The Saxons were thus attacked on both flanks, as well as in front. Bernadotte's attack was not more successful than those of the centre, and, by 11 P.M., he had been forced back from Wagram on to Aderklaa.

There remains Davout's attack on the right. His orders also were late in arriving. His cavalry advanced first against the hussars in Ober-Siebenbrünn and the left of the Austrian cavalry reserve below the bank which runs north from Markgrafneusiedl. The divisions of Morand and Friant crossed at Glinzendorf, behind the cavalry, and then moved against the eastern side of Markgrafneusiedl. Simultaneously, Gudin and Puthod attacked in front across the Russbach from Grosshofen. Nothing, however, came of the attack. The cavalry were unable to make way against the four regiments of Nostitz, and the other attacks never got beyond an artillery duel. Looking to the darkness and the gradual subsidence of the sound of the attacks in the centre, Davout withdrew his corps to Glinzendorf for the night. Thus Napoleon's attack on the Russbach position was everywhere repulsed, in parts disastrously. That accounts for the fact that the whole affair is slurred over, in the 25th bulletin, in a few words regarding the attack on Wagram. The Emperor occupied practically the same positions as he held before the attack on the Russbach.

Towards midnight Charles issued his orders for the continuation of the battle on the 6th July.

He now determined to make an early attack with his right wing on the corps of Masséna, and his orders were to the following effect.

III. corps (less one brigade left on the heights of Stammersdorf) to advance by Leopoldau on Breitenlee against the left flank of the French marching against Wagram. Klenau would be on its right, towards the Danube.

Grenadiers to move with the same object on Süssenbrünn.

Cavalry Reserve between Aderklaa and Süssenbrünn, linking the III. corps to the I.

I. corps to advance against Aderklaa, with its left on the Russbach at Wagram.

II. to hold on to the Russbach position to the last, and, as the III. gained ground, to cross the stream. A heavy artillery fire was to be maintained against the French. IV. corps to attack the French right. V. corps to hold Am-Spitz and other posts on the Danube opposite Vienna. Great silence was enjoined, in order to conceal the movements, the earliest of which was to be Kolowrat's (III. corps) at 1 A.M., whilst the advance of the I. corps was to begin at 4 A.M. The Archduke himself would be with the I. corps. Rosenberg's attack on Davout was also to begin at 4 A.M.

Of the Archduke John nothing was known at headquarters, though he was presumably nearing Marchegg. As a matter of fact, the first orders, of 7 P.M. on the 4th, had only reached him, owing to the terrible weather during the night, at 5 A.M. on the 5th at Pressburg. He had, on the 4th, acted on orders of the 2nd, requiring him to make a diversion from the Pressburg bridge-head. Consequently, when the new orders reached him, many of his troops were on the south bank of the Danube. He had also numerous posts out towards the Schütt island, etc. This was some excuse for John's failure to at once march on Marchegg, but it was not enough, even taken with the confusion which may have arisen owing to the constantly varying orders of the last day or two. He did not even reply to the first order, and it was only on receipt of the second (of 5.30 A.M. on 5th) at 6 P.M. that he wrote that he would march at 1 A.M. on the 6th. He stated his force, after deduction of a garrison left at Pressburg, at a little over 13,000 men. His last orders were to rest three hours at Marchegg, but now there was no time to spare for this, so, at 2 A.M. on the 6th, orders were despatched to him to march straight on through Ober-Siebenbrünn.

Napoleon's orders of this night appear all to have been verbal.[1] There is some disagreement as to what they were in the case of Davout, but, on the whole, the accounts of Pelet and Laborde seem more reliable than that of Koch, who says Davout was ordered to make an outflanking attack on Markgrafneusiedl.

Accepting Pelet's account, we find that Davout was ordered to draw rather closer to the centre, calling in his detachment from Grosshofen. Masséna was to move, at 2 A.M., towards Aderklaa, leaving only Boudet to cover Aspern and the bridges. The Emperor was, in fact, concentrating towards his centre, so as to be ready, as the Austrian intentions became clearer, to move in any direction; it was the strategical "bataillon carrée" applied to tactics.

According to Pelet, Napoleon's design at first was for Davout to take Markgrafneusiedl, Oudinot the heights between it and Parbasdorf, which place was to be stormed by Marmont. Macdonald would follow the same direction as on the previous evening, and Bernadotte would attack Wagram. The whole attack would be frontal only. Yet he wished to make no final decision till the last moment, till he saw more plainly the condition of affairs. Wrede, who was still in the Lobau, kept asking for orders and being put off. He got them at last, namely, to cross from the Lobau, but to hold fast for the moment at Enzersdorf, till he got further orders.

The Austrian attack broke out first from the extreme left where Rosenberg, at 4 A.M., as ordered, led forward the IV. corps,[2] which he divided into three columns. Six battalions marched across the Russbach on Gross-

---

[1] Unfortunately Col. Saski's collection of official documents does not yet extend beyond the battle of Essling. On the other hand, it is generally observable that written orders in the French archives are infrequent on days of battle and probably few were issued, if any.

[2] Including Nordmann's advance guard, which was put under Rosenberg when it fell back from Essling on the 5th.

hofen, 16 more took Glinzendorf as objective. Ten battalions and 8 squadrons formed the advance guards of these columns, half in front of each, but the whole advance guard was commanded by Radetzky. The 3rd column, of 38 squadrons under Nostitz, was ordered to outflank the enemy's right, and form a link with the Archduke John when he arrived. Nostitz sent a detachment of hussars under Fröhlich to Ober-Siebenbrünn, as on the previous day. Riese, with 11 battalions and a heavy battery, remained in the position as reserve. Rosenberg, with his main body still behind the Russbach, directed Radetzky, who had driven in Davout's outposts, not to hurry his advance too much. As for Davout, when the storm broke on him he was on the move towards the centre. Friant's left and Gudin's right were in Glinzendorf, Puthod was in Grosshofen. Between the two villages were artillery and skirmishers.

The light cavalry on Davout's right moved out in part to meet Nostitz in front, whilst part made for Ober-Siebenbrünn, so as to threaten his flank and rear.

It was about 5 A.M. when the Austrians, after some time spent in skirmishing with the French, advanced to the attack of Grosshofen and Glinzendorf, into the nearer parts of which they penetrated.

This early attack on Davout was somewhat surprising, and seemed to point to the early advent of John on the field. Napoleon at once sent Nansouty's and Arrighi's (late Espagne's) cuirassiers to Davout's assistance, and even marched the Guard in the same direction, whilst Nansouty's horse artillery opened on the right flank of the advancing Austrians.

Charles had prescribed a fixed hour for Rosenberg's advance, thinking that by that time both the attack of Kolowrat and that of Klenau would have begun, and John would be nearing the field. But there had been delays; the Austrian right was still a long way off, and

John not likely to be up for hours, if at all. Therefore, Charles, whose intention was to begin the attack with his right, sent orders to Rosenberg to return to his position. But that general was already too deeply involved with Davout to allow of his withdrawal without the appearance of defeat. His main body was already involved in support of the advance guard, and Davout was making a vigorous counter-attack. When, therefore, they found the Austrians retiring the French naturally pressed forward. Radetzky covered the retirement, losing 1000 men in doing so. The whole affair was over by 6 o'clock, and Rosenberg's force was back beyond the Russbach.

Napoleon, being now assured that there were no signs of John, resolved to send Davout to a front and flank attack on Markgrafneusiedl, which was one of the keys of the Austrian position on the Russbach. Davout required two hours to prepare the attack, as he had to get two of his divisions across the Russbach lower down, out of range of the Austrian guns, for the flank attack. Napoleon left Arrighi's cuirassiers to support him, but again withdrew the Guard and Nansouty to the centre, whither he himself returned. Davout was quite safe to be trusted with an affair of this sort.

The Emperor directed Eugène and Oudinot to be prepared to storm the heights in front of them, so soon as Davout's flank attack was developed. When he got back to his centre, he found the Austrians had occupied Aderklaa, which was of vital importance to himself.

Bellegarde, with 15 battalions and 8 squadrons, had moved on Aderklaa soon after 3 A.M., leaving Dedowich behind with 7 battalions. About 4 A.M. Bellegarde's advanced troops observed the Saxons evacuating Aderklaa, no doubt under Bernadotte's orders. The Austrian advance guard occupied the place unopposed, and their main body took post between it and Wagram. By 6 A.M. the grenadiers also had come up and taken post on the opposite side of the village. The Reserve cavalry (less one cuirassier regiment sent to the II. corps) stood in rear of the infantry. But there were still no signs of the Austrian right wing, the III. and VI. corps, which had been delayed in various ways.

A tremendous cannonade was maintained on both sides, and Bernadotte, whose flank was exposed towards Aderklaa, felt it necessary to draw back his Saxons. Masséna was now coming into line, and Napoleon, thoroughly appreciating the serious loss to his line in the Austrian occupation of Aderklaa, just at the angle between his wings, ordered Masséna and Bernadotte to retake it, and then, when Davout should have passed Markgrafneusiedl, to storm Wagram. He was, at this time, entirely ignorant of the approach of the Austrian III. and VI. Corps. His attention was directed chiefly to the square tower marking the position of Markgrafneusiedl. When the line of smoke in that direction should show that the village was taken by Davout, he knew that the Austrian left would have been turned, and the whole position, from Wagram to Markgrafneusiedl, jeopardised. Then would be the time to storm Wagram and the line of heights.

Masséna entrusted the attack on Aderklaa to Carra St Cyr. That general pressed forward with his division in closed columns, whilst Bernadotte's Saxons advanced on his right, suffering terribly from the fire of the Austrian artillery on their right flank.

On Carra St Cyr's right were his Hessian battalions, which behaved splendidly under the great trial of the Austrian artillery fire. The attack had been delayed by Carra St Cyr, though the recapture of Aderklaa was of supreme importance. Masséna was furious at the delay. He had himself been disabled two days previously by a fall with his horse, but had insisted on commanding his corps from a carriage, with which he pressed into the very centre of his troops, launching them against Aderklaa. The village was carried triumphantly; not only that, but the 24th and 4th regiments poured out of the farther side in hot pursuit of the fleeing Austrians. Presently the two regiments, finding themselves almost in the midst of Bellegarde's troops without support, halted and began firing, whilst the Austrians, rallying from their panic, attacked them furiously in front and on both flanks. They could do nothing but fall back on Aderklaa, into which the enemy followed them.

But there had been moving for some time across the plain east of the Bisamberg a glittering line of bayonets, the Austrian III. and VI. corps. At about 8 A.M., the III. corps was on the line Breitenlee-Süssenbrünn, whilst the advance guard of the VI. had driven Boudet's outposts back between Stadlau and Aspern, and the main body was surging through the space between Hirschstetten and Stadlau.

Charles, posted on the heights of Wagram, had been witness of the French attack on Aderklaa and galloped to this critical spot. It was by his orders that Bellegarde, with the Reserve cavalry and the grenadiers supporting him, had again advanced to the recapture of the lost village. Before him he drove Carra St Cyr and the Saxons, and, after a desperate fight, finally remained master of the place; for Masséna could not support his leading division, on account of the threatened attack of Liechtenstein on one flank, and the fire of Kolowrat's batteries from north of Breitenlee on the other. The French left wing was in imminent danger had the Austrians followed up their victory, as the French themselves would have done. But that was not the Austrian way, and they proceeded to draw up their line with Bellegarde between Aderklaa and Wagram, whilst the grenadiers occupied a line from Aderklaa towards Breitenlee.

Masséna, still hoping to recover Aderklaa, sent Marulaz and Lasalle against the two batteries which the Austrians had in front of it. The light cavalry rode down the Austrian gunners and captured the batteries ; but the threatening attitude of Liechtenstein's cavalry compelled them to fall back again. Then Molitor attempted to storm the place. The fighting in the streets and houses raged with the fury of that of Aspern and Essling seven weeks before. Finally, the French fell back in confusion, leaving the Austrians in possession of the hotly contested village.

As a temporary measure to support the French left, Eugène turned Macdonald's corps and most of his guns westward, whilst the news of the serious danger was sent to Napoleon, who was farther east intently watching the progress of Davout's attack on Markgrafneusiedl. He at once galloped back to Masséna and was instrumental in stopping, by his presence, the flight of his troops. It was 9 o'clock when the Emperor first became aware of the danger which threatened him on the left, in the advance of the Austrian III. and VI. corps. There was not a moment to lose, for Kolowrat's right was already in Breitenlee, whilst his left touched the grenadiers. Klenau, too, with the VI. corps, had attacked Boudet about Aspern, and his hussars by a happy charge on Boudet's artillery, forming that general's right wing, had captured the whole of it. Boudet himself, deprived of the support of his guns, was driven into the bridge-head on the Mühlau. Thus, between 9 and 10 A.M., two fresh Austrian corps were advancing against the empty space between the Stadlau arm and Neu-Wirtshaus. Klenau even had posts in Essling. The Austrian right wing was advancing almost in rear of the French centre and left.

2 A

It was well for Napoleon that he held his reserves massed in the centre, whence he could move them to either wing, or to fill a gap.

Once more, as at Eylau, the Emperor decided to use his heavy cavalry to gain time. Bessières was ordered to charge, with the cuirassier divisions of Nansouty and St Germain (late St Sulpice), and the cavalry of the Guard commanded by Walther. Bessières, charging at the head of these great lines of cuirassiers and carbineers, made for the point of union of Liechtenstein's grenadiers and the left of Kolowrat.

Whatever may be said of the inefficiency of Napoleon's cavalry as purveyors of intelligence, no one has ever doubted their bravery and efficiency on the battlefield, at least in these days when the horses obtainable were still good. Again and again the line of mail-clad warriors descended upon the Austrians between Süssenbrünn and Aderklaa. In one charge Bessières' horse was shot under him, and his men rushed with redoubled fury to the rescue of a leader to whom they were devoted. At one moment they had again overwhelmed the Austrian batteries in front of Aderklaa, which were only saved by their infantry. Heavily as the cavalry lost, their charges were effectual in forcing back the right of the grenadiers and the left of Kolowrat, whose advance they brought to a standstill.

Screened by them, Napoleon was busy completing the re-arrangements necessitated by the new state of affairs. Obviously, the first thing to be done was to provide a force to meet the movement of Kolowrat and Klenau against the French left and rear. For this Masséna must be used, and his corps must make a flank march of extreme difficulty across the front of Kolowrat, under fire of his artillery. To Masséna were attached the light cavalry of Lasalle and Marular and the cuirassiers of St Germain. Next to him was Bernadotte, and the movement of these two southwards would leave a gap in the centre which must be filled.   In the first line there the Emperor ranged on an arc of a circle an immense battery of 100 guns, made up of those of Macdonald's corps and of the Guard.   These were opposite the space between Süssenbrünn and Breitenlee.   Macdonald and the Guard infantry formed behind them, and Wrede was hurried up to Raasdorf.   Liechtenstein had just had orders to attack when the deployment of this great line of artillery effectually stopped his doing so.   But Napoleon, though his attention was now largely concentrated on the centre, did not neglect his attack on the Russbach position.   Davout was urged to press on his attack on Markgrafneusiedl, whilst Oudinot was told to hold the Austrians with artillery fire for the present.

The Austrian offensive had now nearly exhausted itself. Klenau contented himself with re-occupying the works at Aspern and Essling, his main body, very slightly in advance of the line Aspern-Breitenlee, awaiting the development of affairs in the centre.   In the moment of victory the enterprise of the Austrians failed.   Klenau's inactivity gave time to Masséna for his flank march.

We must now look to what was happening on the extreme left of the Austrian line.   It was about 10 A.M. when Davout was ready to attack.   The tremendous cross fire of artillery which he had brought to bear on the Austrian guns at and about Markgrafneusiedl had almost reduced them to silence.   To the east of the village, Montbrun, Grouchy, and Pully, having driven Fröhlich from Ober-Siebenbrünn, were moving towards Sichdichfür.   Arrighi was in the centre of the right wing.   On their left, the divisions of Morand and Friant marched against the heights north of Markgrafneusiedl on the left bank of the Russbach, whilst Gudin and Puthod advanced on the village from the right bank. To meet this double attack, Rosenberg had thrown back his second line and his cavalry " en potence " on his left. In vain he sent for help from Charles and Wimpffen in this position, which he felt to be doubly dangerous after the collapse of his artillery before that of Davout. Davout himself led the frontal attack across the Russbach. The fighting was very severe, for the Austrians made a brave defence of Markgrafneusiedl, but by 11 A.M., the French had stormed the village and were pushing up against the square tower in its rear which the Austrians had fortified. The tower, threatened in rear by the advance of Morand and Friant, was stormed and the Austrian counter-attack against it failed. The fighting at the tower was desperate ; on the Austrian side Vecsey and Nordmann met their death, and four other generals were wounded. Davout's horse was killed under him, and Gudin, close beside him, was wounded four times. Whilst Davout, with Puthod and Gudin, was advancing northwards, Morand and Friant were capturing the heights facing east. Morand was at first repulsed, but then, supported by Friant, he reached the heights. Friant, too, only succeeded on his second attempt in mounting the curtain and driving the Austrian infantry out of their half completed entrenchments. As the Austrians formed a fresh line in rear, Arrighi charged them with his cuirassiers, but was repulsed with loss.

At this juncture, Charles arrived in person, bringing up, from Hohenzollern's corps (II.), a reinforcement of five batallions and two cavalry regiments (one of cuirassiers). The II. corps had, so far, only had to oppose Oudinot's artillery fire, and had had rather the better of the duel. Therefore, it was able to spare these reinforcements. With the cavalry thus collected, including that of Rosenberg, Charles sought to defeat the dragoons and light cavalry on Davout's right, and to threaten the right flank of his infantry. But the cavalry attack was mismanaged, and, instead of the whole force of over 40 squadrons attacking the French dragoons and light cavalry, only one regiment of dragoons and one of cuirassiers charged them.   The first line drove back the French first line and captured 10 guns, but then the French second line charged, drove back the Austrians, and recaptured the guns.

It was noon when Davout had crushed in the Austrian left, and Napoleon saw that he was debouching from Markgrafneusiedl.   That was the signal for the decisive manœuvre by which he hoped to break the Austrian centre and secure victory.

As for the attack on his left by Klenau, he had done more than sufficient in sending Masséna to deal with it, and obviously his own success in the centre must cause it to collapse completely.   Binder v. Krieglstein considers that, with the armies of Austerlitz and Jena, he would not even have sent Masséna.   But his troops were not what he had in 1805 and 1806, and there was the fear that they might not stand as the news reached them of the enemy in rear, threatening their retreat to the island.

For the great effort in the centre Macdonald was selected, mainly, probably, because he happened to be in the right position.

It was noon when the Emperor saw that Davout had possession of the tower at Markgrafneusiedl.   At once, an officer was despatched at his topmost speed to tell Masséna to attack " and that the battle was won, since the Archduke John had not yet appeared."   Oudinot was ordered to storm the heights in front of him.   Macdonald's column, which had been prepared behind the great battery, was of an extraordinary formation.   In front, eight battalions, of the divisions of Broussier and Lamarque, were deployed one behind the other.   Behind the right were the six remaining battalions of Broussier in column of battalions.   Lamarque's seven remaining battalions were in similar formation behind the left.   The rear of this great square was closed by Serras' nine battalions. The battalions were extremely weak, for the whole thirty only amounted to 8000 men.

The attack was covered on the right by Walther with the cavalry of the Guard, on the left by Nansouty's cuirassiers and carbineers. It was directed, as had been that of the cavalry, on the point of junction of Kolowrat (III. corps) and the grenadiers. In front of this tremendous column the Austrian first line could but yield; yet it was not routed, and the regiments fell back on either side of Macdonald's column, into both flanks of which they poured a terrible fire, whilst the second line treated its front in like manner. Macdonald could not get forward, even with the help of attacks by his cavalry. He complained bitterly of the cavalry not doing all they might have done. He was in very evil plight, and the numbers of his infantry column were presently reduced to some 1500 men.

Meanwhile, however, Davout had been making rapid progress, once he had debouched from Markgrafneusiedl and begun to roll up the Austrian left on the centre. As their extreme left fell back before Davout's cavalry threatening their rear, it became necessary for those above the Russbach, between Markgrafneusiedl and Parbasdorf, also to retreat on Bockflüss. That in turn compelled Hardegg, who had so far successfully held Parbasdorf against Oudinot's attacks, to evacuate the village and seek safety, partly towards the Helmahof, partly towards the IV. corps at Bockflüss.

Masséna, too, had made rapid progress against Klenau, who, by 2 P.M., had been forced to evacuate even Aspern, and to commence his retreat along the Danube.

Where was John all this time? We know that Napoleon was satisfied that he was not near enough to be a serious danger. From Marchegg he wrote, at 10.30 A.M., to Charles that he had arrived there with part of his corps, but was still awaiting its rear, and especially the artillery which was behind. He could not hope to recommence his march before 1 P.M., twelve hours after he had left Pressburg. He hoped at the latest to reach Leopoldsdorf by 5 P.M. That, however, was much too late for him to be of any use to Charles.

Soon after 2 P.M., Napoleon had poured up reinforcements to the assistance of Macdonald's shattered column. Pacthod's division of the Army of Italy was ordered to attack Wagram on Macdonald's right, whilst Durutte on the left was to storm Breitenlee. To the direct support of Macdonald Wrede was sent, and how seriously Napoleon thought of the situation is shown by his words to the Bavarian general : " You see the unfortunate position of Macdonald. March ! save the corps, and attack the enemy ; in fine do as seems to you best." [1]

Even the Young Guard was ordered to Macdonald's assistance, and, as he sent them off, Napoleon said to Reille : " Do not risk anything ; for I have nothing as a last reserve but the two regiments of the Old Guard." Marmont was marched into the gap on Oudinot's left.

But the end had almost come ; for Charles recognised that there was now no hope of John's arrival in time. He had seen, too, the successful advance of Davout against his left, of Masséna against his right. To save himself from decisive defeat, he must retreat at once, and his orders for that were, Bellegarde with the I. corps, to fall back towards Gerasdorf, whilst Liechtenstein remained with the cavalry on the plain in front of that village covering him. Kolowrat moved back towards the heights of Stammersdorf ; the grenadiers on Hagenbrünn ; Klenau between Gerasdorf and Leopoldau. Charles himself would go to Stammersdorf. The IV. corps was ordered to take post by evening to the west of Pyrawarth.[2]

[1] Heilmann : *Feldmarschall Fürst Wrede.*
[2] Six or seven miles north of Bockflüss near the source of the Russbach.

Just as the retreat was beginning, Napoleon's fresh advance started. Pacthod, moving against the I. corps, had a severe struggle, in which he was assisted by Tharreau, the left division of Oudinot. The other divisions only came into contact with the enemy as he retreated through Sässenbrünn and Breitenlee. At Gerasdorf, where the I. corps was to make a stand, there was more severe fighting. The French cavalry were driven off momentarily, and then the retreat was continued, before the infantry, to the Stammersdorf heights.

Thither also had retreated Klenau, hotly pursued by Masséna's cavalry under the intrepid leadership of that "beau sabreur" Lasalle. As he led one of the many cavalry charges, Lasalle fell dead with an Austrian bullet in the middle of his forehead. His was the last of the many grievous losses which Napoleon suffered amongst his favourite leaders in the two great battles before Vienna.

On the French right progress had been easy since the capture of Markgrafneusiedl and its tower. As Davout advanced across the open plateau on the left bank of the Russbach, Oudinot joined his left. Oudinot's left division (Tharreau) carried Wagram, and, as already mentioned, brought aid to Pacthod. The other two divisions, north of Wagram towards Helmahof, drove the Austrians before them across the upper Russbach, this time from the left to the right bank.

On Davout's right, Montbrun and Grouchy could not penetrate beyond the edge of the wooded heights about Auersthal and Bockflüss. Friant attacked and captured Bockflüss about 6 P.M.

By 8 P.M. the battle was over along the whole line. The French army at that hour stood thus :—

From the Danube near Jedlersdorf through Leopoldau stretched Masséna's corps, his two divisions of light cavalry, the Saxons, Wrede's Bavarians, and Eugène's army. Nansouty and the Guard cavalry were about

Gerasdorf. Marmont and the divisions of Gudin and Puthod were at Wagram, with Oudinot between them and the Wendlingerhof. Davout had Morand's and Friant's divisions, and the cavalry of Grouchy, Pully, and Montbrun to the south-east of Bockflüss and Auersthal. What remained of Dupas' division was at Raasdorf, collecting fugitives and stragglers. Napoleon, as usual, encamped in the midst of the Guard infantry.

The day had been oppressively hot, and many men had been struck down by sunstroke, for the plain was waterless in most parts. All were exhausted, and, in addition to this, Napoleon still feared the arrival of John, whose force he erroneously estimated at 30,000 men, Therefore, no attempt was made to pursue that night. Another reason against pursuit was the defensive strength of the Austrian positions on the heights of the Bisamberg, and of those about Bockflüss.

As for John, he had started from Marchegg, according to promise, at 1 P.M. and endeavoured with his cavalry to get into touch with Rosenberg, He found, however, that that general had retreated, and, finally when he reached Ober-Siebenbrunn about 5 P.M., he received a message from Rosenberg that all was over and he was too late. He was isolated on the plain, his men had marched 26 miles since 1 A.M., and he could do no good, either by moving towards the Lobau or by attacking the French rear, seeing that he had but 13,000 men. Therefore, he resolved to let his men rest till dark and then to return to Marchegg, which he reached at 7 A.M. on the 7th. So bad was the state of the French army that the appearance of some of John's cavalry created a panic, and thousands of men fled towards the Lobau.[1]

At nightfall the rest of the Austrian army stood thus: V. corps at Strebersdorf; VI. north of Stammersdorf; III. corps on the right of VI., with the I. behind it;

[1] It was these men whom Dupas had to rally and collect. See above.

Cavalry Reserve between Seiring and Hagenbrünn; Grenadiers at Hagenbrünn; Nostitz's cavalry division between Enzersfeld and Königsbrünn; main body and II. corps at Enzersfeld; IV. corps, and 11 battalions of II., on the heights across the Brünn road, with Radetzky and 4 battalions south of them.

Charles, having no intention of fighting a third day's battle, proposed to start during the night on his retreat into Bohemia again. At 8 P.M., orders were issued for retreat at 10, to the heights north of Korneuburg, covered by Klenau, standing till midnight on the line Am Spitz—Stammersdorf—Erdesbrünn.

The losses in this great battle of two days are, as usual, difficult to estimate accurately. The Austrian returns are confusing, as they relate to the period 29th June to 11th July. They are, however, much more reliable than the French, which Napoleon always intentionally reduced.

Binder v. Krieglstein has devoted a great deal of care to working out the losses as nearly as possible. Without following his details, we may accept the following table of Austrian losses as a fair approximation :—

	Losses of all sorts.	Percentage of strength.
Advance guard	7,000-7,500	50
IV. corps . . .	5,600-6,000	30
II. „ . . .	9,500	30
I. „ . . .	7,000	30
Grenadiers .	1,769	16
Cavalry Reserve .	1,877	21
III. corps . . .	1,900	11
VI. „ . . .	2,500	15
	37,146	26

The Austrian account gives 31,335 killed, wounded, and prisoners, besides several thousand missing, who rejoined later. This does not differ widely, when these missing are included, from the Prussian writer's estimate. Four generals (Wukassowich, Nordmann, D'Aspre and Vecsey) were killed and 13 wounded, including the Archduke Charles himself. The French accounts only allow of a guess at their losses.

Binder v. Krieglstein, after careful consideration of all available sources of information, including Martinien's nominal lists of officers killed and wounded, estimates the loss in killed and wounded alone at 27,500, or about 15 per cent. on a total of 180,000, inclusive of artillery and departmental troops.

The Austrians lost, in killed and wounded, about 24,000 officers and men, 16 per cent. on a total of 150,000. Of French and allied generals no less than 40 were killed or wounded, amongst whom the death of Lasalle was the most notable loss.

Perhaps the most significant fact in the losses is the proportion of officers to men in the killed and wounded. The Austrians lost, according to their own account, 730 officers, whilst we know, from Martinien, the French loss was 1822. In the former case one officer killed or wounded to every 32 men, in the latter one to every 14. The French had more officers proportionately, but these figures still point to the probability that the French officers had to sacrifice themselves more freely on account of the quality of their troops.

The total loss on both sides in the two days' battle, including prisoners and missing, will probably not be overestimated at between 65,000 and 70,000, out of a total of about 320,000 engaged.

The Austrians carried off 7000 prisoners, and, curiously enough, they had more trophies to show than the conquerors; for they had 12 eagles or standards and 21 guns, whilst the French had only 10 or 11 of the former and 20 guns.

CHAPTER XVIII

THE PURSUIT TO ZNAIM, AND THE ARMISTICE

DAYBREAK of the 7th July saw Napoleon in the saddle, still uncertain whether he would not have to fight a third day's battle on the slopes of the Bisamberg. Soon, however, it became clear that Charles had evacuated those heights, and the Emperor was free to give rein to a somewhat vivid imagination as to the decisiveness of his victory. The Austrian army was certainly not "en pleine dêroute et poursuivie sur toutes les directions" as he chose to represent it to Cambacérès. His own army was exhausted and incapable of the active pursuit he would have wished, and he neither knew the direction of Charles' retreat, nor what had become of the Archduke John, whose advent on the field of Wagram, with forces whose numbers the Emperor greatly over-estimated, he had so much dreaded. Napoleon presently transferred his headquarters to Wolkersdorf, whence only that morning the Emperor Francis had departed on realising the defeat of his army.

Orders were dictated in large numbers by Napoleon, but very little was said about active pursuit. To Masséna he wrote, "we are still not very certain of the direction the enemy has taken." Masséna was to advance meanwhile to the Korneuburg road seeking information in that direction, occupying also Am Spitz, thus coming into direct communication with Vienna. Bernadotte was sent back to Gross Enzersdorf to be on the watch for John.

About 7 P.M., Masséna's Baden troops stormed
Korneuburg after it had been fired by artillery. It was
occupied by Klenau's rearguard. Here Masséna stopped
his advance, on seeing the heights beyond occupied by
strong Austrian forces. On the other flank, the cavalry
came, at Gaunersdorf, upon Radetzky's rearguard of
Rosenberg's corps, which was retreating on Mistelbach
and Laa on the Thaya. Radetzky, after holding
Gaunersdorf till evening, fell back to Schrick.

From these events Napoleon inferred that Charles
was retreating partly on Stockerau, partly on Nikolsburg.
For the pursuit on Nikolsburg the Emperor detailed
Marmont with his own corps, Wrede's division, and the
cavalry of Montbrun and Colbert. His orders were to
start at midnight and cover on the 8th as much as possible of the 32 miles to Nikolsburg. Montbrun was to
reconnoitre also to the left towards Znaim, so that if the
enemy were retreating thither, Marmont might operate
on his left flank.

Practically very little had been done on the 7th
towards pursuing Charles who, in the afternoon, had
issued orders for retreat from Ober-Rohrbach. During
the night, Gollersdorf was to be reached, where the III.
corps would occupy the centre, with the V. corps on its
right, the I. on the left, the Grenadiers in reserve, and
cavalry in front at Sierndorf. Klenau, with the VI.
corps, was to fall back before daybreak, leaving a line of
outposts on the line Stockerau-Gross Russbach, and
occupying strongly the former place.

Hohenzollern, with the II. corps, to retreat by Gross
Russbach to Jetzeldorf on the Pulka, there to unite with
Charles on the 10th. He was to keep in touch with
Rosenberg, with whom was part of the II. corps. The
latter was informed of the intentions of headquarters,
and was to retreat as slowly as possible on Brünn and
Olmütz. He was at Laa when he got the order, at

10 P.M. on the 8th, having moved thither in accordance with orders of the 6th requiring him to cover the left of the army retreating on Znaim.

All were informed that the Archduke intended making another stand in the Jetzeldorf position.

To his brother John, Charles wrote that he was now to act independently, to hold the line of the March, and to have under him, for the defence of Hungary, the forces of Gyulai and Chasteler. In this letter Charles reproaches John with his delay at Wagram. He tells him that, had he arrived even with only a few thousand men a few hours earlier, he would have decided the battle in favour of the Austrians. To the Emperor Francis, Charles wrote somewhat dismally as to his losses, which grew daily in the form of stragglers and marauders, and the exhaustion of the army after its two days' battle. To that Francis replied next day that he had decided to despatch Liechtenstein to Napoleon, and Charles was to arrange with the outposts for his passage.

During the 8th, Marmont compelled Rosenberg to retire on Laa, and, after driving Radetzky from Mistelbach in the evening, bivouacked opposite that commander between Mistelbach and Poisdorf on the Nikolsburg road. Radetzky had held out so well at Mistelbach that Napoleon hurried up to Marmont's support Davout's corps, Grouchy's dragoons, and Arrighi's cuirassiers. He plainly thought there was a stronger enemy on this line than there really was.

Masséna attacked Stockerau at 9 A.M. with Legrand's division, but did not get possession of it till 11, when he reported that the Austrians were retreating northwards. This, added to Marmont's report of Rosenberg's direction, set at rest all doubts of the Austrian destination. They were clearly marching for Znaim. Napoleon, therefore, resolved to despatch stronger forces against them, whilst taking precautions in his rear against a possible raid on Vienna by John, Gyulai, and Chasteler. Bernadotte was left behind for the latter purpose, as well as the Viceroy and Pully's dragoons. There was a slight skirmish between the Saxons and John's outposts when the former, quite unnecessarily, fell back to Unter-Siebenbrünn. Meanwhile, Charles had issued orders in the morning for retreat on Schöngrabern during the ensuing night. Klenau, who was to start with the rearguard at 1 A.M. on the 9th, reported his corps in very bad condition, and Liechtenstein said his brigades did not number over 400 men. There was much straggling. Hohenzollern had fallen back on Kummersdorf; Rosenberg was to cover the Brünn road.

By midday on the 9th, Masséna's advance guard had forced Klenau back on Ober-Hollabrünn. Here a flag of truce demanded passage for Liechtenstein carrying proposals for peace. Whilst he was being taken to Masséna, the fight began again at Ober-Hollabrünn, which was stormed in the evening by the Baden troops. Charles, finding it impossible to make a stand at Jetzeldorf, fell back across the Pulka. Now came news from the Emperor Francis that French cavalry had reached Erdberg and were threatening Znaim. These appear to have been Marmont's men. Rosenberg had now been separated from the rest of the army and was retiring towards Brünn. He halted across the road, with his left almost on the field of Austerlitz. He was not pursued. Charles' retreat on Znaim was seriously threatened by the advance of Marmont and Davout by Laa, and he was again obliged to abandon the idea of fighting behind the Pulka. Marmont was in Laa, Davout in Nikolsburg this night, neither having encountered serious resistance. During the night, orders were issued by Charles for the retreat on Znaim, which was to be covered against Masséna by a strong rearguard of the V. and VI. Corps and Wartensleben's cavalry brigade, all under Klenau, on the heights south of Guntersdorf.

Hohenzollern, with the II. corps, had been ordered, if he did not find the enemy too strong, to attack Marmont at Laa. But he had already retreated on Mailburg where he received the rest of his corps, sent back by Rosenberg to whom it had been attached. He had 20,000 infantry, but only 300 cavalry and 3 batteries, as part of his artillery was still with Rosenberg. The Reserve corps was ordered to occupy the heights east of Znaim on either side of the Thaya ; the I. to cross at Pumlitz, below Znaim ; the III. at Oblas ; the VI. to await the coming in of the rearguard, which it was hoped would be able to keep back Masséna till the night of the 10th. Hohenzollern was to cross to the road from Laa on the north bank of the Thaya and fall back on Znaim by it.

Napoleon was still at Wolkersdorf in the early morning of the 10th. He had ordered the Guard to Wilfersdorf ; Nansouty, followed by Oudinot, on Nikolsburg. The Emperor was now sure, from the reports of Marmont and Masséna, that the greater part of the Austrian army was making for Znaim, and that Marmont was dangerously exposed. Therefore, he ordered Davout, leaving only a small force at Nikolsburg, to hasten at his best speed to support Marmont.

Walther with the Guard was to reach Laa by 1 P.M., Nansouty to march there from Schrick. Napoleon himself rode on to Wilfersdorf, where he warned Masséna of the position of affairs. In the evening he reached Laa. It was not possible, in the wet weather now again prevailing, for Davout, the Guard, and Oudinot to reach Znaim before the afternoon of the 11th. The battle had begun before noon on the 10th.

The Archduke Charles reached Znaim between 8 and

9 A.M. on the 10th with the Reserve corps which he posted, fronting eastwards, to cover the bridges against the French who were reported to be arriving from Laa.[1] The Reserve corps stood with its right on the Thaya near Kl. Tesswitz, its left towards Zuckerhandl, and a brigade on the right bank of the river. Cuirassiers covered its left, and a weak brigade was sent on to the Iglau road behind Znaim. As the II. corps came up, it also was to leave a brigade south of the Thaya. The V. and VI. corps were to fall back to Znaim from the south. The V. corps made a stand with artillery fire about 9 A.M., against Masséna at Schöngrabern. About noon Masséna, joined by St Cyr, for whom he had been waiting, pushed on through Guntersdorf. Marmont, meanwhile, started from Laa at daybreak, practically the whole of his corps moving by the road on the north bank of the Thaya. Arriving before the position of the Austrian Reserve corps, he sent the Bavarians against Kl. Tesswitz, Clausel on their right towards Zuckerhandl, holding Claparède in reserve in the centre.

The Bavarian skirmishers were repulsed, and their main body was held at Kl. Tesswitz till Austrian reinforcements came up from the west. On the right of the Bavarians, Clausel had taken Zuckerhandl, and Montbrun had driven back the light cavalry, but was brought to a standstill by the appearance of the cuirassiers on his right flank. During this fighting, the III. corps crossed the river by the main road and took post on the left of the Reserve, facing nearly north at Brenditz. The I. corps, trying to ford at Pumlitz, was met by the artillery fire of the Bavarians on the heights east of Kl. Tesswitz, which place they had now taken. The advance guard of the Austrian corps bravely pushed on through the river and retook Kl. Tesswitz, which, however, was again stormed by the Bavarians.

[1] *I.e.* Marmont.

2 B

This fight had given time to the rest of the I. corps to cross and march to the support of the Austrian left against Clausel towards Brenditz, north of which place the III. corps arrived at the same moment. Marmont, with visions of his marshal's baton floating before his eyes, had hoped in the morning to win an easy victory over a weak Austrian rearguard, and perhaps to bar the retreat of the army. Now, at 5 P.M., he found he had an army, which he reckoned at 40,000 men, before him, and that all he could do was to try and hold his ground till the help which he urgently demanded from Davout arrived. He felt convinced that the Austrians would disappear from in front of him during the night, and Charles would really have retreated had he thought it possible. But the II. corps was still south of the Thaya, and the V. could not reach Znaim before morning. Moreover, the train which had gone ahead, was stuck in the defiles north of Znaim. Marmont was probably rather relieved when an Austrian officer demanded an armistice, on the ground that Liechtenstein was treating for peace.

This was refused with the usual " bluff " regarding an immediate attack and the arrival of Napoleon in person at any moment. There was no more fighting of any importance that night, but Montbrun had to fall back with his cavalry before the vastly superior force now facing and threatening to outflank him. At nightfall the Austrians stood thus—III. corps on the left between Brenditz and Winau ; I. corps between Brenditz and the Galgenberg, less one brigade in reserve at Znaim ; VI. corps (which had crossed the Thaya) behind these on the Iglau road ; grenadiers, and the brigade of the I. which had taken Tesswitz in the morning, on the heights east of Znaim up to the Thaya ; II. corps and Nostitz's cavalry division on the heights of Pumlitz south of the river ; V. corps and Wartensleben's cavalry brigade marching from Guntersdorf to Znaim, which it began to reach at 11 P.M.

At 10 P.M. Charles issued his orders for the next day (11th). The V. corps was to guard the left (north) bank of the Thaya and the eastern side of Znaim; II. to cross behind the V. and go behind the extreme left, consisting of the cavalry, west of Winau, augmented by Nostitz; III. to remain where it was; I. on the heights between Brenditz and Znaim; VI. across the Iglau road to the north. Headquarters at Wolframitzkirchen. Thaya bridges to be destroyed after all troops were across. The army was thus posted in a semicircle round Znaim.

At midnight[1] Napoleon dictated from Laa a furious letter to Marmont. The marshal had left not a man at Laa, where the bridges were open to destruction by any stray handful of hussars. He had sent very little news, and that not in duplicate. He had not even named the village (Kl Tesswitz) which had been taken and retaken. "You did not learn this carelessness when serving under me." Even at 5 P.M., he had not written sufficiently strongly to hurry up Davout, who, like all generals, would have no particular anxiety to play second fiddle to another. Finally, Marmont was to undertake nothing serious till the Emperor was within reach. At 2 A.M., Napoleon, who had written urgently to Davout to hurry up, started for Znaim with the heavy cavalry of Nansouty, Arrighi and the Guard, and their 42 horse-artillery guns.

At 6 A.M., Marmont, misunderstanding the crossing of the Austrian V. corps, wrote that the enemy was in full retreat, and only 30,000 men remained in front of him.

Soon after that hour, whilst the Austrian V. corps was getting into position and had not yet destroyed the bridges, Masséna's light cavalry began to appear on the

---

[1] The contents show that it was only sent off at 2 A.M.

heights south of the Thaya. Masséna himself, hearing from the Emperor of Marmont's predicament, had
started at 4 A.M., with Legrand and St Cyr. Of
his other two divisions, Boudet's had been left at
Stockerau, and Molitor's was too far behind to come
up on the 11th.

It was between 9 and 10 A.M. when Legrand, reaching the Thaya, was sent forward to the attack, whilst
Marmont's men also moved against Zuckerhandl, where
the resistance proved too strong for them.

About 10 A.M., Napoleon reached the field with the
cavalry. The position he found was a difficult one, in
which it was impossible to do much more than keep the
Austrians from retreating, until the arrival of Davout
and Oudinot, who could hardly be expected before the
small hours of the 12th. The cavalry were sent forward,
north of Kukrowitz, against the III. corps with this
object.

Though this was the position of affairs on the French
side, the Austrians were under the impression that the
enemy had been strongly reinforced, and, therefore,
made no attempt to take the offensive.

On the south of Znaim, Legrand's fight raged with
the utmost fury, his being the only one of Masséna's
divisions yet up. It was 2 P.M. before he had succeeded
in getting across the river and breaking into the suburbs
of Schallersdorf and Klosterbruck. At this hour Carra
St Cyr also began to arrive.

Charles sent some grenadiers to reinforce the V. corps,
but his mind was only set on getting away by the Iglau
road, as soon as the defiles were clear of the train. He
proposed to reach Budwitz with the I., II. and III. corps
across the road, the grenadiers behind them, and the
VI. corps still farther north. The Reserve cavalry
would follow, holding on till the V. corps could pass.
The retreat was to be begun by the VI. at 6 P.M. The

fight with Legrand grew still hotter after 2 P.M., when the French general, with his Baden troops on the left of the main road, and the French on the right, began to press on. Just as he neared the gate of Znaim there broke a perfect deluge of rain which damped the primings of the muskets and prevented firing. The Austrians heavily repulsed the bayonet attack, drove the French and Badeners back in confusion on the bridge, and took many prisoners, Masséna himself narrowly escaping.

Just at this moment, St Germain's cuirassiers, who had crossed by a ford, fell upon the pursuing Austrians, taking many prisoners and two guns, and driving the rest back into the town in such confusion that, but for the opportune intervention of a Viennese volunteer battalion, the cuirassiers would have passed the gate with the fugitives.

Masséna now supported Legrand with the French regiments of Carra St Cyr in the fight for the gate. At the same time (about 5 P.M.) three Hessian battalions were sent to the right of Pumlitz to the assistance of the Bavarians fighting in the vineyards between Znaim and Kl Tesswitz.

Between 6 and 7 P.M., French and Austrian officers passed between the lines of combatants shouting " Peace ! Peace ! Cease fire ! " Marbot on the French side, and D'Aspre on the Austrian, were both wounded as they performed this duty in front of the attack of Masséna. By 7 all firing had ceased.

The cause of this sudden suspension of a battle which could hardly have led to any decisive results before the Austrians had got away on the Iglau road, was the grant of an armistice by Napoleon to Liechtenstein, who had reached the Imperial headquarters only at 1 A.M. During the greater part of the fighting, negotiations had been carried on between the headquarters of the armies.

Napoleon, on this occasion, had held a council at which he allowed those present to speak freely. As evening came on without any signs of the arrival of Davout and Oudinot, the Emperor saw that the continuation of the battle could only end in Charles' retreat, drawing the French still farther away from Vienna. That was probably the principal motive which influenced him in finally casting his vote in favour of an armistice. Its chief terms were—

(1) Retirement of the Austrians behind the Bohemian and Moravian frontiers, the March, and the Raab.

(2) Immediate Austrian evacuation of Brünn and Graz.

(3) Withdrawal of Austrian troops from the Tyrol and the Vorarlberg, and evacuation of Sachsenburg.

(4) In Poland, the armies to keep their present positions.

(5) The armistice to be for one month certain, with 15 days' notice of termination after that.

Binder v. Krieglstein reckons the Austrian loss at Znaim at 5000, the French at 3000.

A few words are necessary as to what had been happening in the rear as Napoleon followed Charles with Masséna, Marmont, Davout, Oudinot and a mass of cavalry.

The Emperor was disturbed by the presence of John, Bianchi, Jelacic, Chasteler, and Gyulai in his rear, and he knew that, once united, they could march on Vienna with between 40,000 and 50,000 men. But, as long as John was on the march, it was not certain whether he would cross to the south of the Danube, or move north to seek a junction with his brother in Moravia. Gyulai had not been inactive, had relieved the citadel of Graz, and compelled Rusea, who was blockading it, to fall back towards Vienna. Napoleon entrusted the protection of his rear to Eugène, to whom he gave an army of from

40,000 to 50,000 men. It was composed of the following elements :—

(1) The Saxon corps under Reynier. Bernadotte's IX. corps was dissolved and its commander sent back to France in disgrace.[1] Into Napoleon's quarrels with him we need not here enter. Whatever the merits, we may feel certain that Bernadotte had not omitted to play, as he always did, for his own hand.

(2) Macdonald's and Grenier's corps.

(3) Baraguay d'Hilliers (before Pressburg).

(4) Vandamme's Wurtembergers, now to be drawn in towards Vienna.

(5) Pully's dragoons.

With his main body between Leopoldsdorf and Ober-Siebenbrünn, the Viceroy was to send a strong advance guard across the March on the 10th.

John, meanwhile, had on the 7th proposed to hold the March with the 'Insurrection,' whilst he himself, crossing at Komorn and joining Chasteler and Gyulai south of the Danube, would compel the enemy to detach against him. No sooner was this plan approved than he changed his mind (on the 9th), or the Emperor Francis did so for him. He had retired from the March on Pressburg in the afternoon of the 8th, having, as he believed, found out that the whole French army was gone in pursuit of Charles, leaving Vienna and the Lobau very weakly occupied. He proposed to issue on the 10th from the Pressburg bridge-head, to brush aside Baraguay d'Hilliers, and to march on Vienna, calling up Chasteler to Oeden-burg, and sending Gyulai to blockade Raab. On the 10th, he gave up the idea when he ascertained that Eugène was in great force on the March. On the 11th, ordering Bianchi to abandon the Pressburg tête de pont, he started for Komorn. On the 12th, Eugène drove

---

[1] Dupas' weak division, of which very little was left after Wagram, was divided between Boudet and Legrand, one regiment to each.

back John's rearguard and established himself at Stampfen beyond the March. On the 13th, news of the armistice stopped operations.

Napoleon had also issued orders for the preservation of Vienna. Its garrison was raised to 6000 men, the guns on the Lobau were used to bring its artillery up to 100 pieces. A powerful bridge-head was ordered at Am-Spitz, covering the new bridge connecting it with the capital. Measures were taken for guarding the magazines there against internal disturbances, as well as external attack.[1]

With events subsequent to the armistice this history is not concerned. There was no renewal of fighting, except in the Tyrol against Hofer, though at times it seemed imminent. The armistice was not ratified by the Austrian Emperor till the 18th July. Francis had come completely under the influence of Stadion and the war party, and this led him to dispense, on the 18th July, with the services, as commander-in-chief, of his brother. He expressed his intention of taking over the command himself.

On the 30th, Charles handed over command of the army in Bohemia to Prince John Liechtenstein. So ended the military career of the best general Austria then had, probably the best she ever had.

---

[1] For an account of local affairs in Vienna, after its capture in May, see Savary, and also the interesting brôchure of P. Müller entitled " L'espionnage militaire sous Napoleon Ier" (Paris, 1896). The latter gives all the available information regarding Charles Schulmeister, the remarkable man who for years acted as Napoleon's principal spy. He had much to do with the surrender of Mack in 1805, and one cannot but regret that he left no reliable memoirs. His adventures would have proved at least as interesting as Marbot's; but his profession did not encourage him to throw much light on his movements. The only memoir he wrote was after the fall of Napoleon when the Austrians and Prussians, who knew him well, were thirsting for his blood. Consequently, his memoir is an attempt to make out he was something quite different from what he really was, and to represent himself in a favourable light.

Charles never served in the field again, though he lived till 1847.

The negotiations for peace dragged on till the 14th October, through a period varied by many incidents, the battle of Talavera, the failure of the Walcheren expedition, the struggle in the Tyrol, and, finally, Stáps' attempt on Napoleon's life.

The terms of the treaty of Schönbrünn (ratified by Napoleon on the 15th, by Francis on the 19th October) are thus summarised by Dr J. Holland Rose: "Austria thereby recognised Joseph as King of Spain, and ceded Salzburg and the Inn-Viertel to Napoleon, to be transferred by him to Bavaria. To the French Empire she yielded up parts of Austrian Friuli and Carinthia, besides Carniola, the city and district of Trieste, and portions of Croatia and Dalmatia to the south of the River Save. Her spoils of the old Polish lands now went to aggrandize the Duchy of Warsaw, a small strip of Austrian Galicia also going to Russia. Besides losing 3,500,000 subjects, Austria was mulcted in an indemnity of £3,400,000, and again bound herself to exclude all British products. By a secret clause, she agreed to limit her army to 150,000 men."

CHAPTER XIX

CONCLUDING REMARKS ON THE SECOND HALF OF THE CAMPAIGN

ON the 24th April, the Archduke Charles wrote to Francis I. that he was retreating to Cham, there to unite his army, including the corps of Kolowrat and Bellegarde. At Cham he would be guided by circumstances as to whether he would fight a battle, or would continue his retreat.

On the 27th, he wrote again from Cham. He was now assured that Napoleon was marching direct on Vienna, and meditating no serious pursuit of the defeated army on the north bank of the Danube. Charles considers that three operations are open to him.

(1) An advance on Ratisbon with the object of falling on Napoleon's rear. The objections to this were the difficulty, owing to loss of pontoons, in crossing the Danube, the further difficulty of subsisting in the now exhausted country south of Ratisbon, and, finally, the danger of a battle fought and lost with the Austrian front towards Vienna. Charles felt that meant the end of the House of Habsburg, as well as of Austria, and he quailed before the responsibility.

(2) A bolder plan would be to move westward by Suabia towards France. To that the objection was that Napoleon would be at Vienna long before Charles could reach Paris.

(3) To retreat by Budweis, to rejoin Hiller, and resume the offensive against Napoleon.

394

The two first plans Charles considered impossible of execution, and he had decided to adopt the third as the safer.

Of the retreat we need not speak further, unless to call attention to Charles' unnecessary sensitiveness for his rear, which induced him to send Kolowrat back to meet a possible advance from Saxony, and afterwards to leave him with a whole army corps to meet Bernadotte. Charles' use of strong flank guards on his right had the effect of deceiving Davout who, till a very late date, suspected him of barricading himself in Bohemia.

Davout's great caution is very remarkable. It seems clear from his actions that he did not agree with the Emperor's decision to march on Vienna, disregarding Charles once his retreat into Bohemia was certain. Napoleon was convinced as to Charles' direction long before Davout was satisfied on the point, and the marshal's doubts induced the Emperor, on several occasions, to leave his subordinate some discretion as to the rapidity of his advance by the right bank.

There was always the danger that Charles might yet break back across the Danube in rear of Napoleon, and unite with the Archduke John and Chasteler to fight that battle " à front renversé," the issue of which must be almost as momentous for Napoleon as for Francis. That was what Davout evidently feared when he thought Charles was stopping in Bohemia. It was the plan which, in a modified form, the Austrian commander-in-chief contemplated when he sent Kolowrat towards Linz, and ordered John to co-operate with him from the south. Who can doubt that it is the one which Napoleon himself, in Charles' position, would have followed?

Napoleon, too, clearly shows how much anxiety the safeguarding of his long line of communications caused him. His frequent orders to Lefebvre to act vigorously in the Tyrol, his eagerness for the commitment of John

to a retreat on Hungary, his orders for the construction
of an almost impregnable bridge-head opposite Linz, his
instructions to Beaumont and the new reserve division at
Augsburg, and to Kellerman and Jerome, all point in the
same direction. Once he was assured that Charles was
marching towards Vienna, or Moravia, with the greater
part of his army, that John was bound for Hungary, that
Chasteler and Jelacic were driven out of the Tyrol, he
felt little anxiety about Kolowrat, whose attack of the
17th May on the Linz bridge-head was easily disposed of
by Vandamme and Bernadotte. In his inmost soul
Napoleon perhaps regretted the advance on Vienna, even
before Essling. After that repulse, with its disclosure
of the greatly increased strength of Charles, it is difficult
to doubt that he must have done so. Even Wagram was
too little of a decisive victory to obliterate the memory
of Essling.

After Essling, Napoleon's position was one of extreme
anxiety. The news of the reverse spread like wildfire
throughout the continent, offering every encouragement
to the brave spirits who were for a bold stroke for
liberty. The news from Spain, and the gallant fight of
the Tyrolese peasants, gave them still further encouragement. Perhaps their worst enemy, and Napoleon's best
friend, was the feeble and selfish Frederick William of
Prussia. Even Russia must have been a source of
anxiety to Napoleon, for her alliance was, to take it at
the best, but half-hearted.

For the defeat of Essling the Emperor had himself to
blame. He had certainly been careless in his preparations for the crossing, once more a result of his unbounded
pride and his contempt for his enemy. He had been
amply warned of the dangers of a sudden rise of the
Danube, the fate of the Austrian bridge at Mauthausen[1]
should have warned him of the danger to a bridge of

[1] *Vide supra*, p. 244.

boats from barges and other masses floated down the rapid stream. Yet he trusted his army to a single bridge of boats without any protection by stockades, or by boats cruising about to arrest such floating masses above the bridge. His information regarding Charles' position seems to have been bad and to have led him not to expect serious resistance immediately after the passage. Even on the morning of Essling, his cavalry had failed to detect the advance of the whole Austrian army.

Napoleon was always preaching the advantages of field fortification ; yet he neglected it before Essling. It is true he at once began a bridge-head at the northern end of his last bridge, but he took no measures to fortify the greater bridge-head of Aspern-Essling and the line between them. Had he spent the night at that work, it is doubtful whether the Austrians would ever have effected a lodgment in either village. The church and churchyard at Aspern might have been rendered almost impregnable, and the same may be said of Essling.

Perhaps Napoleon's escape from still greater disaster at the battle of Essling was due as much to the Austrian failure as to his own efforts. Charles devoted all his energies to the attack on the two strong positions of Aspern and Essling, almost neglecting the attack on the weak, and weakly held, curtain between them. A successful attack on the centre would have broken the Emperor's army in two, and, possibly, have resulted in annihilation of everything on the left bank on the 21st May. As it was, the more or less disjointed attacks on the two villages were never completely successful, and Napoleon was able, thanks to the splendid conduct of Masséna's men on the one flank and Lannes' on the other, to retire in good order to the Lobau. His desperate attack on the Austrian centre, on the 22nd May, narrowly missed success, and that thanks, to a great extent, to Charles' personal valour and influence. It is all very well to blame him for playing the part of a regimental officer, instead of a commander-in-chief, but it must be remembered that he had had unpleasant experiences of the rout into which an Austrian repulse was apt to degenerate, and he probably felt that the crisis was approaching which would convert an orderly retirement into a panic flight, ending in the separation and ruin of his army. Essling was the first great success of an Austrian army against Napoleon in person. Still, a great deal more was made of it than it deserved; for, after all, it was but a partial success, gained by immensely superior forces, which should have been able to absolutely destroy the 22,000 men whom alone Napoleon was able to utilise on the first day of the battle. On the other hand, Napoleon had no justification for attributing his defeat solely to the breaking of the bridge. His attack on the Austrian centre was fairly beaten off before the arrival of Davout became hopeless.

Charles' proposed attacks on the Lobau after Essling were palpably a make-believe, and could not possibly have succeeded.

There is no clearer proof that Napoleon realised his own rashness in the first crossing than the infinite care which he bestowed on his preparations for the second, and the perfection with which they were carried out. The thoroughness of the way in which he turned the Lobau into a great entrenched camp, the success of his endeavours to deceive Charles as to the point of passage, are admirable. The Austrian general had seen the results of Napoleon's failure to fortify the Aspern-Essling position, and had not failed in the same way. Where he did fail was in presuming that the Emperor would dash his head against the front of an almost impregnable fortified position, when Charles had left the bank opposite the whole eastern side of the island practically undefended. The Emperor would not even have had space to deploy in front of the works at Aspern-Essling. Napoleon of course saw all this and determined to turn the fortified position, to debouch by the eastern side of the island, and to unfold his army like a fan, turning the Austrian left. To conceal his real intentions, he resorted to every possible device. By keeping Davout and Eugène before, or to the east of Pressburg, and then marching them to Ebersdorf by a circuitous route, he succeeded in making Charles believe, almost up to the last moment before Wagram, that the real crossing was to be above or below Lobau, where there would be nothing but a feint. When it was no longer to be concealed that the crossing was to be from the Lobau, the Emperor still withdrew the Austrian attention from the real point of passage by ostentatiously moving the greater part of his troops on the island towards the old bridge. Then Legrand was sent over to the Mühlau as a further evidence of his intention to cross there. The bridges and boats for the crossing of the lower part of the Stadlau arm were all kept carefully hidden behind the islands in it.

At the Austrian headquarters divided counsels ruled. Charles disagreed with Wimpffen and Grünne as to the place where Napoleon would cross. He wrongly persisted in expecting a crossing elsewhere than at Lobau. Then, again, the two parties disagreed as to whether, if the crossing were from Ebersdorf, the enemy should be attacked in the act of crossing, or whether he should be left to deploy on the Marchfeld, and then received in a defensive battle in the strong positions of the Russbach and the hills on the north and west of the plain. Here Charles seems to have been in the right, but the result of his failure to firmly impose his own views was that he was almost insensibly drawn into following those of Wimpffen. His situation resembled that of Brunswick in 1806, when Massenbach was striving to commit him to crossing to the right bank of the Saale.

Napoleon's arrangements for the crossing of the lower Stadlau arm worked perfectly smoothly. Jomini has remarked that there was very nearly being fearful confusion, owing to the crossing of Davout's and Oudinot's corps on the left bank. The blame is thrown entirely on Berthier, who is supposed to have miscopied Napoleon's orders. Any stick seems to be considered good enough to beat this poor dog with! It seems to us, however, doubtful if the responsibility must not rest on other shoulders.

Jomini does not point out that the orders provided for a good deal more crossing of corps. Oudinot passed on the extreme right, though destined for the centre in the deployment beyond the river. By the next bridge on Oudinot's left passed Masséna's infantry, destined for the left in the deployment. The next bridge on the left of Masséna's infantry was assigned to Davout, who had to take the extreme right beyond the river. On Davout's left was the bridge for Masséna's cavalry and artillery. Thus Davout would,

(1) pass between Masséna's infantry and cavalry, or,

(2) he would cross right into Masséna's infantry if they had advanced as far as Davout's bridge when he crossed, or,

(3) at the best, he would pass across the rear of Masséna, and very close to it.

It seems difficult to attribute all this crossing of corps to a clerical error of Berthier. What we would suggest is this: Napoleon's whole scheme depended on the first crossing being made on the extreme right. At the same time, he wanted to have Masséna and Davout, his two most trusted commanders, on his wings at the critical points. To send Davout across on the right was out of the question, for Oudinot was already there, and he was to have mastered the passage before Davout could even reach his bridge. Masséna, equally, could not be sent across on the right if he was to take the left beyond the river. Therefore, Oudinot must pass on the right.

Why not send Masséna's infantry over the bridge which was assigned to Davout? The reasons probably were, (1) that the great bridge, swung in one piece, was only for infantry, and, therefore, would not have taken Davout's cavalry and artillery; (2) that, if this transposition had been made, Davout and Masséna's infantry might have crossed on the Lobau, at least if there was any delay on Masséna's part. For these reasons we think that the throwing of the blame on Berthier is not justified.

Napoleon probably realised the objections to the arrangement, but expected Masséna to be clear of Davout's bridge before the latter crossed.[1] As for Davout and Oudinot, the risk could not be avoided under all the circumstances. It must be accepted, in the hope either that Oudinot would have reached his place in the centre before Davout crossed his line, or else that Davout would have crossed Oudinot's front in time to avoid confusion. As it was they met, and it was only the good sense of men and officers which saved the difficulty.

On the Austrian side the view prevailed which favoured retirement, before decisive action, to the strong positions in rear of the Marchfeld; yet, as a result of the mere existence of divergences of opinion on this matter, a half measure was adopted. The fortified line Aspern-Essling-

[1] This is probably what happened, as there is no mention of danger of confusion between Davout and Masséna. The author has been unable to ascertain exactly where, relatively to Masséna's infantry position, Davout passed. That will perhaps be cleared up when Col. Saski's fourth volume is published.

Count Yorck, without stating his authority, says that Masséna, by 4.30 A.M., was opposite the northern end of the Ile Alexandre, well beyond Davout's bridge. Oudinot only moved into line at 8 A.M., after Davout had reached his place on the right (*Napoleon as a General*, ii. 89).

2 C

Enzersdorf was occupied by a force of some 30,000 men, with instructions to hold it as long as possible. There was very little use in this, for the holders of this line were to be left unsupported, and there could be no doubt that nothing but defeat could lie before them. The capture of the position from a force of this strength was a foregone conclusion, especially when it had been turned by the direction of the French crossing. The rather feeble defence of Enzersdorf seems to point to the realisation by the Austrian advance guard of the hopelessness of their exposed position.

Charles would probably have done much better to insist on following his own scheme of attacking the French in the act of crossing, or before they could deploy, as they did unmolested, on a line facing north. But if he did so the attack should of course have been with his whole force, not with an isolated corps. Once Masséna was established on the left flank of the fortified position, its garrison was powerless to delay the French deployment, covered as it was by the overwhelming fire of the batteries on the Lobau. The only result of the defence of the line was the retreat of two beaten forces, one towards each wing of the Austrians, placed respectively on the Russbach position and that of the Bisamberg. Charles, instead of using all his available forces on the battlefield, left the V. corps and a brigade of the III. on the Bisamberg heights. Any serious attack in that direction was improbable, looking to Napoleon's system. Schustekh might have been called up from Krems, but he paralysed Vandamme's larger force opposite him, and was therefore, perhaps, better left where he was.

Up till 6 or 7 P.M. on the 5th July there was no hindrance to the French worth mentioning. The attack which then took place on the line of the Russbach was manifestly mismanaged. Time pressed, if a decisive result was to be obtained before dark, and each corps was hurried into action irrespective of the others. The position was a strong one, the attack on it, owing to want of time, was simply frontal, and, though success was nearly attained at one moment, the French were beaten off all along the line, and there was a disgraceful panic.[1]

The Austrian right wing could do nothing in time to help the left, a fact which, no doubt, led Charles to the decision to have no more to do with Wimpffen's "pair of pincers" scheme.

The 6th July began with an event very fortunate for the Austrians, the abandonment of Aderklaa by Bernadotte and its occupation by the enemy. It was of extreme importance to Napoleon, but he was unable to get permanent possession of it again till the close of the battle. Each side, on this second day of the battle, endeavoured to turn the enemy's left. Napoleon's new attack on the Russbach position was to be by Davout marching against its left, by the left bank of the stream, with part of his corps, whilst the rest of the corps attacked Markgrafneusiedl in front. The frontal attack on Davout's left was only to be pushed home when the Duke of Auerstädt had broken down the support of the Austrian left by the capture of Markgrafneusiedl. For the advance of the III. and VI. corps from the Bisamberg against his own left, the Emperor does not seem to have been prepared. He apparently thought Boudet, in the Aspern-Essling position, was quite sufficient to guard the bridges in that direction, as well as to keep off any enterprises against his left and rear. He had moved the rest of Masséna's corps farther to the right. Yet he was careful to keep his reserves in mass towards his centre, whence they could most easily be sent in any direction required. He actually, at one moment, was moving the Guard to Davout's support. Finding it not required

---

[1] There was another after the battle was won on the 6th; clear evidence of the deterioration of the French troops.

there, he took it back, to be employed later in the centre. The attack of the III. and VI. corps necessitated the flank march of Masséna to the left, and the 100-gun battery seems to have been intended as much to protect that operation as to make a breach in the enemy's centre, into which the Emperor could pour his infantry and cavalry.

Though his scheme now was to break through the Austrian centre, he still kept his eye constantly on the progress of Davout's advance, designed to roll the Austrian left back upon the centre. The Austrian left was the point to which he looked for the decision of the battle, and, as he saw the line of smoke from Davout's muskets pass west of Markgrafneusiedl, he said to an aide-de-camp : "Gallop ! Tell Masséna that the battle is won, since the Archduke John has not yet appeared." Charles, too, saw, as Davout and Oudinot moved westwards, that there were but two alternatives left to him, to retire defeated but not annihilated, or to make a last effort for victory, with utter ruin staring him in the face if he failed. Napoleon would, perhaps, in Charles' place, have accepted the latter alternative. Charles seeking, not for the conquest of fresh empires, but for the preservation of his country and his House, wisely chose the first. By retreating he could still keep in hand a respectable army, capable of further action, and of gaining terms which from a Napoleon victorious as in 1806 he could never expect. He had attacked on a widely extended line, the necessary consequence of a turning movement such as his. Napoleon, on a shorter line, holding his masses in a central position, was able to break through the weakened Austrian line.

The battle ended in victory for Napoleon, but not decisive victory such as he gained at Austerlitz and at Jena.

Immediate pursuit there was none, and, tired though

his troops were, its absence seems to point to a decadence in Napoleon's thoroughness.

The Archduke John was, throughout the day, on Napoleon's mind. His arrival, with the force he actually had, would probably not have turned the scale in the Austrian favour ; but Napoleon believed he had a very much larger army, and his own reserves had been largely drawn upon. When he sent Reille with the Guard to Macdonald's aid, he said to him, " Do not run risks ; for I have nothing with me as a last reserve but the two regiments of the Old Guard." Though John might not have saved the battle, that is no excuse for his delay in arriving. Charles, in his report on the battle of Wagram, blames his brother's delay in starting from Pressburg, and asserts that his arrival at Ober-Siebenbrünn would have protected the left of the army against Davout.

The consequence of the absence of immediate pursuit was that, for two days after Wagram, Napoleon was in uncertainty as to the direction of Charles' retreat. When he sent Davout and Oudinot towards Nikoloburg, he was ignorant that only one corps (Rosenberg's) was in that direction. When Charles had decided to stand at Znaim, Napoleon had moving against him only the weak corps of Marmont from Laa, and Masséna's echeloned far along the road to the Danube.

Marmont's attack on the Austrian left at Znaim, on the 10th July, was certainly rash, and exposed him to the risk of very severe treatment at the hands of a more enterprising enemy. His conduct generally at this time was very rash and negligent, and he could not justly complain of the severe terms in which Napoleon censured his neglect in leaving the passage of the Thaya, at Laa, in his rear, absolutely unprotected against any stray body of cavalry. On the 11th, Napoleon was abel to bring to his support a strong body of cavalry, but, even with that, it was not possible to hope for any decisive result. Masséna, too, arrived from the south, though, for the first part of the day, he had only Legrand's division available, and, later, only that and Carra St Cyr's. Napoleon saw clearly that, until Davout and Oudinot should arrive, he was powerless to defeat the six[1] Austrian corps in position about Znaim. The French reinforcements could hardly be ready for action before the early hours of the 12th. The Emperor could not even hope to prevent the Austrians from retreating on Iglau ; if they did so, as Charles intended, the French army would be once more drawn far to the north, away from Vienna. That was probably what induced Napoleon to accede to Liechtenstein's demand for an armistice. Had he seen his way to holding Charles at Znaim till the 12th, it seems certain he would not have granted it.

With the armistice of Znaim the campaign was at an end, though it took several months of negotiation before peace was finally concluded.

Brilliant as many of Napoleon's manœuvres had been, the campaign differed very widely in the degree of its success from its predecessors of Austerlitz and Jena. Its comparative failure must be attributed largely to Napoleon's preconceived idea of marching on Vienna, irrespective of the enemy's movements, an idea to which he obstinately adhered when Charles retreated through Ratisbon into Bohemia. Had Napoleon followed him to Cham with the corps of Davout, Masséna and Lannes, it is difficult to doubt that the result must have been the defeat of the Austrian army, with its complete break-up in the Bohemian Forest. Hiller could have easily been dealt with by Bessières' force and Lefebvre, behind whom the Guard was beginning to arrive.

With the army of Charles destroyed, Napoleon might have marched on Vienna as he marched on Berlin in

[1] V., I., and III. in first line, II. and Grenadiers in second line, VI. on the road to Iglau.

1806. "There is nothing better than to march on the enemy's capital after a decisive victory; before it, no!"[1]

The failure to gain a decisive victory over Charles in April led only to the barren occupation of Vienna, to the repulse of Essling, to the indecisive victory of Wagram, and to the armistice of Znaim.

It seems remarkable that, with the incompleteness of his success, Napoleon should have in the end been able to dictate such terms as those of the Treaty of Schönbrünn. Francis and his friends of the war party would have renewed operations had they dared, but they had thrown away, by the dismissal of the Archduke Charles, their best, perhaps their only general, and probably they felt that a renewal of the struggle could but end in fresh and more decisive defeat, with the inevitable consequence of the obliteration of Austria from the map of Europe, and of the House of Habsburg from the list of reigning families.

[1] *Bonnal*, p. 346.

INDEX